ALTER ICONS

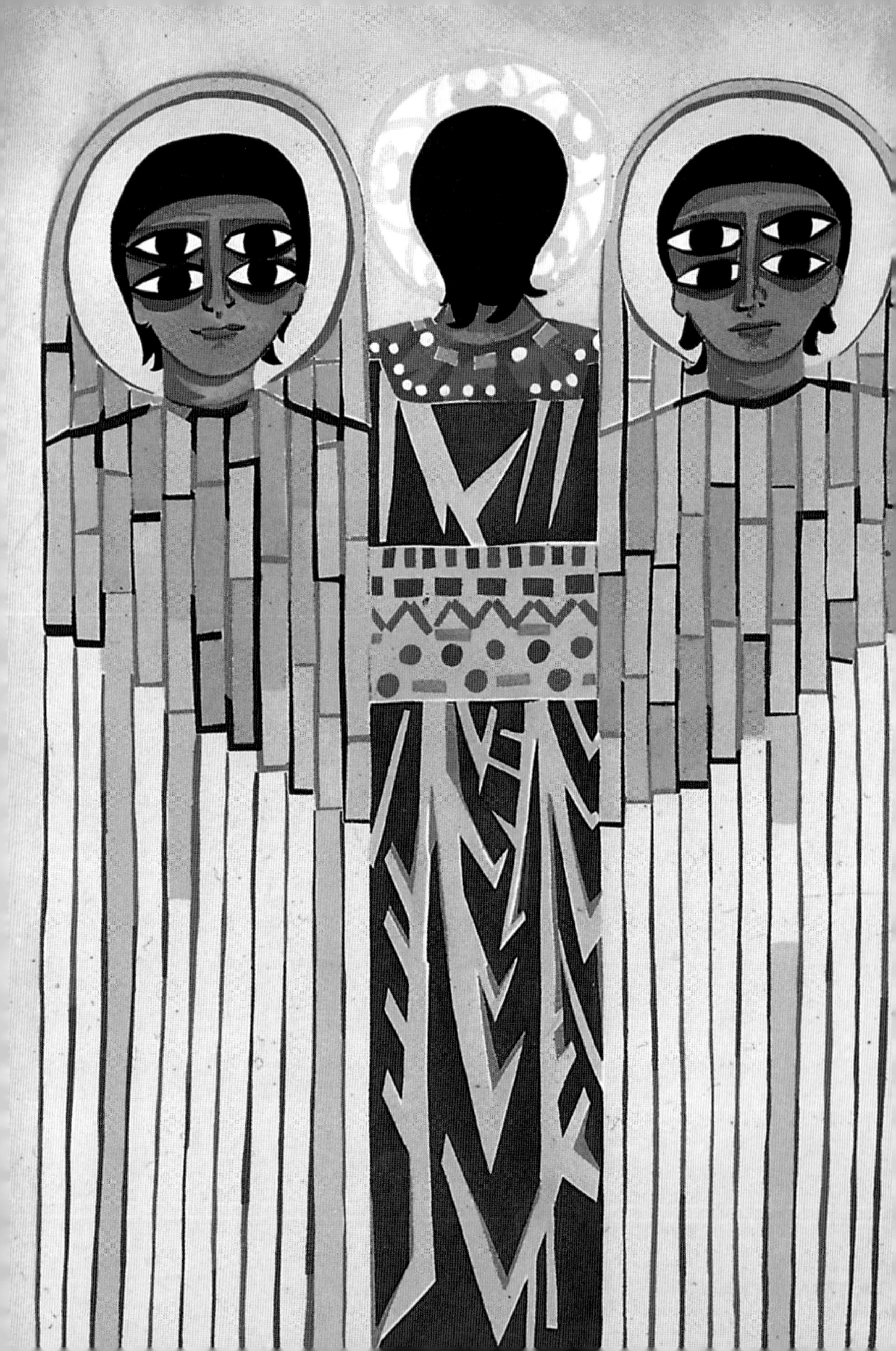

ALTER ICONS

THE RUSSIAN ICON AND MODERNITY

EDITED BY
Jefferson J. A. Gatrall and Douglas Greenfield

The Pennsylvania State University Press
University Park, Pennsylvania

Studies of the Harriman Institute,
Columbia University

Library of Congress Cataloging-in-Publication Data

Alter icons : the Russian icon and modernity / edited by Jefferson J. A. Gatrall and Douglas Greenfield.
p. cm.
"Studies of the Harriman Institute, Columbia University."
Includes bibliographical references and index.
Summary: "A collection of essays by eleven scholars of Russian history, art, literature, cinema, philosophy, and theology that track key shifts in the production, circulation, and consumption of the Russian icon from Peter the Great's Enlightenment to the post-Soviet revival of the Orthodox Church"—Provided by publisher.

ISBN 978-0-271-03677-9 (cloth : alk. paper)
1. Icons, Russian.
2. Art and society—Russia.
I. Gatrall, Jefferson J. A.
II. Greenfield, Douglas M.
III. Title: Russian icon and modernity.

N8189.R9A76 2010
704.9'4820947—dc22
2010010380

Published by The Pennsylvania State University Press,
University Park, PA 16802-1003

The Pennsylvania State University Press is a member of the Association of American University Presses.

It is the policy of The Pennsylvania State University Press to use acid-free paper. Publications on uncoated stock satisfy the minimum requirements of American National Standard for Information Sciences—Permanence of Paper for Printed Library Material, ANSI Z39.48–1992.

Frontispiece: Goncharova costume sketch (detail, Plate 12)

Image on page x: Mother of God icons (detail, Plate 7)

Studies of the Harriman Institute, Columbia University

The Harriman Institute, Columbia University, sponsors the Studies of the Harriman Institute in the belief that their publication contributes to scholarly research and public understanding. In this way the Institute, while not necessarily endorsing their conclusions, is pleased to make available the results of some of the research conducted under its auspices.

CONTENTS

ILLUSTRATIONS

FIGURES

PLATES

(following page 172)

ACKNOWLEDGMENTS

It is a pleasure to thank the many people who have shared their time and knowledge to make this book possible. The volume grew out of a conference and exhibit held in 2003 at Columbia University and sponsored by the Harriman Institute. Catharine Theimer Nepomnyashchy, then the Institute's director, enthusiastically supported our efforts, and among the staff we especially wish to thank Ronald Meyer, Alla Rachkov, and Natalia Novikova. The Harriman Institute also provided a generous subvention toward the volume's publication.

The chapters included here convey only in part the challenging and wide-ranging contributions that enlivened the conference. The editors are grateful to all the scholars who took part, including Konstantin Akinsha, Brian Baer, Karin Beck, David Borgmeyer, Vitaly Chernetsky, Laura Engelstein, Richard Gustafson, Stephen Hutchings, Myroslava Mudrak, Svetlana Rakic, Jane Sharp, Rebecca Stanton, Oleg Tarasov, Mark Von Hagen, James West, and Richard Wortman. Alex Melamid opened the conference with a presentation on the relation between art and religion. Eileen McGuckin, John Walsted, and the masters and students of the Prosopon School of Iconology exhibited their contemporary icons. Arsen Pankovich generously loaned us paintings and drawings by the late Serbian American artist Alexander Markovich.

The staff at Penn State Press provided superb assistance throughout the process. Eleanor Goodman, our editor, supported the book from the start. She has matched our enthusiasm for this project and lent it her long experience. Danny Bellet and Cali Buckley worked closely with us in readying the manuscript, and Cherene Holland, Patricia A. Mitchell, and Laura Reed-Morrisson shepherded it through production. Martin White prepared the index.

We wish to thank the authors for their vision, their commitment, and their humor. It has been a joy and an education to collaborate with them. In addition, we are grateful to Rupa Bhattacharya, Felicia Greenfield, Nicole Rizzuto, and Karin Zitzewitz for their editing and support, and to Kristin Romberg for her help in tracking down images. Finally, we owe a special debt of thanks to our friend and colleague Natalia Ermolaev. The success of the conference that resulted in this book would have been impossible without her inspiration, energy, and grace.

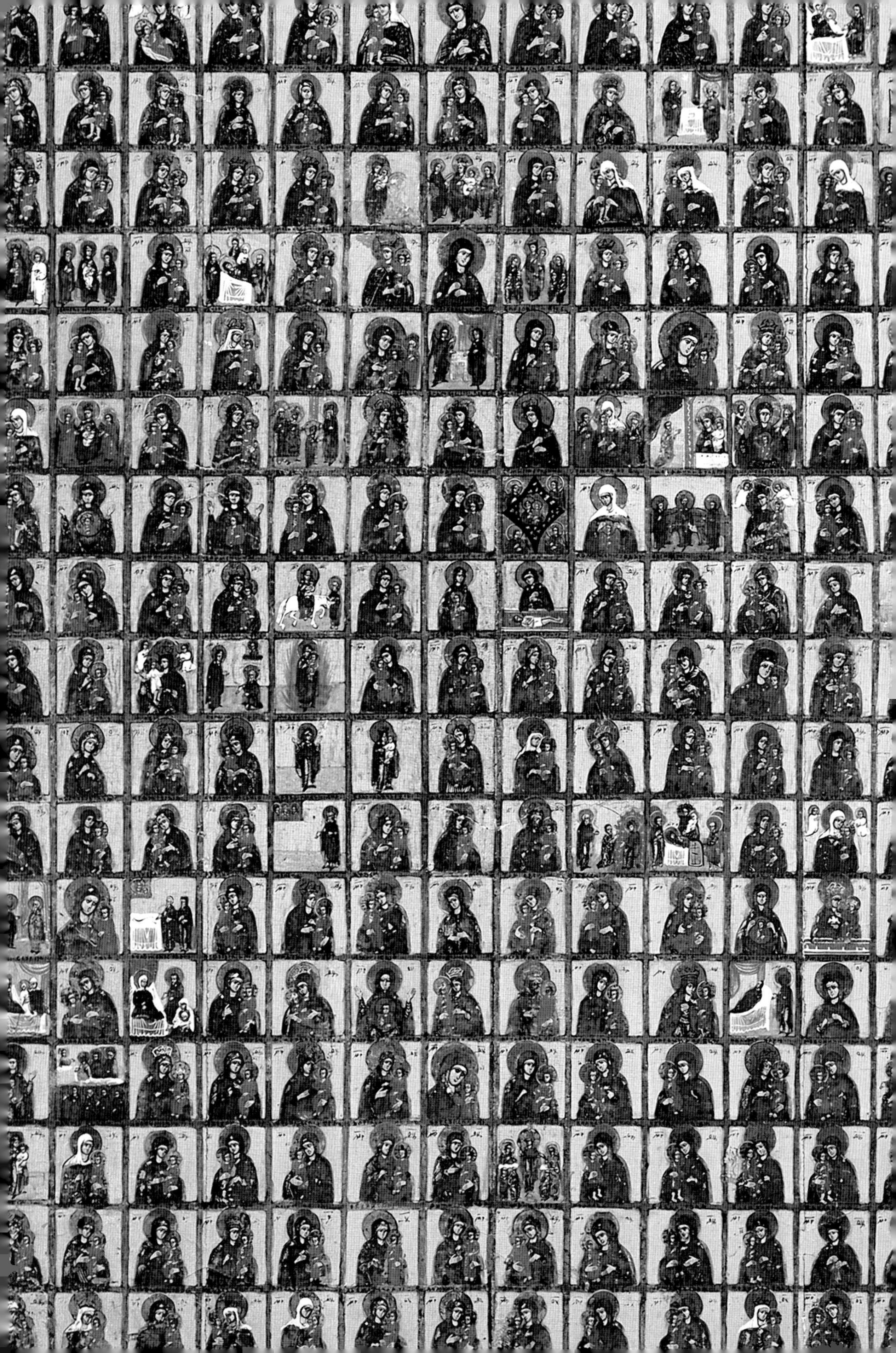

JEFFERSON J. A. GATRALL

INTRODUCTION

The Russian icon has led a storied existence since entering the modern world. The vicissitudes of passage have shaped even what it means to be an icon. Within the Orthodox community, of course, the icon did not cease to be a venerated image, as it had been in Russia since the eleventh century. Yet over the past two hundred years, the icon fell into new hands. Once under the care of their latter-day handlers, icons began to migrate en masse from churches and monasteries to museums, public exhibitions, and private collections. By the 1930s, the combined efforts of archeologists, art historians, restorers, curators, and collectors had succeeded in reconstituting the Russian icon as a globally recognized art form, one with distinct schools and its own history of styles. At the same time, the means of producing icons also changed hands. In the final decades of tsarist Russia, traditional icon painters, working in provincial centers, faced competition at both the high and low ends of their trade: while painters from the St. Petersburg Academy of Arts were winning the lion's share of major new church commissions, Moscow factories were churning out household icons at reduced cost for mass consumption. Lastly, if the Russian icon has had its modern defenders, it has also endured modern waves of destruction, from the iconoclasm of revolution and civil war to the bombs and vandals of World War II. Indeed, a number of medieval icons that were sold or smuggled abroad for safekeeping during the Soviet period are only now returning to Russian soil, notably the Tikhvin Mother of God, an icon whose legendary peregrinations—from the paintbrush of Saint Luke to fourteenth-century Rus—include, in modern times, exile to Chicago in 1944 and repatriation to the village of Tikhvin in 2004.

Alterability has been a conspicuous feature of the icon's modernity. Modernity here refers not simply to a series of events unfolding through an empty chronological time; on the contrary, modernity defines itself against a past that it has created in its own counterimage. As the icon took on new forms and meanings, and as it attracted an increasingly diverse array of acolytes, the boundaries of its modernity, its fateful before and after, were continually redrawn. Not only does the demarcating line between the modern and the premodern shift with each new way of seeing; the icon itself alternately falls on one side or other of this moving divide. In one view, the icon embodies tradition, both as a monument to a medieval worldview and as a bulwark against an advancing modernity. In another view, the icon partakes of a living culture, one whose rituals and outward aspect adapt to changing times, whether in line with a dominant mainstream or as a viable alternative. For one side, the icon's modernity is a contradiction in terms; for the other, it is its ineluctable condition. Even more difficult to track are those underlying structures in the longue durée that have slowly and anonymously shaped the icon's material culture. In this respect, those historical stretches when the icon seems to disappear from view are as significant as the dazzling and recurring spectacles of its rediscovery.

Current criticism on the concept of modernity opens further vistas for surveying the icon's recent history. Following a standard division in the critical literature, the icon can be said to have experienced both a social modernization and a cultural modernity, each with its own subdivisions and periodization.[1] In terms of modernization, the icon, like any other commodity in imperial Russia (1721–1917), was subject to such processes as the international flow of capital or the industrialization of production. More so than aesthetics or theology, for instance, analysis of changing media technologies across Europe helps account for the Russian icon's remarkable material transformations—wood panels, paper prints, tin plates—from the seventeenth to the nineteenth century. As a sacred object, in contrast, the icon circulates within a system of cultural or "religious" capital that is seemingly irreducible to the economic base, in a Marxist sense, or that retains a certain autonomy from what Pierre Bourdieu terms the "field of power."[2] This autonomy is never absolute, however. Even within the economy of the sacred, large social processes have had a demonstrable impact on the aggregate value of icons and their rituals. In particular, the Russian icon presents a compelling case study for the ongoing secularization debate in the humanities and social sciences.[3] For Max Weber, writing in the early twentieth century, modern Western culture, through a long process of intellectualization, had arrived not so much at increased knowledge as at the "disenchantment of the world" (*Entzauberung der Welt*), that is, the decline of magic and mysticism as forms of substantive reason.[4] In the Russian context, the conjunction of modernization and secularization has clear heuristic appeal, whether in relation to state campaigns to regulate or suppress icon veneration from Peter I (r. 1682–1725) to the Soviet period or in terms of the evolving views of specialists and the general public regarding the icon's otherworldly orientation—its evocation of a divine prototype, its magical powers of protection and healing, and so on. The post-Soviet revival of Russian Orthodoxy, including the return of icons to the pageantry of state power,[5] nevertheless exemplifies the challenges currently facing classic secularization theory. The veneration of icons, like so many traditional church practices, survives and even flourishes in modernity, appearing to disconfirm secular projections. This state of affairs lends potential support to attempts at reconceiving modernity as either "incomplete,"[6] obsolete (postmodernity), untenable (antimodernity), or heterogeneous (multiple modernities).

Moreover, even within secular ideologies and institutions there would seem to be ample room for the sacred and the profane—the binary that Émile Durkheim considered "fundamental to all religious organization."[7] As icons were withdrawn from the church, literally and figuratively, new values—art, nation, the people—began to accrue to them. Although very much of this world, these values were arguably no less sacred than the Orthodox dogmas and lay beliefs that they displaced. In terms of the conventional periods of cultural modernity, perceptions of the Russian icon, from the Enlightenment to postmodernism, have changed in response to international trends in the arts and letters. Modernism in particular vastly expanded the icon's artistic horizons. From the 1880s to the 1930s, the Old Russian icon, long neglected by a Western-educated gentry, was transformed from a parochial craftwork into a world masterpiece, from an antiquarian curio into an avant-garde aesthetic model, and from a medieval cult object into a modernist prism for seeing the world anew. The enduring success of this aesthetic revaluation is perhaps matched only by the icon's repositioning as a national symbol. As the subtitle of our volume indicates, the modern Russian state—in its imperial, Soviet, and post-Soviet incarnations—represents the specific site of the critical interventions undertaken in the chapters that follow. For our contributors, the Russianness of the "Russian icon," far from being taken for granted, represents a central problem for analysis. In a variation on the Romantic cult of the medieval, the icon emerged in the nineteenth century as an emblematic expression of the peasant's traditional worldview and, by extension, the true essence of what it meant to be Russian. Especially in the wake of major upheavals—the French invasion of 1812, the 1917 Revolution, or the 1991 dissolution of the Soviet Union—Russia's political and cultural elite have repeatedly conferred on the icon and its folk traditions a leading role in competing formulations of national identity.

No less important to investigate are the ways in which modernity has realigned the icon's interfaces with the profane, both in the sense of the commonplace and the contaminating. In the latter sense, a marked anti-Western orientation can be included among the icon's modern values. From the anti-Enlightenment sermons of clergy to the antirealist manifestos of the avant-garde, the icon's modern defenders have sought to protect it from Western influences while at the same time defining its most authentic attributes in opposition to those same influences; at the limit of this binary logic, the icon becomes what the West is not, and vice versa. Opposition to the West does not necessarily imply an antimodern outlook, however, as if Western Europe were the sole global source of modernity, or the backward East its vast inassimilable Other. The trend in postcolonial and transnational studies over the past two decades toward "counter," "alternative," or "multiple modernities" offers useful models for rethinking the often contentious identity politics surrounding the Russian icon.[8] In decoupling the West and the modern, it becomes easier to observe the formation of alternative modernities in Asia, Africa, the Americas, and even Europe. For a Western theorist such as

Theodor Adorno, aesthetic modernism found much of its justification in an uncompromising critique of social modernization and its reified cultural by-products.[9] The turn to the icon in Russian modernist aesthetics likewise represents not a retreat into the premodern but an alternative path of resistance, one in which traditional templates are not so much given as dreamed into being.

No single anthology could retrace all the winding paths of the icon in the modern period. Through a range of methods and subject matter, this volume seeks to introduce the modernity of the Russian icon as a distinct field of interdisciplinary inquiry.

HIDDEN AND REVEALED

The theme of "discovery" figures prominently in most accounts of the Russian icon's recent history.[10] Two events stand out in particular. The first surrounds the scientific restoration of Andrei Rublev's *Old Testament Trinity* (*Troitsa*) (c. 1410 or 1425–27) in 1904–6 (pl. 2). At the time, this icon—in which the three visitors to Abraham (Gen. 18:1–8) are depicted as a Christian allegory of the Trinity—was still housed in the place for which it had been originally painted, namely, the Trinity Cathedral in Sergiev Posad, northeast of Moscow. The icon hung on the lower left side of the cathedral's iconostasis—the distinctive wall of icons, usually with several rows, separating the nave from the sanctuary in Eastern Orthodox churches. Rublev's *Trinity* would have faced the laity during services. Yet despite its well-defined visual role in one of the holiest sites in Orthodox Russia, the icon appeared, for a certain type of viewer at the turn of the century, as if hidden from view. The icon had been repainted at least three times, while layers of protective varnish (*olifa*), which darkened with time, had been regularly applied over the years. Moreover, as was common for most revered icons, a gilded metal casing, or *oklad,* overlay most of the icon's surface. Under the direction of Vasily Gurianov, restorers removed this gilded frame and began the painstaking task of scraping away centuries of overpaint and varnish. What they found underneath was the astonishing vibrancy of Rublev's original colors—the light pinks, blues, and greens adorning the three figures, with bright yellow and gold replacing drab brown in the background. In a sort of secular apocalypse, a false veil of outmoded church practices had been pulled away to reveal true art, as Gurianov and his colleagues became the first moderns to see the genius of a long-neglected master, one whose name—hitherto little known beyond clergymen and antiquarians[11]—soon attained national and international renown.

The partial cleaning of the *Trinity* prompted a flurry of further restoration projects,[12] not least a hunt through rural Russia for lost and unattributed works of Rublev. Such wealthy patrons as Ilya Ostroukhov and Stepan Riabushinsky employed a new generation of *ikonniki,* hereditary icon painter-restorers, to work on icons in their private collections, while the church made available many icons under its control. The fruits of these combined restoration projects were presented in March 1913 at the Exhibition of Old Russian Art, which took place in the decidedly secular setting of Delovoy Dvor (literally, "business court") near Red Square in Moscow. The exhibition introduced fifteenth- and sixteenth-century icons, cleaned and unframed, to critical acclaim as well as to a large and highly receptive public. The icons of these two centuries were presented as a uniquely Russian artistic legacy, at once distinct from earlier Byzantine models and not yet overrun by the norms of the Western Renaissance. In an influential review, the art critic Nikolai Punin wrote, "This exhibition is an event. More than that, a revelation to us all! Has not a new artistic consciousness begun in Russia?"[13]

In retrospect, a better case could be made for considering the 1913 exhibition the final in a series of pivotal discovery events. Over the past two decades—due in large part to Gerold Vzdornov's masterly 1986 monograph on nineteenth-century icon scholarship—the beginning of the icon's rediscovery has been considerably pushed back in time. Long-lost murals were being unearthed in Russian cathedrals as early as the end of the eighteenth century; restoration of ancient churches in Kiev and elsewhere was under way by the 1840s; museum collections of ancient icons were organized in Moscow and St. Petersburg in the 1860s; the first exhibition devoted to ancient Russian art took place not in 1913 but in 1898; and so on.[14] This protracted and largely unheralded process of scholarship and restoration laid the groundwork for the more celebrated turn-of-the-century rediscovery. In his review of the 1913 exhibition, Punin grudgingly grants earlier scholars priority of discovery, observing that their research found no response in the "artistic strivings of their contemporaries": "Scholars studied, while we remained cold."[15] As these words suggest, Punin and other commentators, not without some justification, distinguished the modernist rediscovery from its nineteenth-century precursors by its aesthetic emphasis. Before the 1880s, and especially during the height of realism, the art of icon painting had few apologists.[16] Recent literary critics have pointed to the icons that adorn the classic realist novel, from *A Sportsman's Sketches* (1852) to *War and Peace* (1869) to *The Brothers Karamazov* (1880).[17] Icons also appear frequently in the genre and historical paintings of Russian realist painters in the 1860s and 1870s. Yet it remains a matter of debate the extent to which Fyodor Dostoevsky, the early Lev Tolstoy, or first-generation Itinerants (*Peredvizhniki*) conceived of the icon specifically in aesthetic terms,[18] let alone as an artistic model for their own work. Even Fyodor Buslaev, in his groundbreaking *General Remarks on Russian Icon Painting* (1866), draws on realist criteria to account for the icon's "low level of artistic development": "It's as if it were afraid of reality."[19]

This question of precedence aside, the 1913 exhibition played an undeniable role in repositioning the icon at the forefront of Russian avant-garde art. Running parallel to the efforts of restorers, or even slightly behind (in the logic of avant-gardism), a significant number of Russian artists, critics, and poets were turning to the icon as a source of artistic inspiration. Thanks to research begun in the 1970s by such art historians as John Bowlt in the United States and Olga Tarasenko in Russia, the avant-garde's extensive engagement with the icon is now widely recognized.[20] For the avant-garde, the icon represented both a new myth of origins and a future horizon. On the one hand, as Alexander Rodchenko put it in 1919, "Russian art has its origin in the icon";[21] in other words, the Russian avant-garde traced its genealogy not to the derivative canvas painting of the St. Petersburg Academy of Arts, an eighteenth-century Western import, but to an indigenous, nonrealist art form. On the other hand, in the studios of Neoprimitivist, Cubo-Futurist, Suprematist, and Constructivist artists, the icon was reconceived as a paragon of abstractionism. Such leading artists as Mikhail Larionov, Vladimir Tatlin, and Kazimir Malevich, in their common cause against realism, appropriated different formal aspects of the icon, from its hieratic and free-floating figures to its flattened perspective and monochrome coloring. Natalia Goncharova's religious compositions, including *Coronation of the Virgin* (1910) and *Evangelists* (1911), as well as her set and costume designs for the ballet *Liturgy* (1915) (pl. 12), proved especially provocative in their deformations of traditional Russian and Byzantine iconography. On a number of occasions, the Holy Synod, the governing body of the Orthodox Church in imperial Russia, led efforts to block the exhibition of Goncharova's works because of their perceived blasphemy. In her iconlike paintings, Goncharova plays on the angular and anatomically irregular figures of the Virgin, saints, and angels, employing a color scheme evocative of the cleaned Old Russian icon.[22] On this last point, she had the tacit blessing of Henri Matisse, a global authority on all things primitive, who had enthused about the "wealth of pure color" he discovered in the icons of Moscow and St. Petersburg.[23]

Despite resistance at times from the official church, the avant-garde did find fellow travelers in the burgeoning Russian religious renaissance—a revivalist movement in Orthodox theology. Evgeny Trubetskoy, Pavel Florensky, and Sergei Bulgakov, among others, contributed to the development of a critical vocabulary for understanding the Russian icon as an Orthodox alternative to the paradigms of Western visual art. As recent translations by Wendy Salmond and Robert Bird attest,[24] Florensky's writings, notably "Reverse Perspective" (1920) and "Iconostasis" (1921), have had an enduring impact on not just icon studies but the general field of Russian visual culture. In images organized through reverse perspective—a term coined in 1907 by Oscar Wulff[25]—parallel lines appear to diverge from the picture plane, rather than converging on a vanishing point, as in linear perspective. In making this new term his own, Florensky expanded reverse perspective from a formal feature of Orthodox art into an indictment of the Western Enlightenment, including its positivist science and realist art. In gazing at a Russian icon, the viewer does not preside, in the "predatory and mechanical"[26] manner of perspectival vision over a lifeless mirror of the material world. On the contrary, the viewer submits to, and is transformed by, the beauty of a higher reality, as if the viewer were the icon's vanishing point and the icon board heaven's window. As for his opinion of Rublev, Florensky could not have been more anti-Cartesian: "There exists the icon of the Holy Trinity by Saint Andrei Rublev; therefore, God exists."[27]

In sum, over the first two decades of the twentieth century, the Old Russian icon reappeared in its full glory. That restorers, artists, or exhibition visitors could rediscover the artistry of the Old Russian icon at all nevertheless says at least as much about what they were looking for as it does about what they saw. Without detracting from its importance, the cleaning of Rublev's *Trinity* serves as a convenient metaphor for a far more pervasive, and multifarious, revaluation: the view of Old Russian icons as works of art. In this revaluation, the roots of which predate the modernist rediscovery, the spirit of modern science dovetailed with a no less modern artistic sensibility, as new specialists—restorers, archeologists, art historians, collectors, and curators—furnished material for the formal experiments and manifestos of artists and critics.

Moreover, if the Old Russian icon was a discoverable object, something whose true essence could be revealed, then this is because it had somehow disappeared from view. The notion that the icon had been long hidden pervades the writings of its modern discoverers. As in the case of Rublev's *Trinity,* this disappearance could be quite literal. In "What Do Icons Teach?" (1916), the critic and writer Maximilian Voloshin describes the icon's rediscovery as something akin to an exhumation: "Pious barbarians, who understood nothing about the beauty of tone or colors, each year covered icons with a layer of varnish. . . . Varnish was the tomb that preserved this ancient art and transported it untouched to this day."[28] Voloshin here pits a secular modernity against the superstitions of a backward populace. Many art historians assumed this enlightened position in relation to the Orthodox Church, which was accused of letting its own ancient icons rot and perish. As old icons darkened from soot and varnish, to the point of illegibility, clergymen were in the habit of relegating them to the status of "black boards" (*chernye doski*); as such, they were consigned to storage, where they could be fetched for fuel or used to patch holes in church walls.

In a 1930 article, Alexander Anisimov, a leading Soviet icon scholar, argued that the task for his field was "to establish on a really scientific basis, chronologically dating for the main periods, the history of Russian Icon-Painting, its bloom, its over-refinement, and, finally, its decay."[29] Crucial to that task was saving Old Russian icons from the church. The institutions responsible for the icon's storage, maintenance, study, and valuation indeed underwent a profound secularization, in a very literal sense, as control over the most ancient of Russian icons passed to a new class of secular priests (*cleris sæculum*). The migration of icons from churches to museums was already well under way by the reign of Nicholas I (r. 1825–55). In the wake of the 1917 Revolution, when the new Soviet government began to seize church lands in a systematic manner, this migration became a rout. Rublev's *Trinity,* for example, was relocated in 1929 to the Tretiakov gallery, where it still remains. For the Orthodox Church, the icon had been an object that could be cleaned, repainted, encased, and even destroyed, all according to codified rituals.

The application of varnish took place annually on the first Sunday of Lent,[30] while in the wake of the seventeenth-century schism in the church, elaborate and austere public ceremonies were developed for defacing and burying icons that failed to conform to newly instituted iconographic standards.[31] In the church, the icon is sacred, yet not of its own power; rather, what infuses the icon with sacred value is the absent prototype it evokes. In the museum, by contrast, the body of the icon itself becomes inviolate, subject to rituals of preservation no less sacred for being secular. These rituals serve to set the icon apart from the profane circulation of everyday goods. Whereas old churches generally went unheated, the icon's new environment was carefully controlled for light, humidity, and temperature. It was likewise necessary to remove the profane traces of the icon's material history, so as to restore it, inasmuch as this was possible, to the authenticity of its original created state. In the museum, the value of icons depends less on the identity of their holy figures than on that of their creators, whether "the people" (*narod*) at large, particular schools, or, more rarely, individual artists—artists whose names curators and art historians often took great pains to ascertain.

Other scholars attributed the modern disappearance of the Russian icon to the invidious effects of Western influence. In his authoritative *The Russian Icon* (1927), Nikodim Kondakov writes that "two centuries of neglect, beginning in Peter's time, have sundered the Russian people from the last flourishing period of icon-painting and destroyed a greater number of examples than all the town fires or devastations of the countryside."[32] Kondakov, writing from exile in Prague, attributed the decline of icon painting from the late seventeenth century onward to the increasing Westernization of educated Russian society, of which the clergy represented only one small part. Suffering from an "excessive admiration of everything Western," educated Russians "ceased to care for [icons], forgot them, and no longer looked after them . . . they were put away into store." This culpable neglect affected even where icons were made. Icon painting, once centered in Moscow and Novgorod, "hid itself in the depths of the Russian countryside," that is, in the towns of Palekh, Kholui, and Mstera in the Vladimir province, where the icon, once a high art form, had degenerated into a "handicraft or *kustar'* product."[33]

Most important, the educated elite—with certain noteworthy exceptions[34]—failed to protect the art of icon painting from the corrosive influence of the Renaissance. From the end of the sixteenth century onward, the Russian icon gradually began to lose its aesthetic purity. In churches and the homes of the aristocracy, icons took on naturalized figures, darker hues, decorative flourishes, and rudimentary elements of perspective. In describing such icons, Kondakov uses the common term "Frankish" (*friazskii*), a style he criticizes as an "unsatisfactory compromise" between "late Greek" and "Western art."[35] For the twentieth-century theologian Leonid Ouspensky, such Western stylistic corruptions are inseparable from an underlying "secularisation of religious consciousness": "In the XVIIth century the decline of Church art sets in. . . . Loss of the consciousness of the dogmatic meaning of art inevitably led to the distortion of its very foundations and no artistic gift, no exquisite technique proved able to replace them."[36] The icon's long "neglect" (Kondakov), "decline" (Ouspensky), or "decay" (Anisimov) reaches its nadir only in the nineteenth century. Yet on both aesthetic and theological grounds, the Russian icon's earlier exposure to the Western Renaissance set in motion this tragic fall into modernity.

A double chronology of hiding and revealing thus underlies the logic of the icon's modernist rediscovery. Modernism made possible the widespread recognition of the Old Russian icon as an art form. By the very terms of aesthetic modernism, however, the modernity of the icon would seem to have begun much earlier. One set of modern forces—secular scholarship, the science of restoration, avant-garde aesthetics—precipitated the recovery of a lost artistic patrimony. Yet a second set of modern forces—Westernization and a secular disregard for native religious traditions—had resulted in its long hiding. Most classic monographs on "the Russian icon"—Rovinsky (1857), Kondakov (1928–33), Lazarev (1983)[37]—do not extend past the seventeenth century. This volume begins where the standard historiography of the Old Russian icon ends. Between these two chronologies, in the period of the icon's supposed neglect and disappearance, lie important yet understudied chapters in the icon's modernity.

ICON AND IDENTITY

From the point of view of cultural practice, it is hard to imagine an object less in need of discovery than the icon in imperial Russia. For the Orthodox and non-Orthodox alike, icons were everywhere. As the pioneering icon scholar Ivan Snegirev explained in an 1862 article, holy faces, watching over the faithful from the cradle to the grave, were always in the visual field: at church, at home, at work; on city gates and bridges; in the marketplace; interceding for soldiers on land and at sea; presiding at births, marriages, and deaths; and mediating family disputes.[38] More recently, Oleg Tarasov, in his cultural history *Icon and Devotion* (1995), has underscored the challenges that the "burden of numbers" poses for the study of imperial-era icons, millions of which were produced annually from the mid-nineteenth century onward in Palekh, Kholui, and Mstera: "It seems certain that in no other place or period was icon production so massive."[39] These imperial icons may not have fit as well as their Old Russian predecessors in modernist canons of art history; yet at the time, their mass production ensured a constant rate of replacement at levels that more than made up for any loss of aging models. By their near ubiquity, icons cast a sacral veil (*pokrov*)—to borrow a familiar symbol of intercession in Mother of God icons—over everyday life in imperial Russia.

This veil did not extend evenly to all corners of the empire, however. In the wake of the iconoclastic controversies of the eighth and ninth centuries in Byzantium, icon veneration was affirmed in Orthodox dogma as a requirement for all members of the church. In imperial Russia, the icon continued to confer the sign of Orthodoxy on those who venerated it. In her research on Russian Orthodoxy in the prerevolutionary period—the "largest Orthodox culture of modern times"—Vera Shevzov makes the compelling case that icon veneration, even more so than attending mass or receiving the Eucharist, played a dominant role in fostering an "ecclesial identity" among the laity; thus peasants in rural areas who might go years without stepping inside a church or never once see a bishop in their lifetime identified with the sacred community of the church by means of icons.[40] In an Orthodox household, one or more icons were generally placed in the so-called beautiful corner (*krasnyi ugol*) of the main room, ideally on a small, elevated shelf facing the entrance from the east and lit by a prayer candle. At the same time, homes that lacked an icon corner bore the mark of its absence. The non-Orthodox included "those of other faiths" (*inovertsy*)—Jews, Muslims, Buddhists, members of polytheistic religions—as well as dissenters, such as the Dukhobors[41] and Tolstoyans, who in rejecting icons as idolatry rendered manifest their break with official Orthodoxy. The role of the icon in identity formation extended as well to rites of inclusion and exclusion at the threshold between the Orthodox and the non-Orthodox. Thus missionaries incorporated icons in the baptismal ceremonies of new converts at the far reaches of empire,[42] while as part of an annual rite commemorating the Orthodox victory over the iconoclasts, anathemas were proclaimed in parish churches, not least against those who, in old ways and new, mock or profane holy images.[43]

Through prayers, blessings, hymns, and other rituals, all subsections of the Orthodox community, from the tsar and the Holy Synod to the vast peasant laity, participated in the veneration of icons. Yet different constituent groups identified with the icon for different reasons, not all of which had Orthodoxy as their foremost concern. In sermons and ecclesiastical writings, local and national clergy, in endless variations on the same theme, promulgated the incarnational theology adopted at the Seventh Ecumenical Council in Nicea (787); just as the Word became flesh (John 1:14), so, too, holy beings or "prototypes"—Christ, the Mother of God, and the saints—may be legitimately venerated through their human likeness in icons. To confuse the image for its prototype constitutes idolatry, that is, the worship of graven images (Exod. 20:4–5), while to pray before the wrong kind of image borders on heresy. The ability of the church to police correct usage was nevertheless limited in practice. In *Likeness and Presence,* Hans Belting argues that Christian traditions of image veneration, both Catholic and Orthodox, ultimately derive from popular rites foreign to the "church's institutions"; theology, at first unable to ban the people's favorite cult images, instead settled "for issuing conditions and limitations governing access to them."[44] Be that as it may, the Russian Orthodox Church remained a relatively decentralized institution in the imperial period, with standardized rites supplemented by a patchwork of local practices. Thus individual parishes tended to have their own "revered" (*osobochtimye*) icons, icon processions, and favored saints, and while the laity did look to the clergy to consecrate any new "miracle-working" (*chudotvornye*) icons in their midst, the church lacked a single standard for adjudicating all claims, and official disapproval did not necessarily curb rumors surrounding a popular icon's magical appearance or healing powers.[45]

Under Peter I (r. 1682–1725) and his successors, the church hierarchy, motivated in part by an Enlightenment distrust of superstition, struggled to contain the sacred within officially approved channels, confiscating nonsanctioned icons, submitting miracle-working icons to empirical tests, and blocking the veneration of church icons in public spaces.[46] During the course of the nineteenth century, official responses to popular forms of icon veneration nevertheless became gradually more accommodating. As Shevzov observes, church intellectuals, in Russia and elsewhere, were actively relocating the institutional center of their respective sacred communities in the "people"; as patriarchs of the Eastern churches explained to Pope Pius in an 1848 encyclical, "Neither Patriarchs nor Councils could introduce novelty among us, because the protector of religion is the very body of the Church, the people themselves."[47] In Russia, this conceptual shift toward the peasant laity, as formulated by both secular and clerical authorities, contributed to a fin-de-siècle flourishing of popular rituals and legends involving icons. Thus the number of rural icon visitations, in which revered icons are led from church to church or to private homes, measurably increased, while prominent church leaders, offering their protection and theological support, often welcomed reports of new miracle-working icons beyond the few dozen that the Holy Synod officially recognized.[48]

Top-down campaigns to regulate icon veneration, in contrast, had a mixed record at best. From 1653 to 1656, to note a major example, Patriarch Nikon of Moscow, with the approval of Tsar Alexis I (r. 1645–76), forced through a number of liturgical revisions in an attempt to bring Russian practices in line with Greek Orthodox models, including on matters of iconography. Thus the spelling of Jesus' name on icons was changed from *Isus* to *Iisus,* and the number of fingers used in making the sign of the cross increased from two to three. At church councils in 1656 and 1666–67, those who refused to support the revised rite—and its accompanying iconography—were anathematized, a judgment that the state backed with force of arms. This combined front nevertheless failed to prevent, and even arguably accelerated, the formation of independent "Old Believer" churches (as the dissenters came to be collectively known). Under Nicholas I (r. 1825–55), state authorities redoubled their efforts to suppress Old Believer practices, in the process confiscating large numbers of "heretical" icons from before and after the schism. Yet by the mid-nineteenth century, the fate of Old Believer icons was no longer exclusively a matter of church and state. For a small group of scholars and private collectors, Old Believers had performed an invaluable national service not only in protecting pre-Nikonian icons from official acts of iconoclasm but also in continuing to paint new icons using the methods and iconography of the "old style." Wealthy Old Believers discreetly amassed private icon collections, and scholars of varying religious persuasion relied on Old Believer sources to rewrite the sacred history of the icon along national and secular lines.[49] Even within the government Old Believer icons found allies; thus, instead of being ritually destroyed, as had been the norm two centuries earlier, many confiscated icons from the Ministry of Internal Affairs ended up in state museums.[50]

For all sides concerned, a national reframing of the icon's significance furnished common ground for a new connoisseurship. At a pragmatic level, discussion of the schism remained tightly censored. In Dmitry Rovinsky's *Survey of Icon Painting in Russia Through the End of the Seventeenth Century* (1856), the first general monograph of its kind, religious censors expurgated all references to Old Believers.[51] Yet in a larger sense, a unified national narrative—one grounded in a common valorization of Russia's folk heritage—displaced an otherwise still very real controversy over the conflicting icon traditions of the Old Believers and the official church. In terms of semantics, "Russian" (*russkoe*) and "Old Russian" (*drevnerusskoe*) emerged as master qualifiers for "the icon" (*ikona* or *obraz*) in publications and exhibitions, a development no less significant than the prevalent substitution of "art" (*iskusstvo*) and "painting" (*zhivopis'*) for "icon painting" (*ikonopis'*) a half century later. In 1905, after an edict on religious tolerance permitted Old Believers to open their churches, fresh caches of pre-Nikonian icons were made public and restored by specialists.[52] The 1913 Exhibition of Old Russian Art not only brought together icons from both sides of the schism; neither "Orthodox" nor "icon" even appeared in the exhibition title.

The 1913 exhibition, which was enthusiastically supported by Nicholas II (r. 1894–1917) and proved a highlight of the celebrations for the Romanov dynasty's tercentenary, also illustrates the role of the state in nationalizing the icon. This role can further be tracked in relation to Ukrainian church art. The Russian and Ukrainian branches of the Orthodox Church, both descended from Kievan Rus, had for nearly two hundred years existed independently prior to the Russian acquisition of eastern Ukraine in the 1620s–1640s. Among the precipitating causes of Nikon's liturgical reforms had been the need to harmonize Moscow's liturgy with that of the Ukrainian Church.[53] Inasmuch as they were thought to resemble Greek models, Ukrainian icons ended up on the opposing side of the schism from those defended by predominantly Russian Old Believers. Despite the official favor that the Ukrainian liturgy enjoyed following the schism, decisions affecting Ukrainian churches were increasingly made by state authorities in Russia. In 1686–87, the Kievan Metropoly became subordinate to the Moscow Patriarchate, while in 1721, Peter I abolished the Moscow Patriarchate and replaced it with the Most Holy Governing Synod in St. Petersburg, the new imperial capital, effectively rendering the Orthodox Church a department of the state. By the mid-nineteenth century, as in the case of Old Believer icons, the restoration of Ukrainian churches in Kiev was contributing in significant ways to a growing appreciation of icons in Russia. In the fall of 1842, Nicholas I visited the Monastery of the Caves (*Pechers'ka lavrato*) in Kiev to inspect frescoes in the eleventh-century Dormition Cathedral, which recently had been repainted under the auspices of the Kievan metropolitan. Unhappy with what he saw, the tsar ordered that all church renovations henceforth be approved by the Holy Synod. As Vzdornov notes, the tsar's displeasure, for better or worse, marked a key moment in the transition from repainting to restoration in the empire. With Nicholas I's approval, Fyodor Solntsev, a Russian painter from the St. Petersburg Academy of Arts, employed secular techniques in the restoration of the Dormition Cathedral and, shortly thereafter, the even more ancient and revered Saint Sophia Cathedral in Kiev.[54]

Under Nicholas I, "Orthodoxy, Autocracy, and Nationality"—a formula developed by Sergei Uvarov, his minister of education—became the official doctrine of the Russian Empire. A coincidence of Orthodoxy and nationalism, on one hand, and the collaboration of state, church, and academy, on the other, can be observed in many church commissions at the time. For major construction projects, the Holy Synod generally turned to academy-trained painters (*zhivopistsy*), who enjoyed a higher level of professional prestige than did traditional icon painters (*ikonopistsy*) from Palekh, Kholui, or Mstera. In two prominent cases—Saint Isaac's (1818–58) and Christ the Savior (1838–81), the largest cathedrals in St. Petersburg and Moscow, respectively—teams of academy painters applied Western-style religious painting more or less directly onto the walls of Orthodox churches. By contrast, in a Russian iteration of Pre-Raphaelitism, the focus toward the end of the century noticeably shifted from the Renaissance to Byzantium. Thus Viktor Vasnetsov studied Old Russian icons as well as the Byzantine frescoes and mosaics of Rome and Istanbul in preparation for designing the murals of the Saint Vladimir Cathedral in Kiev. Built from 1885 to 1896, this cathedral was commissioned to commemorate the nine-hundredth anniversary of the conversion of Rus to Christianity in 988 under Vladimir, Grand Prince of Kiev and a canonized saint (pl. 8). Vasnetsov lent visual form to an official reading of church history that positioned Russia as the rightful heir to Kievan Orthodoxy, the first church of the East Slavic peoples, and he himself emerged as the leader of a reform movement within Orthodox iconography, as his Byzantine-inspired murals were widely reproduced in lithograph form and in other churches.

In short, those branches of Orthodoxy that were nonconforming (Old Believers), non-Russian (Ukraine), or even pre-Russian (Byzantine) were to varying degrees assimilated into emerging narratives about the Russian icon. Despite the central role assigned to the Russian people in such narratives, the church and the intelligentsia nevertheless maintained a certain ambivalence toward popular means of icon production. In his 1866 study, Buslaev praises the "artistic ideals" of the traditional Russian icon painter, an ascetic folk figure who does not "consciously strive toward refinement" or "artificial poetry": "in such ideals . . . the Russian people expressed its understanding of human worth." These same ideals had enabled Russian icon painters, at least until the seventeenth century, to "remain true to Byzantine traditions": "our ancient icon painting has the indisputable advantage over Western art inasmuch as fate guarded it . . . from that artistic upheaval commonly known as the 'Renaissance.'"[55] Traditional icon painters appeared to have accomplished this extraordinary feat of preservation through an ethos of similitude: the icon reveals the likeness of its prototype; new icons, as copies of copies, preserve that likeness by transcribing it from other icons. For midcentury icon scholars across Europe, research on Greek icon-painting manuals and Russian pattern books (*podlinniki*), which provided verbal or pictorial schemas for canonical holy figures, further explained the perceived stylistic continuity of the Eastern icon over the centuries and across the Orthodox world. In Russia, where pattern books were still in use, the 1869 publication of the pre-schism Stroganov *podlinnik* had the telling, if unintended, consequence of reinforcing a growing stereotype of the icon painter as a mere copyist. In Leskov's *The Ensealed Angel* (1873), a popular novella about a desecrated Old Believer icon, one icon painter pointedly rejects such a view: "It's an offense to us to think that we simply use set patterns as if they were stencils. In the pattern book [*podlinnik*], we're given a rule, but how it's followed is left to the freedom of the artist."[56]

As these comments suggest, a reliance on sanctioned models seemed at odds with the criterion of originality dominant in secular canons of high art. Elizabeth Valkenier, for example, observes that first-generation Peredvizhniki painters, for all the populism of their subject matter, did not borrow from such peasant art forms as the *lubok,* a type of woodcut used for making anything from domestic icons to shop signs.[57] Indeed, *lubochnyi* ("lubok-like") served as a derogatory term for coarse art among professional painters and critics.[58] In a similar manner, as Robert Nichols has shown, icon scholars and enthusiasts from Moscow and St. Petersburg tended to be appalled at the ominous signs of mass production they found on visiting provincial icon centers. In order to keep up with overwhelming demand, icon painters in Palekh, Mstera, and Kholui were increasingly forced to sacrifice individual craftsmanship in favor of a collective division of labor; in a given workshop, where the underpaid workers often included women and children, each icon was constructed in a piecemeal fashion, passing from one station to the next.[59] In a 1901 report "on the contemporary state of Russian folk icon painting," Kondakov laid out for Nicholas II the extent to which the craft of icon painting had deteriorated due to the ignorance and poverty rampant in such workshops. Even worse, foreign firms in Moscow were producing tintype icons by means of metal presses and chromolithography, a practice that Kondakov and his allies subsequently campaigned, without much success, to have banned.[60] In the age of mechanical reproduction, the painting of Western Europe confronted its perspectival double in the photograph; the icon, a sacred copy, instead attained a sort of *reductio ad absurdum* in the canning factories of Moscow.

On the eve of modernist rediscovery, the art of icon painting, for a small but influential minority, was in desperate need of revival. The diverging fates of the Old Russian icon and the imperial icon were inextricably linked at the turn of the twentieth century. The cultural elite celebrated the folk traditions of the first, even as they abhorred the means through which the second was made available to the masses. Five years after Kondakov's report, Gurianov, an award-winning icon painter in his own right and a fellow proponent of the craft's revival, published the results of the cleaning of Rublev's *Trinity*. Upon removing the icon's metal casing, and before witnessing Rublev's underlying colors, Gurianov recounts his "surprise" at the sheer artlessness of the overpainting: "We saw an icon painted in the new Palekh manner of the nineteenth century."[61] In the landmark restorations of Old Russian icons, not only did the hidden become revealed, but something that had been everywhere visible became unworthy of view. The imperial icon was the first layer modernism scraped away.

REFRAMINGS

The meaning of the icon depends on its contexts. These contexts include the spaces in which icons reside and move, the processes of production and maintenance they undergo, as well as their discursive environment—the words written about them, spoken in their presence, or inscribed on their surface. On the importance of language in particular, semiotics concurs with theology. Boris Uspensky and Leonid Ouspensky, in otherwise very different monographs, both emphasize the writings of the Church Fathers in constituting the icon's meaning and content.[62] The icon's potential for meaning is nevertheless not foreclosed by any single interpretative structure, be it a body of dogma or a system of signs. On the contrary, the removal of old frames clears the way for new ones. With a shared attention to dynamic processes, as well as a critical orientation toward one-sided narratives of loss, the authors in Parts I and II of this volume explore the changing meaning of icons in their modern contexts.

In a chapter on Mother of God icons, Elena Boeck brings fresh insight and theoretical sophistication to the long-standing problem of the Russian icon's relationship to Western images. As Boeck demonstrates, cross-cultural exchanges proved conducive to the production of entirely new iconographic types. At the turn of the eighteenth century, disparate images of Mary from across Christendom—which were making their way to the Russian market via print media—laid the foundation for the emergence of compendia icons, a type unknown to earlier Byzantine iconography. In such icons, multiple miniature miracle-working icons are displayed in a well-ordered grid, each icon labeled to indicate its provenance. Such an arrangement, in its concern for cataloging and universality, betrays a taxonomic impulse typical of the Enlightenment. As modern innovations, Russian compendia icons are not intended to be perceived as miraculous in themselves; rather, their purpose is to affirm existing traditions of miracle-working icons. As Boeck argues, the first compendia icons appear to have participated in eighteenth-century campaigns against the church reforms of Peter I, including his efforts to put purportedly miracle-working icons to the test. By the end of tsarist Russia, in contrast, the compendium icon had fully entered the Orthodox mainstream, becoming a patriotic expression, officially sanctioned, of Russia's favored status beneath the Mother of God's veil.

Vera Shevzov pursues this emphasis on the politics of tradition within church liturgy, documenting the modern evolution of the annual celebration of icon veneration on the first Sunday of Lent, a feast day known as the Triumph of Orthodoxy. As Shevzov argues, icons are framed not only materially but also rhetorically, that is, according to the sacred language of liturgy. Since its inception in ninth-century Byzantium, the liturgical rite that was conducted for the occasion of this feast linked icons with the "triumph" or "victory" of the Orthodox faith. It did so by reiterating the incarnational theology on which the veneration of icons was based; by remembering those who defended images and this theology; by condemning iconoclasts and their views; and by lauding the emperor and patriarch or local bishop as the defenders of Orthodoxy. In the mid-eighteenth century, church officials streamlined and standardized this rite in order to make its celebration uniform throughout Russia. Reading these revisions in light of the modern account of the icon's history, Ouspensky concluded that the new rite obscured the confessional content of the icon, thereby reflecting the general decline to which the icon in modern Russia was subject. Through close analysis of the modern celebration of the Triumph of Orthodoxy, Shevzov maintains instead that while the content of the new rite did indeed focus less on the icon, it did not lose sight of it. Rather, the icon's theological meaning was liturgically recast, enabling latent meanings to come into relief.

In a chapter on Nicholas II, Robert Nichols extends this focus on icon traditions to the imperial court. Specifically, Nichols demonstrates that the last emperor's abiding preoccupation with miracle-working icons, far from representing a political anachronism, as has been commonly argued, contributed to a well-crafted national persona. As a future head of the church, Nicholas had been raised as a child with an appreciation for all forms of liturgical worship, and throughout his life he maintained a belief in the miraculous powers of icons. Nichols situates the tsar's iconophilia within the context of an emerging twentieth-century aesthetics of power, one in which the cult of the medieval served as a thoroughly modern alternative to competing ideologies based on the principles of the Enlightenment. This synthesis of the old and the new is especially evident in Nicholas II's behind-the-scenes involvement in the canonization of Saint Seraphim of Sarov, an early nineteenth-century elder (*starets*), whose freshly minted icon the tsar used to bless Russian troops as they departed for war with Japan in 1904. In keeping with his national persona, Nicholas also endorsed efforts to revive the traditional art of icon painting. For Nicholas and Alexandra, icons, particularly those of warrior saints, harked back to an earlier era when the tsar and the people were spiritually united, and thus embodied the faith, military strength, and established order key to Russia's continued greatness.

Nicholas II's new synthesis did not survive his reign, of course. After the collapse of the Romanov dynasty in 1917, control over pre-Petrine icons shifted decisively from the church to the museum. Shirley Glade, John-Paul Himka, and Wendy Salmond explore the causes and consequences of this process from three different starting points. In a chapter on Alexander Anisimov, Glade selects the work of a single scholar-champion (*uchenyi-borets*) to highlight the high stakes surrounding the rediscovery of the Russian icon in the first decades of the twentieth century. As a scholar and one of the founders of the Soviet science of restoration, Anisimov was an early and outspoken proponent of the view of Old Russian icons as artistic masterpieces. In 1912, he launched the first public attack on the Orthodox Church for its mismanagement of the icons in its care. Just a few years later, Animisov found himself fighting instead the indiscriminate iconoclasm unleashed by the revolution. In 1918, Anisimov was appointed scientific director for the newly founded Commission for the Preservation and Uncovering of Monuments of Ancient Painting. Thanks to the nationalization of church holdings in the 1920s, he and his colleagues gained unprecedented access to the most ancient icons in Russian cathedrals. Through numerous publications, Anisimov was instrumental in rewriting the history of the Russian icon and, by extension, Russian painting. Perhaps his single greatest feat was the restoration and scientific dating of the Vladimir Mother of God, among the first icons to reach Russia from Byzantium. While Anisimov's thoroughgoing secularism may have corresponded well to the spirit of times, he eventually fell victim to Stalin's purges, and his name was virtually forgotten.

In a chapter on the National Lviv Museum, John-Paul Himka chronicles the hundred-year history of a major icon collection against the background of recurrent political upheaval. At the time of the museum's founding in 1905, the destruction of aging icons was commonplace in Catholic churches in Galicia. For such iconophiles as Andrei Sheptytsky, the archbishop of Lviv, it was a matter of great urgency to seek out endangered icons and place them under the auspices of the new museum. Like the city of Lviv itself, which was ruled successively by Austria-Hungary, Poland, Nazi Germany, the Soviet Union, and independent Ukraine, the museum found itself in the continual crossfire—at times literally—of opposing ideological forces. The shifting political landscape influenced everything from the makeup of the curatorial staff, many of whom suffered arrest and exile, to the location of the museum's collection, a subject of bitter dispute as recently as 2005. Despite such hardships, secular scholarship on the icons of Galicia flourished at most stages of the museum's existence. Himka's research on the museum's Ukrainian Catholic icons offers suggestive parallels for rethinking the museum collections of Orthodox icons elsewhere in the former Soviet Union as well. As with the Russian icon, the reconceptualization of the Ukrainian icon from sacred image to folk art proved amenable to Communists and nationalists alike, helping the museum's collection outlive the regimes around it.

Among many other points of contact, Himka and Glade—focusing on a single scholar and a single museum, respectively—each chronicle the immense and protracted labor required to effect a revaluation of the medieval icon, which saw its perceived artistic worth rise steadily over the early decades of the twentieth century. In a chapter on the traveling exhibition "Masterpieces of Early Russian Painting," Wendy Salmond follows this process of revaluation to its logical conclusion, examining how Soviet scholars, including Anisimov, repackaged the icon for the global art market. Working in conjunction with the State Trading Agency (Gostorg), Soviet icon scholars and restorers organized the first-ever exhibitions of Old Russian "painting"—that is, *zhivopis'*, a term preferred to *ikonopis'* or "icon painting"—in Western Europe and the United States. Igor Grabar, the guiding force behind the enterprise, conducted numerous interviews with the foreign press, while the exhibition catalog showcased Soviet advances in the science of restoration. Focusing on the American stage of the tour in 1930–32, Salmond makes two provocative claims about the exhibition's aims and results. First, its hidden agenda was to raise hard currency for the cash-strapped Soviet state by instilling an appreciation for the icon as a fine art in bourgeois collectors. Second, the exhibition version of the Russian icon's rediscovery became the dominant narrative in the American academy. Ironically, as Salmond documents, the exhibition failed in its mercantile mission. In a larger sense, however, the exhibition did succeed in securing a permanent place for the Russian icon on the world stage. Salmond provides a timely genealogy of the international study of the Russian icon.

Since the seventeenth century, myriad ideological forces have been brought to bear upon the icon, from Enlightenment taxonomies to anti-Enlightenment anathemas and from an imperial cult of the medieval to a Soviet cult of science. In the process, the meaning of the icon has been repeatedly reframed: old icons must be restored, not repainted; preserved for posterity, not put to ritual death. Most crucially, the icon, once within the walls of the museum, becomes a painting, a work of art, even a masterpiece. Looking back, with whatever blind spots and vantage points such hindsight affords, the aesthetic value of the Old Russian icon, rather than representing something neglected and then rediscovered, can be recognized as modernity's own seal of authenticity.

INTERMEDIAL ICON

Not only did Russian icons acquire new discursive frames in modernity; they also changed medium. In *Icon and Icon Veneration* (1931), to cite a telling example, the theologian Sergei Bulgakov transforms the icon into a new phenomenology by way of film: "In a lifetime, a person manifests an innumerable number of icons of his spirit, unfolding the endless film reel of his phenomenology."[63] For Bulgakov, the human form is like an icon, while the icon, in turn, is like a moving image (as opposed to a static portrait). Setting aside the intricacies of Bulgakov's incarnational theology, his conjunction of icon and film here is symptomatic of a fundamental shift in the understanding of what constitutes an icon. In modern art, criticism, and the notion of theology, the icon began to refer not just to a certain type of holy image depicting the set figures of Christian iconography, one made by church-sanctioned producers and consecrated as worthy of veneration for the faithful. In addition, icons, whether whole or in part, readily morphed into word pictures, paintings, posters, photographs, and stage sets. They were projected on film, in dreams, from the retina of the eye, or, as in Bulgakov, into the recesses of the soul.

Beginning in the nineteenth century and culminating in the art of the avant-garde, the icon emerged from a long-standing, if only ever relative, artistic isolation and entered into an ever-widening scope of intermedial contacts with the secular arts. Intermediality, a term that has gained currency in word/image studies, can be defined as the network of relations, both internal and external, connecting cultural productions of one medium with those of others.[64] In the case of the icon, its appropriation by other media could result in an eclectic syncretism or a totalizing synthesis (*Gesamtkunstwerk*), depending on the artist in question. Yet whether an artist accented or effaced its otherness, the Russian icon, in its new media, became both more and less than what it had been before. The authors in Parts III and IV of this volume critically examine the aesthetic and ideological ramifications of the icon's protean intermediality in modernity.

Jefferson Gatrall explores the different ways that late nineteenth-century Russian writers and painters attempted to modernize the iconography of Christ, tracking in particular a convergence of scholarly and artistic projects over the field of early Christian iconography. In preparation for his painting *Christ and the Adulteress* (1887), Vasily Polenov consulted catacomb frescoes as well as Byzantine icons and miniatures in a quixotic effort to reconstruct the physical appearance of the historical Jesus—a conspicuously modern Christ type. Polenov's work parallels that of the archeologist Dmitry Ainalov, who in the 1890s conducted firsthand research on Byzantine mosaics in Italy, where, among other things, he singled out a fourth-century blond-haired, blue-eyed Christ as the oldest extant instance of the "historical type." In the novel *Julian the Apostate* (1896), by contrast, Dmitry Merezhkovsky's fourth-century protagonist, the last pagan emperor of Rome, encounters a host of Christ images from Constantinople to Cappadocia, none of which captures whole the True Face and yet all of which carry a potential trace of its original meaning. In different media and with disparate results, Polenov, Ainolov, and Merezhkovsky thus each extended the nineteenth-century quest of the historical Jesus to an updating of the iconography of Christ. In the process, they modernized the traditional link between an icon and its prototype: the true likeness of the historical Jesus, inasmuch as it is recoverable at all, must be sought in his earliest surviving afterimages.

In contrast with this iconographic focus, typical for nineteenth-century scholars and artists, the Russian avant-garde appropriated the icon's formal properties to an unprecedented degree. In her chapter, Sarah Pratt detects and analyzes "invisible icons" embedded in select poems by Vladimir Mayakovsky, Velimir Khlebnikov, and Nikolai Zabolotsky. These icons are not legible on a cursory reading yet emerge from within the visual logic of each poem. Moreover, different poems encode quite specific icon types—Christ Pantocrator, Our Lady of the Sign, and so on—without, however, being just poems *about* icons. In other words, none of these poems are ekphrases. Instead, they preserve the intermedial otherness of the icon through a complex semiotic operation. Borrowing Charles Sanders Peirce's terminology, Pratt analyzes how each poem, as a "symbol" or third-order sign, both obscures and reveals the presence of an imaginary icon, that is, a first-order sign. This icon, as if buried beneath layers of text, forms one part of a "mixed-media palimpsest"; thus the poem does not cancel out its own semiotic thirdness but rather expands to accommodate the firstness of the icon. The reader, as an "interpretant," is transformed into a viewer and, in an Orthodox sense, even a supplicant. At the same time, these invisible icons serve thoroughly heterodox purposes, whether to glorify Soviet Man (Zabolotsky), poetic language (Khlebnikov), or the poet himself (Mayakovsky).

Unlike traditional icon painters, who worked as members of the church, avant-garde poets and painters of iconlike art, whatever their individual belief systems might be, remained secular producers. Pavel Florensky, priest and polymath, worked from the opposite direction, bringing theology into dialogue with profane realms of knowledge in order to reconcile the icon's dual claims as art form and sacred object. Douglas Greenfield and John McGuckin both situate Florensky's theory of icons in relation to understudied aspects of his life and writings. Greenfield takes up Florensky's philosophy of technology. Connecting Florensky's thoughts on such eclectic topics as Aegean archeology, the physiology of the eye, puppet theater, and even Siberian permafrost, Greenfield sheds light on the neglected material substratum of Florensky's theological interpretation of reverse perspective. For Florensky, tools not only reflect, as symbolic reagents, a given culture's worldview; they also represent organ projections, literal extensions of the body. Florensky tellingly demonstrates the dual aspect of the symbol-tool in relation to a recently discovered binocular-shaped vessel from ancient Crete. In Florensky's view, this symbol-tool belongs to the cult of a deity and simultaneously evinces an advanced awareness of binocular disparity. As Greenfield argues, the Orthodox icon, as a symbol-tool in its own right, expresses a similar awareness of the disparity between the images received by each eye. In his essay "Reverse Perspective," Florensky contends that Western painting, in its dependence on linear perspective, presupposes a monocular worldview. By contrast, the icon, which integrates multiple perspectives on a given object over time, remains faithful to the doubleness of human vision, a superiority with both symbolic and technological consequences. The icon, as the projection of two eyes, not one, is a powerful tool for suprasensible perception.

In his chapter on Florensky's theory of dreams, McGuckin makes the provocative claim that Florensky himself, through the totality of his words and deeds, represents both an icon and its commentary. In keeping with his own understanding of Divine Wisdom as a cosmic unity in diversity, Florensky undertook a personal journey through the empirical and theoretical sciences—from mathematics to art history to linguistics and beyond—in search of a synthetic worldview that could accommodate the heterogeneity of the material world. These studies, moreover, were inseparable from his vocation as an ordained priest. Even after the revolution, when he was forced to give up his position in the church, he remained a conspicuous witness to the spirit of ecclesiality, wearing his cassock to scientific lectures and even at party meetings. As McGuckin argues, this liminality, straddling the secular and the clerical, the spiritual and the material, also informs Florensky's understanding of the icon. In his essay "Iconostasis," Florensky, through the concept of iconic dreaming, presents an arch-psychoanalytical interpretation of dreams to illustrate the liminality of icons. As in a dream state, the icon painter, in an ascending moment, enters an imaginary space in which the visible and invisible, the phenomenal and the noumenal, coexist. It is only in the descent toward waking, however, that the dreamer/icon painter, passing back across the threshold, lends revelation the form of symbolic imagery. The icon, indeed all true art, is materialized dream.

In the final chapter of this volume, Robert Bird emphasizes the circumspection with which Andrei Tarkovsky approached the icon in his 1969 film *Andrei Rublev.* In his writings, Tarkovsky does identify certain formal qualities common to film and the icon: both are imprints of absent originals, whether a negative image or a divine prototype; both are torn between the demands of image and narrative. At the same time, however, film is an utterly profane art form. As Tarkovsky observes, film was born at the fairground, and there is a long tradition of desecrating icons in Soviet cinema. Any attempt to capture icons on film runs the double risk of either profaning or aestheticizing the sacred. Tarkovsky instead uses the medium of film, as both narrative and image, to illuminate the religious significance, common to all sacred arts, of aesthetic experience. In *Andrei Rublev,* icons remain passive, background objects in the narrative of Rublev's life. This narrative, though profane, nevertheless crucially situates his icons in the material world and provides occasion for their presence to become manifest—most paradoxically, in scenes where they are destroyed. Through the pauses in the fragmentary narrative of *Andrei Rublev,* Tarkovsky thus pushes film toward a transcendent image of that which must ultimately lie beyond its own grasp. The "celluloid icon," as Bird puts it, does not replace the icon but rather marks the break where film, in a gesture of intermedial sacrifice, cancels itself out.

In the six decades between the cleaning of Rublev's *Trinity* and the making of Tarkovsky's *Andrei Rublev,* the icon became a model of color and perspective, of human vision and the human visage, for the secular arts in Russia. Just as any backward gaze at the golden age of Rublev must pass through the lens of modernist rediscovery, it is now difficult, in retrospect, to think of the Russian icon apart from all its modern couplings. The icon is like painting, folk art, or a masterpiece. But the reverse is also true: painting, photography, film, poetry, prose, or even dream can become like an icon. Forgoing a return to the origin, the authors in this volume instead unravel the manifold operations through which the icon has been reframed and reshaped in the workshops of modernity.

NOTES TO INTRODUCTION

1. See especially Daniel Bell, *The Cultural Contradictions of Capitalism* (New York: Basic Books, 1976), 31–171; Marshall Berman, *All That Is Solid Melts into Air: The Experience of Modernity* (New York: Simon & Schuster, 1982), 87–130; Maurizio Passerin d'Entrèves and Seyla Benhabib, eds., *Habermas and the Unfinished Project of Modernity: Critical Essays on the Philosophical Discourse of Modernity* (Cambridge, Mass.: MIT Press, 1997); S. N. Eisenstadt, ed., *Multiple Modernities,* Proceedings of the American Academy of Arts and Sciences 129, no. 1 (Cambridge, Mass.: American Academy of Arts and Sciences, 2000); Dilip Parameshwar Gaonkar, ed., *Alternative Modernities* (Durham: Duke University Press, 2001).

2. On the concept of "religious capital," see Pierre Bourdieu, "Genesis and Structure of the Religious Field," trans. Jenny B. Burnside, Craig Calhoun, and Leah Florence, *Comparative Social Research* 13 (1991): 10, 22–23.

3. On the secularization debate, see, for example, Steve Bruce, ed., *Religion and Modernization: Sociologists and Historians Debate the Secularization Thesis* (Oxford: Clarendon Press, 1992); Talal Asad, *Formations of the Secular: Christianity, Islam, Modernity* (Stanford: Stanford University Press, 2003); Charles Taylor, *A Secular Age* (Cambridge, Mass.: Belknap Press of Harvard University Press, 2007). In the Russian context, see Laura Engelstein, "Holy Russia in Modern Times: An Essay on Orthodoxy and Cultural Change," *Past and Present,* no. 173 (2001): 129–56.

4. See Max Weber, "Science as a Vocation," in *From Max Weber: Essays in Sociology,* ed. and trans. Hans H. Gerth and C. Wright Mills (1918; repr., New York: Oxford University Press, 1946), 129–56.

5. Prime Minister Vladimir Putin and President Dmitry Medvedev are regularly shown with icons on Russian television. See Adrian Blomfield, "Orthodox Church Enters Unholy Alliance with Putin," *Daily Telegraph* (London), 23 February 2008; Kyra Latukhina, "Vlast' smenilas'," *Vedemosti,* 8 May 2008.

6. Jürgen Habermas, "Modernity: An Unfinished Project," in *Habermas,* 38–55.

7. Émile Durkheim, "Concerning the Definition of Religious Phenomenon," in *Durkheim on Religion: A Selection of Readings with Bibliographies,* ed. W. S. F. Pickering, trans. Jacqueline Redding and W. S. F. Pickering (1899; repr., London: Routledge, 1975), 90.

8. See, for example, Paul Gilroy, *The Black Atlantic: Modernity and Double Consciousness* (Cambridge, Mass.: Harvard University Press, 1993), 1–40; Arjun Appadurai, *Modernity at Large: Cultural Dimensions of Globalization* (Minneapolis: University of Minnesota Press, 1996); Tani E. Barlow, ed., *Formations of Colonial Modernity in East Asia* (Durham: Duke University Press, 1997); Dipesh Chakrabarty, *Provincializing Europe: Postcolonial Thought and Historical Difference* (Princeton: Princeton University Press, 2000); Gaonkar, "On Alternative Modernities," in *Alternative Modernities,* 1–23.

9. See, for example, T. W. Adorno, *Aesthetic Theory,* ed. Gretel Adorno and Rolf Tiedemann, trans. C. Lenhardt (London: Routledge, 1984), 48–51.

10. For an excellent overview of the early twentieth-century rediscovery, see Shirley A. Glade, "A Heritage Discovered Anew: Russia's Reevaluation of Pre-Petrine Icons in the Late Tsarist and Early Soviet Periods," *Canadian-American Slavic Studies* 26, nos. 1–3 (1992): 145–95; for a succinct synopsis in Russian, see V. N. Lazarev, "Otkrytie russkoi ikony i ee izuchenie," *Russkaia ikonopis'—ot istokov do nachala XVI veka,* 6 vols. (Moscow: Iskusstvo, 1983), 1:11–18.

11. Lindsey Hughes, "Inventing Andrei: Soviet and Post-Soviet Views of Andrei Rublev and His Trinity Icon," *Slavonica* 9, no. 2 (November 2003): 84–85.

12. Restoration on the icon resumed in 1918.

13. N. Punin, "Vystavka drevnerusskogo iskusstva (ustroennaia Moskovskim Arkheologicheskim Institutom imeni Imp. Nikolaia II)," *Apollon* 5 (1913): 38.

14. G. I. Vzdornov, *Istoriia oekrytiia i izucheniia russkoi* *srednevekovoi zhivopisi: XIX veka* (Moscow: Iskusstvo, 1986), 22–23, 28–46, 81–86, 209.

15. Punin, "Vystavka," 38.

16. Among writers, Nikolai Leskov was a rare and important exception. See Vzdornov, *Istoriia otkrytiia i izucheniia russkoi srednevekovoi zhivopisi,* 204, 275.

17. For scholarship on icons in the novels of Tolstoy and Dostoevsky, see especially Richard F. Gustafson, *Leo Tolstoy, Resident and Stranger: A Study in Fiction and Theology* (Princeton: Princeton University Press, 1986), 202–13; Diane Oenning Thompson, *The Brothers Karamazov and the Poetics of Memory* (Cambridge: Cambridge University Press, 1991), 76–83; Amy Mandelker, *Framing Anna Karenina: Tolstoy, the Women Question, and the Victorian Novel* (Columbus: Ohio State University Press, 1994), 76–80; Jefferson J. A. Gatrall, "The Icon in the Picture: Reframing the Question of Dostoevsky's Modernist Iconography," *Slavic and East European Journal* 48, no. 1 (2004): 1–25.

18. The Peredvizhniki were a group of realist painters, founded in 1870, that organized exhibitions independently of the St. Petersburg Academy of Arts. For recent research on the Peredvizhniki and church art, see Marina Shumalova, "Novoe priobretenie GTG—ikona V. G. Perova 'Spas,'" *Materialy pervoi nauchnoi konferentsii* (Moscow, 1996), 114–21; Tat'iana Iudenkova, "Troitskii iconostas I. N. Kramskogo," *Russkaia galeriia* 1 (2001): 56–61; Ol'ga Atroscenko, "Vasilii Polenov i Aleksandr Ivanov: k istorii tserkvi Kologrivenskogo uchilishcha," *Sobranie,* no. 1 (2004): 104–15.

19. F. I. Buslaev, "Obshchie poniatiia o russkoi ikonopisi," in *Drevnerusskaia literatura i pravoslavnoe iskusstvo* (St. Petersburg: Izdatel'stvo Russkogo Khristianskogo gumanitarnogo instituta, "Liga-Plius," 2001), 36–186: 50.

20. See John E. Bowlt, "Orthodoxy and the Avant-Garde: Sacred Images in the Work of Goncharova, Malevich, and Their Contemporaries," in *Christianity and the Arts in Russia,* ed. William C. Brumfield and Milos M. Velimirovic (Cambridge: Cambridge University Press, 1991), 145–50; O. Tarasenko, "K probleme natsionalnykh istokov v russkoi zhivopisi kontsa XIX-nachala XX veka," *Sovetskoe iskusstvoznanie* 27 (1991): 156–82; Verena Krieger, *Von der Ikone zur Utopie: Kunstkonzepte der russischen Avantgarde* (Cologne: Böhlau Verlag, 1998); Andrew Spira, *The Avant-Garde Icon: Russian Avant-Garde Art and the Icon Painting Tradition* (Burlington, Vt.: Lund Humphries, 2008).

21. Alexander Rodchenko, quoted in Krieger, *Von der Ikone zur Utopie,* 7.

22. See Jane Ashton Sharp, *Russian Modernism Between East and West: Natal'ia Goncharova and the Moscow Avant-Garde* (Cambridge: Cambridge University Press, 2006), 238–53.

23. Henri Matisse, quoted in Jack D. Flam, ed., *Matisse on Art* (New York: Phaidon, 1973), 296.

24. Wendy Salmond, trans., *Beyond Vision: Essays on the Perception of Art by Pavel Florensky,* ed. Nicoletta Misler (London: Reaktion Books, 2002); Robert Bird, trans., *The Trinity–St. Sergius Lavra and Russia,* by Pavel Florensky (New Haven: Variable Press, 1995).

25. Oscar Wulff, "Die umgekehrte Perspektive und die Niedersicht," in *Kunstwissenschaftliche Beiträge, August Schmarsow gewidmet* (Leipzig: Hiersemann, 1907), 1–40.

26. Florensky, "Reverse Perspective," in *Beyond Vision,* 218.

27. Pavel Florensky, *Iconostasis,* trans. Donald Sheehan and Olga Andrejev (Crestwood, N.Y.: St. Vladimir's Seminary Press, 1996), 68.

28. M. V. Voloshin, "Chemu uchat ikony?" in *Liki tvorchestva,* ed. V. M. Manuilov, V. P. Kupchenko, and A. V. Lavrov (Leningrad: Nauka, 1988), 292.

29. A. I. Anisimov, "Russian Icon-Painting: Its Bloom, Over-Refinement and Decay," in *Masterpieces of Russian Painting,* ed. Michael Farbman (London: Europa, 1930), 65.

30. Glade, "A Heritage Discovered Anew," 146.

31. Boris Uspensky, *The Semiotics of the Russian Icon,* PdR Press Publications in Semiotics of Art 3, ed. Stephen Rudy (Lisse: Peter de Ridder, 1976), 22n18.

32. Nikodim Pavlovich Kondakov, *The Russian Icon,* trans. Ellis H. Minns (Oxford: Clarendon Press, 1927), 2.

33. Ibid., 2, 3.

34. In the seventeenth century, the archpriest Avvakum Petrov (Kondratiev) famously polemicized against the sort of "pot-bellied German" seen on new icons, which were painted in a "carnal way" so as to seem "alive." Quoted in Uspensky, *Semiotics of the Russian Icon,* 14.

35. Kondakov, *Russian Icon,* 3n2, 9.

36. Leonid Ouspensky, "The Meaning and Language of Icons," in Leonid Ouspensky and Vladimir Lossky, *The Meaning of Icons,* trans. G. E. H. Palmer and E. Kadlouborsky (Crestwood, N.Y.: St. Vladimir's Seminary Press), 47, 48.

37. D. A. Rovinskii, *Obozrenie ikonopisaniia v Rossii do kontsa XVII veka* [A Survey of Icon Painting in Russia Through the End of the Seventeenth Century] (1856; repr., St. Petersburg: Izdatel'stvo A. S. Suvorina, 1903); V. N. Lazarev, *Russkaia ikonopis'—ot istokov do nachala XVI veka* [Russian Icon Painting from Its Origins to the Beginning of the Sixteenth Century]. The fourth volume of the Russian edition of Kondakov's *Russian Icon* ends with the seventeenth century. N. P. Kondakov, *Russkaia ikona,* 4 vols. (Prague: Seminarium Kondakovianum, 1928–33).

38. I. M. Snegirev, "Vzgliad na pravoslavnoe ikonopisanie," in *Filosofiia russkogo religioznogo iskusstva XVI–XX vv.: Antologiia,* ed. N. K. Gavriushina (Moscow: lzdatel'skaia gruppa "Progress-Kul'tura," 1993), 101–12.

39. Oleg Tarasov, *Icon and Devotion: Sacred Spaces in Imperial Russia,* ed. and trans. Robin Milner-Gulland (London: Reaktion Books, 2002), 37–57.

40. Vera Shevzov, "Icons, Miracles, and the Ecclesial Identity of Laity in Late Imperial Russian Orthodoxy," *Church History* 69, no. 3 (2000): 611–12.

41. The Dukhobors, or "spirit wrestlers," were religious pacifists who rejected the state and many Orthodox rituals and dogmas, including the doctrine of Christ's divinity. Persecuted in the 1890s, the majority of the Dukhobors emigrated to Western Canada, thanks in part to Tolstoy's intervention on their behalf.

42. On missionaries in imperial Russia, see especially Robert P. Geraci and Michael Khodarkovsky, eds., *Of Religion and Empire: Missions, Conversion, and Tolerance in Tsarist Russia* (Ithaca: Cornell University Press, 2001).

43. On the connection between icons and anathemas in the modern rite for the Sunday of Orthodoxy, see Vera Shevzov's chapter in this volume.

44. Hans Belting, *Likeness and Presence: A History of the Image Before the Era of Art,* trans. Edmund Jephcott (Chicago: University of Chicago Press, 1994), 1.

45. Vera Shevzov, *Russian Orthodoxy on the Eve of Revolution* (Oxford: Oxford University Press, 2004), 173.

46. See Gregory L. Freeze, "Institutionalizing Piety: The Church and Popular Religion, 1750–1850," in *Imperial Russia: New Histories for the Empire,* ed. Jane Burbank and Daniel L. Ransel (Bloomington: Indiana University Press, 1998), 210–49.

47. Shevzov, "Icons, Miracles, and Ecclesial Identity," 611.

48. Ibid., 626. See also Shevzov, "Iconic Piety in Russia," in *Modern Christianity to 1900,* ed. Amanda Porterfield, Vol. 6, *A People's History of Christianity* (Minneapolis: Fortress Press, 2007), 199–203.

49. Vzdornov, *Istoriia otkrytiia i izucheniia russkoi srednevekovoi zhivopisi,* 59–68.

50. Ibid., 117.

51. Ibid., 73–78.

52. Lazarev, *Russkaia ikonopis',* 13.

53. See Serge A. Zenkovsky, "The Russian Church Schism: Its Background and Repercussions," *Russian Review* 16, no. 4 (1957): 44–47.

54. Vzdornov, *Istoriia otkrytiia i izucheniia russkoi srednevekovoi zhivopisi,* 28–36.

55. Buslaev, "Obshchie poniatiia o russkoi ikonopisi," 41, 42, 56, 57.

56. N. S. Leskov, "Zapechatlennyi angel," in *Sobranie sochinenii,* 6 vols., ed. L. Anninskii (Moscow: Ekran, 1993), 5:269.

57. Elizabeth Kridl Valkenier, *Russian Realist Painting: The State and Society: The Peredvizhniki and Their Tradition* (Ann Arbor: Ardis, 1977), 122.

58. On the *lubok* and its early twentieth-century rediscovery, see Alla Sytova, *The Lubok: Russian Folk Pictures, 17th to 19th Century,* trans. Alex Miller (Leningrad: Aurora Art Publishers, 1984).

59. Robert L. Nichols, "The Icon

and the Machine," in Brumfield and Velimirovic, *Christianity and the Arts in Russia,* 131–44. See also Oleg Tarasov, "The Russian Icon and the Culture of the Modern: The Renaissance of Popular Icon Painting in the Reign of Nicholas II," *Experiment* 7 (2001): 73–101.

60. Nichols, "The Icon and the Machine," 141–43.

61. V. P. Gur'ianov, *Dve mestnye ikony Sv. Troitsy v Troitskom Sobore Sviato-Troitsko-Sergievoi Lavry i ikh restavratsiia* (Moscow: Pechatnia A. I. Snegirevoi, 1906), 6.

62. Leonid Ouspensky, *Theology of the Icon,* 2 vols., trans. Anthony Gythiel (Crestwood, N.Y.: St. Vladimir's Seminary Press, 1992), 1:151; Uspensky, *Semiotics of the Russian Icon,* 9.

63. S. N. Bulgakov, *Ikona i ikonopochitanie: dogmaticheskii ocherk* (1931; repr., Moscow: Russkii put', 1996), 86.

64. The word "intermediumality" was first used by Samuel Coleridge and reentered critical discourse in a 1966 article by Dick Higgins, reprinted in *Horizons: The Poetics and Theory of the Intermedia* (Carbondale: Southern Illinois University Press, 1984), 18–28. For recent criticism, see Peter Wagner, "Introduction: Ekphrasis, Iconotexts, and Intermediality—the State(s) of the Art(s)," in *Icons—Texts—Iconotexts: Essays on Ekphrasis and Intermediality,* ed. Peter Wagner (Berlin: Walter de Gruyter, 1996), 1–40; Werner Wolf, *The Musicalization of Fiction: A Study in the Theory and History of Intermediality* (Amsterdam: Rodopi, 1999); Sabine Gross, "Image and Text: Recent Research in Intermediality," *Monatshefte* 93, no. 3 (2001): 355–66.

PART I

EMPIRE OF ICONS

ELENA BOECK

1

STRENGTH IN NUMBERS OR UNITY IN DIVERSITY?

COMPILATIONS OF MIRACLE-WORKING VIRGIN ICONS

This chapter examines the origin and diffusion of icons containing multiple, miracle-working images of the Virgin Mary (or Mother of God) in prerevolutionary Russia.[1] It is not often that the emergence of a new icon type can be clearly delineated in historical documentation. While the origins of most icon types are shrouded in mystery or miraculous narratives, this novel icon type can be traced to a specific period of transition in early modern Russian history. Highly unusual for their combination of numerous miniature images of miraculous Marian icons, these compendia also deviate from established assumptions about icons of the Virgin as central or large single-image panels, or as central and hieratic images.[2]

A particular challenge in understanding and evaluating Russian compendia icons is their amalgamation of old and new. Icons with multiple, miniature, labeled representations of the Mother of God are unknown in medieval and early modern Russia, or in other post-Byzantine Orthodox cultures. While the cult of the Virgin in the Christian world was officially sanctioned in the fifth century, no systematic attempt to catalog and compile a comprehensive visual record of her miraculous manifestations appeared until the Counter-Reformation. Compendia icons arise at a particular historical moment, reflecting and coinciding with an intellectual ferment within Russian society as established traditions of relating to the divine were being challenged and modified. These icons, I will argue, belong to the category of what Eric Hobsbawm has termed "invented traditions"; such icons use "ancient materials to construct invented traditions of novel type for quite novel purposes."[3] As Hobsbawm further notes, invented traditions arise as "responses to novel situations which take the form of reference to old situations, or which establish their own past by quasi-obligatory repetition."[4] Russian compendia icons achieve repetition by using ancient, revered icons as tesserae to create a mosaic with modern appeal. What follows is an attempt to document three significant stages in the development and reception of the compendium icon type: its emergence, rise to popularity, and final acceptance into official Orthodoxy.[5]

IN SEARCH OF ANTECEDENTS: MEDIEVAL AND MODERN, EASTERN AND WESTERN

From the surviving evidence of Byzantine and post-Byzantine Orthodox icon painting up to the eighteenth century, only one icon presents a suitable parallel to the Russian compendium icon: a twelfth-century hexaptych measuring 49 x 36 cm (19 x 15 in.) that is housed at Saint Catherine's monastery on Mount Sinai (fig. 1).[6] The upper part of this icon contains five representations of the Mother of God in the top register and thirty-six smaller images representing scenes from the life of Christ below. The central image is that of the enthroned Mother of God holding a frontal Christ Child on her lap, with the tiny figure of a donor prostrate at the foot of the throne. The four flanking images of the Mother of God are all famous miracle-working icons from Constantinople.[7] These icons are arranged symmetrically around the enthroned Virgin and Child in the center: two images of the Virgin alone (Hagiosoritissa and Chemevti) in a supplicatory position are turned toward the center on the viewer's right, while two other images of the Virgin and Child (Blachernitissa and Hodegetria) are positioned on the left.

The central image is inscribed simply as "Mother of God," and thus is not identified as a particular miracle-working image.[8] It bears a resemblance, however, to the apse mosaic of the Virgin and Child in the Hagia Sophia.[9] The image of the Virgin and Child in the Hagia Sophia was a landmark—its creation celebrated the Triumph of Orthodoxy in the ninth century.[10] The reverential positioning of the four Constantinopolitan miraculous Marian images signals the primacy of the central Mother of God. This panel evokes the sacred topography of Constantinople, reinforcing its special place in the Christian world through the miraculous icons of the Mother of God and their privileged placement in relation to Christ's miracles and passion below.[11]

Despite some typological similarities, there are crucial conceptual differences that set Russian compendia icons apart from this isolated medieval predecessor. Unlike the Sinai panel, the Russian icons showcase a multiplicity of minuscule images of the Virgin, rather than highlighting a select group of particularly privileged images from the capital. The overall appearance of Russian compendia icons is quite flexible, ranging from miniatures as the exclusive subject of a panel to compositions in which Marian icons frame a Menologium or a Christological central image. Their hallmark is the presence in the same panel of dozens of miniature icons of the Virgin or Virgin and Child, each of them individually labeled as to its name or provenance. This neatly arranged and labeled display is exemplary of a "museum mentality." In her

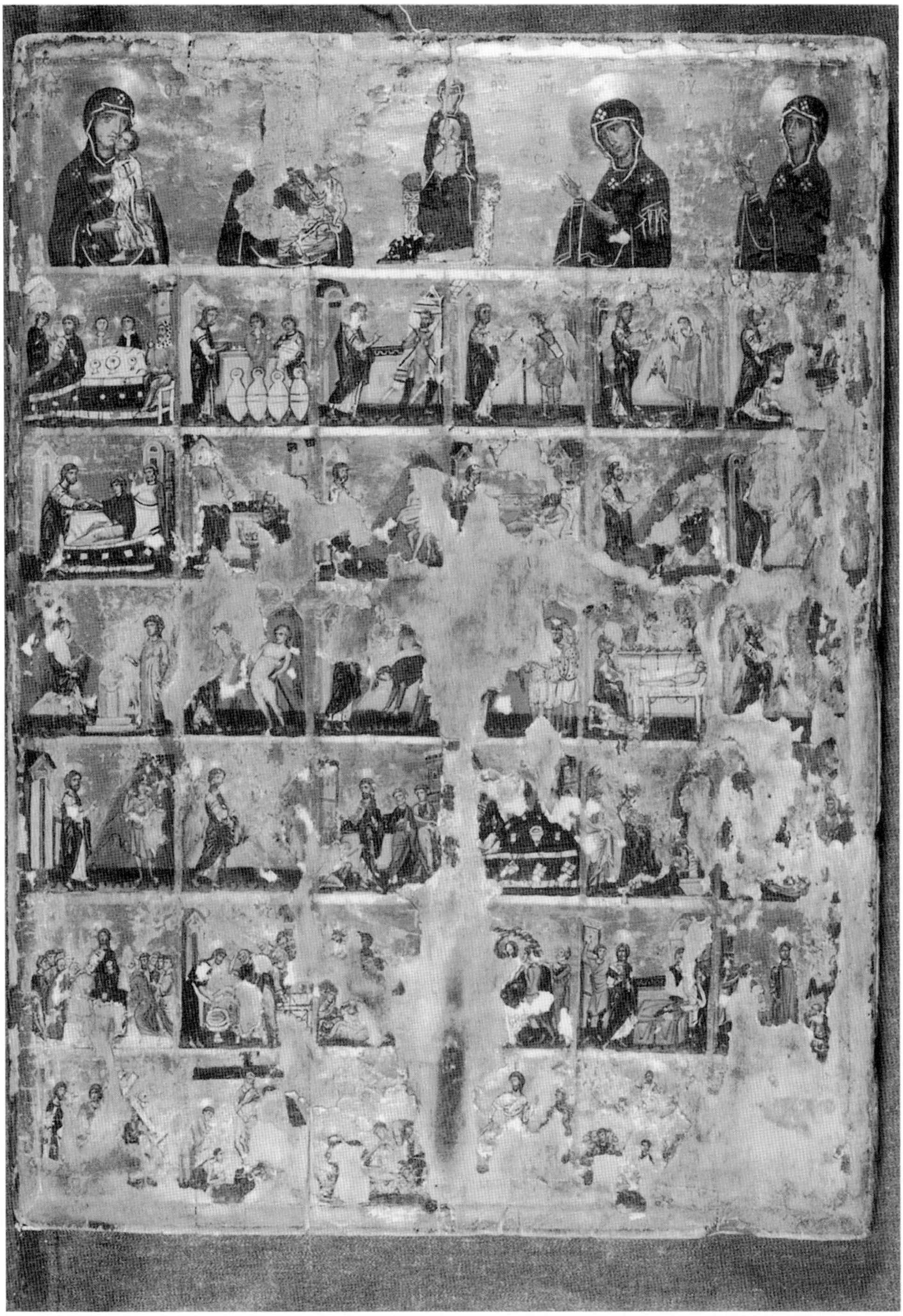

FIG. 1 Hexaptych icon, Byzantine, twelfth century. Monastery of Saint Catherine, Sinai, Egypt. Reproduced courtesy of the Michigan-Princeton-Alexandria Expedition to Mount Sinai.

discussion of museum formation, Susan Pearce observes that the "crucial idea is that of selection, and it is the act of selection which turns a part of the natural world into an object and a museum piece."[12] A compendium icon can include more than two hundred individual Marian icons of the same size, or privilege a particular image (such as the Virgin of the Burning Bush) surrounded by multiple smaller images (pl. 6). As in a museum display, selection is the distinguishing feature of this assembled collection, comprehension of which is guided by identifying labels for each image.

This fascination with assembling a comprehensive range of miraculous images has intellectual antecedents in the encyclopedic scope of collecting, displaying, and cataloging exhibited in the *Kunst-* and *Wunderkammern* of early modern Western Europe.[13] The sixteenth and seventeenth centuries witnessed an intense desire to collect and display marvelous objects, with universal scope being either an implicit or explicit goal.[14] Although collecting and displaying marvelous objects has complex roots, it was particularly inspired by the desire to witness God's presence in the most unusual and miraculous manifestations.[15] The so-called Christian marvelous,[16] that is, relics and objects related to miracles, counted among collectors' most prized possessions.[17] Such an intellectual climate was distinguished by an intense fascination with the medieval marvelous, a desire for compilation,[18] and an encyclopedic approach to decoding the divine plan. Crucial as well was a fashion for displaying marvelous objects from the Age of Discovery.[19] These trends converged to produce early museums, which sought to "reappropriate and reassemble reality in miniature."[20] The power of print culture—cataloging and illustration—was tapped to spread knowledge of these collections and to increase their status.

This fascination with assembling, displaying, arranging, and labeling objects is also reflected in various European engravings from the sixteenth to the eighteenth centuries. For instance, if we look at the engraving *Cries of Rome* (1582) by Ambrosius Brambilla (fig. 2), we find the same method of organizing images as in Russian compendia icons.[21] *Cries of Rome* represents 199 specialized street vendors of the city. Within a precise symmetrical grid, each figure inhabits a minuscule rectangular space. Each vendor is represented with the unique attributes of his trade and is clearly labeled. Thus the potentially bewildering array of urban activities is integrated into a structured and encyclopedic collection. Like the compendia icons, such engravings reflect a collecting and categorizing mentality in which even animate beings can be assembled, cataloged, and represented as a group.

ICONS OR IMAGES? PIETY AND AUTHORITY IN A TIME OF TRANSITION

The compendia icons appeared in Russia during a particular historical moment when printed images and texts were flooding in from Europe and when the state was attempting to impose a new vision of Orthodoxy upon the populace.[22] First, under Nikon (patriarch 1652–66), the official church attempted to change and centralize devotional practices. Subsequently, Peter I (r. 1682–1725) asserted governmental control over the church and icon

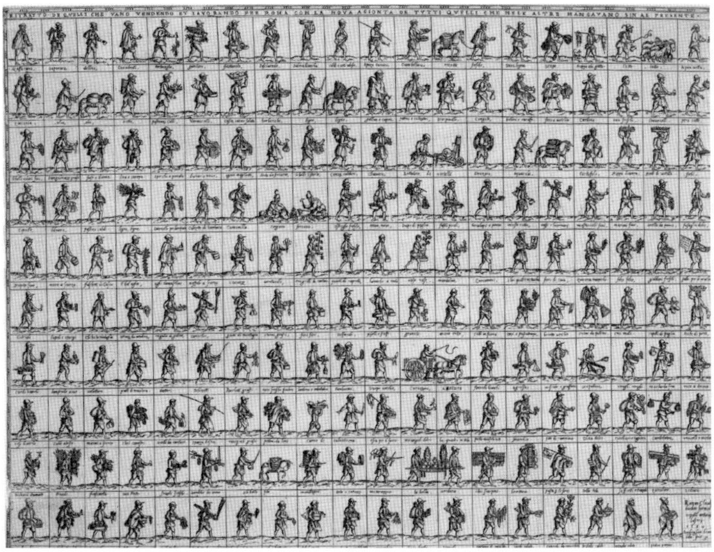

FIG. 2 Ambrosius Brambilla, *Cries of Rome,* 1582, engraving. Rijksmuseum, Amsterdam.

painters.[23] Both were attempting to reshape popular Orthodoxy. Eric Hobsbawm has described such times of transition as particularly fertile for the invention of tradition: "[W]e should expect the invention of tradition to occur more frequently when a rapid transformation of society weakens or destroys the social patterns for which 'old' traditions had been designed . . . or when such old traditions and their institutional carriers and promulgators no longer prove sufficiently adaptable and flexible, or are otherwise eliminated: in short, when there are sufficiently large and rapid changes on the demand or supply side."[24] Precisely such changes were taking place in Russia from the second half of the seventeenth century onward. While fighting against the growing movement of Old Believers in the wake of Nikon's reforms, the official church faced, first of all, an onslaught of new printed imagery from the West.[25] The church implemented restrictive measures against foreign prints in order to retain power over Orthodox devotion through icons. It feared that the flood of foreign materials, labeled "heretical prints," could enable local dissenters to bypass the official church and undermine its control over religious imagery.

In the late seventeenth and early eighteenth centuries, Western engravings and printed images were a source of great fascination and made a notable cultural impact in Russia. Printed books, most notably illustrated bibles such as Piscator's, actively and successfully entered the Russian market.[26] Their influence was apparent in the church frescoes and icon painting of the Armory School in Moscow, revealed in such techniques as perspective, European architectural motifs, and depth in facial features.[27] The painterly manner of the Western-inspired icons was met with stiff opposition by leading Old Believers, who refused to venerate naturalistic-looking icons and condemned the erosion of sacred Orthodox tradition: "The contemporary icon painters," complained one such Old Believer, "do not draw icons from the old sacred prototypes of Greek and Russian miracle-working images, but from rational conjurings. They fatten the body of Christ the Savior, and the saints . . . not according to the ancient sacred icons, but according to the pictures published in Latin and other printed bibles, and those painted on canvases."[28]

Both church and state officials monitored and attempted to control icon painting with measures ranging from the distribution of authorized pattern books (*podlinniki*) in the late sixteenth century to the government's exclusive employment of officially recognized icon painters in the late seventeenth century.[29] Nonetheless, innovations were filtering into icon painting (such as the Lord of Sabaoth) in spite of the fact that unauthorized images were sternly banned at the highest levels by the patriarch and the church councils.[30] The plight of the Orthodox authorities is most vividly exemplified by a statement from Patriarch Joachim in 1674:

> Paper images printed by German heretics are being bought and sold [in Moscow, etc.], [images made] by Lutherans and Calvinists in accordance with their false and damnable opinions, and [depicting] persons like those of their country, in their peculiar German clothes, and not in accordance with the old originals used by the Orthodox; and these heretics do not venerate holy icons, but revile and ridicule [them], and with their prints discount the holy icons done on panels, thus scorning icon veneration; but venerating icons has long been commanded and established by the holy church and the tradition of the fathers; and it is ordered that [icons] be depicted on panels, not paper.[31]

In his rejection of foreign images, the patriarch articulated an official Orthodox definition of an icon. He emphasized the paramount importance of both style and material in the creation of icons. Only religious imagery executed on panels in accordance with Orthodox traditions ("old originals") could be considered worthy of veneration. Thus style became a bearer of meaning. This definition of an icon leaves no room for foreign pictures: only icons painted in the traditional (old) style, using the traditional materials, and adhering to the traditional iconography were classified as suitable for veneration. In defining an icon, the patriarch was attempting to neutralize the power of foreign images and to guide the faithful to true Orthodox icons.

The patriarch was alarmed for good reason. In the seventeenth century, an onslaught of foreign prints challenged the church's unity and monopoly over religious imagery; by the eighteenth century, the government was also tackling issues of Orthodox devotion and church authority. Peter I abolished the vestiges of autonomy of the church by incorporating it into the bureaucratic structure of the state. He refused to appoint a new patriarch, instead instituting a Holy Synod (College of Ecclesiastical Affairs), which answered to the ruler.[32] The tsar reaffirmed earlier laws establishing governmental control over the sale of religious images in printed form, and governmental censorship continued to regulate the sale of printed matter, including engravings from "papers of Franks" (Western prints).[33] Peter not only promoted Western styles in Russia but also maintained strict supervision over icon painting, ordering that a "'superintendent' of icon painters, responsible to the Synod, was to be appointed."[34]

The struggle to rein in iconography continued throughout the eighteenth century. Gregory Freeze has noted that "from the 1740s the Church waged an unrelenting struggle against 'newly manifest icons' and any cleric who abetted popular veneration."[35] Again and again, authorities would campaign for the "purification" of religious images. The sweeping campaigns ranged from confiscating "ugly" and improperly painted icons,[36] to prescribing icons suitable for veneration, to attempting to license icon painters. These harsh measures were often met with popular resistance,[37] and despite their application the state was unsuccessful in its fight against print media and popular devotion.

Peter was personally uncomfortable with some Orthodox practices, especially the cult of icons. In line with Protestant image theory, he was purportedly "only for keeping the picture of Christ, but that it ought only to be a remembrance and not an object of worship."[38] John Perry, an English engineer employed by the tsar, reported that Peter introduced other Protestant-leaning devotional practices into his own household and circle of associates, as well as among the populace. For instance, upon finding numerous icons in the cabins of his newly built naval fleet, Peter allegedly decreed that "one of those pictures or images was enough [for sailors] to cross themselves to, and therefore he ordered that all the rest should be taken away, for he would have no more than one in each ship."[39]

These Petrine policies challenged major aspects of popular piety by characterizing them as inappropriate, irrational, and superstitious.[40] Miracle-working icons were confiscated from private houses and investigated for their authenticity.[41] Peter's measures caused great consternation within pious circles. In the court of public opinion, Peter was viewed as dismissive of miracle-working icons. According to a historical anecdote, upon hearing of a miracle-working icon in St. Petersburg, the tsar rushed to demonstrate that the icon in question, far from producing miracles, was, in fact, rigged with mechanical devices.[42] He was thus assaulting Orthodoxy at its popular core. In this context, following the Counter-Reformation example, defense of tradition would include proving the authenticity, universality, and true power of miracle-working icons.

CROSS-CULTURAL CONNECTIONS AND COMPILATIONS

The first step toward a compilation was the gathering of information about known miracle-working icons and their locations. For instance, in 1665 the Ukrainian monk Ioanykii Haliatovskyi published a work titled *The New Heaven,* which was inspired by Counter-Reformation treatises and discussed some of the many images dedicated to the Virgin Mary.[43] Another significant text produced in Russia around the same time or slightly later attempted to provide a more comprehensive compendium of miracle-working icons.[44] The catalog bore the full title "List of holy icons of our Most Holy Virgin and Mother of God and their various appearances in various towns and cities in various years." The first part of the list is written in Russian and describes seventy-four images of the Virgin. The second part is numbered separately and incorporates a list of forty-seven images. It is partially derived from Western sources, as a few of the entries display Ruthenianisms such as *rok* and are dated according to the Gregorian calendar. While some of the entries are terse and provide only the name of an icon, other entries are accompanied by more extensive descriptions, such as: "On Cyprus island there is an icon, [the Mother of God] seated on a throne and holding Christ on her lap, and two angels; and one Arab shot at the knee of the Mother of God, and blood came out."[45] The latest event relating to an icon in the list is dated 1666, which suggests a convenient *terminus post quem* for the text.[46]

The first known compendium of images of the Mother of God in Russia was produced by Grigory Tepchegorsky, a fairly prominent and prolific Moscow engraver (active 1702–18).[47] His oeuvre was influenced by Western prints and included numerous engravings for bibles and other devotional literature. One set of his engravings, which is now housed in the State Pushkin Museum in Moscow, consists of three pages of Marian icons. Two of the pages contain twelve icons, while the third has eight. Each of the icons is clearly labeled and has a short vita attached to it. The precise origins and purpose of these engravings is still uncertain; it remains unclear whether they were intended for individual circulation or belonged to a larger opus. Igor Kochetkov, who recently examined these engravings, suggests that they could have been prototypes for some of the later compendia icons. He also notes an inscription on one of the pages in an eighteenth-century hand: "Icons of the Holy Mother of God, which are working miracles in many countries."[48] Many of the icons that Kochetkov considered unknown in Russia in the early eighteenth century (such as Arapskaya, Maletinskaya, Siluamskaya, and Florenskaya) are featured in the "List of holy icons" discussed above, which would suggest that literary lists shaped early attempts to provide visual compilations.

A second set of Tepchegorsky's engraved Marian icons is found in a handwritten volume dating from 1715–16. The volume was compiled by Simeon Mokhovikov, a guard at the Moscow Annunciation Cathedral, who may have been either an Old Believer sympathizer[49] or perhaps a member of Stefan Yavorsky's circle.[50] The manuscript, which was discovered and first studied by Irina Pozdeeva, consists of 539 pages of text by different hands and has ninety-three engravings glued into it. Tepchegorsky produced seventy-seven of its surviving eighty-seven images of the Virgin. The thirty-two disparate texts of the volume are unified by the overarching theme of miracle-working icons as well as frescoes of the Mother of God and the saints. For instance, a section titled "Tale about holy miracle-working icons . . . of the Holy Mother of God" incorporates 139 numbered entries documenting their appearance.[51] These entries include the date, place, and circumstances of the appearance of each icon, as well as follow-up comments regarding each icon's last known location, miracles, and recent history.

The defense of imperiled Orthodoxy and the refutation of impious iconoclasts were the central objectives of the volume. Mokhovikov declares his desire to "expose the iconoclasts, enemies of the Cross of Christ, who rose like sea crocodiles and are shaking Russia" and "to expose the heretics and iconoclasts [who] . . . were swayed by the Latin [dogma] of their teacher heretics Calvin, Luther, Iakunts, Martyshenko."[52] The references to Calvin and Luther as well as to their counterparts in Orthodox territories point to Counter-Reformation rhetoric as Mokhovikov's inspiration.

During the sixteenth century, the Catholic Church found itself on the defensive against real and rhetorical Protestant assaults on its established practices and images. Luther, for example, referred to medieval Mariology as "abominable idolatry . . . not praising Mary, but slandering her in the extreme and making an idol of her."[53] Forced to defend church practices, ranging from the authenticity of contemporary miracles to the orthodoxy of cult images, Catholic publicists insistently affirmed the centrality of the Virgin Mary in Catholic worship.[54] Hans Belting identifies two distinct strategies in the defense of image veneration that emerged during the Counter-Reformation: "[Catholic theologians] could adopt the Reformed kind of image, stripped of its offensive features—an image that stimulated theological reflection by a speculative content presented in artistic guise. Or they could push the matter to the extreme by using wonder-working images in the manner of relics, commanding acceptance because of their age."[55] The latter position would be implemented with great success in Rome and elsewhere.[56]

Following the Council of Trent in 1563, the Catholic Church went on the offensive to reclaim souls lost to Protestantism.[57] The new orders, particularly the Jesuits, would play a crucial role in bringing significant parts of Europe back into the Catholic fold, "reconquering Europe," so to speak.[58] Once again, images became "a means of propaganda."[59] The reclamation of lost sheep had both a visual and verbal strategy. The Virgin, it would seem, took on a missionary role by actively cementing and expanding the frontiers of Catholicism through her miraculous images.[60] Collections of miracles and biographies of miracle-working Marian images proliferated during the Counter-Reformation as the Jesuits compiled, organized, and codified texts and images. These compilations attested to the authenticity and the power of Marian miraculous images—proof of the Virgin's unceasing work.[61] Beyond revealing the manifold divine grace and the intercessory power of the Virgin, these compilations mobilized Marian images against the Protestant challenge. These icons were to be understood not as mere representations, but as actual manifestations of sacred power.[62]

To legitimize "the religious marvels of the post-Biblical period,"[63] Counter-Reformation intellectuals described, witnessed, and depicted them in the same fashion as the marvels of the physical world were arranged, cataloged, and represented in *Kunst-* and *Wunderkammern* of the sixteenth and seventeenth centuries.[64] In the spirit of the age, these compilations can themselves be seen as "a microcosm of the marvels"—ambitious in their goal of comprehensive legibility, encyclopedic in scope, and animated by a desire to record,

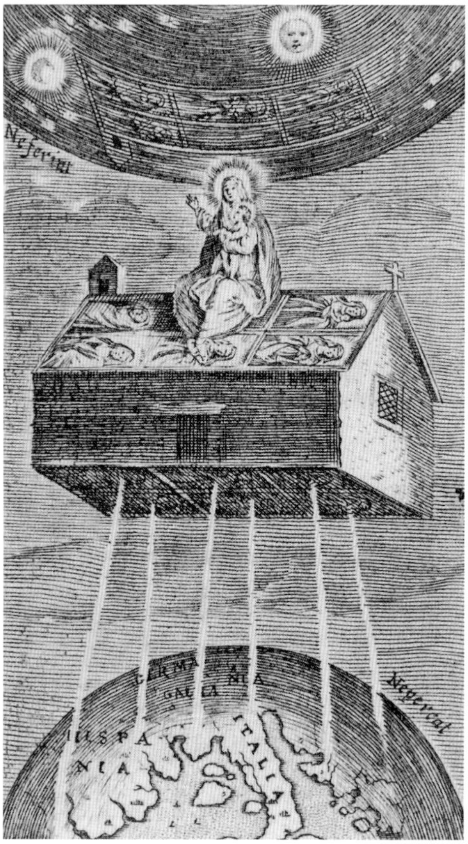

FIG. 3 The Virgin Seated on the Roof of the Church, in Wilhelm Gumppenberg's *Atlas Marianus, sive De imaginibus Deiparae per orbem Christianum miraculosis* (Ingolstadt, 1657). By permission of Houghton Library, Harvard University.

document, and authenticate divinely manifested wonders.[65]

The Jesuit Wilhelm Gumppenberg's *Atlas Marianus, sive De imaginibus Deiparae per orbem Christianum miraculosis*, published in 1657, exemplifies the taxonomy of miraculous Marian images and their vitae that would appear in Russian compilations in the eighteenth century and continue into the twenty-first century.[66] The diminutive *Atlas* (12.7 x 7.4 cm or 5 x 3 in.) is a two-volume publication assembled under one cover. Each volume includes a description of twenty-five icons active in Catholic countries from Spain to Lithuania. Discussion of each icon is preceded by its illustration. Factual information is emphasized, including the first appearance of each image, its subsequent history, documented miracles (along with the names of witnesses), and features of its cult at the time of compilation. The scientific approach and the catalog-style format of the publication are reinforced at the end of each volume by an index of images, which are grouped according to individual countries.

Each *Atlas* volume opens with an identical engraving that shows a central, frontal, seated Virgin Mary with Christ Child on her lap (fig. 3). Quite unconventionally, the Virgin is positioned on the roof of a church, which is propelled from earth toward heaven. The foundation and the roof of the structure are formed with images of the Virgin. The roof is tiled with five different images. As a sign of respect for her representations, the Virgin herself is seated on a blank panel. Thus the iconographically distinct rectangular icons are conjoined to form a unified covering and foundation for the church.

The seated Virgin raises her hand upward, piloting the church toward the heavenly sphere, while her haloed head overlaps with heaven. The celestially bound vessel is the reflection of the heavenly sphere: the same five images of the Virgin (save the space on which the Virgin sits) are revealed in the heavenly sphere. The entire Catholic edifice is centered on the Virgin, and her images literally serve as the building blocks for the structure. While its roof mirrors the heavenly sphere, the six faintly visible icons of the foundation link the church to the earthly world below. From the center of each image, a stream of light beams down to the Catholic countries: Italia and Hispania are most prominently labeled, with Gallia and Germania also legible.

This iconic arrangement eloquently transmits the Counter-Reformation message. The Virgin and the veneration of her images form the foundation of proper Christian devotion and the true link between Christians and God. The Virgin bridges the gap between the terrestrial and celestial worlds; she validates the authenticity of her images, which not only compose the Catholic edifice but also come directly from heaven. Divinely sanctioned devotion elevates the Catholic countries and links them to heaven; the Catholics are united in the Virgin, and the Virgin unites the Catholics with God.

What then connects the *Atlas Marianus* with Russian compendia icons? Just like the icons of *Atlas Marianus,* many icons of the Mokhovikov volume and "List of holy icons" display heightened activity in the seventeenth century: they were making numerous appearances and performing miracles.[67] By documenting the careers of miraculous images, these Marian compilations articulate divine opposition to a changing political and cultural climate. By actively performing marvelous deeds, the miraculous icons resist marginalization. The Catholic and Orthodox treatises employ similar structural and narrative tactics in their efforts to protect the tradition of Marian devotion and images against iconoclasts.

Although the iconoclasts of Mokhovikov's verbal invective are clearly identified, the profile of his target audience is less certain. In the twentieth century, the volume was discovered in an Old Believer enclave in the Briansk region.[68] This evidence suggests that even if the Old Believers were not Mokhovikov's intended audience, they were receptive to his approach. Old Believers embraced and propagated paper images for their own purposes. They selectively reproduced older images and created new ones to reinforce their vision of tradition. Subjects for these prints ranged from religious to didactic to patriotic/historical.[69] Some Old Believers accepted and used images on paper as icons, such as hand-colored lithographs and engravings. The use of paper images as icons was in direct opposition to the policies of the official church, which decreed once again in 1721 that "the holy images for the purposes of veneration are painted on panels, but not printed on paper . . . which are acceptable for looking, but not for veneration."[70]

Although engravings of Marian images from Mokhovikov's compilation (or a similar volume) serve as an important link between established and invented traditions, these images could not become fully integrated into mainstream Orthodox veneration until they made the leap from paper to panel.[71] The intellectual content of Mokhovikov's volume, however, clearly establishes the ideological argument that also propelled Russian compendia icons. The miraculous icons located in Russian territories predominate in both his volume and in the compendium icon type. Although foreign icons also appear, their function is arguably twofold: they reinforce (by their marginality) the universality of the cult of the Mother of God, and they affirm Russia's unique destiny in the divine plan.

THE LEAP FROM PAPER TO PANEL

Much remains to be learned about the earliest compendia icons. It is difficult to tabulate the number of surviving examples, since icons of the eighteenth and especially nineteenth centuries are still poorly cataloged.[72] Many of these icons can only be seen in church settings and private collections.[73] With the exception of preliminary studies by Pozdeeva and Kochetkov, they have not been systematically researched.[74] Very little is known about the crucial transition from engravings to paintings on panels.

At some intermediate point between the Tepchegorsky-Mokhovikov collaboration and the year 1817, compendia started to be painted on panels and set up in churches. A document from 1817 provides a clear *terminus ante quem* for their acceptance into churches. That year, a Russian aristocratic traveler to Kiev recorded an extensive and frustrating encounter with a compendium icon:

> While at the Vydubitsky monastery, in the monastery church my eyes inadvertently beheld a wide painting representing up to fifty different varieties of the Mother of God. Among others, according to inscriptions, I found the appearance of the Spanish and Pochaevskaya Mother of God, both of whom belong more to the Catholic Church than to ours. After glancing at them, I wanted to put a question to all our pastors and teachers: why, as it appears, do icons of the Mother of God manifest themselves incessantly and in each and every location, while I have not seen anywhere miraculously appeared icons of Christ under adjectival titles? In our country, every town, every monastery has its own icon of the Mother of God, but Christ is one and the same everywhere. He is not called Tambovsky, nor Podolsky, nor Revelsky. At the same time, what a multitude of allegorical images exist of the Mother of God! Painters do not exercise their imagination to that extent on any other image save the Mother of God. The matter even sometimes achieves the most reprehensible forms of seduction [i.e., artistic license]. Tell me, my lords, in tall hats, wide garments, and stoles, why do you tolerate this, why do you not put up obstacles to the escapades of these icon painters, or to put it more aptly "besmearers of god" from Kholui [*Kholuiskie bogomazy*], who, if not abated, will promptly drag into our churches such things that could not even be found in heathen idol sanctuaries [*kumnitsy*]?[75]

The educated beholder approached the compendium icon from the position of an enlightened aristocrat steeped in Western aesthetics. Simultaneously intrigued and repelled by a novel "painting" (*kartina*), he attentively studied each image and accompanying inscription. He navigated the icon with the help of labels, since he was able to categorize "Catholic" icons according to their inscriptions, as opposed to their iconography. The educated viewer did not appreciate the system of categorization displayed by this icon. Unlike the icon painter, he drew boundaries between Orthodox ("our") images of the Mother of God and Catholic ones of the Virgin Mary. As the beholder impugned the ignorance of the painter, he revealed his own lack of familiarity with popular piety. For the aristocratic viewer the presence of Catholic images indicated backwardness and artistic license, but to the painter the Catholic images were necessary to reinforce the idea of Russia's unique place in the divine plan. Foreign images had to be present for the full ideological impact of a compendium icon, which assembled a wide range of miraculous icons and thereby celebrated Russia's controlling share of divine benediction. The invented tradition of this icon type, which drew upon older traditions of Marian icons, innovative Counter-Reformation imagery and compilations, and a culture of collecting, had now been accorded legitimacy by believers and accepted into an Orthodox Church.

The critical viewer also immediately established the icon's provenance and assessed the quality of workmanship against elegant society's standards of good art: the offensive image was indeed made by the "besmearers of god" from Kholui.[76] After the Petrine reforms and official efforts at Westernizing visual culture, villages in the Vladimir region remained the most significant center of traditional icon painting in Russia. There icon painting became an enormous industry, with thousands of Vladimir icons traded in every part of Russia.[77] Before the mid-nineteenth century, these icons circulated primarily among the lower social classes and Old Believers, reaching as far as the Balkans.[78] The educated viewer above did not yet embrace this imagery and still expressed an Enlightenment-era disdain. For him, popular piety, refracted through this particular image, was a dangerous and misguided force that needed to be more directly controlled by the official church. Thus he implored church authorities to rein in imagery in the face of popular corruptions.

A few decades later the cultural climate within elite circles would shift dramatically as a taste for "authentic" Russian culture (Russophilism) came into vogue. Although the educated elite would continue to reject many of the icons produced in Vladimir for "the simple Russian people," by the early twentieth century the region came to be recognized as "the only preserve of Russian icon painting."[79] Thus Vladimir icons were embraced by the elites as true icons, that is, as examples of a living, ancient, authentic tradition.[80] The region's icon painters were not only acknowledged as Russia's finest in competitions at St. Petersburg exhibitions but also were lionized as master fresco painters and restorers of medieval icons.[81] The populace accepted their works because of the long-standing tradition of icon painting in the region, while the higher classes esteemed them now that it had become possible to put icon painting "on the level of art."[82] In short, sometime during the second half of the nineteenth century, popular and educated tastes converged.[83] Surviving compendia icons, which invariably date from this period, are consistently attributed to the workshops of the Vladimir region.

Why did these icons proliferate in the nineteenth century? Internationally, intellectual trends had changed course rather rapidly. The eighteenth century's skepticism and rationalism gave way to Romanticism and nationalism with their selective idealization of the past.[84] In mid-nineteenth-century Russia, a spate of popular publications promoted the special relationship of the Virgin with Russia, such as *Protective Veil of the Most Holy Virgin Mother of God over Russia* (*Pokrov Presviatoi Devy Bogoroditsy nad Rossiei*) of 1843. James Billington notes that Russian intellectuals were moving in the same direction: "When a trickle of intellectuals began to return to the Church in the late imperial period, one of the converts likened the process to an exchange of the Sistine Madonna for the icon of Our Lady of Vladimir."[85] In 1846, Nikolai Nadezhdin advanced an idea that would arguably be central to the increasing popularity of compendia icons: "Especially here in holy, pious Rus, the image of the Mother of God has many particular forms, which from ancient times were blessed by the church. It is impossible to enumerate all of the named versions [*naimenovanii*] that the affectionate child has lavished upon the loving mother."[86] Pious texts justified Russia's particular favor with the Mother of God and its unique place in the divine plan; visual compendia actualized these texts.

The mid-nineteenth century was the moment in which innovation started to be confused with tradition. Moreover, during the nineteenth century, the style of the compendia became diversified. These icons began to appear in both the "painterly," fleshy, academic, Western style and the traditional, two-dimensional, "old" style of icons. After the Petrine reforms, style was an important cultural indicator. Despite the systematic suppression of grassroots objections to the Western style after the seventeenth century, the traditional style continued to coexist with the Western style preferred by elites. For instance, in a 1759 document two men are called upon by the Synod to paint icons: one, Alexander Durakov, is called a painter (*zhivopisets*), while the other, Gavrilo Ivanov, is characterized as an icon painter (*ikonopisets*).[87] The production of compendia icons in different styles indicates that they began to appeal to diverse segments of the market for devotional images.

A remarkable and particularly rich icon, which represents 238 miniature icons of the Mother of God, deserves particular consideration (pl. 7). This late nineteenth-century icon was produced in Kholui, Vladimir province.[88] The diminutive size of each image (5.6 x 5.4 cm or 2.2 x 2.1 in.) impedes traditional veneration, making one-on-one interaction with the gaze of the holy person virtually impossible.[89] The arrangement of the inscriptions indicates that the icon was to be viewed instead as a catalog-like whole. A prominent Greek inscription, *Meter Theou* (Mother of God), is placed by the head of each Virgin, thus clearly articulating her universality in the multiplicity of images. The second inscription, in Russian, on the lower frame of each image, identifies each icon's provenance or type. Together, the inscriptions express the primary and secondary identities of every icon: the immutability of the universal Mother of God and the variability of her local manifestations. The inscriptions impart the idea of unity in diversity, integrating individual images into a whole. Like the engraving of the Virgin in Gumppenberg's *Atlas Marianus,* the multiple tessarae of her individual images compose a universal mosaic of the Mother of God.

As the search for a uniquely Russian past intensified, both intellectuals and ordinary believers invoked the Virgin's role as a symbol of Russian identity and as a special protector of the nation. Aimed at a broad readership, pious compilations celebrating the images and miracles of the Mother of God became overtly patriotic. While reassuring the faith of believers, they assembled "relics of the past" to create an ideologically transformative vision of the past and future.[90] One such volume by Sofia Snessoreva was first published in 1891 and reprinted in 1897 in expanded form. Its reissue in the 1990s attests to the revival of Orthodoxy in the post-Soviet period.[91] The authoritative revised edition was intended as a catalogue raisonné of miracle-working icons of the Mother of God in Russia. The first edition had included 293 icons. The author, however, was criticized for settling on this number by the *Theological Bibliographical Newsletter*, which noted that the generally accepted number of miracle-working icons of the Virgin is 364.[92] Snessoreva defended her number by appealing to the infinity of the divine: "There are as many miracle-working icons of the Mother of God as there are stars in the sky; nobody has yet been able to count them and only the Queen of Heaven knows their number."[93] This appeal to uncircumscribable divinity was tempered by the author's quasi-scientific approach to her data, as she claimed to draw only on "reliable historical sources."[94] Snessoreva dealt with the conundrum of the infinite nature of the divine by assembling a representative sample of iconic specimens. Her methodology, like that of Gumppenberg and Mokhovikov before her, fuses devotion and scholarly systematization. Like the compendia icons, this publication represents a collector's desire to reconcile in a finite format the infinite varieties of divine manifestation.

Snessoreva's work represents a curious mixture of piety and patriotism. As she declares, "Our Russia can be called the temple of the Mother of God, the place primarily chosen by her for her stay on earth. Nearly all Russian towns and areas are dedicated to her through their main churches, which for the most part are built in the name of the Most Holy Virgin." She writes further: "On account of particular divine benevolence, Russia received many miracle-working icons, which serve to fortify the faith of Russians in the intercession of the Mother of God."[95] Thus she verbalized the idea inherent in every compendium icon: the Virgin favors Russia above all other countries.[96] The compendia icons and popular piety would be co-opted into the ideological service of the state.

THE COMPENDIUM ICON IN THE EMBRACE OF EMPIRE AND ORTHODOXY

The final stage in the life history of the Marian compendia icons in late imperial Russia was their glorification by official Orthodoxy. Within one century, compendia images went from being the lowly "distortions" of Orthodoxy excoriated by an aristocratic traveler to Kiev in 1817 to prominent frescoes in the state-sponsored Cathedral of Christ the Savior (*Khram Khrista Spasitelia*), the great patriotic memorial to the victory over Napoleon in 1812.[97] This Moscow cathedral was one of the most important imperial monuments of the nineteenth century and served as both a church and a political symbol.[98] The complex interconnections between the building, the Romanov dynasty, and official Orthodoxy sealed its fate after the revolution. Once Moscow's grandest building, it was destroyed by Stalin's orders in 1931 to clear space for the grandiose Palace of the Soviets, which was never built. For decades the site of the world's largest swimming pool, built under Nikita Khrushchev in 1960, the cathedral has since been reconstructed in the post-Soviet period under Moscow's mayor Yury Luzhkov, though not without controversy over its funding and materials.[99]

This extravagant testament (completed in 1883) to the divine elevation of Russia featured frescoes of several miraculous icons of the Mother of God in a chapel dedicated to Saint Alexander Nevsky, the patron saint of three of the four Russian emperors who oversaw the cathedral's construction (Alexander I, Alexander II, and Alexander III).[100] This thirteenth-century prince was particularly celebrated by later generations for his "patriotism" and military prowess in defeating the Swedish forces on the Neva River in 1240 and the Teutonic knights in the battle on the ice in 1242.[101] Peter I drew parallels between his confrontation with Sweden and Alexander Nevsky's medieval exploits. Peter strengthened the imperial cult of the saint by transferring his relics to St. Petersburg and founding a monastery in his name.[102]

The Saint Alexander Nevsky chapel (located in the north wing of the church) was a grand narrative of Russia's divinely sanctioned destiny. Its decoration included images of Alexander Nevsky, scenes from his life, images of his princely relatives, Russian princely saints, and other Russian saints and martyrs who died for their country. Finally, it also featured "the most important miracle-working icons of the Mother of God, which are particularly honored in Russia."[103]

Twenty-eight frescoes of miraculous Marian icons were arranged in four groupings between the windows of the chapel. In each compendium, a large (297.2 cm or 117 in.), central, full-length icon of the Mother of God was surrounded by six smaller icons (one on each side and four below).[104] The smaller icons were uniform in size (169.5 cm or 66.7 in.), each representing a half-length image of the Virgin. The role of these monumental compendia icons in this chapel was highly political, as they were incorporated into a densely patriotic visual matrix. Devotion to the Mother of God was now officially imbued with the patriotic message of Russia's unique destiny.

The compendium icon type gained slow but steady acceptance by Russian Orthodox believers. From small, humble collections of paper engravings first produced on the fringes of Russian society, they were ultimately elevated to three-meter-tall embodiments of the official ideology of the Russian state. The compendia took on a variety of meanings as they came to fulfill different functions. First used in defense of embattled popular piety, they became a part of the patriotic culture of late imperial Orthodoxy. Their diversity of styles suggests their adoption by diverse segments of society. Ultimately, their persistence and popularity, as well as their journey from the margins to the mainstream, can be attributed to the fact that they reminded beholders of the manifold divine blessings bestowed upon Russia by the Mother of God.

NOTES TO CHAPTER 1

1. The designations "Mother of God" and "Virgin Mary," standard for Orthodox and Catholic terminology, respectively, will be used interchangeably throughout the chapter.

2. The literature on icons of the Mother of God in the medieval period is voluminous. Some important titles include: Hans Belting, *Likeness and Presence: A History of the Image Before the Era of Art,* trans. Edmund Jephcott (Chicago: University of Chicago Press, 1994); Bissera Pentcheva, *Icons and Power: The Mother of God in Byzantium* (University Park: Pennsylvania State University Press, 2006); Maria Vassilaki, ed., *Images of the Mother of God: Perceptions of the Theotokos in Byzantium* (Aldershot: Ashgate, 2005); idem, ed., *Mother of God: Representations of the Virgin in Byzantine Art* (Milan: Skira Editore, 2000); M. Vloberg, "Les types iconographiques de la mère de Dieu dans l'art byzantin," in *Maria,* ed. H. du Manoir (Paris: Beauchesne, 1952), 403–43; V. Lazareff, "Studies in the Iconography of the Virgin," *Art Bulletin* 20 (1938): 26–65; N. P. Kondakov, *Ikonografiia Bogomateri* (St. Petersburg: Tipografiia imperatorskoi akademii nauk, 1914–15).

3. Eric Hobsbawm, *The Invention of Tradition* (Cambridge: Cambridge University Press, 1992), 6.

4. Ibid., 2.

5. This chapter forms part of a book project that explores the transformation of visual culture in early modern Russia under the influence of ideas and images from Western European print culture and the Catholic Reformation.

6. The icon has been discussed by Annemarie Weyl Carr, "Icons and the Object of Pilgrimage in Middle Byzantine Constantinople," *Dumbarton Oaks Papers* 56 (2002): 75–92; G. Soteriou and M. Soteriou, *Eikones tes Mones Sina* [The Icons of Mount Sinai], 2 vols. (Athens: Institut Français d'Athènes, 1956), 2:146–47; Nicolette Trahoulia, "The Truth in Painting: A Refutation of Heresy in a Sinai Icon," *Jahrbuch der Österreichischen Byzantinistik* 52 (2002): 271–85.

7. Soteriou and Soteriou, *Eikones,* vol. 1, fig. 125. For color reproductions and brief descriptions of selected images of the Mother of God, see Vassilaki, *Mother of God,* 144–46.

8. Weyl Carr identifies this image as the Virgin of the Burning Bush. Weyl Carr, "Icons and the Object of Pilgrimage," 77.

9. Bibliography on the Hagia Sophia is extensive. See especially Robert S. Nelson, *Hagia Sophia, 1850–1950: Holy Wisdom Modern Monument* (Chicago: University of Chicago Press, 2004); Rowland J. Mainstone, *Hagia Sophia: Architecture, Structure, and Liturgy of Justinian's Great Church* (New York: Thames and Hudson, 1988); Robert Mark and Ahmet S. Cakmak, eds., *Hagia Sophia from the Age of Justinian to the Present* (Cambridge: Cambridge University Press, 1992).

10. See Homily XVII of the Patriarch Photius, "An Image of the Virgin in St. Sophia," translated by Cyril Mango in *The Art of the Byzantine Empire, 312–1453: Sources and Documents* (Toronto: University of Toronto Press, 1986), 187–90; Robert S. Nelson, "To Say and to See: Ekphrasis and Vision in Byzantium," in *Visuality Before and Beyond the Renaissance,* ed. Robert S. Nelson (Cambridge: Cambridge University Press, 2000), 143–68. For a discussion of this mosaic, see also Cyril Mango and E. J. W. Hawkins, "The Apse Mosaic of St. Sophia at Istanbul," *Dumbarton Oaks Papers* 19 (1965): 113–51; Robin Cormack, "The Mother of God in the Mosaics of Hagia Sophia in Constantinople," in *Mother of God,* ed. Vassilaki, 107–23; idem, "Interpreting the Mosaics of S. Sophia at Istanbul," Study VIII, in *The Byzantine Eye* (London: Variorum Reprints, 1989); N. Oikonomides, "Some Remarks on the Apse Mosaic of St. Sophia," *Dumbarton Oaks Papers* 39 (1985): 111–15.

11. Weyl Carr proposes the following interpretation for this image: "In sum, the Sinai icon reflects a bouquet of epithets and images honoring Mary, so suggesting icons that served not as accessories to a site but as objects of pilgrimage in their own right. . . . Yet it is only the Hodegetria that can be identified as an icon of an icon; the other images seem to function above all through their names, which refer less to images

than to sites." Carr, "Icons and the Object of Pilgrimage," 81.

12. Susan Pearce, *Museums, Objects, and Collections: A Cultural Study* (Washington, D.C.: Smithsonian Institution Press, 1992), 5.

13. For a more extensive discussion of this subject, see Joy Kenseth, ed., *Age of the Marvelous* (Hanover, N.H.: Hood Museum of Art, Dartmouth College, 1991); Oliver Impey and Arthur MacGregor, eds., *The Origins of Museums: The Cabinet of Curiosities in Sixteenth- and Seventeenth-Century Europe* (Oxford: Clarendon Press, 1985); Adalgisa Lugli, *Naturalia et Mirabilia: Il collezionismo enciclopedico nelle Wunderkammern d'Europa* (Milan, 1983); Maristella Casciato, Maria Grazia Ianniello, and Maria Vitale, eds., *Enciclopedismo in Roma Barocca: Athanasius Kircher e il Museo del Collegio Romano tra Wunderkammer e museo scientifico* (Venice: Marsilio, 1986).

14. Impey and MacGregor, *The Origins of Museums,* 1.

15. See Anthony Alan Shelton, "Cabinets of Transgression: Renaissance Collections and the Incorporation of the New World," in *The Cultures of Collecting,* ed. John Elsner and Roger Cardinal (Cambridge, Mass.: Harvard University Press, 1994), 177–203.

16. Kenseth, "Preface," in *The Age of the Marvelous,* 13. For an extensive discussion of the "Christian marvelous," see Baxter Hathway, *Marvels and Commonplaces: Renaissance Literary Criticism* (New York: Random House, 1968), 133–66.

17. Kenseth, "A World of Wonders in One Closet Shut," in *The Age of the Marvelous,* 94.

18. Kenseth, "Preface," 13.

19. See Shelton, "Cabinets of Transgression," 189–203. See also Stephen Greenblatt, *Marvelous Possessions: The Wonder of the New World* (Chicago: University of Chicago Press, 1991).

20. Giuseppe Olmi, "Science-Honour-Metaphor: Italian Cabinets of the Sixteenth and Seventeenth Centuries," in Impey and MacGregor, *The Origins of Museums,* 5. See also Thomas DaCosta Kaufmann, "From Treasury to Museum: The Collections of the Austrian Habsburgs," in *The Cultures of Collecting,* ed. Elsner and Cardinal, 137–54.

21. The engraving is published in Sean Shesgreen, ed., *The Criers and Hawkers of London: Engravings and Drawings by Marcellus Laroon* (Stanford: Stanford University Press, 1990), fig. 13. For the history of this genre and bibliography, see Shesgreen, *The Criers,* 12; Dwight Miller, *Street Criers and Itinerant Tradesmen in European Prints* (Stanford: Department of Art, Stanford University, 1970); Anna Omodeo, ed., *Mostra di stampe popolari venete del '500: Catalogo* (Florence, 1965), figs. 5, 6.

22. For a very good introduction to the subject, see James Cracraft, *The Church Reform of Peter the Great* (Stanford: Stanford University Press, 1971).

23. For a discussion of the period, see Cracraft, *Church Reform;* Lindsey Hughes, *Russia in the Age of Peter the Great, 1682–1725* (New Haven: Yale University Press, 1998), 335, 348–51, 377–78. For Peter's instructions on the subject matter of icons, the quality of their execution, and the instituting of a supervising authority over the icon painters, see *Polnoe sobranie postanovlenii i rasporiazhenii po vedomstvu Pravoslavnogo Ispovedaniia Rossiiskoi Imperii,* vol. 2 (1722; repr., St. Petersburg, 1872), 466–68.

24. Hobsbawm, *The Invention of Tradition,* 4–5.

25. For the ecclesiastical debate over various forms of printed imagery, see N. Snegirev, *Lubochnye kartinki russkogo naroda v Moskovskom mire* (Moscow, 1861), 14–15.

26. James Cracraft, *The Petrine Revolution in Russian Imagery* (Chicago: University of Chicago Press, 1997), 94. See also Lindsey Hughes, "The Moscow Armoury and Innovations in Seventeenth-Century Muscovite Art," *Canadian-American Slavic Studies* 13 (1979): 204–23.

27. Engelina Smirnova, "Simon Ushakov—'Historicism' and 'Byzantinism.' On the Interpretation of Russian Painting from the Second Half of the Seventeenth Century," in *Religion and Culture in Early Modern Russia and Ukraine,* ed. Samuel H. Baron and Nancy Shields Kollmann (Dekalb: Northern Illinois University Press, 1997), 169–83. The inspiration for the arrangement of the adoring figures around the Vladimir Mother of God in Simon

Ushakov's icon *In Praise of the Vladimir Mother of God* derives from Ukrainian engravings of the second half of the seventeenth century. See Smirnova, 171; V. G. Chubinskaia, "Ikona Simona Ushakova 'Bogomater' Vladimirskaia,' 'Drevo Moskovskogo gosudarstva,' 'Pokhvala Bogomateri Vladimirskoi': Opyt istoriko-kul'turnoi interpretatsii," *Trudy Otdela Drevnerusskoi Literatury* 38 (1985): 290–308; V. G. Briusova, *Russkaia zhivopis' XVII veka* (Moscow, 1984).

28. This is a quote from Andrei Denisov's "Pomorskie otvety" (answer 50, article 20), reproduced in Boris A. Uspensky, "Schism and Cultural Conflict in the XVII century," in *Seeking God: The Recovery of Religious Identity in Orthodox Russia, Ukraine, and Georgia,* ed. Stephen Batalden (DeKalb: Northern Illinois University Press, 1993), 124.

29. See Cracraft, *Church Reform,* 212n5.

30. Quoted in Cracraft, *Petrine Revolution,* 87.

31. Ibid. 90.

32. Cracraft, *Church Reform,* 210, 59. For a discussion of Peter and popular religion, see Paul Bushkovitch, "Popular Religion in the Time of Peter the Great," in *Letters from Heaven: Popular Religion in Russia and Ukraine,* ed. John-Paul Himka and Andriy Zayarnyuk (Toronto: University of Toronto Press, 2006), 146–64. See also E. B. Smilianskaia, *Volshebniki. Bogokhul'niki. Eretiki: Narodnaia religioznost' i "dukhovnye prestupleniia" v Rossii XVIII v.* (Moscow: Indrik, 2003).

33. M. Alekseeva, "Torgovlia graviurami v Moskve i kontrol' za nei v kontse XVII–XVIII vv.," in *Narodnaia graviura i fol'klor v Rossii XVII–XIX vv.* (Moscow: Sovetskii khudozhnik, 1976), 140–41.

34. Cracraft, *Church Reform,* 212.

35. Gregory Freeze, "Institutionalizing Piety: The Church and Popular Religion, 1750–1850," in *Imperial Russia: New Histories for the Empire,* ed. J. Burbank and D. L. Ransel (Bloomington: Indiana University Press, 1998), 229.

36. The issue of the quality of icon painting is summarized in a poignant quote from an anonymous letter written in 1700 and intended for Peter: "In towns and in villages icon painters paint holy icons with the very worst quality of craftsmanship and sell them for a small price and exchange them for eggs; but it is necessary that the holy icons be painted in a true manner of craftsmanship." *Chteniia v Imperatorskom obshchestve istorii i drevnostei rossiiskikh pri Moskovskom universitete* (hereafter ChOIDR) 1888/2, 22.

37. ChOIDR 1914/1, 661–72.

38. Quoted in Cracraft, *Petrine Revolution,* 295.

39. Ibid., 79.

40. See N. B. Golikova, *Politicheskie protsessy pri Petre I. Po materialam Preobrazhenskogo prikaza* (Moscow, 1957). See also a historical survey on the subject in A. S. Lavrov, *Koldovstvo i religiia v Rossii 1700–1740 gg.* (Moscow: Drevlekhranilishche, 2000), 9–21.

41. Cracraft, *Church Reform,* 212.

42. D. S. Merezhkovskii, *Petr i Aleksei,* vol. 3 of *Khristos i Antikhrist* (Moscow, 1914), 48. In the latter part of Peter's reign, a wide-ranging campaign against religious "superstition" unfolded. A special point in the Ecclesiastical Regulation instructed bishops to "observe that . . . false and invented miracles are not attributed to holy icons." Cracraft, *Church Reform,* 290. See also Vera Shevzov, "Miracle-Working Icons, Laity, and Authority in the Russian Orthodox Church, 1861–1917," *Russian Review* 58, no. 1 (1999): 26–48.

43. Ioanykii Haliatovskyi, *Nebo novoe, s novymi zvezdami sotvorennoe, to est' Preblagoslovennaia deva Maria bogoroditsa s chudami svoimi* (Lviv, 1665). For a brief consideration of Ukrainian influences, see Engelina S. Smirnova, "Icone miracolose della Madre di Dio," in *Icone Russe,* ed. Carlo Pirovano (Milan: Electa, 1999) cat. no. 58. For further discussion of Haliatovskyi, see Paul Bushkovitch, *Religion and Society in Russia: The Sixteenth and Seventeenth Centuries* (Oxford: Oxford University Press, 1992), 126. For a detailed discussion of the Ukrainian impact on Russian Orthodoxy, see K. V. Kharlampovich, *Malorossiiskoe vliianie na velikorusskuiu tserkovnuiu zhizn'* (Kazan, 1914), especially 435–49. See also Serhii Plokhy, *The Cossacks and Religion in Early Modern Ukraine* (Oxford: Oxford University Press, 2001).

44. Before the revolution the text was located in the library of the St. Petersburg Theological Academy.

It was published in ChOIDR 1893/1, 8–13.

45. "List of holy icons of our Most Holy Virgin and the Mother of God," ChOIDR 1893/1, 11.

46. I am grateful to Brian Boeck for bringing this document to my attention.

47. D. A. Rovinskii, *Podrobnyi slovar' russkikh graverov XVI–XIX vekov* (St. Petersburg, 1895), vol. 2, col. 1000.

48. I. A. Kochetkov, "Svod chudotvornykh ikon Bogomateri na ikonakh i graviurakh XVIII–XIX vekov," in *Chudotvornaia ikona v Vizantii i Drevnei Rusi,* ed. A. M. Lidov (Moscow: Martis, 1996), 405.

49. I. Pozdeeva, "Vnov' naidennyi sbornik Simeona Mokhovikova s graviurami G. P. Tepchegorskogo," in *Narodnaia graviura i fol'klor v Rossii XVII–XIX vv.* (Moscow: Sovetskii khudozhnik, 1976), 175–76.

50. Stefan Yavorsky, a controversial figure in Russian scholarship, may have intended to introduce Catholic Marian miraculous images into the Russian liturgical calendar. Kochetkov, "Svod chudotvornykh," 409–10; Lavrov, *Koldovstvo i religiia,* 231. For a more detailed discussion of Yavorsky, see Kharlampovich, *Malorossiiskoe vliianie na velikorusskuiu tserkovnuiu zhizn',* 467–69; Iu. F. Samarin, "Stefan Iavorskii i Feofan Prokopovich," in *Izbrannye proizvedeniia* (Moscow, 1996), 228–39.

51. Pozdeeva, "Vnov' naidennyi sbornik," 177.

52. Ibid., 179. In invoking Calvin and Luther, our author followed the same rhetorical strategy as Feofan Prokopovich in his Prolegomena. For excerpts of Prokopovich's treatise, see Samarin, "Stefan Iavorskii i Feofan Prokopovich," 78.

53. Jaroslav Pelikan, *Mary Through the Centuries: Her Place in the History of Culture* (New Haven: Yale University Press, 1996), 154.

54. For a good introduction to Protestant attitudes toward images, see Belting, *Likeness and Presence,* 458–65; C. C. Christensen, *Art and the Reformation in Germany* (Athens: Ohio University Press, 1979).

55. Belting, *Likeness and Presence,* 484.

56. Ibid.

57. See David Freedberg, "The Hidden God: Image and Interdiction in the Netherlands in the Sixteenth Century," *Art History* 5 (1982): 133–53; "The Structure of Byzantine and European Iconoclasm," in *Iconoclasm,* ed. A. Bryer and J. Herrin (Birmingham, UK: Center for Byzantine Studies, 1977), 165–77.

58. Émile Mâle, *L'art religieux de la fin du XVI siècle, du XVII siècle et du XVIII siècle* (Paris, 1951), 21.

59. Belting, *Likeness and Presence,* 485.

60. A considerable number of miracles are attested in the border regions between Catholicism and Protestantism. See Jean De Viguerie, "Le Miracle dans la France du XVIIe siècle," *XVIIe Siècle* 140 (1983): 313–31. As Zirka Zaremba Filipczak noted: "This interconnection between image and miracle, Catholics thought, would demonstrate to the Protestants (foremost among them Calvinists) who barred the use of paintings and sculptures in churches that God permitted such works to be vehicles of his mercy or power, either directly or through saints." Filipczak, "A Time Fertile in Miracles," in *The Age of the Marvelous,* 203.

61. Some important works include Ferreolus Locrius, *Maria Augusta* (1608), Maselli, *Vita della Beata Vergine* (1610), Astolfi, *Historia universale delle imagini miracolose della gran Madre di Dio* (1624).

62. See Belting, *Likeness and Presence,* 484.

63. Kenseth, "Preface," 13.

64. One of the most prominent collectors of the seventeenth century was the Jesuit Athanasius Kircher. See Silvio Bedini, "Citadels of Learning: The Museo Kircheriano and Other Seventeenth-Century Italian Science Collections," in *Enciclopedismo in Roma Barocca* (Venice, 1986), 249–67.

65. Kenseth, "A World of Wonders," 95, 84.

66. Wilhelm Gumppenberg, *Atlas Marianus, sive De imaginibus Deiparae per orbem Christianum miraculosi* (Ingolstadii, 1657). For descriptions of this often-misunderstood atlas, see Belting, *Likeness and Presence,* 485.

67. During the Counter-Reformation, reports of miracles performed by images of the Virgin increased dramatically. See Jean de Viguerie, "Le Miracle."

68. Pozdeeva, "Vnov' naidennyi sbornik," 176.

69. E. I. Itkina, ed., *Russkii risovannyi lubok kontsa XVIII-nachala XX vekov: iz sobraniia Gosudarstvennogo istoricheskogo muzeia, Moskva* (Moscow: Russkaia Kniga, 1992), 7, 11.

70. Quoted in N. Snegirev, *Lubochnye kartinki russkogo naroda,* 8.

71. Another intermediate link can be found in an engraving recently published by Vera Shevzov, *Russian Orthodoxy on the Eve of Revolution* (Oxford: Oxford University Press, 2004), fig. 6.9.

72. See Oleg Tarasov, *Ikona i blagochestie: ocherki ikonnogo dela v imperatorskoi Rossii* (Moscow: Progress-Kul'tura, 1995); Pirovano, ed., *Icone Russe*; Ivan Bentchev and Eva Haustein-Bartsch, *Muttergottesikonen* (Reklinghausen, 2000); Yuri Piatnitsky et al., eds., *Sinai, Byzantium, Russia: Orthodox Art from the Sixth to the Twentieth Century* (London: Saint Catherine Foundation in association with the State Hermitage Museum, St. Petersburg, 2000).

73. Reproductions appear in the following publications: D. A. Rovinskii, *Russkie narodnye kartinki,* vol. 3 (St. Petersburg, 1881–93); Father Vladimir Ivanov, *Russian Icons* (New York: Rizzoli, 1988); Pirovano, *Icone Russe; Pozdniaia russkaia ikona konets XVIII–XIX vek* (St. Petersburg: Limbus Press, 1994).

74. For discussion of these icons, see Tarasov, *Ikona i blagochestie,* 395–97; Shevzov, *Russian Orthodoxy,* 254–57; Smirnova, "Icone miracolose della Madre di Dio." A brief description of these icons can also be found in Ivan Bentchev and Eva Haustein-Bartsch, *Muttergottesikonen.*

75. *Dnevnik puteshestviia v Kiev 1817 goda* (ChOIDR 1870/2, 1870), 140–41.

76. The derogatory term *bogomaz* survived into the nineteenth century to refer to icons produced for the mass market. See N. P. Kondakov, *Sovremennoe polozhenie russkoi narodnoi ikonopisi* (St. Petersburg: Tipografiia I. N. Skorokhodova, 1901), 2.

77. For statistics on distribution, see Kondakov, *Sovremennoe polozhenie,* 31–32.

78. See V. A. Bakushinskii, *Iskusstvo Palekha* (Moscow and Leningrad, 1934).

79. D. K. Trenev, *Ikonopis' Mstertsev* (Moscow, 1903), 3.

80. Kondakov, *Sovremennoe polozhenie,* 11.

81. Trenev, *Ikonopis' Mstertsev,* 3, 7.

82. Kondakov, *Sovremennoe polozhenie,* 2.

83. See Trenev, *Ikonopis' Mstertsev,* 6, 8, 9. See also Kondakov, *Sovremennoe polozhenie,* 1.

84. James H. Billington, *The Icon and the Axe: An Interpretive History of Russian Culture* (New York: Vintage Books, 1970), 346–47. Goethe's Romantic interest in popular culture was responsible for drawing the attention of many educated Russians to the Vladimir province icons. Goethe owned a number of icons from the region. Kondakov, *Sovremennoe polozhenie,* 1n.

85. Billington, *The Icon and the Axe,* 351.

86. Nikolai Nadezhdin, "Izobrazhenie Bozhiei Materi," in *Filosofiia russkogo religioznogo iskusstva XVI–XX vv.: Antologiia,* ed. N. K. Gavriushin (Moscow: Izdatel'skaia gruppa "Progress-Kul'tura," 1993), 66.

87. ChOIDR 1914/1, 360. For an example of a compendium icon in Western style, see Ivanov, *Russian Icons,* no. 136. For an example of a traditional compendium icon, see *Pozdniaia russkaia ikona. Konets XVIII–XIX vek,* no. 17.

88. The icon was published in Pirovano, *Icone Russe,* 216.

89. The importance of directly encountering and meditating upon the image of the Mother of God is summarized by Pavel Florensky: "I am looking at an icon and saying to myself: 'This—is She Herself'—not a depiction of Her, but She Herself, seen through a medium, with the aid of the iconic art. As if through a window I see the Mother of God . . . and I am praying to Her, face to face." Florenskii, *Ikonostas* (Moscow, 1994), 67.

90. Pearce states: "They take . . . the role of acting as a tangible means by which past history can be selectively rearranged so that continuity is stressed while dislocation and fragmentation is denied, and a romantic wholeness and significance is achieved." Pearce, *Museums, Objects, and Collections,* 197–98.

91. See Sof'ia Snessoreva, *Zemnaia zhizn' Presviatoi Bogoroditsy i opisanie sviatykh chudotvornykh ee ikon, chtimykh pravoslavnoi tserkov'iu, na osnovanii sviashchennogo pisaniia i tserkovnykh predanii, s izobrazheniiami v tekste prazdnikov i ikon Bozhiei Materi* (Yaroslavl, Verkhne-Volzhskoe knizhnoe izdatel'stvo, 1999).

92. Snessoreva, *Zemnaia zhizn' Presviatoi Bogoroditsy,* 3. The number of miracle-working icons has increased to seven hundred in one of the most recent counts. Ivan Pankeev, *Presviataia Bogoroditsa: Chudotvornye ikony i molitvy v zhyteiskikh nuzhdakh* (Moscow, 2002), 7.

93. Snessoreva, *Zemnaia zhizn' Presviatoi Bogoroditsy,* 3.

94. Ibid., 433.

95. Ibid., 81, 86.

96. For the intersection between devotion and nationalism in late imperial Russia, see Shevzov, *Russian Orthodoxy on the Eve of Revolution,* 244–48. For a discussion of late imperial popular piety, see Shevzov, "Icons, Miracles, and the Ecclesiastical Identity of Laity in Late Imperial Russian Orthodoxy," *Church History* 69, no. 3 (2000): 610–31; Valerie Kivelson and Robert Greene, eds., *Orthodox Russia: Belief and Practice Under the Tsars* (University Park: Pennsylvania State University Press, 2003).

97. Recent publications on this cathedral include Konstantin Akinsha and Grigorij Kozlov, with Sylvia Hochfield, *The Holy Place: Architecture, Ideology, and History in Russia* (New Haven: Yale University Press, 2007); *Khram Khrista Spasitelia v Moskve: istoriia proektirovaniia i sozdaniia sobora: stranitsy zhizni i gibeli, 1813–1931* (Moscow: "Planeta," 1992).

98. *Khram Khrista Spasitelia v Moskve,* 99, 140–41.

99. Akinsha and Kozlov, *The Holy Place,* x–xii, 121–23, 140–41, 154–65.

100. M. S. Mostovskii, *Istoriia Khrama Khrista Spasitelia v Moskve* (Moscow, 1891), 100–101.

101. For the nineteenth-century perspective on Alexander Nevsky, see M. Khitrov, *Sviatyi blagovernyi velikii kniaz' Aleksandr Iaroslavich Nevskii: podrobnoe zhizneopisanie s risunkami, planami i kartami* (Moscow, 1893). For a more recent appraisal, see John Fennell, *The Crisis of Medieval Russia, 1200–1304* (New York: Longman, 1983), 109–24.

102. Khitrov, *Sviatyi blagovernyi,* 194–201; Hughes, *Russia in the Age of Peter,* 276–77.

103. *Khram Khrista Spasitelia v Moskve,* 57.

104. For the four groupings, see Mostovskii, *Istoriia Khrama Khrista pasitelia,* 101–2.

VERA SHEVZOV

2

BETWEEN PURITY AND PLURALISM

ICON AND ANATHEMA IN MODERN RUSSIA, 1860–1917

Leonid Ouspensky's two-volume *Theology of the Icon* is one of the most influential and widely consulted works in Western scholarship on the subject of the icon in modern Russia. In many ways, however, his presentation of the icon during this period raises more questions than it answers. On the most basic level, Ouspensky's account depicts a theological world associated with the icon that reaches its clearest formulation and richest visual manifestation following the iconoclastic period in Byzantium and in early medieval Russia, especially in the fourteenth and fifteenth centuries. The subsequent history of the icon in modern Russia, according to Ouspensky, is one of decline: from the seventeenth century, "the spiritual decay that ravaged the entire Orthodox world resulted in a complete loss of the Orthodox conception of the image"; "The image ceased to be a revelation of God, 'a revelation and manifestation of what is hidden.'"[1]

Ouspensky presents his narrative primarily in light of the icon's appreciation and understanding by educated and "enlightened" Russian society. His attention to the meaning and function of the icon within the Orthodox faith community in Russia is relatively minimal. Writing from the well-known though not unchallenged point of view that the church had been transformed into a department of state in the eighteenth century, Ouspensky depicts the clergy and the church as relatively ineffectual in the preservation of the icon's authentic form and meaning. Clergy had their "ecclesial sense disabled by scholasticism," and the icon's "Orthodox content was gradually and systematically deleted from [their] awareness."[2]

Ouspensky's presentation of the meaning and function of the icon in modern Russia leaves unanswered the question of precisely how the Orthodox Church officially thought about icons in the modern period. This chapter offers some preliminary insights into this issue by examining the church's commemoration of the annual feast, celebrated on the first Sunday of Great Lent, dedicated specifically to the icon and its veneration. Generally known as the "Sunday of Orthodoxy" (*Nedelia Pravoslaviia*) or the "Triumph of Orthodoxy" (*Torzhestvo Pravoslaviia*), this ancient feast marked the defeat of iconoclasm. It was reportedly celebrated in a rudimentary form for the first time in Constantinople in 843 with the support of Empress Theodora.[3] The liturgical service for this feast—the "rite of Orthodoxy"—linked the notion of triumph with icons and their veneration. The rite communicated the notion of triumph in three ways: by remembering all those who had defended images and the devotional logic associated with the veneration of icons; by condemning iconoclasts and their views; and by lauding the living emperor and patriarch or local bishop as defenders and protectors of icons and the faith.[4] The celebration of icons became synonymous with the Triumph of Orthodoxy because the theology and veneration of the icon were seen as crowning several centuries of theological developments that had come to define Orthodoxy. Although icons were not mentioned in the Nicene-Constantinopolitan Creed, their veneration came to be treated as dogmatic; according to the Seventh Ecumenical Council, those who refused to venerate icons were not considered Orthodox.[5] Consequently, Byzantine Orthodox Christians soon applied the notion of triumph in the celebration of icons to the entire Orthodox faith, and not simply to icon veneration itself. The celebration of the two—icon and Orthodoxy—effectively merged.

As an annual sacred anniversary of the icon, the Sunday of Orthodoxy offers a unique context for examining the modern Orthodox presentation of the icon. Its liturgical rite, simply by virtue of its being prescribed on this occasion, officially framed and liturgically contextualized the icon. Although we do not have sufficient sources to consider in detail how Orthodox believers at large might have interpreted or understood this rite, we can say something about the ideas, images, and emotions that the rite communicated and that offered meaning to the icon in modern times. How was the victory of icons liturgically remembered in modern Russia? What was the character of the rite for this day and in what way did icons figure into its logic? Perhaps more important, we also have a vast body of sermons, pastoral discussions, and devotional literature that "translated" and interpreted this rite for believers.[6] How, we might ask, did clergy present the icon in their exposition of the meaning of the rite or feast? Finally, what does the celebration and interpretation of this feast tell us about understandings of the icon and Orthodoxy in light of the challenges posed by modernity?

THE EMERGENCE OF THE MODERN RITE

Although prerevolutionary church historians were not sure precisely when the Triumph of Orthodoxy was first celebrated in Russia, they agreed that it was initially celebrated according to the rite as conducted in Constantinople in the twelfth century.[7] While the rite in Russia retained the basic format of its ancient Byzantine counterpart, it was gradually modified to reflect Russia's own realities—with respect to both church and state.

Before the eighteenth century, the celebration of the Triumph of Orthodoxy in Russia could vary from region to region, and within any region it could change over time.[8] In part, this had to do with the nature of the liturgical service. Certain key themes characterized the rite from its inception in ninth-century Byzantium: namely, thanksgiving to God for victory of the Orthodox faith over so-called heresies; the intonation of the names of heretics (or heretical beliefs) and the proclamation of anathemas against them; and remembrance of those in the sacred community, both living and deceased, who had helped to preserve the faith.[9] During the initial celebrations of this feast in the ninth century, the understanding of "triumph" was associated almost exclusively with the use of icons; the subjects of the anathemas and commemorations, therefore, were those involved in the iconoclastic controversies. Later, both in Byzantium and in Russia, the list of heretical beliefs, the names of dissenters, and the list of defenders of the faith all expanded or contracted as historical circumstances necessitated. For this reason, no single final version was ever composed in Byzantium, and Russia never inherited a set rite. In addition, by the seventeenth century, translations of three different versions of the Greek rite circulated within Russia. Consequently, celebration of the rite also varied according to the translation.[10]

On two occasions in the mid-eighteenth century—in 1749 and 1766—the Holy Synod took measures to revise the rite in order to bring uniformity to its celebration. Although it is unclear precisely what motivated churchmen to revisit the rite in 1749, by 1766 members of the Synod were looking to standardize it so as to ensure that changes could not be made impromptu by a diocesan bishop, and to avoid incidents like the one that took place in the diocese of Rostov in 1763. The metropolitan of that diocese, Arseny (Matseevich), was one of the few hierarchs of the Russian Orthodox Church who took an openly oppositional stance toward Peter the Great's ecclesiastical reforms and Empress Catherine II's policy of secularizing church lands. In that year, Arseny used the anathemas as a political and spiritual statement by inserting a clause that condemned those who confiscated church land, hence implicating the empress herself. In order to avoid further incidents such as this, the Holy Synod requested that diocesan bishops send the texts of the rite they used for the service of the Triumph of Orthodoxy to it for immediate correction.

The annual rite of Orthodoxy in its modern form was composed in 1766 and forwarded to diocesan bishops in 1767. It was never published in the Lenten service book (*Triodion*) in the nineteenth or early twentieth century.[11] With only minor revisions in 1840 and again in 1869, the modern version of the rite retained its fundamental form: thanksgiving; condemnation of "adversaries and defamers" of the church; remembrance of the defenders of the faith; and lauds for the living members of the imperial family, patriarchs, metropolitans, and bishops.

The modern form of the rite altered the tenor of the ancient rite in several significant ways. First, as Ouspensky had observed, the modern rite shed its overt and intimate association with the Seventh Ecumenical Council and with the final ninth-century defeat of iconoclasm. The modern rite no longer prescribed a series of prayers (canon) or introductory readings and hymns about the veneration of icons and the evils of iconoclasm. The question remains, however, whether this omission was as consequential as Ouspensky has suggested. Mikhail Gorchakov, the well-known prerevolutionary historian of canon law at St. Petersburg University, has raised doubts about whether such prayers were universally part of the rite of Orthodoxy in Russia before the seventeenth century. In regions where the canon had been conducted, its elimination might have indeed significantly altered the character and content of the ritual celebration.[12] Yet if the canon, with its emphasis on icons and the iconoclastic controversy, was only sporadically prescribed in the seventeenth century, then its omission a century later would not have been as uniformly marked.[13]

Moreover, the premodern rite sometimes incorporated icons into more elaborate ritual acts. In the seventeenth century, for instance, the rite as celebrated in Moscow's Dormition Cathedral involved processions with icons from other parish churches to a space specially set up outdoors behind the cathedral's altar.[14] Because of this movement from neighboring churches to the diocesan cathedral, the rite of Orthodoxy had also traditionally been referred to as "Assembly Sunday" (*Sbornoe voskresen'e*).[15] Bell-ringing from the city's churches would continue for approximately one hour during these processions.[16] In contrast, from the mid-eighteenth century, the modern rite was conducted primarily indoors and involved no procession.

More significant, in the seventeenth century, more than half of the anathemas concerned iconoclasts and their ideas; in the modern rite, only one of twelve anathemas concerned this topic. While certainly not dismissing icons as a public marker of Orthodox identity, the modern rite repositioned them and placed them alongside several other aspects of the faith. Even without considering the canon and its introductory prayers, the modern version of the rite, therefore, lost much of its overt thematic connection to the iconoclastic controversy and to the little-known Byzantine iconoclasts specifically named by the hymns. Such developments led Leonid Ouspensky to trace the gradual elimination of the "confessional content of the image" from the rite of Orthodoxy in modern Russia.[17]

A second noteworthy difference between the seventeenth-century rite and its eighteenth-century counterparts was that the modern rite contained a greatly shortened list of individuals named during both the anathemas and the commemoration of the living and the dead. The pre-Petrine rites consisted of the recitation of names among which were not only Byzantine emperors and empresses, Eastern patriarchs, and particular saints, but also Russian grand princes and princesses, patriarchs, metropolitans, bishops, founders of monasteries, and troops who "courageously fought and fell for the Orthodox faith."[18] By the seventeenth century, a rite of Orthodoxy could include more than four thousand names of deceased and living "defenders" of Orthodoxy.[19] The recitation of names from the annals of Russian church and state history, along with many holdovers from Byzantine history, led Gorchakov to consider the commemoration of the living and the dead the high point of the premodern rite. Such lengthy commemorations, he maintained, were an exercise in historical memory. In his view, they could not help but have left a "tremendous impression" on believers and have "powerfully aroused and strengthened within them a feeling of patriotism and impressed in their memories the names of heroes of the fatherland." The recollection of names of past heroes and events helped to nourish the thought among believers that "to die for the fatherland, for holy Rus, means to die for the holy faith."[20] Accordingly, by no longer reciting hundreds of names, the modern rite no longer drew as much on the memory of particular people and of past events in order to affirm and strengthen community bonds.

The elimination of personal names is particularly noteworthy with respect to the anathemas. By the second half of the nineteenth century, the anathemas no longer referred to *any* named individuals; the final two names, the political traitors Grishka Otrepiev and Ivan Mazepa, were deleted in 1869. The removal of the numerous names altered the tenor of the proclaimed anathemas since the object of ecclesial censorship became not particular individuals but mainly ideas and ways of thinking. It also contributed to the general weakening of the mnemonic power of the modern rite and led to its impersonalization. To a large extent, the list of beliefs that were the subject of the anathema in the modern rite read like an anti-Enlightenment, antimodernist declaration in the nineteenth-century context. The beliefs (and by association, those persons who held these beliefs) that were targeted included those who denied the existence of God; those who denied the Trinity; those who denied the Incarnation or the salvific nature of Christ's birth, death, and resurrection; those who did not believe in Mary's ever-virginity; those who denied the immortality of the soul; and of course, those "who cast reproaches on the holy image . . . in remembrance of the works of God . . . those who say that they are idols."[21]

Generally, the anathemas were directed against beliefs that stood in opposition to those conveyed in the Creed. They were, however, also directed against those who opposed the institutions that were the supposed guardians of the "right faith"—church and tsar. The institutional church was guarded by an anathema against those "who reject the council of the holy fathers and their traditions . . . which the Orthodox Catholic Church piously maintains." The inclusion of an anathema against "those who think that Orthodox sovereigns do not ascend their thrones by the special favor of God toward them" ensured that the proposed linkage between Orthodoxy and the tsar was at least publicly maintained. Because virtually no individuals were specifically named, the practical effects of the new form of anathemas were quite modern: they left the test of heresy during the rite up to individual conscience.

Finally, the celebration of the modern rite was an exclusively urban event; the privilege of conducting the modern Russian rite lay with diocesan bishops and no longer extended to heads of monasteries as it had prior to 1767.[22] Despite the fact that by all accounts the urban event was exceptionally well attended in the Russian Empire up to the revolutions of 1917, and despite the fact that most of those present were common people, many of whom traveled to provincial capitals for the occasion of the feast, it is doubtful that the majority of Russia's Orthodox population would have witnessed the rite during their lifetimes.[23] Yet, if the number of published sermons is an indication of the status of a particular feast day or holiday, then the rite of Orthodoxy was more than a passing curiosity for an urban few. It garnered more attention in the extensive and expanding world of published sermons than many of the twelve major official feast days of the Orthodox Church. Although clergy were under no directive to preach on the occasion of this rite, it is clear from the number of published sermons (by both urban and rural clergy) and the frequency with which such sermons annually appeared that many priests felt compelled to do so.

THE MODERN RITE AND THE ICON

The modern rite took place either before the beginning of the Divine Liturgy or right after its completion. It began with a member of the presiding clergy carrying out an icon of Christ and an icon of the Virgin and placing them in the middle of the church. With altar servers prescribed to hold sacramental fans over the icons, the images of Christ and Mary remained at the visual center of the rite, despite the fact that the textual references to icons and their veneration within the rite were minimal. The modern rite was divided into roughly two parts: prayers of thanksgiving to God as creator and benefactor of the church, which included psalms, several special prayers, an epistle reading (Rom. 16:17–21), and a Gospel reading (Matt. 18:10–19); and the recitation of the newly revised Synodicon (*Sinodik*), which included the Nicene-Constantinopolitan Creed, twelve anathemas, and commemorations of the living and deceased protectors of the faith.[24] Focusing on these textual revisions, Leonid Ouspensky has maintained that the "vital significance of the icon was no longer perceived."[25] Yet each part of the rite took place in front of the centrally placed icons. Insofar as all those present during the performance of this rite were aware of its connection to the victory of icons, everything stated would be linked to the icon, if only by association.

Moreover, in their understanding of the feast, believers could draw upon the broader liturgical context of the celebration of the first Sunday of Lent, which included the vespers and matins services—both of which retained the iconic theme—and the sermon preached after the completion of the rite of Orthodoxy by the presiding bishop (or appointed priest). The hymns of the vespers and matins services in particular provided a rich liturgical context for the celebration of the icon. Vespers was celebrated on Saturday evening; matins either immediately followed vespers or was celebrated on Sunday morning before the Divine Liturgy. Virtually every classical theological justification for the icon's use in worship articulated by Saint John of Damascus and by other churchmen during the proceedings of the Seventh Ecumenical Council was conveyed through the hymns.[26]

Three features of the icon's meaning and function in particular were highlighted.

First, hymns associated the making and veneration of the icon directly with the Incarnation and consequently with human salvation; only because the divine nature was "pleased to take flesh and be circumscribed" could and did believers depict the form of the Son of God incarnate.[27] Representations of Christ in the flesh were said to lead believers "to a desire for and love of God."[28]

Second, alongside the purely theological reflections that situated the icon in the context of the economy of salvation, the services also alluded to the experiential aspect of icon veneration. This aspect was most graphically conveyed in a prescribed homily that was to be read during matins; in the words of the homily, "From Thine icon, we receive grace of healing." The homily recounted the campaign against the use of icons in the Byzantine East, led primarily by its emperors, and the dramatic reversal of that campaign during the reign of Empress Theodora.[29] The establishment of this feast, according to this account, was based neither on theological debate nor on a campaign for the defense of a perceived truth. Rather, it rested on the experience of icons. It portrayed the feast's protagonist, Empress Theodora, as a woman of deep faith and piety, as well as a loyal wife who was haunted by fears about the fate of her deceased husband in the afterlife.

According to the homily, Emperor Theophilus, Theodora's husband and a staunch iconoclast, became ill with a horrid intestinal disorder in which "his mouth opened so wide that his internal organs were visible."[30] On his deathbed, Theophilus underwent what appeared to be a conversion and confessed that "it is good to venerate holy icons." In order to confirm Theophilus's change of heart and mind, Theodora brought icons from her own bedchamber for him to venerate. He did so and then died. Theophilus's act, however, in and of itself did not move Theodora to a public condemnation of iconoclasts and related proclamation of the victory of icons. That proclamation came only after two further events. First, ascetics and recluses (as opposed to philosophers or theologians) inspired her to condemn iconoclasts publicly. Second, it was only after she was assured through a dream (which included an icon) of the divine forgiveness of her own husband and his eternal rest that she announced the public celebration of the victory of icons on the first Sunday of Lent. According to this homily, then, the proclamation of the victory of icons resulted from religious experiences as much as from any political or theological factors. As one hymn from the matins maintained, icons made "use of the heart as well as the eye."[31]

Finally, hymns for both vespers and matins spoke about icons as the church's "precious adornment." As objects of sacred beauty, they embellished the church with divine glory and inspired the faithful to "rejoice with holy joy." But they did more than simply gild the church; they clothed it. The identification of the icon with clothing and garments implied that without them the church was naked, vulnerable, and susceptible to destructive elements. Icons formed the church's "facade," so to speak, as a type of shield and defense. They were "safeguards of the Orthodox faith" by whose grace and splendor heretics were driven away. Hymns celebrated icons as signs of the Orthodox faith's victory over its adversaries. Icons marked a successful struggle with the "heretics," who brought "dark despondency" and the "violence of impiety." Accordingly, the services reminded believers that if they "hold fast to the icon of the Savior . . . they shall not go astray." The faith community, in turn, would remain intact.

Within the church, the victory of icons signified unity of faith. Victory over "adverse powers" meant an end to internal division and enmity: "Divided members . . . have been brought to unity." Accordingly, the hymns hailed agreement, unity of mind, and harmony. Liturgically, the icon and its veneration were associated with "right faith" and the censure and "failure" of other ways of thinking. Here the hymns intersected with the modern rite's emphasis on the theme of victory over Orthodoxy's adversaries. The rituals and texts that focused on the iconoclasts were left out in the eighteenth-century revised version. For this reason, if believers were not present for vespers or matins on the first Sunday of Lent and participated only in the rite of Orthodoxy, the connection between the incarnational theology of the icon and the experiences associated with its veneration may not have been immediately evident.

This vital connection nevertheless survived thanks to preaching. Clergy often addressed the theological and experiential aspects of icon veneration in their sermons at the end of the rite. Indeed, the celebration offered churchmen the opportunity publicly to educate their flock about icons, and many took the occasion to do so. Most churchmen, even if they did not choose to focus on the subject of icons in their sermon, began with a brief note on the historical circumstances surrounding the establishment of this feast. In doing so, some recalled the story of Empress Theodora and her husband, Theophilus;[32] others chose to situate the practice of icon making and veneration in a broader tradition that extended back to Christianity's early years. In such cases, they preferred to draw upon the narrative tradition regarding Abgar, King of Edessa, and the story of the Evangelist Luke's painting of Mary, which were presented uncritically as part of what one priest erroneously called the "New Testamental witness to the necessity of icons."[33]

Some churchmen reiterated the "Orthodox content" of the icon and its veneration, occasionally quoting passages from hymns contained in the vespers and matins services in their defense. Such sermons routinely addressed the relationships between icons and the Incarnation,[34] the image and the prototype,[35] the written word (scripture) and drawn image (icon), and sight and sound in the human quest for the knowledge of and communion with God.[36]

Other churchmen focused more on the experiential aspect of icon veneration and on the power of the human gaze. In so doing, they introduced a particular anthropological view. Since the human person consisted of body and soul, the priest Andrei Tretiakov from the Perm diocese noted, the fullest human experience, including the experience of the sacred, had to involve both. Being clothed in a body, maintained another priest in a sermon published in 1877, a person was unable fully to understand heavenly truths except by means of images. As biblical accounts convey, he argued, God himself had often chosen to communicate with humans through the visual.[37] Moreover, because of its close association with the body, the soul could not be content in its relationship to God living simply in empty space. For instance, in 1917, Faddei, the archbishop of Tver, argued that most humans could not live a full life in a completely empty home in which there was nothing to look at except bare walls. Such an environment would provide no spiritual or physical rest; a person would in fact become exhausted by boredom and emptiness. The same held true for a person's religious life. In order to flourish and grow, a soul needed icons in order to have occasion to pause, to think, to be comforted, and to hope.[38]

Churchmen also promoted icons for their ability to enkindle the human imagination and to orient a person toward whomever or whatever the icon depicted.[39] Recollection here was connected with a sense of presence. The priest Ioakim Romanov, a teacher at the Aleksandrovsky Institute in St. Petersburg, suggested that when a person gazed at an image of Christ, Christ's physical absence became easier to bear. It was as if a person saw him, heard him, and "received his mercy as if from his hands."[40] Gazing upon an icon, asserted Father Mikhail Skriabin from the Perm diocese, "enlivened memory and placed those depicted as if before our eyes."[41]

In addition to drawing a person outward and engaging the believer with the subject depicted, the icon, claimed Orthodox clergymen, could also affect a believer's internal, psychological disposition. The act of gazing at an icon could awaken a "sacred disposition" that either enabled a person to pray or induced a feeling of comfort.[42] Father Porfiry Bazarianinov from the Ekaterinoslavl diocese taught that icons gradually helped to shape a person internally. Similarly, Father Ioann Yakimov from the Voronezh diocese insisted that one simple gaze could instill in the soul a sense of reverence and fear of God.[43] Churchmen's belief in an icon's ability to alter a person's disposition—their sentiments and habits—led to a defense of their ritual aspect in general. In 1887, Tikhon, the bishop of Eniseisk, claimed that icon veneration provided for a "freedom of feeling" in the human act of worshiping and glorifying God; as such it should be defended as inviolable.[44] From this perspective, Byzantine iconoclasm could be interpreted as an attempt to deny Christians the freedom of expression of their religious sensibilities before God.

Despite the modern intellectual suspicion of miracles, Orthodox clergy in the late nineteenth and early twentieth centuries did not hesitate to draw upon both ancient and recent miracle stories in support of icon veneration. Miracles occurred, clergymen maintained, either as testimony to God's mercy and goodness or as testimony to divine favor with respect to icons.[45] In 1884, in demonstration of the fact that icons were not mere art, Father Skriabin spoke about the experiences of a thirty-year-old university graduate who, soon after marrying, came down with an extraordinarily severe case of hemorrhoids. One night, in a dream, the young man found himself in a church that contained the relics and an icon of Saint Tikhon of Zadonsk. The sick man watched an elderly peasant man venerate the icon of the saint. After the man departed, it was as if the image of the saint came alive and said to him: "You should do the same." The sick man became frightened and cried out, "O bishop of God! Help me! How long am I to suffer?" The saint responded that he should be patient, and the vision ended. According to this story, the sick man then set out on a pilgrimage to Zadonsk, after which he was finally healed.[46]

Clergy also pointed out that although the first Sunday of Lent technically commemorated the ninth-century victory over the iconoclasts, iconoclasm as such was not merely an ancient matter; it was alive and well in modern Russia, not only among the non-Orthodox, but among Orthodox believers themselves. Some clergy referred to everyday occurrences, such as dirty icon corners and dusty icons, as signs that believers were not treating icons in an appropriate way.[47] In the 1870s, the priest V. Bandakov from the Kharkov diocese condemned the sale of icons to non-Christians as a form of iconoclastic desecration. The same priest also noted that self-destructive behavior—especially any that affected the human body, such as alcoholism—was a form of iconoclasm insofar as it was set on destroying the image of God within the person.[48]

Most common in sermons were the clergy's comments on what they perceived as the growing absence of icons in modern life. Priests addressed the embarrassment or discomfort that the display of icons in the home appeared to cause many modern educated people. Clergy claimed that by removing icons or hanging them in an inconspicuous place, it was as if people were trying to free themselves from an Orthodox worldview in order to follow a modern one that allowed for actions and behaviors that Orthodoxy did not. Modern believers, claimed the priest A. Zamiatin in 1915, had lost their need to gaze upon the face of Christ or the saints.[49] Clergy also defended icons against those modern Orthodox Christians who maintained that their use was superfluous to the Orthodox ideal that advocated interior prayer. In a defense of the physicality of prayer, one priest offered the image of Christ, who prayed in the garden of Gethsemane until he bled.[50] Manifestations of modern forms of iconoclasm, according to another priest from the Kievan diocese, simply pointed to a gradual erosion of love toward God and Christ in the modern world. After all, a person usually chooses not to gaze at a depiction of someone he or she does not like.[51]

By expanding our analytical frame beyond the prescribed text of the rite or the Synodicon for the Sunday of Orthodoxy, we can see that the icon in modern Russia was not severed from its patristic and conciliar roots. Although the rite itself no longer dwelled on the icon, other liturgical services and sermons for the occasion of this feast preserved the consciousness of the incarnational and experiential dimensions of the icon's place in Orthodox life. Far from ceasing to be a "revelation and manifestation of what is hidden," as Ouspensky maintained, the icon—in whatever style it was written—not only retained its revelatory role within Orthodoxy but also became in this capacity a countercultural emblem that defied and challenged modernity's anthropological axioms.[52]

THE ICON REPOSITIONED

In spite of the widespread evidence of sermons that associated the rite of Orthodoxy with the theological and experiential aspects of icon veneration, the icon as such was not the most popular topic in sermons on this day. Even when sermons for the feast of the Triumph of Orthodoxy discussed the icon, they usually did not focus solely on it. Clergy often coupled the subject of the icon with the theme of Orthodoxy or "right faith" and referred to icons as symbols of the fullness of that faith. As one author noted in 1899, the Byzantine controversy about icons was not merely about devotional practices, but about the sacred truth to which such practices testified.[53]

Insofar as "sacred truth" implied dogma, the modern celebration of the icon came to be associated with the reaffirmation and defense not merely of specific doctrinal teachings such as the Incarnation, but of the very notion of dogma itself. The term "dogma," from the Greek meaning "that which seems to be good," refers to that body of teachings that had been deemed definitive for the Orthodox worldview by the seven ecumenical councils. Insofar as it suggests a body of knowledge that had been handed down by ecclesiastical authorities and that cannot be rationally proven, the very notion of dogma found itself largely discredited in the minds of modern Western intellectuals. One has only to recall Jean-Jacques Rousseau's young priest of Savoy from his novel *Émile* in order to understand the challenges that modernity posed to dogma. "What was the purpose of their dogmas but to create new obscurity?" the priest asks. "They have made men proud, intolerant, and cruel, and instead of establishing peace on earth, they bring to it fire and the sword. I wonder what is the use of all that."[54] In contrast to church authority and revelation, the priest of Savoy professed self-reliance, self-examination, skepticism, reason, and intuition as values necessary to a genuine religious quest.

Russia's Orthodox churchmen saw no lack of threat from the intellectual and spiritual trends associated with modernity. They warned their parishioners about "free thought and skepticism" and "foreign false thinking," which they identified with the West. In their estimation, these notions infected "inexperienced souls" with their "noxious poison."[55] They cautioned listeners about the current climate that demanded "progress" and "development" in all realms of human life and that characterized the church in terms of "immobility, lifelessness, and backwardness."[56] In the view of the priest Dmitry Sliusarev from the diocese of Kiev, self-willed behavior and self-willed thought—that is, reasoning and actions left unguided by Christian principles—were among the most difficult "ulcers" to "cure" within the church environment.[57]

In many ways, the ancient rite of Orthodoxy served as the modern Orthodox Church's official, public response to such intellectual trends, a response that did not entirely shed its iconic associations. A description of the feast printed in the Yaroslavl diocesan newspaper in 1912 enjoined believers to imagine an unmoving bluff or cliff amid the swelling waves of free thought and skepticism. This rock was the church, which could not be leveled by such waves. The feast of the Triumph of Orthodoxy captured this sense of the church as a stronghold. Ecclesial unity was understood here from a defensive perspective. Those who distorted and rejected the faith were positioned on the "outside"; those who remained steadfast were directed to understand the tenets of their faith through their minds and their hearts in order to fortify that bastion from within.[58] The icon and the act of its veneration, by virtue of their association with this feast, signified one of the buttresses by which the church was to withstand the onslaught of modernity.

The central concern of the feast was the unity and integrity of the faith. It was by this one faith that all holy men and women in the church were saved.[59] Accordingly, many churchmen turned to the rite to think about the nature and function of right faith, of dogma, and of Orthodoxy. Alexander Preobrazhensky, a priest and professor from Kazan University, argued in 1909 that dogma was central to unity in church life. Taking stock of the emphasis that modern religious discourse placed on feelings, Preobrazhensky maintained that feeling and act were rooted in thought and idea. Without the defined worldview offered by dogma or creed, the sacred community or church would be left only with an amorphous religious "mood" (*nastroenie*), one too unstable to secure ecclesial unity. Dogma, in Preobrazhensky's view, provided the norms that identified the limits of what was permissible and "healthy" with respect to life itself.[60]

In contrast to modern notions of "progress" and "development" as signs of something positive and good, churchmen argued for a notion of dogma that was immutable and unchanging.[61] In 1897, Archimandrite Pavel, the dean of the St. Petersburg Theological Academy, defended the immutable quality of dogma as an essential aspect of Orthodoxy. Not denying that human thought developed and changed over time, the archimandrite argued that change and development in terms of revealed truth were only human perceptions. Truth remained one, undamaged and unchanged.[62] Similarly, in 1903, Anastasy, bishop of Olonets, compared dogmas to the laws of science. In drawing this comparison, he pointed out that society usually did not dismiss those who recognized and accepted the unchanging laws of science as ignoramuses. If science could not exist without its unchanging laws, why, he rhetorically asked, did people expect that religions must?[63]

Notions of purity, preservation, and sanctity implied the awareness of their opposites: corruption, destruction, and depravity. Since the victory of icons commemorated the church's victory over opponents of the Christian faith, clergymen frequently likened the rite to a drama that enacted the struggle between believers and their various "enemies."[64] Linking icons and dogma, churchmen sought a common strand that tied the earliest Christian era, the iconoclastic period, and the present together. In 1905, for instance, the priest Mikhail Izvolsky interpreted the movement against icons in the eighth and ninth centuries as part of a broader activity of "the mystery of lawlessness" that had sought the destruction of the Christian faith since the earliest times.[65] If, in the earliest times, "evil forces" sought this destruction from the outside—through outright persecution—from the fourth century, their tactics changed. Izvolsky and other preachers saw those forces as insinuating themselves within the Christian community in the forms of heresy and schism.[66] Izvolsky presented dogmatic differences and heresies among Christians as manifestations of the same principle of lawlessness that stood behind early Christian persecutions, but as much more effective ways of ruining the community. These same forces, he reminded his readers, were actively at work in contemporary times.

THE ANATHEMAS

Icons provided the visual focal point of the celebration of Orthodoxy in modern Russia; the proclamation of the "anathemas," in turn, served as the rite's auditory highlight and drew the crowds. In describing the feast as it took place in the Dormition Cathedral in the year 1900, one Moscow newspaper noted the "enormous mass of believers" that had gathered both in the cathedral and in the square outside.[67] Andrei Muraviev, writing in the 1830s about his visit to Kazan, referred to the rite as a "show."[68] Clearly what brought out the crowds and gave the rite its sensational quality were the anathemas.[69]

The theatrical aspect of the anathemas was captured in the story "Octava," published in 1902 by a Russian writer from a peasant background, Stefan Gavrilovich Petrov (1868–1934), also known by the pseudonym Skitalets or "Wanderer."[70] Petrov depicts a provincial cathedral overflowing with a crowd of a thousand who await the commencement of the rite with "some sort of mysterious anticipation." When the deacon intones prayers, it seems as if "inexorable fate, destiny itself, was passing a somber sentence that no one had the power to change. . . . In this tone, his mighty voice became like a massive, threatening cloud with a distant thunder, which was approaching."[71] The "threatening cloud" alludes to the anathemas, the words of which are read as if "hammering them with nails." His pronouncement of the actual word "anathema" rings out with a force that seems to make everything sway. The thousand faceless people present simultaneously sigh, "apprehensively and mournfully." As the twelve anathemas proceed one after another, with the clergy and choir each chanting "anathema" in response to each clause, "a strange, sorrowful murmur passed through the crowd, a general groan. Sobbing could be heard and someone hysterically called out. Tears streamed down the faces of those people standing in front."[72]

Petrov's perhaps overly dramatized account nevertheless was in large part confirmed by many clergy in their sermons. In 1883, Father Nikolai Kratirov admitted that it was difficult to listen to the anathemas without shuddering and feeling a deep heartache. A believer wanted to weep, he noted, when he heard the word pronounced in church. Much strength and effort of will was needed to control oneself during the course of the service.[73]

Although the rite was usually well attended, it also endured much public criticism, especially among the educated, and especially following the Holy Synod's public anathematization of Lev Tolstoy in 1901.[74] Against the backdrop of modern principles of freedom of conscience, humanism, religious tolerance, and pluralism, the anathema had a harsh, oppressive ring to it. Preachers were very aware of the public perception of this rite.

As Archimandrite Vissarion from the Samara diocese stated in 1910, not one feast of the Orthodox Church was subject to as much criticism and attack as the feast of the Triumph of Orthodoxy.[75] Priests noted that the rite was seen as impinging on the principle of freedom of conscience and as displaying "fanatical intolerance to diverse beliefs and opinions."[76] People complained that the anathema was anachronistic and manifested an unreasonable degree of stringency with respect to church rules.[77] Some saw it as "medieval."[78] Parishioners associated it with vengefulness and considered it as totally incongruous with the Christian principle of love.[79] It appeared to counter everything modernity stood for.[80]

From the mid-nineteenth century, many churchmen turned their attention to the anathemas in order to define and explicate their meaning in a way more agreeable to the modern ear. Although not denying the sense of dread the anathema instilled, they attempted to distinguish it from an act of damnation or consignment to perdition. The interpretation of the anathemas as an act of damnation was a meaning that at least some churchmen attributed to historical developments dating to late antiquity.[81] They argued that, unlike a curse, the anathema was not inherently an expression of anger, hatred, or revenge, nor was it pronounced in a moment of passion or in a spirit of hostility. Rather, as it was positioned in the rite, it signified a calmly calculated separation or a removal of a one-time believer from the sacred community—in short, excommunication. Clergymen defined the anathema as the act of placing someone outside the boundaries of the faith community, of severing someone from that community as with a "spiritual sword."[82] It was an official recognition of someone who, once "one of us," was now, because of his or her views, considered foreign or "other" (*chuzhimi*).[83] A missionary from the Perm diocese maintained that in then-current language, the notion of anathema should be understood to mean "leave us alone; separate yourself from us, for there is nothing left in common between you and us."[84]

Defined in this way, the rite was an act of public identification of ideas and views that were considered incompatible with Orthodoxy, that is, contrary to dogma. Clergy argued that its function was pedagogical rather than punitive.[85] In 1907, the rector of the Tobolsk seminary maintained that the rite played a healthy role in the life of the church; it forced modern Christians to choose between two mind-sets—that designated by church tradition or that offered by "this age." For those believers who knew little about their faith, the rite often served as a stark reminder and helped them to distinguish between truth and falsehood with respect to the various philosophical trends or ways of thinking about their faith.[86]

From the Orthodox perspective, what was at stake in this rite was the issue of salvation. Those who were outside the boundaries of the community for all practical purposes were seen as having deprived themselves of the means by which personal salvation could be attained. As one priest stated, "The person who finds himself severed from the church finds himself under the authority of the evil one, who has full access to him, since such a person does not enjoy the protection of the grace of

God."[87] Consequently, being "outside," they were deprived of even the hope for salvation.[88] Not surprisingly, this act of formal separation was spoken of as both frightening and mournful.[89] The pastor's task was to ensure that as many of the flock as possible averted this path to self-destruction.

Although conceding that the anathema was a threatening and frightening act, clergymen also routinely insisted that it was a word and act of love.[90] They reminded believers that the church in whose name this ritual was being performed was a feminine principle and was referred to as "mother." As such, she sought the safety and salvation of its members. The judgment should be thought of, said one priest, not in terms of the anger of a harsh and unyielding ruler, but of "a child-loving mother."[91] The anathema, said another, should be heard as a "painful cry of a mother's heart."[92]

The anathemas were proclaimed against beliefs that were contrary to ancient dogmas of faith. Yet contemporary heresies, churchmen maintained, offered nothing new as far as Christians were considered. The ideas underlying contemporary religious "deviations," in their view, had already been anticipated and addressed by the ancient church councils. In this sense, the rite of Orthodoxy was not an antiquarian relic but a modern expression of the church's collective wisdom. As one priest argued in 1892, if the church had seen something new in the current thinking of nihilists, naturalists, and Westernizers in general, it would not have remained silent; church authorities would simply have added another clause to the list of anathemas: "to Büchner, Feuerbach, Renan, and their followers, anathema." The church did not do so because the worldviews of these thinkers were based on principles that Orthodoxy had deemed foreign long before and that were already rejected by the existing anathemas, among them being one against iconoclasts.[93]

The anathemas and their defense of dogma also challenged the modern view that all religions were essentially the same but simply expressed truth in different forms. Russia's churchmen ardently denied the idea of a plurality of truths shared by the world's religious traditions. Such a view, they maintained, would make the church superfluous.[94] Facing charges of intolerance and exclusivity, churchmen retorted that the notion of tolerance did not mean indifference or coldness to matters of faith.[95] If there were indeed a truth that was one and unchanging, it was rationally impossible to hold this truth alongside any views that contradicted it. Consequently, while clergymen encouraged Orthodox Christians to show respect toward other people's beliefs and convictions, they also warned members of the flock about developing a posture of religious nonchalance. Indifference in spiritual matters, claimed one priest from the Yaroslavl diocese in 1910, could be compared to indifference to the taste of food. More often than not, such indifference was a sign of illness.

As mentioned above, Gorchakov maintained in his 1881 essay on the rite of Orthodoxy that the commemorations for the living and the dead had dominated believers' attention in the pre-Petrine rite. In contrast, modern Orthodox believers seem to have been mesmerized by the anathemas. While not losing its associations with history and memory, the modern form of the rite and the sermons that followed more often than not related Orthodox collective identity to revisionist notions of the anathema as a caring act of love. In this context of active love, the icon, as testimony to the preservation of a "pure, undefiled ecclesial faith," found itself discussed in light of equally ancient themes of threat and defense, exposure and protection, and ultimately defeat and triumph.[96]

A NEW CONTEXT?

The anathema and the sermons that defended its use continued to be part of the rite of Orthodoxy that was served in diocesan cathedrals right up to the 1917 revolutions. Beginning in the 1870s, the celebration of the Sunday of Orthodoxy took on a somewhat different meaning when the Orthodox Church harnessed the feast to its expanding missionary efforts. In 1871–72, Innokenty, the metropolitan of Moscow, petitioned the Holy Synod to direct parish priests to hold annual discussions about missionary work in order to propagate zeal for the effort. The Missionary Society, in turn, presented the Holy Synod with four model sermons that could be used as guidelines for talks delivered on that day, which the Holy Synod proceeded to send in multiple copies to dioceses throughout Russia.[97] Most of Russia's bishops came to choose the Sunday of Orthodoxy as the occasion on which to encourage their pastors to deliver such homilies. In 1888–89, the Holy Synod reiterated this appeal and published a total of seven additional model sermons. These model sermons (or versions thereof) would then occasionally be reprinted in diocesan newspapers as much as fifteen or twenty years later.

The missionary theme somewhat altered the image of the church as a stronghold in a threatening sea. Instead of calling attention to modern threats to the faith from "foreign thoughts," preachers turned to those who belonged to other faiths (*inovertsy*) and began focusing on the relationship between the Orthodox and the religious Other. When considering those of other faiths—mostly Muslims and so-called pagans (*iazychniki*)—they thought primarily in terms of peoples living within the boundaries of the Russian Empire. Here "outsider" had a slightly different connotation than a "Westerner" or a "deviant" from within the Orthodox community. In the missionary context, the outsiders were not ones to be avoided but rather met and incorporated into the fold of Orthodoxy: "If these people who are now entirely foreign to us become Orthodox, they will become our brethren."[98]

The emotional appeal of sermons that focused on the missionary effort was somewhat different from those that focused on the anathema. Here clergy were less on the defensive and appealed to what they considered to be the fortune of having been born into the Orthodox faith. Such fortune, they maintained, should be shared with those whom they considered less fortunate. How many millions of people exist who "wander in darkness and in the shadows of death," people who "live not somewhere in China or India, but in our own homeland, in Siberia and Turkistan and even closer in the eastern provinces of Perm, Orenburg, Ufa, and Kazan?"[99]

Whether politically or spiritually motivated—and these sermons were clearly both—unity of faith, when considered in the missionary context, was thought of more in terms of engagement than defense and preservation. Sermons for this feast began emphasizing the missionary effort as a responsibility of every Christian, both individually and collectively. Individually, believers were encouraged to think about the non-Orthodox as the suffering, the hungry, and the poor, but in a spiritual sense.[100] Collectively, believers were to consider the broader social and political implications of transforming "not our own" into "our own" within the Russian Empire. Preachers held the prospects of foreigners "reborn as Orthodox Russian people" before their eyes.[101]

The increasing trend to use the occasion of the celebration of the icon to speak about missionary activity in parish churches, both urban and rural, led to a situation in which two variants of the rite for the Triumph of Orthodoxy were being performed simultaneously throughout Russia. In 1897, the third annual meeting of the Missionary Society in Kazan claimed that for missionary activity within Russia to be successful, the power of collective prayer was needed. Six years later, in 1903, the Holy Synod responded to this request by directing that the rite of Orthodoxy be carried out in all monasteries and urban and rural parish churches in an abbreviated form, without the anathemas. The two celebrations, one with the anathemas and commemorations and one without, presented as it were two faces of Orthodoxy in the modern age: one that sought strict boundaries and definitive limits and another that sought inclusion and longed-for universal unity. It is difficult to tell whether this was a short-term modification or a long-term trend that eventually would have influenced the way in which the feast was celebrated in the cathedrals. In little more than a decade, the new Soviet realities would make proclamation of the anathemas in Russia's cathedrals impossible and the issue a moot point.

CONCLUSION

It might be tempting for the historian of Orthodoxy in Russia to conclude from sermons for the feast of the Triumph of Orthodoxy that the celebration of the icon became lost beneath discussions about "right faith." Leonid Ouspensky drew such a conclusion. He connected the eighteenth-century revisions of the service for the feast—revisions that excluded portions of the service that concerned the icon's confessional content—with a general blurring of the understanding of the icon during the synodal period.[102]

I would argue, instead, that the modern rite of Orthodoxy in prerevolutionary Russia reflected not so much a blurring of the understanding of the icon among Orthodox clergy as it did a shift in significance that was no less sacramental and no less traditional than the incarnational understanding about which Ouspensky wrote. In 1915, Father Zamiatin from the Podolia diocese emphasized the social and communal aspect of icon veneration. By gazing at an icon, believers sensed their belonging to a single community. "In making and decorating icons and in venerating them," he maintained, "we express our entire belonging to the church, our inseparability from her in soul and in body. Not to venerate icons means to be alienated from the living body of the church."[103] By merging with the celebration of the Triumph of Orthodoxy, the icon, as Zamiatin's words show, became linked with thinking about the church—one of the most challenged Christian ideals and institutions in the modern age. The feast, and the victory of icons that stood as its subtext, celebrated the integrity of the faith community in a rather bold insistence that such integrity was still possible.

Moreover, the Seventh Ecumenical Council was not only about the icon's visual depiction. It was also very much rooted in the experiences that believers had had with icons, experiences that related to the veneration and presence of the icon itself. Given the way that Orthodox preachers spoke about the icon in their sermons, it seems that it is this dimension of the icon—that is, the icon not only as medium but as object, as a tangible article of faith and "objective" bearer of the holy—that gained ascendancy in modern Russia. If the theology that countered iconoclasm in the eighth and ninth centuries stood for a perceived sense of objective truth, for the perceived reality of the Incarnation, then the modern period, it might be argued, saw the development of another, related layer of meaning regarding the icon. The icon, irrespective of the particulars of its depiction, had become in itself an affirmation of dogma—the non-negotiable Orthodox teachings—as well as the ontological antecedent of those teachings as a whole. In other words, the icon became the affirmation of the existence and very knowability of truth, and the historical manifestation of that truth, over against the skepticism and relativism of post-Enlightenment thought.

Finally, because of the historical link between the celebration of the icon and the celebration of Orthodoxy, thinking about the icon and the religious Other continued to be associated in modern Russia. While the liturgical rite performed on this day spoke explicitly about icons only in the context of the anathemas, the entire service commenced with a procession of icons into the center of the church, and the chanting of the service took place in front of them. Moreover, clergy generally fostered the association between icons and the celebration of the Triumph of Orthodoxy by mentioning the victory over iconoclasm in their sermons. Consequently, the commemoration of the victory of icons offered churchmen an occasion to consider the issue of unity of faith and the modern challenges to that unity and faith. In turn, differing dispositions toward perceived threats generated different readings of the icon. Indeed, it is at the various fronts at which preachers situated this feast—vis-à-vis the Christian West, vis-à-vis Enlightenment ideals, vis-à-vis the non-Russian, non-Orthodox peoples of the empire, or even vis-à-vis the state and ethnic Russians—that the modern meanings or revelations of the icon are to be found.

NOTES TO CHAPTER 2

1. Leonid Ouspensky, *Theology of the Icon,* trans. Anthony Gythiel, 2 vols. (Crestwood, N.Y.: St. Vladimir's Seminary Press, 1992), 2:362, 368.

2. Ibid., 2:425.

3. The most exhaustive history of this rite remains the classic study by Konstantin Nikol'skii, *Anafematstvovanie (otluchenie ot tserkvi), sovershaemoe v pervuiu nedeliu velikogo posta* (St. Petersburg, 1879); also see F. Uspenskii, "Konstantinopol'skii sobor 842 goda i utverzhdenie pravoslaviia," *Ocherki po istorii Vizantiiskoi obrazovannosti* (St. Petersburg, 1891), 3–89; D. E. Afinogenov, *Povest' o proshchenii imperatora Feofila i Torzhestvo Pravoslaviia* (Moscow: Indrik, 2004), 63–78.

4. Jean Gouillard, "Le Synodikon de l'Orthodoxie, Édition et commentaire," in *Travaux et Mémoires* 2 (Paris, 1967); F. Uspenskii, *Sinodik v nedeliu Pravoslaviia. Svodnyi tekst s prilozheniiami* (Odessa, 1893). See also Andrew Louth's translation of the early twelfth-century text of the Synodicon of Orthodoxy: http://web.ukonline.co.uk/ephrem/synodikon.htm.

5. "Obriad anafematstvovaniia," *Voskresnyi den'* 6 (1914): 64–66.

6. In addition to the liturgical texts, this chapter is based on the reading of more than 250 sermons and pastoral discussions published during the period 1860–1917.

7. Scholarship on the rite of Orthodoxy disagrees on the history of the rite's introduction into Russia. For different opinions on this question, see Nikol'skii, *Anafematstvovanie,* 22; M. I. Gorchakov, *Anafematstvovanie ot tserkvi, sovershaemoe v pervuiu nedeliu velikogo posta* (St. Petersburg, 1881), 5; Grigorii Georgievskii, comp., *Prazdnichnye sluzhby i tserkovnye torzhestva v staroi Moskve* (1896; repr., Moscow: Mezhdunarodnyi izdatel'skii tsentr Pravoslavnoi literatury, 1995), 55; S. S. Averintsev, ed., *Khristianstvo: Entsiklopedicheskii slovar',* 3 vols. (Moscow: Bol'shaia Rossiiskaia entsiklopediia, 1995), 2:191; N. Snegirev, "Nedelia Pravoslaviia ili Sbornoe voskresen'e v Moskve," *Pravoslavnoe obozrenie (Zametki)* 2 (1865): 61–71; Uspenskii, *Ocherki po istorii Vizantiiskoi obrazovannosti,* 127.

8. Nikol'skii, *Anafematstvovanie,* 25–36.

9. K. N., "Chin Pravoslaviia," *Pribavleniia k tserkovnym vedomostiam* 11 (1888): 284–88.

10. Gorchakov, *Anafematstvovanie,* 5.

11. The redactions of 1749 and 1766 were the work of bishops Gavriil (Kremenetsky) of Kolomna and Gavriil (Petrov) of Tver, respectively, but included the collective effort of the Holy Synod as well.

12. Among the twenty eighteenth-century manuscripts of the rite of Orthodoxy I examined from various dioceses throughout Russia, only some prescribed the canon attributed to Theodore the Studite. RGIA, f. 834, op. 1, d. 989, lines 1–3; d. 991, lines 1–5; d. 994, line 1 ob; d. 1005. The only manuscript I found that contained the full text of the canon was that from Moscow's Dormition Cathedral.

13. Gorchakov, *Anafematstvovanie,* 40.

14. Nikol'skii, *Anafematstvovanie,* 53. For a brief description of the rituals associated with the celebration of the Triumph of Orthodoxy in Moscow's Dormition Cathedral, see Georgievskii, comp., *Prazdnichnye sluzhby,* 53.

15. Churchmen maintained that it was also referred to as "Assembly Sunday" since the feast was established during the ecumenical councils. See Snegirev, "Nedelia Pravoslaviia ili Sbornoe voskresen'e v Moskve," 63; Kafedral'nyi protoierei Semenov, "Slovo v Nedeliu Pravoslaviia," *Orenburgskie eparkhial'nye vedomosti,* otdel neofitsial'nyi 5 (1874): 185–90.

16. Nikol'skii, *Anafematstvovanie,* 53–57.

17. Ouspensky, *Theology of the Icon,* 2:363, 467. Despite Ouspensky's claim, even a cursory review of the hymns that comprised this canon shows that there was strikingly little reference to the confessional content or actual theology of the image. See Nikol'skii, *Anafematstvovanie,* 63–71. Ouspensky dates the changes in the rite of Orthodoxy to the seventeenth century.

However, according to historians such as Nikolsky and Gorchakov, such changes were instituted in the eighteenth century.

18. For a copy of the commemorative part of the rite (the so-called Synodicon) for the year 1684 as recited in Moscow, see Nikolai Novikov, ed., *Drevniaia Rossiiskaia Vivliofika,* 2nd ed. (Moscow, 1788), 420–506.

19. "Anafematstvovanie: Kratkii istoricheskii ocherk," *Voskresnyi den'* 7 (1912), 4.

20. Gorchakov, *Anafematstvovanie,* 2, 8.

21. The list of anathemas can be found in "Obriad anafematstvovaniia," 64–66; "Torzhestvo Pravoslaviia," *Iaroslavskie eparkhial'nye vedomosti,* chast' neofitsial'naia 7 (1901): 97–100. English translations can be found in John Glen King, *The Rites and Ceremonies of the Greek Church in Russia* (London, 1772), 403–4.

22. In 1767, by Synod decree, four copies of the newly revised rite were sent to diocesan bishops with the directive that only they were to carry out the rite. "Chin Pravoslaviia," *Pribavleniia k tserkovnym vedomostiam* 9 (1903): 329; Nikol'skii, *Anafematstvovanie,* 52.

23. V., "Anafematstvovanie," *Penzenskie eparkhial'nye vedomosti* 5 (1866): 139–44.

24. Synodicon refers to the names of individuals, both living and deceased, who are to be commemorated at a particular prayer service. The list designated for the rite of the Triumph of Orthodoxy is referred to as the "Synodikon of Orthodoxy."

25. Ouspensky, *Theology of the Icon,* 2:467.

26. Believers would have heard that icons were not idols and would have been reminded more than once of Saint Basil of Caesarea's well-known maxim that the honor shown to the icon passes to the prototype it represents.

27. For the Slavonic text, see *Triod' Postnaia* (Moscow, 1897), 143–50; for a translation of the hymns, see *The Lenten Triodion,* translated from the original Greek by Mother Mary and Archimandrite Kallistos Ware (London, 1978), 299–310.

28. For an analysis of the *kontakion* hymn for the Sunday of Orthodoxy, see Ouspensky, *Theology of the Icon,* 2:179–229.

29. For a historical presentation of the details of the story related by the homily, see Afinogenov, *Povest' o proshchenii imperatora Feofila;* Martha Vinson, "The Terms ἐγκολπιον and τἐνάντιον and the Conversion of Theophilus in the *Life of Theodora* (BHG 1731)," *Greek, Roman, and Byzantine Studies* 36, no. 1 (1995): 89–99.

30. The prescribed homily or Synaxarion was situated between the sixth and seventh odes of the canon for the feast. The Synaxarion reading is still included in contemporary rubrics for the matins service. See *Triod' Postnaia,* 147–50. It is unclear, however, whether or not clergy actually read this homily during the service.

31. "Pouchenie v Nedeliu Pravoslaviia," *Poucheniia k poselianam prikhodskogo sviashchennika Permskoi eparkhii Andreia Tret'iakova* (Moscow, 1875), 83.

32. For example, see "Pouchenie v Nedeliu Pravoslaviia," *Sbornik pouchenii na vse voskresnye i prazdnichnye dni goda i na osobennye sluchai tserkovnoi i obshchestvennoi zhizni* (Kiev, 1877): 417–27; Sv. I. G. Pospelov, "Pouchenie 1-e v Nedeliu Pravoslaviia," *Poucheniia i rechi* (Kostroma, 1878): 239–41; S.N.R., "Pouchenie v Nedeliu Pravoslaviia," *Orenburgskie eparkhial'nye vedomosti,* otdel neofitsial'nyi 7 (1882): 276–80; "Nedelia Pravoslaviia," *Voskresnyi den'* 7 (1889): 89–90; Sv. Pavel Shumov, "Pouchenie v Nedeliu Pravoslaviia," *Khristianskaia beseda* 2 (1895): 99–104; Sv. Ioann Troitskii, *Pouchitel'noe chtenie v Nedeliu Pravoslaviia* (Kiev, 1898); O.E.V., "Nedelia Pravoslaviia," *Voskresnyi den'* 5 (1915): 50–51; Inspektor Permskoi Dukhovnoi Seminarii Nikolai Znamirovskii, "Slovo v Nedeliu Pravoslaviia," *Permskie eparkhial'nye vedomosti* 7 (1915): 183–88.

33. "Pouchenie v Nedeliu Pravoslaviia," *Sbornik pouchenii,* 417–27. For the story of King Abgar of Edessa, see Jefferson J. A. Gatrall's chapter in this volume. For examples of sermons that referred to this story, see "Pouchenie v Nedeliu Pravoslaviia," *Poucheniia k poselianam prikhodskogo sviashchennika Permskoi eparkhii,* 81–85; Prot. Iakov Burlutskii, "Beseda v Nedeliu Pravoslaviia," *Penzenskie eparkhial'nye vedomosti,* chast' neofitsial'naia 7 (1880): 1–10; Sv. Porfirii Bazarianinov, "Pouchenie v Nedeliu Pravoslaviia," *Sbornik slov i pouchenii sviashchennosluzhitelei Ekaterinoslavskoi eparkhii* vyp. 1 (Ekaterinoslav, 1875), 60–61; Arkhimandrit Vladimir, nyne episkop Sarapulskii, "Beseda v Nedeliu Pravoslaviia o pochitanii sviatykh ikon," *Pastyrskie trudy za tridtsat' piat' let sluzheniia sv. Tserkvi (1866–1901)* (St. Petersburg, 1901): 191. For scholarly treatment of the narrative of King Abgar, see Averil Cameron, "The History of the Image of Edessa: The Telling of a Story," in *Okeanos: Essays Presented to Ihor Ševčenko,* ed. C. Mango and Omeljan Pristak (Cambridge, Mass.: Ukrainian Research Institute, Harvard University, 1983), 80–94; Herbert L. Kesslar and Gerhard Wolf, eds., *The Holy Face and the Paradox of Representation* (Bologna: Nuovo Alfa, 1998). For examples of sermons that referred to the story of the Evangelist Luke painting Mary, see "Pouchenie v Nedeliu Pravoslaviia," *Poucheniia k poselianam prikhodskogo sviashchennika Permskoi eparkhii,* 81–85; Arkhimandrit Vladimir, "Beseda v Nedeliu Pravoslaviia," 192. For a discussion of the narrative of Luke's painting of Mary, see Hans Belting, *Likeness and Presence: A History of the Image Before the Era of Art,* trans. Edmund Jephcott (Chicago: University of Chicago Press, 1994), 47–59.

34. Prot. A. Zamiatin, "Slovo v Nedeliu Pravoslaviia," *Pravoslavnaia Podoliia,* neofitsial'naia chast' 8 (1915): 389–93.

35. Burlutskii, "Beseda v Nedeliu Pravoslaviia," 1–10; "Pouchenie v Nedeliu Pravoslaviia," *Sbornik pouchenii,* 419.

36. Sv. Ioann Iakimov, "Pouchenie v nedeliu 1-uiu posta," *Prostonarodnye poucheniia sel'skim prikhozhanam* (Voronezh, 1887), 164–66; Arkhimandrit Vladimir, "Beseda v Nedeliu Pravoslaviia," 188.

37. "Pouchenie v Nedeliu Pravoslaviia," *Poucheniia k poselianam prikhodskogo sviashchennika Permskoi eparkhii,* 81–85; Prot. Feodor Vasiutinskii, *Slovo v Nedeliu Pravoslaviia* (Chernigov, 1900); "Pouchenie v Nedeliu Pravoslaviia," *Sbornik pouchenii,* 417–27.

38. Faddei (Uspenskii), arkhiepiskop Tverskii, "Slovo v Nedeliu Pravoslaviia v pervuiu nedeliu Velikogo Posta," *Vladikavkazskie eparkhial'nye vedomosti* 6 (1917): 158–62.

39. "Pouchenie v Nedeliu Pravoslaviia," *Sbornik pouchenii,* 419; Arkhimandrit Vladimir, "Slovo v Nedeliu Pravoslaviia," 181–85.

40. I. K. Romanov, "Poucheniia v 1-uiu nedeliu Velikogo Posta: O torzhestve pokloneniia ikone Spasitelia," *Polnoe sobranie pouchenii* (St. Petersburg, 1880): 207–8.

41. Sv. Mikhail Skriabin, "Slovo v Nedeliu Pravoslaviia," *Permskie eparkhial'nye vedomosti,* otdel neofitsial'nyi 9 (1884): 133–40.

42. "Pouchenie v Nedeliu Pravoslaviia," *Sbornik pouchenii,* 422.

43. Bazarianinov, "Pouchenie v Nedeliu Pravoslaviia," 60–61; Iakimov "Pouchenie v nedeliu 1-uiu posta," 164–66.

44. Episkop Tikhon, "Slovo v Nedeliu Pravoslaviia," *Eniseiskie eparkhial'nye vedomosti,* otdel neofitsial'nyi 5 (1887): 61–69; Nikanor, episkop Khersonskii i Odesskii, "Beseda v Nedeliu Pravoslaviia: O pochitanii sv. ikon," *Orenburgskie eparkhial'nye vedomosti* 12 (1885): 410–19.

45. Bazarianinov, "Pouchenie v Nedeliu Pravoslaviia"; Voskresenskii, "Beseda v Nedeliu Pravoslaviia," *Pribavleniia k Khersonskim eparkhial'nym vedomostiam,* 207–25; "Pouchenie v Nedeliu Pravoslaviia," *Sbornik pouchenii,* 417–27.

46. Skriabin, "Slovo v Nedeliu Pravoslaviia," 137–38.

47. Bazarianinov, "Pouchenie v Nedeliu Pravoslaviia," Iakimov, "Pouchenie v nedeliu 1-uiu posta," 164–66.

48. Bandakov, "V 1-uiu nedeliu sv. Chetyredesiatnitsy," *Prostye i kratkie poucheniia,* vol. 4 (Kharkov, 1879), 85–86.

49. Zamiatin, "Slovo v Nedeliu Pravoslaviia," 389–93. See also A.A., "Slovo v den' Pravoslaviia," *Moskovskie tserkovnye vedomosti* 8 (1885): 144–45; Burlutskii, "Beseda v Nedeliu Pravoslaviia," 1–10.

50. S.N.R., "Pouchenie v Nedeliu Pravoslaviia," 276–80.

51. "Pouchenie v Nedeliu Pravoslaviia," *Sbornik pouchenii,* 425.

52. K. Kiparisov, "Slovo v Nedeliu Pravoslaviia," *Omskie eparkhial'nye vedomosti,* chast' neofitsial'naia 6 (1912): 4–10; A. Liubomudrov, "Slovo v Nedeliu Pravoslaviia," *Penzenskie eparkhial'nye vedomosti,* chast' neofitsial'naia 5 (1868): 140.

53. I. Nikolin, "Pochemu tserkov' v ustanovlenii dogmata ob ikonopochetanii vidit osoboe 'Torzhestvo Pravoslaviia,'" *Dushepoleznoe chtenie* 3 (March 1899): 483.

54. Jean-Jacques Rousseau, *The Creed of a Priest of Savoy,* trans. Arthur H. Beattie (New York: Frederick Ungar, 1957), 52.

55. "Slovo v Nedeliu Pravoslaviia v den' vosshestviia na prestol Blagochestiveishego Gosudaria Imperatora Aleksandra II," *Podol'skie eparkhial'nye vedomosti* 9 (1865): 247; Burlutskii, "Slovo v Nedeliu Pravoslaviia," 170.

56. Episkop Vissarion, "Torzhestvo istiny: Slovo v Nedeliu Pravoslaviia," *Golos pastyria* (Moscow, 1893), 35–41; Prot. M. Zlatoverkhovnikov, "Slovo v Nedeliu Pravoslaviia," *Kievskie eparkhial'nye vedomosti,* chast' neofitisal'naia 4 (1895): 152–53; Prot. V. Nechaev, "Torzhestvo istiny," *Dushepoleznoe chtenie* 3 (1887): 357.

57. Sv. Dimitrii Sliusarev, "Pouchenie v Nedeliu Pravoslaviia," *Kievskie eparkhial'nye vedomosti,* chast' neofitsial'naia 5 (1898): 180; Arkhiepiskop Vasilii (Luzhinskii), "Slovo v Nedeliu Pravoslaviia," *Slova, rechi i arkhipastorskie poslaniia k dukhovenstvu Polotskoi eparkhii* (St. Petersburg, 1866), 40, 43.

58. "Slovo v Nedeliu Pravoslaviia na den' vosshestvie na prestol," *Podol'skie eparkhial'nye vedomosti,* 247.

59. Originally in *Kholmskaia tserkovnaia zhizn'* 3 (1908): 79–86; repr. in Arkhiepiskop Andronik, *O tserkvi Rossii* (Friazino, 1997), 39–45. The theme of unity characterized sermons throughout the late imperial period. For another example, see Arkhimandrit Varfolomei, "Slovo v Nedeliu Pravoslaviia," *Kievskie eparkhial'nye vedomosti* 5 (1866): 165.

60. A. Preobrazhenskii, *Tserkovnoe otluchenie (*anafema*) v svoei istorii i v svoikh osnovo-motivakh* (Kazan, 1909), 24–25.

61. Kliment, Novoierusalimskii arkhimandrit, "Pouchenie 15: v pervuiu nedeliu Velikogo Posta," *God v novom Ieruslaime ili sobranie pouchenii* (Moscow, 1856), 95–102; Sv. Ksenofont Delektorskii, *Propovedi, 1822–1842* (St. Petersburg, 1901), 107–8.

62. Arkhimandrit Pavel, "Slovo v Nedeliu Pravoslaviia," *Pribavleniia k tserkovnym vedomostiam* 9 (1897): 313–15. Prot. A. Nikol'skii, "Slovo v Nedeliu Pravoslaviia," *Tul'skie eparkhial'nye vedomosti,* chast' neofitsial'naia 4 (1882): 132–36.

63. Episkop Anastasii, "Khranite pravoslavie, kak verneishee i sovershenneishee ispovedanie Bogootkrovennoi istiny i kak luchshee dostoianie russkogo naroda," *Olonetskie eparkhial'nye vedomosti,* neofitsial'nyi otdel 5 (1903): 145–47.

64. Semenov, "Slovo v Nedeliu Pravoslaviia," 185; Sviatitel' Ignatii Brianchaninov, "Slovo v Nedeliu Pravoslaviia," Palamarchuk, comp., *Anafema: istoriia i XX vek,* 4–12.

65. Mikhail Izvol'skii, "Ikonoborchestvo i Torzhestvo Pravoslaviia, v sviazi s sobytiiami nashikh dnei," *Pravoslavno-russkoe slovo* 5 (1905), 379–410.

66. For views similar to Izvolsky's, see Prot. Dimitrii Abriutskii, "Slovo v Nedeliu Pravoslaviia," *Slova i rechi* (St. Petersburg, 1859), 157–66; *Slovo v Nedeliu Pravoslaviia i v den' vosshestviia na prestol Blagochestiveishego Gosudaria Imperatora Aleksandra II* (Kamenets-Podol'sk, 1865), 1; Eparkhial'nyi missioner, Iv. Klimiuk, "Slovo v Nedeliu Pravoslaviia," *Irkutskie eparkhial'nye vedomosti* 10 (1914): 344–56; Preosviashchenneishii Nikodim, Episkop Astrakhanskii, "Slovo v Nedeliu Pravoslaviia," *Astrakhanskie eparkhial'nye vedomosti,* otdel neofitsial'nyi 8 (1914): 189–96; V.P., "Pouchenie v Nedeliu Pravoslaviia," *Tavricheskii tserkovno-obshchestvennyi vestnik* 5 (1916): 127–33.

67. "Moskovskaia khronika," *Moskovskie tserkovnye vedomosti* 19 (1900): 120–21.

68. A. N. Murav'ev, *Pis'ma o bogosluzhenii,* 2 vols. (1882; repr., Moscow: Russkii dukhovnyi tsentr, 1993), vol. 1, pt. II, 169.

69. Christian use of the anathema had a long history that was independent from the rite of Orthodoxy. For histories of the anathema outside the context of the rite, see Nikol'skii, *Anafematstvovanie,* 1–13, 272–91; V., "Anafematstvovanie," 139–44; N. Suvorov, *O tserkovnykh nakazani-*

iakh: opyt issledovaniia po tserkovnomu pravu (St. Petersburg, 1876), 148–74; Sv. E. Ovsiannikov, "O smysle i znachenii tserkovnoi anafemy," *Donskie eparkhial'nye vedomosti* 8 (1902): 160–61; Vladimir (Bogoiavlenskii), Mitropolit Kievskii i Galitskii, *Ob anafeme ili tserkovnoe otluchenie* (Moscow: Otchii dom, 1998), 14–20.

70. Skitalets, "Oktava," *Rasskazy i pesni* (St. Petersburg, 1902), 170–239.

71. Ibid., 204.

72. Ibid., 206.

73. Sv. Nikolai Kratirov, "Slovo v Nedeliu Pravoslaviia i den' prazdnovaniia vosshestviia na prestol Gosudaria Imperatora Aleksandra Aleksandrovicha," *Donskie eparkhial'nye vedomosti,* otdel neofitsial'nyi 6 (1883): 213–15.

74. See comments by V., "Anafematstvovanie," 139–44. It should be noted that Tolstoy's was an example of an anathematization taking place independently of the rite of Orthodoxy. In that rite, Tolstoy's name was never recited. He was occasionally spoken about, however, in sermons that accompanied the feast.

75. Arkhimandrit Vissarion, "Slovo v Nedeliu Pravoslaviia, skazannoe v Samarskom kafedral'nom sobore," *S tserkovnoi kafedry: slova i rechi* (Samara, 1910), 109.

76. "Obriad Pravoslaviia," *Voskresnyi den'* 7 (1895): 102–3; Prot. V. Strepotov, "Slovo v Nedeliu Pravoslaviia," *Kavkazskie eparkhial'nye vedomosti* 6 (1887): 208–12; V. Klirikov, "Slovo v Nedeliu Pravoslaviia," *Iaroslavskie eparkhial'nye vedomosti,* chast' neofitsial'naia 8 (1888): 121–27; Ieromonakh Kornilii, "Slovo v den' Torzhestva Pravoslaviia," *Iaroslavskie eparkhial'nye vedomosti,* chast' neofitstial'naia 13 (1910): 225–30.

77. VENSKL, "Slovo v Nedeliu Pravoslaviia," *Volynskie eparkhial'nye vedomosti* 8 (1900): 241–48.

78. Ovsiannikov, "O smysle i znachenii tserkovnoi anafemy," *Donskie eparkhial'nye vedomosti* 7 (1902): 137; Episkop Vissarion, "Slovo v Nedeliu Pravoslaviia i v den' rozhdeniia Gosudaria Imperatora Aleksandra Aleksandrovicha," *Golos pastyria,* 105–11. This sermon was read in February 1889.

79. "Nedelia Pravoslaviia ili Sbornoe voskresen'e v Moskve," 63.

80. Prot. G. Kramarev, *Slovo v Nedeliu Pravoslaviia* (Kiev, 1866), 2–3.

81. Preobrazhenskii, *Tserkovnoe otluchenie,* 15; "Slovo v Nedeliu Pravoslaviia," *Voskresnoe chtenie* 49 (1853): 454–48; Makarii, episkop Tambovskii i Shatskii, *Slova i rechi,* vol. 2 (St. Petersburg, 1859), 254–61; Sv. D. Lebedev, "Slovo v Nedeliu Pravoslaviia," *Smolenskie eparkhial'nye vedomosti* 6 (1869): 394–403; Prot. A. Lukanin, "Slovo v Nedeliu Pravoslaviia," *Permskie eparkhial'nye vedomosti,* otdel neofitsial'nyi 10 (1881): 101–2; Kratirov, "Slovo v Nedeliu Pravoslaviia," 215; Aleksandr Vlasov, "Slovo v Nedeliu Pravoslaviia," *Donskie eparkhial'nye vedomosti,* otdel neofitsial'nyi 6 (1884): 228; Vasiutinskii, *Slovo v Nedeliu Pravoslaviia,* 4. There were exceptions to this general trend. See, for instance, the sermon of Bishop Isaac from Eniseisk diocese, who referred to the anathemas as "thunders of ecclesial malediction" (*gromy prokliatiia tserkovnogo*), in "Slovo v Nedeliu Pravoslaviia," *Eniseiskie eparkhial'nye vedomosti,* otdel neofitsial'nyi 6 (1885): 92; Sv. A. Lotskii, "Anafematstvovanie v Nedeliu Pravoslaviia, ego smysl i znachenie," *Volynskie eparkhial'nye vedomosti,* chast' neofitsial'naia 9 (1911): 195–97.

82. Semenov, "Slovo v Nedeliu Pravoslaviia," 188.

83. Ovsiannikov, "O smysle i znachenii tserkovnoi anafemy," *Donskie eparkhial'nye vedomosti* 9 (1902): 178–79.

84. Eparkhial'nyi missioner, Permskogo Uspenskogo zhenskogo monastyria, sv. Stefan Lukanin, "Slovo v Nedeliu Pravoslaviia," *Permskie eparkhial'nye vedomosti,* otdel neofitsial'nyi 6 (1893): 121–25.

85. Rektor seminarii, prot. M. Shcheglov, "Slovo v Nedeliu Pravoslaviia," *Podol'skii eparkhial'nye vedomosti,* chast' neofitsial'naia 10 (1895): 269.

86. Rektor seminarii Arkhimandrit Nikolai, *Tobol'skie eparkhial'nye vedomosti* 8 (1907): 212–17; Klimiuk, "Slovo v Nedeliu Pravoslaviia," 347–48. For similar arguments, see Anatolii, Arkhiepiskop Mogilevskogo i Mstislavskogo, "Slovo v Nedeliu Pravoslaviia," *Slova i besedy* chast' 2 (St.

Petersburg, 1854): 75; Episkop Isaakii, "Slovo v Nedeliu Pravoslaviia," *Eniseiskie eparkhial'nye vedomosti,* otdel neofitsial'nyi 6 (1885): 93; Sv. Dimitrii Klepikov, "Pouchenie v Nedeliu Pravoslaviia (15 fevralia 1909)," *Omskie eparkhial'nye vedomosti* 5 (1909): 33.

87. K.P., *Orenburgskie eparkhial'nye vedomosti,* no. 6 (1887): 221.

88. Vysokopreosviashchenneishii Dimitrii, arkhiepiskop Khersonskii i Odesskii, "Slovo v nedeliu Pravoslaviia," *Khersonskie eparkhial'nye vedomosti,* chast' neofitsial'naia 8 (1863): 169–76.

89. Semenov, "Slovo v Nedeliu Pravoslaviia," 189.

90. S., "Voskresnye besedy: Nedelia Pravoslaviia," *Moskovskie eparkhial'nye vedomosti* 8 (1872): 60–61; Arkhmandrit Sergii, "Slovo v Nedeliu Pravoslaviia, proiznesennoe v Isaakievskom sobore 18 fevralia 1901," *Pribavleniia k tserkovnym vedomostiam* 8 (1901): 264.

91. Klepikov, "Pouchenie v Nedeliu Pravoslaviia," 33; Morev, "Slovo v Nedeliu Pravoslaviia," 23.

92. Sv. Feodor Bazhanov, "Pouchenie v Nedeliu Pravoslaviia," *Orenburgskie eparkhial'nye vedomosti* 10 (1911): 239.

93. E.F., "Chin Pravoslaviia," *Dushepoleznyi sobesednik* 2 (1892): 45–48.

94. Liubomudrov, "Slovo v Nedeliu Pravoslaviia," 137–44; Sv. P. Shumov, "Ob anafeme: Pouchenie v Nedeliu Pravoslaviia," *Dushepoleznoe chtenie* 3 (1891): 367–71; "Slovo v Nedeliu Pravoslaviia, proiznesennoe sviashchennikom Zverevym v Bol'shom Uspenskom sobore, 9-go marta, 1880," *Moskovskie tserkovnye vedomosti* 12 (1880): 163–66; Ovsiannikov, "O smysle i znachenii tserkovnoi anafemy," *Donskie eparkhial'nye vedomosti* 11 (1902): 217–20; Preobrazhenskii, *Tserkovnoe otluchenie,* 27; Kornilii, "Slovo v den' Torzhestva Pravoslaviia," 225–27.

95. Kornilii, "Slovo v den' Torzhestva Pravoslaviia," 227–30.

96. Andronik, *O tserkvi Rossii,* 30.

97. *Penzenskie eparkhial'nye vedomosti* 3 (1899): 62.

98. Ieromonakh Nikon, "Tri poucheniia v Nedeliu Pravoslaviia," pouchenie 1; Prot. Sergii Modestov, "Tri poucheniia v Nedeliu Pravoslaviia," pouchenie 3, *Prilozhenie k tserkovnym vedomostiam* 5 (1889): 8.

99. Nikon, "Tri poucheniia v Nedeliu Pravoslaviia," 1; Konstantin Ozerov, "Chetyre poucheniia odobrennye Sviateishim Pravitel'stvuiushchim Sinodom dlia povsemestnogo proiznosheniia v tserkvakh, v Nedeliu Pravoslaviia, s tsel'iu vozbuzhdeniia v narode userdiia k delu rasprostraneniia sv. Pravoslavnoi very," pouchenie 4, *Pribavleniia k tserkovnym vedomostiam* 6 (1888): 137; "Pouchenie v Nedeliu Pravoslaviia," *Omskie eparkhial'nye vedomosti,* chast' neofitsial'naia 2 (1901): 1–5; Prot. Nikolai Voinov, "Pouchenie v Nedeliu Pravoslaviia," *Moskovskie tserkovnye vedomosti* 6 (1886): 122.

100. Ozerov, "Chetyre poucheniia," 137–41.

101. Nikon, "Tri poucheniia v Nedeliu Pravoslaviia," 1; Prot. Mikhail Vozdvizhenskii, "Tri poucheniia v Nedeliu Pravoslaviia," pouchenie 2, *Prilozhenie k tserkovnym vedomostiam* 5 (1889) 4; Modestov, "Tri poucheniia v Nedeliu Pravoslaviia," 8.

102. Ouspensky, *Theology of the Icon,* 2:467.

103. Zamiatin, "Slovo v Nedeliu Pravoslaviia," 391.

ROBERT L. NICHOLS

3

NICHOLAS II AND THE RUSSIAN ICON

We heard of many people being cured today and yesterday. Another cure happened in the cathedral, while the holy relics were being carried round the altar. God is miraculous through his saints. Great is his mercy towards dear Russia; there is inexpressible comfort in the evidence of this new manifestation of the Lord's grace towards us all; let us put our hope in the Lord forever and ever. Amen!

—DIARY OF NICHOLAS II, 19 JULY 1903

Emperor Nicholas II linked himself closely with the Russian icon in the final decades of imperial Russia. From childhood, he was surrounded with icons, which formed an integral part of the love of liturgical worship that he shared with his father as he was growing up. At the time of his marriage to Alexandra, icons decorated their apartments, especially their bedroom, where they served as a sacred connection between God and their domestic lives.[1] With his ascent to the throne in 1894, the emperor began to make frequent public appearances at Russia's holy shrines: the Chapel of the Iberian Mother of God near the Moscow Kremlin, to point to the most prominent one. After 1903, the year of Serafim of Sarov's canonization, he kept an icon of the new saint above his desk in the Alexander Palace to stay connected with the

I would like to thank the National Council for Eurasian and East European Research (NCEEE), under authority of a Title VIII grant from the U.S. Department of State, for the generous funding that made this research possible. I also thank the American Academy of Religion and Smith College's Committee on Faculty Compensation and Development for funding earlier stages of research for this chapter.

The epigraph to this chapter is quoted in Andrei Maylunas and Sergei Mironenko, *A Lifelong Passion: Nicholas and Alexandra: Their Own Story,* trans. Darya Galy (New York: Doubleday, 1997), 230.

thaumaturgic power the saint had mediated, a power that allowed the empress to conceive an heir to the throne and the emperor to be reassured about Russia's sacred mission in Asia.[2] He used Serafim's icon to bless the troops as they departed European Russia for war against Japan. Nicholas became a patron of the icon by supporting the work of collectors, restorers, and painters at a time when the Russian icon was bursting onto the international art scene and by giving focus to domestic intellectual debates about reconciliation with Russia's past and the Orthodox faith. He sought to protect the traditions of icon painting against the new industrial mass manufacturing of icons. In honor of his father, Alexander III, he opened a special wing of the Russian Museum devoted to Old Russian sacred art. At a special "village," Fedorovsky Gorodok, the royal family built a complex of medieval-style buildings that housed many old and new icons. The Church of Saint Theodor itself was a reminder of the connection between the Romanov dynasty and the icon of the Mother of God in Kostroma, where Michael I (r. 1613–45), the first tsar of the Romanov dynasty, acknowledged his readiness to assume the crown in 1613. In the months immediately preceding the Great War, Nicholas sponsored the publication of an expensive bimonthly journal, *The Russian Icon* (*Russkaia ikona*), issued through the Russian Museum in St. Petersburg. During the period of exile, the royal family kept more than sixty icons at the Ipatiev house in Ekaterinburg, where in July 1918 the family was held under arrest and then executed. Eventually, Nicholas, in a manner of speaking, became an icon, when he and the other members of his family were "glorified" as martyr saints, first by the Russian Orthodox Church Abroad (1981) and then by the Moscow Patriarchate (2000).

In all of these ways and more, Nicholas II was more prominently associated with the icon than any previous modern Russian ruler, including his father, Alexander III. How are we to explain this, and what significance, if any, are we to attach to it as part of an inquiry into the relationship between the icon and modernity? Of course, we expect the emperor as head of the Russian Church to be seen reverencing icons and employing them as part of his traditional symbolism of authority. Yet Nicholas's regard for icons seems to go beyond traditional usage. Richard Wortman places this royal interest in the icon into the context of Nicholas's "scenario of power."[3] Through myth and ceremony, the emperor sought to construct a public image of himself as a "national persona." This interpretation has rightly shifted attention from the view current at the time of the Russian Revolution and sustained during the Soviet period: namely, that such public demonstrations of imperial godliness were simply a retreat from reality into mystical fantasy. Unable to cope with the real problems of the empire, Nicholas and Alexandra found comfort and reassurance in a medievalism that had no place in the modern world. These public demonstrations were an anachronism to be swept away by the forces of progress. Students of the period as diverse as Lev Trotsky and Nicholas Zernov saw the royal couple and their devotion to the icon in precisely this way. Trotsky believed that the religiosity of Nicholas and Alexandra was merely a function of a medieval monarchy that had somehow survived into the twentieth century, but would inevitably be destroyed by socialist revolution. Zernov makes a similar point when he writes: "They lived in a world of their own, endeavouring to return to the atmosphere of the Muscovite Tsardom, when the sovereigns of Russia and their people were united in their membership in the Church and shared the same outlook."[4] In such a view, Nicholas's identification with the icon is understood as a withdrawal from reality into an imagined earlier time of miracle and faith. He invoked the traditional powers of God, the Mother of God, and his saints by way of surmounting Russia's pressing problems.

Yet, as Wortman suggests, the myth of the pious national tsar is a modern myth. And when we consider the deliberately archaizing features of the post–World War I era—Fascist appeals to past Roman glory, the medieval crusading spirit cultivated by the Nazi Third Reich, Stalin's wedding-cake Gothic makeover of Moscow—then one might argue that in using visual images as an enhancement of power Nicholas was, perhaps, a pioneer in this aspect of modern politics. Stalin and those who supported his cult drew more on the images and techniques first developed in the last imperial reign than we might suppose. In this chapter, I will explore another aspect of Nicholas II's relationship to the icon, namely, his belief in its miraculous power. In doing so, I think it is important to understand that this belief did not constitute some abiding medievalism among the Romanovs or an anachronism without place in the modern world. Nor should this relationship be viewed too narrowly as a cynical strategy formulated as an ideological alternative to competing claims for political power. Rather, Nicholas's belief in the miraculous power of the icon, already evident early in his life, is deeply rooted in a broad reaction to the Enlightenment, which had been gaining strength in Russia and Europe since the Napoleonic Wars.

AN AGE OF MIRACLES

The rise of Napoleon was accompanied by growing opposition to the rationalism of the eighteenth-century Enlightenment and the revolutionary upheaval linked to it. One aspect of the reaction was the emergence of Protestant pietism and a mysticism of the sort that became prominent in England with the establishment of the British and Foreign Bible Society in 1803 and in Russia with the life and policies of Tsar Alexander I after 1815. But the reaction was by no means confined to these two countries or to Protestantism. In France, as elsewhere in Catholic Europe, many interpreted the defeat of the French Revolution as a sign of God's providential concern. Miracles and prophecies abounded. Pilgrims began to visit shrines in large numbers to experience healings through the miraculous intercession of the Virgin Mary. George Tavard points out that in France alone the Mother of God appeared in at least twenty-one locations between 1803 and 1899, most notably in 1830, 1846, 1858, and 1871: "All of these dates correspond to periods of social turmoil and stress that gave the visions political significance."[5] Lourdes became a special focus of pilgrimages after Bernadette Soubirous experienced visions of the Holy Virgin there in 1858. Sacred relics, sacred waters, and sacred images regularly healed the sick (physically, mentally, and spiritually) and comforted those who suffered. Apparitions also took place with growing frequency in Belgium and Portugal. Prophecies, too, abounded, seemingly in company with a growing messianic nationalism in Europe. Prophecy provided a key to political legitimacy that fit well with the broader reaction to European rationalism of the eighteenth century.[6]

Throughout the nineteenth century, reports of such miraculous interventions steadily increased, and along with them the number of those who claimed to act as the channel for God's grace. By the end of the century, "medieval" writers and doers were being rediscovered: Jacob Boehme, Thomas à Kempis, Joan of Arc, Jan von Ruysbroeck, Rulman Merswin, and the German Dominican Johannes Tauler, to name a few of the "cloud of witnesses" whose life experiences testified to the mysterious and miraculous ways in which the Holy Spirit crosses humanity's path. The French writer August Jundt, in *Les Amis de Dieu* (1879), recounted how fourteenth-century mystics—mainly monks and nuns—pursued a "divine mission" of popular social and spiritual renewal through an education led by those who believed deeply in the efficacious intercession of the Holy Virgin and saints venerated through their relics. The Friends of God experienced mystical joy and visions and developed an ascetic way of life mirroring the sufferings of the Savior. What these earlier friends of God had achieved, in Jundt's view, was still possible in modern times.[7] Take, for example, Joan of Arc, whose case for canonization in the Catholic Church was being pressed in Rome at the turn of the twentieth century. For many, Joan of Arc represented the native virtues that made France distinctive as a nation. Her humble roots also nostalgically recalled a lost paternalistic agricultural harmony and social hierarchy. Right-wing royalists such as Charles Maurras, founder of Action Française and a Catholic sympathizer, favored Joan's canonization because she was a saint chosen by "the people." Joan of Arc had a high symbolic value to conservative French nationalists during the protracted Dreyfus Affair (1894–1906) and during the discussions leading to the disestablishment of the Church of France by the "Separation" of powers made law in December 1905. For the enemies of Dreyfus, Joan symbolized the absolute authority of the state as represented by the king whom she so faithfully served, whatever his shortcomings. She upheld the idea of a fatherland defended by faith, military strength, and established order.

Faith, military strength, and established order were of course the same qualities that Nicholas and Alexandra felt so deeply connected them with Russia's own saints, particularly its warrior saints, whose miraculous feats and victories were the result of divine intervention on behalf of the Russian land. Even Alexander III, the "peacemaker," could be counted among this mighty army of saintly warriors. Several observers of Nicholas have noted that he was so in awe of his father's strength, discipline, and faith that he felt himself in the presence of a saint. He wrote in his diary when his father died, "This was the death of a saint!" The next day, he added that his dead father's face was "miraculous [*chudnoe*], smiling, as if he wants to laugh!"[8]

Saintly intervention gave proof to prophecy. This prophetic connection held true in the case of the Tsarevich Alexis, whose remissions from hemophilia, a miracle of personal and national significance, were attributed to the mediation of Serafim of Sarov. Nicholas found it meaningful that Serafim (1754–1833), an ascetic and elder (*starets*) renowned during his lifetime for his healing powers, had prophesied that "the church [has] no vice of any sort. For the sake of its virtues, Russia will forever be renowned and terrible to its foes, and invincible; with faith and piety as a shield and with truth for armor, the gates of hell shall not prevail against it."[9] Moreover, the emperor's interest encouraged others to elaborate their own prophetic beliefs in a manner that stressed their relevance to the Russia of his day. Father Leonid Chichagov (1856–1937), who had been placed in charge of preparing the documentation for Serafim's glorification in 1903 at Nicholas's request, linked this reclusive monk from a monastery outside Nizhny Novgorod with holy Moscow 250 miles to the west: Ivan the Great's Bell Tower, the symbol of Russian Tsardom, would one day miraculously travel from Moscow to Serafim's relics in the town of Sarov, where the tongue of the Tsar Bell would ring joyously, exceeding the sound of a thousand bells and inspiring rejoicing throngs of people to descend on Serafim's shrine, making the shrine national. Pilgrims—everyone from the highest-born royalty to the poorest cripple—would come from all corners of the empire to worship, venerate the saint, experience healing, and celebrate a spiritual and communal solidarity. The royal couple, Nicholas and Alexandra, summoned by the Tsar Bell for worship in this sacred place, would signify how the holiness of Serafim was bound up with the fate of Russia. The saint's shrine would be understood as an icon of Holy Russia, bringing the "joy of all joys" to the people through the compassionate mercy and tenderness of the Virgin, aided by her poor Serafim. For others, like Sergei Nilus (a self-styled mystic who, among other things, was responsible for publishing the full text of the anti-Semitic *Protocols of the Elders of Zion* in 1905), prophecy came in the form of a dream signifying military glory. In the dream, Nicholas meets Serafim, whose words are subsequently interpreted to mean victory in China at the time of the Boxer Rebellion.[10]

According to V. K. Ollongren, the son of Nicholas's governess, "[Nicholas's] cherished wish was to dress himself in a gold stikharion, to stand near the priest in the middle of the church, and, at the time of anointing, to hold the sacred cup."[11] This love of liturgy and sacrament he shared with his father and with his uncle, Grand Duke Sergei Alexandrovich; probably his sense of the miracle of sacrament owed something to their shared feelings for liturgical drama and public religious ritual. As Grand Duchess Maria, in her memoir, *Education of a Princess,* put it, Sergei was "pious and scrupulous in observance of all rites of Orthodoxy."[12]

Through father and uncle, Nicholas was linked to the growing and deepening current of contemplative spirituality found in nineteenth-century Russian monasteries and cloisters. When as young men Alexander and Sergei traveled to the Trinity Lavra of Saint Sergius, they did so in the company of their mother (and Nicholas's grandmother), Maria Alexandrovna, a frequent visitor there and a great admirer of Metropolitan Filaret. Filaret was renowned for his expressive celebration of the divine liturgy, and both brothers greatly admired the aging bishop. Alexander even risked his father's displeasure when he attended Filaret's funeral despite Alexander II's specific instructions not to go. The territory of the Lavra was also the home of the Gethsemane *skete,* which had been founded in the 1840s by Filaret and his prior at the Lavra Antony (Medvedev, 1792–1877) as an experiment in reviving the traditions of Byzantine contemplative monasticism. Antony had been a personal disciple of Serafim of Sarov.

Alexander and Sergei were also influenced in their love of liturgy and devotion to miracle-working icons by a later prior of the Lavra, Archimandrite Leonid (Kavelin, 1822–1891), one of the outstanding figures among the elders at the Optina hermitage in the 1850s and onetime director of the Russian Orthodox Ecclesiastical Mission in Jerusalem. Leonid recalled long conversations with the two brothers about miracle-working icons, including the icon of the Mother of God in the Boris and Gleb Anosin Convent near Zvenigorod. A nun had brought the icon to the monastery from Kursk. In 1864, it healed the Moscow merchant Simeon Rykov. The abbess of the monastery was an aristocrat of the Ozerov family close to Sergei at court. Leonid tells us that as a young man, Sergei kept an "oratory" (*molennaia*), whose walls were entirely covered with icons, including those of Saint Sergius of Radonezh and Saint Savva, his disciple. Aside from the fact that Saint Sergius was the grand duke's patron saint, these icons were another link for him, as well as for his brother, the future Tsar Alexander III, to the Trinity Lavra of Saint Sergius.

The point of all of this seems to be that the reverence for icons, holy relics, prayer, and liturgical worship so prominently evinced in the lives of the royal couple is linked through the family with the contemplative revival in Moscow, at the Trinity Lavra, and at cloisters and shrines throughout Russia. Through their frequent visits in the company of their mother, Empress Maria Alexandrovna, the brothers regularly came into contact with this current of modern Orthodox spirituality. Filaret often spoke of the miraculous power inherent in sacred things: Eucharist, icons, holy relics. "Does the healing power that proceeds from the Lord Christ during his earthly ministry still proceed from Him today?" he asked in a sermon at the Chudov monastery in Moscow. The answer was, of course, yes. Communion puts one physically in touch with Christ; the relics of His saints mediate divine power through their holy corporeal remains. Filaret personally gave Maria Alexandrovna icons and relics of Saint Panteleimon (her patron saint).

Of course, contemplative and charismatic spirituality, which pointed back to the Muscovite and Byzantine past, was just one more indication of the importance of pre-Petrine Russia in the emperor's religious frame of reference. Devotions as forms of piety could establish an emotional intimacy associated with the seventeenth century, rather than with the eighteenth century and with Russia's Enlightenment. Many historians and other commentators have noted this desire on Nicholas's part to return emotionally to that imagined time of harmony between tsar and people united in a common faith and fate. Mark Steinberg sums up most of this thinking in his discussion of the ideal of the good tsar that Nicholas set for himself and modeled for his son: "With similar intent and meaning, Nicholas named his son and heir, born in 1904, after the ancestor he most admired: the first Tsar Aleksei, father of Peter the Great (the ruler whom Nicholas least admired)."[13] Alexis embodied the mythical ideal of the "gentle tsar" (*tishaishii tsar'*), of the tsar as "saint." It is interesting to note that Count Sergei Sheremetev, several years before the Tsarevich Alexis was born, regarded *Nicholas* as the modern Tsar Alexis because of his pious concern for Russia's sacred art. Nicholas later had himself portrayed as Tsar Alexis in a painting.[14]

All this suggests a certain contemporary playfulness when it came to these comparisons. There are nevertheless at least several reasons to question any identification of the tsarevich's name solely with that of the "saintly" seventeenth-century tsar. First, Tsar Alexis was never made a saint, although he might be thought to have had saintly qualities. Second, it was in his reign that Orthodoxy became divided by schism, hardly the ideal moment to celebrate the seamless religious unity of tsar and people. Third, after the events of 1666–67, Alexis became an ardent Westernizer, ushering in many of those influences that gained great prominence in the reign of Peter the Great. Thus it is possible, as some have suggested, that the royal couple may have had others in mind when naming their son Alexis in 1904. One thinks of the ever-popular early Christian figure Alexis, Man of God, for example, though I know of no direct evidence to link the tsarevich to him.

More pertinent here is Alexei, metropolitan of Moscow, through whose authority and actions Prince Dmitry was able to become grand prince of Moscow in 1359.[15] A number of modern icons support this attribution. Alongside domestic icons of the medieval Moscow metropolitans Pyotr, Ioann, Philip, and Alexei, the emperor and empress arranged such icons as one painted in 1898 by the Mstera icon painter Alexander Tsepkov, in which Saint Nicholas the Miracle Worker and Saint Tsarina Alexandra, the royal couple's patron saints, are painted alongside one another (pl. 9). Together these icons created a tableau of saints linking throne and church as well as past and present. A similar connection can be found in the icon *Fedorovskaya Mother of God* (1913), painted by the Moscow artist Vasily Gurianov, a frequent supplier of icons to the court. In this icon, the attendant saints Michael, Tsarina Alexandra, Metropolitan Alexei, and Nicholas the Miracle Worker stand in front of buildings of the Kremlin, including the Uspensky Cathedral, where Tsar Michael Romanov had been crowned. Gurianov's icon was highly revered by the Romanovs, since its original ("found" in 1239 by a prince of Kostroma) served as the clan's palladium icon.[16]

Thus in addition to the good and "gentle" tsar, the name Alexis evokes the idea of a Holy Russia centered in Moscow, protected by Christ and the Holy Mother of God, and ruled by tsar and tsarina in harmony with the church and its saints. The Tsarevich Alexis, then, was the miraculous heir of this intimate family, whose birth portended a coming era of glory. A few years earlier in 1900, it is noteworthy that new icon-bearing military banners, replacing earlier ones, were designed for various elite army regiments, including the Life-Guard Engineers, His Majesty's Life-Guard Cuirassier Regiment, and the 14th Orenburg Cossack Regiment. These banners displayed a woven image of the Savior Not Made by Hands and the inscription "God Is with Us," suggesting the direct and unmediated divine protection of Russia.[17]

PATRONAGE

Nicholas II may not have admired or cared much for the concerns of the Russian art world of his day. Alexander Benois is often quoted to show that the emperor had no interest in art or in any intellectual pursuit. He describes the young Nicholas during a visit with his parents to an exhibition of watercolors in 1892: "It was all too clear that the Tsarevich was bored, and that he had absolutely no interest in these thoroughly tedious pictures and the dull fellows who had come to trade in them. Let it not be thought, however, that this was the result of the extreme refinement of his tastes. . . . He walked behind his father, looking from side to side rather than at the paintings, and said absolutely nothing to the artists themselves."[18] Benois may well be right that the emperor had no highly refined aesthetic taste in art or that he did not share the modern artist's concern for artistic autonomy and individual aesthetic expression. And it is hard to believe that the emperor could ever have become interested in the ways Russian avant-garde artists tried to reprocess and transmute icon painting and church frescoes into their new aesthetic systems of Neoprimitivism, Cubo-Futurism, Suprematism, and Constructivism.[19] But his connection to the icon did make him an important patron of those artists, art historians, collectors, and restorers whose purpose was to recenter Russia's sacred art tradition in modern life.

At some points one can almost hear the emperor trying to understand what this revival of the icon was all about and how he might support it. In this respect, the activities of Count Sergei Sheremetev (1844–1918) and Nikodim Kondakov (1844–1925) are instructive. As one of the founders of the highly elitist Society of Lovers of Ancient Letters in 1877, Sheremetev sought to advance the recovery of Old Russian sacred art. In 1898, when the Society was renamed to include Ancient Art as well as Letters, Sheremetev became its chairman. He moved the Society and its museum of icons to his palace on the Fontanka. As the art historian Gerold Vzdornov points out, "dozens of icons" confiscated from Old Believers and received by the Society from the Holy Synod formed the basis of this collection. In collaboration with Kondakov, Sheremetev endeavored to elevate the Society from its amateur origins to a position of scholarly preeminence.[20]

In his memoirs, Kondakov writes that Sheremetev was very close to Emperor Alexander III (they had served together in the Hussars). After Alexander's death in 1894, the count sought to cultivate Nicholas, but Alexandra did not favor it. Nonetheless, Kondakov thought that Sheremetev might establish a fruitful relationship with

Nicholas on the basis of their mutual interest in the icon. The moment seemed favorable. The count and Kondakov had just returned from a trip to the famous villages of icon painting, Kholui, Mstera, and Palekh in Vladimir province, a trip both men believed to be of "decisive importance" for the future of Russian icon painting. What they discovered was the hapless state of traditional icon painting, faced with competition from cheap modern mass lithographs produced by foreign manufacturers, such as Jacquot and Bonacoeur in Moscow. In an hour-long interview with Nicholas II, Kondakov reported on their trip and on the alarmingly precarious condition of traditional icon painting. Kondakov complained to the emperor that these businessmen had bribed officials in the Holy Synod in order to gain permission to produce cheap knockoffs of the best models of Russian icons painted by hand. The crisis, Kondakov explained, required the personal intervention of the tsar. Nicholas was "overcome" with concern, even if he was puzzled by their scholarly and antiquarian work. After listening to Kondakov's long appeal, the emperor responded with the lone remark: "I thought about how in Russian you describe your study of icons—*ikonovedenie,* is it not?"[21] Nicholas did eventually agree, apparently at State Council member Vladimir Trepov's suggestion, to create a nongovernmental commission to preserve traditional icon painting. He did not take direct part in its work, but he wanted to know about the commission's progress. Count Sheremetev, who chaired the commission, reported directly to the tsar.[22]

In addition to shoring up the traditional art and craft of icon painting, Nicholas supported the work of secular painters who devoted considerable portions of their careers to portraying in art the life of Christ, the Holy Mother of God, and Russian and Byzantine saints. Pavel Korin, Viktor Vasnetsov, Mikhail Nesterov, and Mikhail Vrubel are just some of the names of professional artists whose religious paintings, mosaics, and frescoes enjoyed the emperor's support. It is of interest that among the avant-garde, probably Natalia Goncharova—who, as far as I know, never enjoyed imperial support—most closely paralleled the emperor's own sense of the divine presence in the holy image. Her album of prints called *Mystical Images of War* (1914) represents the Holy Mother of God, the Archangel Michael, and the other angels as beings "imbued with the magical power to save Holy Russia" (fig. 4). For Goncharova, this sacred art was transfigurative, but not in the "miraculous" way in which Nicholas understood divine intervention in human life. It was the power of the art that changed "human consciousness, and hence reality."[23] Here again, we see how even shared interests did not mean shared views; the elements of miracle and prophecy that shaped the emperor's outlook did not necessarily provide a bridge to educated Russians who were beginning to reassess their attitude toward Russian traditions, including political and religious ones.

Nicholas II also patronized the work of icon collectors and restorers and sponsored efforts to awaken awareness of Old Russia's sacred art. Collectors wanted to show off their large collections as well as to explain

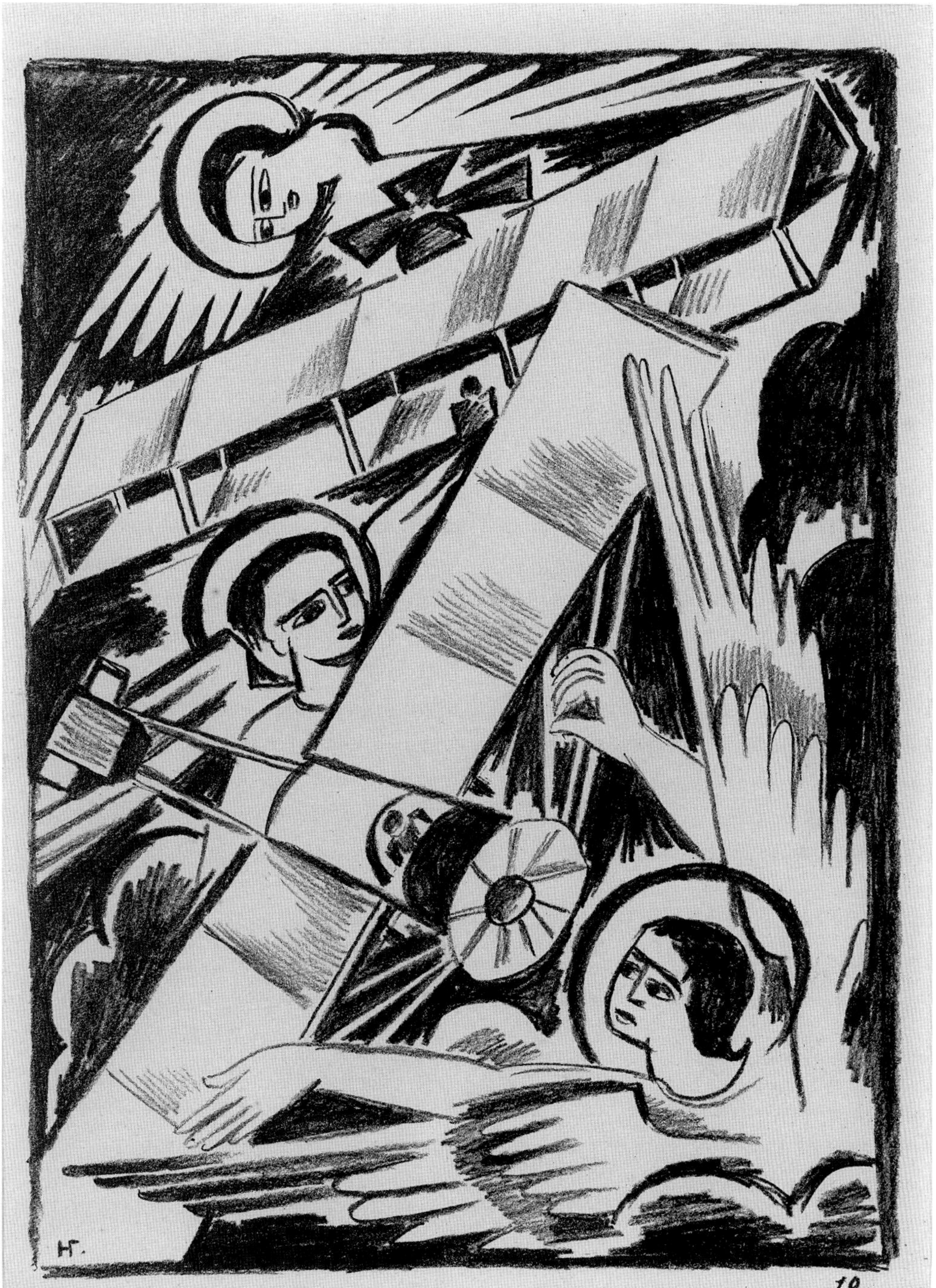

FIG. 4 Natalia Goncharova, *Angels and Aeroplanes,* 1914, lithograph on paper. Mead Art Museum, Amherst College, Amherst, Massachusetts. Gift of Thomas P. Whitney (Class of 1937). © 2008 Artists Rights Society (ARS), New York/ADAGP, Paris.

their significance to the public. In this regard, Nicholas's own reverence for the icon coincided with the growing public interest in pre-Petrine art. The icon could be identified as the truly national essence of Russia's artistic culture, and students of the icon set out to chronicle its history. Nikolai Likhachev (1862–1936), an important collector of icons, published his preliminary survey, *Materials for a History of Russian Icon Painting,* as a first step in this direction.[24] The artist Viktor Vasnetsov (1848–1925) combined his extensive collection with Likhachev's in an exhibition for the First Congress of Russian Artists held in St. Petersburg in the winter of 1911–12. The purpose of the exhibit was to provide an understanding of Old Russian icons by evaluating the monuments of the fourteenth to seventeenth centuries. The approximately three thousand icons in the Likhachev collection were bought by the government. Nicholas also supported the work of such icon painters as Grigory Chirikov (1882–1936), a Moscow-based restorer of icons for state collections. Chirikov worked with the Russian Museum in St. Petersburg, the sole prerevolutionary state institution to collect icons, many of them bought by Nicholas or supplied by the Ministry of Interior from the stockpile it had amassed from confiscations carried out in Old Believer churches, chapels, monasteries, and homes.[25] In early 1914, the deluxe journal *The Russian Icon,* an organ of the Russian Museum, was launched to offer a synthetic or "unitary" history for the museum's vast collection of Old Russian art.[26] Its purpose was to inform Russians and Western Europeans about this sacred art (descriptions of the icons reproduced were in both Russian and French). On 18 March 1914, a new museum wing was consecrated in a religious ceremony with the formal title "The Ancient Repository of Monuments of Russian Icon Painting and Ecclesiastical Antiquities in the Name of Emperor Nicholas II." A solemn prayer service in the presence of the Grand Duke Georgy Mikhailovich preceded the office of sanctification. Four days later Nicholas and his two daughters, Olga and Tatiana, along with other royal dignitaries, were shown around the collection by the museum's director, who presented the tsar with a copy of *The Russian Icon* when the tour was completed. Wendy Salmond has suggested that Nicholas viewed the new wing of the museum in wholly religious terms. In other words, it was not simply a museum but a "church museum" or sacred space.[27]

Many more examples can easily be found to illustrate the important role the emperor played in supporting the return of the icon to national and international prominence. In June of the same year, for instance, Empress Alexandra visited the women's school of icon painting, known as the School of National Art, which opened under the museum's sponsorship.

CONCLUSIONS

Nicholas II was profoundly affected by the revival of the Russian icon in the last decades of the Old Regime. He became fully convinced of the icon's miraculous power as one of several indications of providential concern for the well-being of Russia and its rulers. This conviction probably first took shape under the influence of his parents and some of his aunts and uncles. Along with the numerous glorifications of Russian saints during his reign, especially that of Serafim of Sarov, the world of icons provided reassurance in an uncertain time. That Nicholas held such views is explained partly by the native Russian currents of spirituality that had been growing in the post-Napoleonic era and that found an outlet in a monastic revival. But his views were also part of the wider European reaction to the Enlightenment that seemed to relate miracle, prayer, and prophecy to the growth of the nation-state. In this respect, Nicholas's reverence for "miracle-working" icons brought him into contact with the religious renaissance of the Silver Age, as educated Russians began to reconsider and reevaluate Russia's own traditions in light of the modern world and the experience of the 1905 Revolution. Icons, carefully arranged, created a sacred tableau in which the autocrat and his family participated in the national drama with all of its mysterious signs and symbols for the age to come. While the icon served as the emperor's bridge to the world of art and art scholarship, he remained distanced from the modern reinterpretation of the icon in aesthetic terms. In this way, as in so many others, the longed-for religious unity of tsar and people could not be achieved in the world of art.

Nor could this unity be readily achieved through the institution of the church. For Nicholas, the icon was one clear expression of his broader spiritual quest. He felt most comfortable in the presence of the divine liturgy, the holy shrines of Russia, the cathedrals of the Moscow Kremlin, and in his own private and sacred "village" at Tsarskoe Selo. Added to these were the cloud of witnesses of European mysticism and devotionalism as well as Russia's own saints and spiritual elders. Along with such private influences, the icon was a potent resource in linking God, the autocracy, and the people, yet without the specific mediation of the church as such. Nicholas's relationship to the icon was thus of a piece with his uneasy relationship to the Orthodox Church generally. He felt most drawn to its extra-institutional expressions at a time when he distanced himself from the hierarchy and the modern Orthodox reform movement. He did not favor summoning a reformist national *sobor,* or council; nor did he favor the idea of a restored patriarchate. His relationship to the church's foremost hierarch, Metropolitan Antony (Vadkovsky) of St. Petersburg, was at best a cool one. Something of the same sort could be said for the official royal chaplains. Here again, what characterized the emperor's religious life led not toward unity but toward division in late imperial Russia.

NOTES TO CHAPTER 3

1. "Had lunch together," Nicholas wrote in his diary, "and then spent the whole evening arranging icons in the new icon case." Entry for 1 January 1896, *Dnevnik imperatora Nikolaia II, 1890–1906 gg.*, ed. A. S. Burdykin (Moscow: Polistar, 1991), 121. See a photograph of this room as it appeared in 1917 in *Nicholas and Alexandra: The Last Imperial Family of Tsarist Russia, from the State Heritage Museum and the State Archive of the Russian Federation* (New York: Harry N. Abrams, 1998), 96.

2. See Gregory L. Freeze, "Subversive Piety: Religion and the Political Crisis in Late Imperial Russia," *Journal of Modern History* 68 (June 1996): 312–29; and Robert L. Nichols, "The Friends of God: Nicholas and Alexandra at the Canonization of Serafim of Sarov, July 1903," in *Religious and Secular Forces in Late Tsarist Russia,* ed. Charles E. Timberlake (Seattle: University of Washington Press, 1992), 206–29.

3. Richard Wortman, *From Alexander II to the Abdication of Nicholas II,* vol. 2 of *Scenarios of Power: Myth and Ceremony in Russian Monarchy* (Princeton: Princeton University Press, 2000).

4. Nicholas Zernov, *The Russian Religious Renaissance of the Twentieth Century* (London: Darton, Longman, and Todd, 1963), 167. For Trotsky's views on Nicholas II, see *The History of the Russian Revolution,* trans. Max Eastman (New York: Simon & Schuster, 1932), chap. 1.

5. George H. Tavard, *The Thousand Faces of the Virgin Mary* (Collegeville, Minn.: Liturgical Press, 1996), 178.

6. See Thomas A. Kselman, *Miracles and Prophecies in Nineteenth-Century France* (New Brunswick, N.J.: Rutgers University Press, 1983), 82–83.

7. Auguste Jundt, *Les Amis de Dieu au quatorzième siècle* (Paris: Sandoz, 1879).

8. Nicholas II's diary entries for 20–21 October 1894, *Dnevnik,* 42–43.

9. "Skazanie o zhizni i podvigakh startsa Serafima, ieromonakha sarovskoi pustyni i zatvornika, izvlechennoe iz zapisok uchenika ego," *Maiak* 16 (1844): 86.

10. These prophecies are more fully explained in Robert L. Nichols, "Orthodox Spirituality in Imperial Russia: Saint Serafim of Sarov and the Awakening of Orthodoxy," *Modern Greek Studies Yearbook* 16–17 (2000/2001): 19–42.

11. Quoted in Wortman, *From Alexander II to the Abdication of Nicholas II,* 310.

12. Marie, Grand Duchess of Russia, *Education of a Princess: A Memoir,* ed. Lord Russell (New York: Viking, 1931), 17.

13. Mark D. Steinberg and Vladimir M. Khrustalev, *The Fall of the Romanovs* (New Haven: Yale University Press, 1995), 17.

14. This painting was reproduced in a collection of materials published as part of the Romanov dynasty tercentenary celebrations in 1913. M. S. Putiatin, ed., *Letopisnyi i litsevoi izbornik* (Moscow: Izdatel'stvo S. S. Ermolaeva, 1913). The portrait is also reproduced in Wortman, *From Alexander II to the Abdication of Nicholas II,* 380.

15. *Nicholas and Alexandra,* 60–61.

16. Ibid., 136–37. Probably the icon was painted for the Fedorovsky Cathedral in 1913, but was at one time hung in the Alexander Palace.

17. *Nicholas and Alexandra,* 182–83.

18. Quoted in ibid., 98.

19. On this subject, see the interesting essay by John E. Bowlt, "Orthodoxy and the Avant-Garde: Sacred Images in the Work of Goncharova, Malevich, and Their Contemporaries," in *Christianity and the Arts in Russia,* ed. William C. Brumfield and Milos M. Velimirovic (Cambridge: Cambridge University Press, 1991), 145–50.

20. G. I. Vzdornov, *Istoriia otkrytiia i izucheniia russkoi srednevekovoi zhivopisi. XIX vek* (Moscow: Iskusstvo, 1986), 167–68. After 1923, the large and valuable collection was transferred to the Russian Museum. The Society itself was abolished only in 1932. On the icon collection in the Russian Museum, see Shirley A. Glade's chapter in this volume.

21. N. P. Kondakov, *Vospominaniia i dumy N. P. Kondakova*, ed. I. L. Kyzlasova (Moscow: Indrik, 2002), 178–87. The quotation is from p. 187.

22. I have written about this commission in "The Icon and the Machine in Russia's Religious Renaissance, 1900–1909," in *Christianity and the Arts in Russia*, ed. Brumfield and Velimirovich, 131–44.

23. Quoted in Bowlt, "Orthodoxy and the Avant-Garde," 148–49.

24. L. N. Likhachev, *Materialy dlia istorii russkogo ikonopisaniia*, 2 vols. (St. Petersburg: Ekspeditsiia zagotovleniia gosudarstvennykh bumag, 1906).

25. For a crisp discussion of prerevolutionary collectors, see G. I. Vzdornov, "Kollektsionery i restavratory v Rossii (1905–1917)," in "A Thousand-Year Heritage of Christian Art in Russia. Symposium, Hernen (the Netherlands), September, 1988," special issue, *Slavica Gandensia* 18 (1991): 51–65.

26. *Russkaia ikona*, now a bibliographic rarity, was a bimonthly journal published in St. Petersburg. Apparently only three issues were published before the outbreak of World War I in August 1914.

27. Wendy Salmond argues that the prototype for this innovative museum was Fedorovsky Gorodok, whose religious aesthetic rested on principles identified with the reign of Tsar Alexis. This seems to fit with other aspects of the emperor's spirituality expressed outside the Orthodox Church's specific institutional setting. The religious aesthetic Salmond identifies with the reign of Alexis may be extended to icons and their devotional setting prior to the appearance of Baroque influences on Muscovite sacred art. Wendy R. Salmond, "Nicholas, Alexandra, and the Icons of Fedorovskii Gorodok," paper presented at the annual convention of the American Association for the Advancement of Slavic Studies, Pittsburgh, 21–24 November 2002. I am citing this paper with the author's permission.

PART II

CURATORS AND COMMISSARS

SHIRLEY A. GLADE

4

ANISIMOV AND THE REDISCOVERY OF OLD RUSSIAN ICONS

Civil war was raging across Russia in 1919 when Alexander Anisimov predicted: "In distant years a future historian of the revolution calmly considering all that now is unfolding in such disorder before our eyes ought to note with amazement that, along with the establishment of a new state . . . the ferment of the revolution set in motion a reverse process of 'the gathering of Rus,' which led to the awakening of once-buried immortal cultural conquests and great images of Russia's past from a centuries-old sleep."[1] Anisimov's prediction is at last coming true. From the first decade of the twentieth century to his arrest in 1930, he played a leading role in this scholarly "awakening" of Russia's early icons. For more than five decades, however, his trailblazing achievements were obscured by the "fog of half-remembered history"—Gerold Vzdornov's term for the miasma enshrouding Soviet scholarship during the Stalin era and its aftermath.[2] In 1983, Vzdornov, parting this "fog," initiated Anisimov's rehabilitation with the publication of the first collection of his writings, followed in 1984 by the first article on the scholar.[3] Using materials gathered from previously inaccessible archives, Irina Kyzlasova published the first book on Anisimov six years later.[4] We are deeply indebted to Vzdornov and Kyzlasova for drawing long-overdue attention to the extraordinary accomplishments of this

I am grateful to have had the opportunity to gather material for this chapter at the Summer Research Laboratory on Russia, Eastern Europe, and Eurasia at the University of Illinois in Urbana-Champaign. I also would like to thank Professor Ann Kleimola and Professor Alexis Klimoff for their invaluable advice and assistance.

scholar, teacher, restorer, museum curator, and collector, whom Kyzlasova rightly calls a "scholar-champion" (*uchenyi borets*).[5]

Over the centuries, the Russian custom of overpainting icons buried their original images. When icon boards cracked from the harsh extremes of Russia's climate, varnish darkened, or secular tastes changed, icon painters would be asked to paint the image anew. This process was often repeated over and over on the same panel. As Anisimov explained, "Each [old Russian icon] is not just one but multiple images, one atop the other."[6] There was little interest in disinterring the old icons' earliest images, however, until the victory over Napoleon in 1812 stimulated the curiosity of Russian elites about their native cultural heritage, including icons predating the seventeenth century. This development helped transform early icons into objects of scholarly study.[7] Each old, illegible panel—so-called black boards—also became a potentially valuable antique. This possibility turned untold numbers of old icons into archeological finds that were excavated with lye and pumice under the supervision of icon dealers; less scrupulous dealers would even "age" the cleaned panels to increase their worth.[8] These restorers were generally hereditary icon painters called *ikonniki,* a number of whom proved instrumental in creating safer cleaning methods by the turn of the twentieth century. These parallel developments impelled collectors, amateurs, and scholars to join forces to preserve Russia's early icons.

The rediscovery of this cultural heritage was well under way by the time Anisimov was born on 30 March 1877 in St. Petersburg. He grew up in Moscow, where his social-activist parents, an economist and a medical assistant, were closely involved in the *zemstvo* movement's campaign to bring self-government, health care, and educational services to rural Russia. In 1904, their son graduated from the Department of History and Philosophy at Moscow University, where the rector, Prince Sergei Trubetskoy, was Anisimov's mentor.[9] Following his parents' example, Anisimov became an instructor at a seminary in Grigorovo, teaching history and geography, training elementary-school teachers, and tutoring French and Latin. He spent his rare free hours studying ancient cultural monuments in nearby Novgorod, where the master *ikonnik* Pavel Yukin taught him to restore old icons and frescoes.[10] Yukin's student soon became an active member of the Novgorod Society for Admirers of Antiquity and began exploring every corner of the province in search of old icons and other ecclesiastical objects.[11] Several of his discoveries were displayed at the exhibition of the All-Russian Archeological Congress, which he helped organize in 1911.[12] In addition, Anisimov made significant contributions to the collection of Novgorod's Diocesan Museum, which opened in 1913.[13] His publications from this period reflect his growing knowledge of early icons and frescoes.[14] At the same time as Anisimov's love for Russia's historic and artistic monuments was deepening, he was also developing a connoisseur's eye, and he soon assembled one of Russia's best private collections of icons and ecclesiastical applied art.[15] His experience restoring and collecting old icons in and around Novgorod laid the foundation for a passionate and lifelong campaign to protect and preserve them as a precious part of the nation's cultural inheritance.

In the first decade of the twentieth century, Anisimov shared this mission with a large number of his colleagues, who believed that state and church authorities were not devoting adequate attention and resources to Russia's early icons.[16] In 1912, these concerns were addressed at the Congress of Artists in Petrograd in a session titled "Russian Antiquity and Its Protection." Anisimov opened his address to this group by quoting an anonymous colleague's prediction that someday European museums would seek out early Novgorod icons with the same zeal they had previously devoted to finding old Egyptian and Greek sculptures. He then tempered this rosy forecast by predicting that precious few old icons were likely to survive to that point unless immediate measures were taken to rescue them from the Orthodox Church. When icons became illegible "black boards," or when the church deemed them redundant or stylistically outmoded, they would be tossed in belfries, cellars, and storerooms and left to rot. Anisimov criticized his colleagues for their failure to intervene in this destruction: "Who is guilty when icons perish? *We* are . . . we who consider ourselves lovers of antiquity, setting up commissions, societies, and institutes! Icons only interest archeological societies after they are saved."[17] Congress participants had both a duty and the expertise to help solve this problem, he argued. They would need to chart an agenda to rescue old icons, and he advised first asking the church to itemize "redundant" old icons, which would then be registered and moved to state-run sites.[18] His call for action, which was joined by other Congress members,[19] motivated many participants to petition the state for protection of "this precious property of the people."

Their cause gained broader support in 1913, when the Moscow Archeological Institute sponsored the first public exhibition of cleaned old icons at the Delovoy Dvor during the celebration of the tercentenary of the Romanovs. Freed from accumulated layers of varnish and paint, the brilliant colors and high artistic quality of these resurrected images from Russia's finest private collections astonished exhibition visitors and critics. As the eminent art historian Viktor Lazarev later recalled, "It was as if a veil suddenly fell, revealing the genuine face of Russian painting."[20] The unique beauty and colors of the Delovoy Dvor icons convinced reviewers that Russia's pre-Petrine icons were the equals of works by Giotto and Fra Angelico. Therefore, they deserved recognition as the nation's "Classical Art" as well as "a beautiful branch of the mighty tree of World Art which had now become the property of the nation."[21]

The recovered images also provided evidence that a new generation of scholars could use to challenge the validity of earlier studies based upon written sources, iconography-based analysis, and, most important, overpainted old icons.[22] This academic-archeological approach now seemed irrelevant to younger specialists, who were choosing to focus upon the old icons' newly revealed cultural-historical and aesthetic values.[23] For example, in 1914, art historian Pavel Muratov asserted that the time had come to make every possible effort to clean and study old icons "to preserve their historic place" in Russia.[24]

That same year, Nikolai Shchekotov praised Ilya Ostroukhov for valuing the old icons in his priceless collection not as "archeological artifacts" but for their artistic and aesthetic qualities.[25]

Anisimov advanced the cause of this new approach in 1914, when he published the first substantive articles on Novogorod's icons as works of art.[26] He based his evaluations primarily upon the icons The Praying Novgorodians and The Miracle of the Mother of God, both painted in 1467. They had been recently cleaned by Yukin, with Anisimov's help on the latter. In the nineteenth century, icon scholar Fyodor Buslaev had denigrated early Novgorod icons for their "incorrect drawing, perspective, and coloring," arguing that these shortcomings, along with the images' lack of "intelligent chiaroscuro," doomed them "always to remain stuck at the lowest level of their artistic development."[27] In response, Anisimov pointed out that Novgorod, the so-called Ravenna of the North, was already a recognized center of artistic activity by the time the icons under discussion were created. He also reminded his readers that Buslaev had based his "old-fashioned" conclusions upon examinations of murky overpaintings rather than the original fifteenth-century images. Studying those restored panels, he concluded that their vibrant colors and compositional harmony, as well as their psychological and spiritual resonance, attested to an impressively high level of "artistic development."[28] In addition to reinforcing Anisimov's reputation as a connoisseur of Novgorod icons, these articles emphasized the serious need for more advanced studies of Russia's early art. In 1915, Anisimov stated that if more of Russia's oldest icons were brought into "proper perspective as praiseworthy monuments of great art, Russians no longer would need to question when their art history started."[29] Already in 1910, Anisimov's archeological and scholarly activities had caught the attention of Nikodim Kondakov, a Buslaev protégé and preeminent Byzantinist who had promoted iconographic rather than aesthetic evaluations of old icons and who felt that "fancy divorced from criticism" was leading critics to overrate cleaned icons.[30] Despite their methodological differences, Kondakov, who remained the younger man's revered mentor until his death in 1925,[31] predicted that Anisimov would help "establish the basis of the future science of icon studies."[32] By 1915, it was becoming increasingly difficult for Anisimov to balance the demands of his heavy teaching schedule in Grigorovo with his scholarly work and research in the capital. After being granted a less demanding teaching post in Petrograd in 1916, he moved to Peterhof to prepare for a master's exam in Art History while continuing to visit and write about his beloved Novgorod.[33] As N. P. Porfiridov recalls, "Many elderly Novgorodians considered [Anisimov] a fellow countryman."[34] A year earlier, the artist Boris Kustodiev had underscored Anisimov's attachment to that city by painting a portrait of the scholar with Novgorod's Kremlin in the background (fig. 5). This portrait was hidden away in the Russian Museum until the end of the 1950s, when it was exhibited with other works by Kustodiev.[35] On the eve of the 1917 Revolution, Anisimov published two articles expressing alarm over the state's neglect of Novgorod's

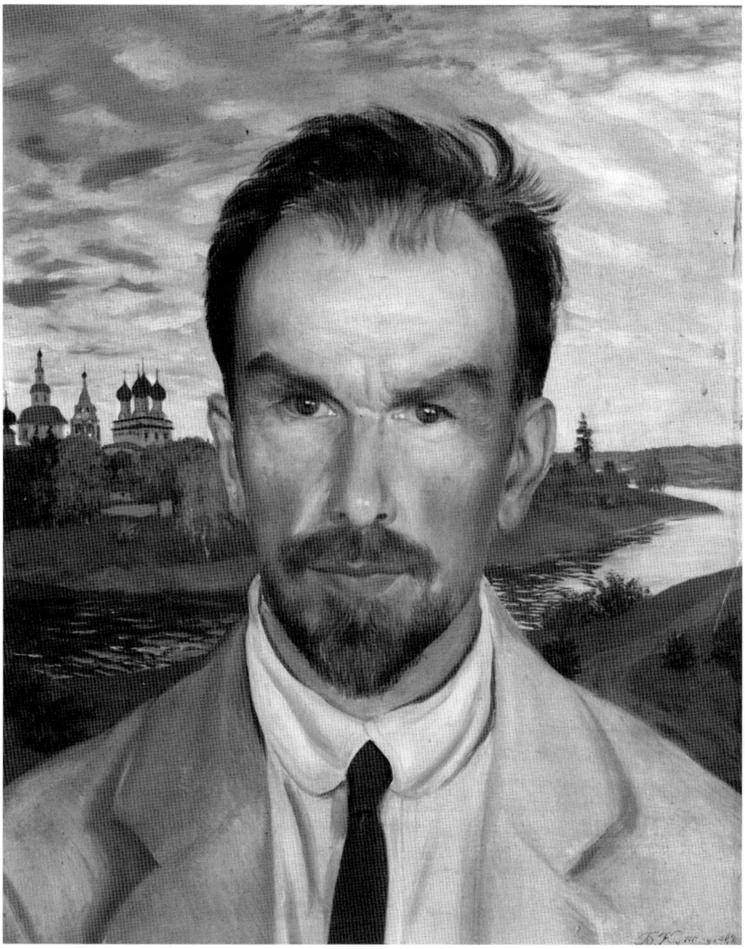

FIG. 5 Boris Kustodiev, *Portrait of A. I. Anisimov, Art Historian and Restorer,* 1915, oil on card-board. © 2010 State Russian Museum, St. Petersburg.

heritage.[36] In the second, he protested the planned construction of a railway line bisecting an ancient part of the city, closing with a pointed quotation from Alexander Pushkin: "Savagery, baseness, and ignorance do not esteem the past; they prostrate themselves before the present alone."[37]

The next year, revolutionary forces unleashed savage and ignorant attacks on an unprecedented scale upon Russia's religious and cultural treasures, making their defense an even more challenging and vital priority. Appalled by the destruction wrought by the February Revolution, Maxim Gorky gathered cultural leaders to advise the Provisional Government on protecting artistic and architectural monuments. He also appealed directly to the public to protect their cultural inheritance and "vigilantly, alertly to guard the 'old culture'" as the foundation upon which to build the new.[38] An epidemic of "outrageous vandalism" in October further exacerbated the cultural crisis.[39] By the spring of 1918, the state was stable enough to respond to the pleas of prerevolutionary cultural leaders for the creation of an agency to protect the nation's cultural legacy. On 26

May 1918, the People's Commissariat for Enlightenment (Narkompros) created a "guardian" of "old culture"—the Board for the Affairs of Museums and Protection of Monuments of Art and Antiquity.[40] The prerevolutionary secular redefinition of old icons as artworks now ensured their protection under the new regime as "Monuments of Russian Painting." A series of decrees nationalized private and institutional icon collections,[41] controlled their export, and, echoing Anisimov's prerevolutionary proposal, mandated their registration at specified "Museum Fund" collection sites, from which they were sent to museums or newly established restoration workshops.[42]

On 10 June 1918, the board founded the Commission for the Preservation and Uncovering of Monuments of Ancient Painting in Russia,[43] whose responsibilities were taken over by the Central State Restoration Workshops (TsGRM) in 1924.[44] Both agencies aimed to rescue, restore, and protect old frescoes and icons, and both were directed by Igor Grabar—artist, art historian, a founder of the "World of Art" (*Mir iskusstva*) movement, former director of the Tretiakov Gallery, and editor of the multivolume *History of Russian Art* (*Istoriia russkogo iskusstva*). Grabar helped establish and then headed the first Soviet icon restoration and research institutions;[45] he also initiated their resumption of work after World War II. In 1918, Grabar invited Russia's best collectors, scholars, and *ikonniki* restorers to join the commission.[46] Five years later, several commission members from Petrograd and Moscow gathered in the Kremlin's restoration workshop for a group photograph in which Grabar, Anisimov, the restorer Dmitry Bogoslovsky, the collector Ilya Ostroukhov, the collector and scholar Nikolai Likhachev, and the Russian Museum's curator of Old Russian painting, Pyotr Neradovsky, are shown, as well as Grigory Chirikov, whom Anisimov called "king among icon painters and restorers,"[47] and his assistant *ikonniki* restorers Pavel Yukin, Ilya Suslov, and Vasily Kirikov.

Anisimov accepted Grabar's invitation to become the commission's scientific director in 1918 because, as he noted, "it coincided with my scientific interests and experience."[48] Thus began a complex relationship between the two most influential forces in the field. Anisimov gratefully acknowledged Grabar's vital role as the first specialist to promote state support for restoration programs by building a bridge between Narkompros and prerevolutionary specialists.[49] In addition, Grabar's prolific writings and lectures echoed Anisimov's own concerns. The personalities of the two specialists were strikingly different, however. Grabar was a politically savvy administrator and consolidator,[50] while Anisimov was apolitical, outspoken, and fiercely independent. Evgraf Konchin later called him "an obstinate, impetuous person who did not hide his impatience with barbarism nor mince words."[51] Despite their occasional clashes,[52] the director and scientific director managed to work together productively.

Between 1918 and 1930, Anisimov made impressive progress toward achieving his goal of transforming the craft of icon restoration into a science.[53] Rejecting the old-fashioned reliance of restorers upon harsh solvents from their "kitchen of alchemy," Anisimov asserted that the restorer's primary tool is not chemistry but craft, the mechanics of "the able hand of a master wielding a small brush and knife." He further warned that the sharper the knife, the greater the skill required of its wielder. Anisimov preferred to use the term *raskrytie* (uncovering) rather than *restavratsiia* (restoration), objecting that the latter implies the icon can be returned to its original appearance, which is impossible.[54] From 1918 onward, the promoters of scientific restoration focused on preventing further damage, reinforcing an icon's layers and board, revealing its earliest image, and preserving that image without any inpainting or additions. N. A. Okolovich, director of the Russian Museum's workshop, put it this way: "Nothing augmented nor altered, and nothing added. The restorer's task is to halt further destruction."[55] Despite the challenging conditions and shortages of the period, specialists did impressive work in the commission's/TsGRM's main restoration workshops in Moscow and Petrograd/Leningrad as well as in the branches that Anisimov set up and administered in Novgorod, Vladimir, Yaroslavl, Vologda, the Trinity Lavra of Saint Sergius, and Pskov.[56]

The removal of precious covers and the accumulated layers of paint, varnish, and soot not only liberated the earliest images on the old icons but also uncovered vital new data for their historical study,[57] which was Anisimov's second major goal. In 1914–15, he gave Russia's first lecture course on Old Russian icon painting at the A. I. Shaniavsky Moscow People's University. After the revolution, Anisimov directed the Old Russian Art division at the Moscow Institute of Art Historical Research and Museology (MIKhIM).[58] He also taught at the Advanced Art-Technical Workshops (VKhUTEMAS), the Scientific-Research Institute of Archeology and Art History at Moscow State University (NIIAiI), and Yaroslavl University.[59] In 1920, he began working on a "Compendium of Exactly and Indirectly Dated Monuments of Old Russian Art," an annotated dictionary for researchers and teachers at the Moscow Institute.[60]

Between 1918 and 1928, Anisimov led expeditions of specialists to monasteries, churches, and chapels in Ferapontovo, Vologda, Vladimir, Belozersk, Kirillov, Riazan, Nizhny Novgorod, Kazan, Solvychegodsk, Staraya Ladoga, Veliky Ustiug, Rostov Veliky, Pskov, Yaroslavl, the environs of Moscow, and other areas.[61] These trips often yielded spectacular finds, repeatedly validating Anisimov's prerevolutionary expression of concern for the church's abandoned "black boards." For example, three illegible panels that Chirikov rescued from a leaky shed in a Zvenigorod churchyard in 1918 turned out to be images of an archangel, the Apostle Paul, and Christ painted in the early fifteenth century by Russia's most revered icon painter, Andrei Rublev.[62] Anisimov reported on restorer Mikhail Tiulin's 1919 discovery of an early thirteenth-century icon of the Mother of God, Velikaya Panagiya (Orant), overpainted in oils and hidden away in a storage room of the Spassky Monastery in Yaroslavl.[63] Anisimov was frequently in Yaroslavl to oversee work at the restoration workshop.[64] In 1922, he went there to select icons and fittings that were too valuable to be melted down by the Commission for the Removal of Church Valuables.[65] The next year he reported on the condition of icons and frescoes in the area.[66] In 1926, he published a catalog for an exhibition of old Yaroslavl icons that had recently been cleaned and put on display in conjunction with the celebration of the city's nine-hundredth anniversary.[67] As inspector of Old Russian painting for the Main Administration of Scientific-Research Institutions (Glavnauk), Anisimov evaluated icons in all of Pskov's churches in June 1926.[68] Cleaning revealed the dynamic lines and distinctive palette (deep greens and reds predominated) of these old images, convincing Anisimov that, from then on, specialists needed to reclassify Pskov's early icons as "Pskovian," rather than continuing to identify them as a subcategory of Novgorod icon painting.[69]

In 1926, Natalia Trotskaya, director of the Museum Division in Narkompros, reported that commission and TsGRM representatives had been threatened in some remote areas by "dark elements of the population" who were suspicious of outsiders, whom they called "Bolsheviks" or "atheists" (*bezbozhniki*).[70] Anisimov and his colleagues at TsGRM faced a threat from their supposed allies as well, however. During the Civil War, the Bolsheviks' own "dark elements" frequently spread terror among local populations, as Anisimov learned on the commission's first expedition to Kirillov and Ferapontovo in 1918. In an early report to Grabar, Anisimov wrote that work was going very well, thanks primarily to Bishop Varsonofy, an icon connoisseur who had provided invaluable help during the inspection and inventory of icons at the Kirillo-Belozersk Monastery. Twelve days later, a shaken Anisimov informed Grabar that Varsonofy, along with the Mother Superior of the Ferapontov Monastery, two villagers, and two peasants, had been shot by the local Cheka in retaliation for the assassination of a Petrograd Cheka leader.[71] In 1919, due to his brief affiliation with the Constitutional Democrats (Kadets) in 1917, Anisimov himself was arrested in Peterhof by the Cheka and sentenced to be shot in Kronstadt. Alerted by telegram, Trotskaya sent an urgent appeal to Yelena Stasova, secretary of the Party's Central Committee, asking her to spare this "irreplaceable servant of Russian science and art."[72] Trotskaya's action saved Anisimov's life at the last minute.

After the revolution, secular specialists gained unprecedented access to the nation's most revered icons at Russia's holiest sites. In 1918, Patriarch Tikhon issued a charter blessing the work of the commission's "toilers of science"—Grabar, Anisimov, and Vasily Georgievsky—as they set out to visit "the ancient holy places of our Fatherland" to study icons painted by "the great masters, Andrei Rublev and Dionysius."[73] That same year Anisimov witnessed the removal of the precious cover from, and the definitive cleaning of,[74] Rublev's revered *Old Testament Trinity*. His subsequent article was among the earliest descriptions of the original image's unexpectedly vibrant color and clarity of line.[75]

In 1922, Anisimov lectured at Moscow State University on new revelations surrounding Russia's most esteemed icon: the original image of the Vladimir Mother of God.[76] Beginning in the 1130s, when the Greek Metropolitan Mikhail ordered this icon from Constantinople as a gift for Prince Mstislav Vladimirovich in Kiev,[77] through its stay in Vladimir (where it acquired its name), and following its installation in Moscow's Dormition Cathedral, this wonder-working image had been a palladium for Orthodox believers. In addition, Anisimov asserted that the icon had served as an "oriflamme," a rallying banner, for medieval Rus and then imperial Russia down through the centuries.[78] By 1918, however, "The past of the monument was wrapped in an increasingly fantastic legend, [while] the monument itself was shrouded in an impenetrable dark veil of overpaintings, touch-ups, and renewals." The icon remained imprisoned beneath a hermetically sealed cover (fig. 6).[79] After removing the cover, specialists discovered a nearly illegible image on a panel ravaged by mold and wood rot.[80] In 1922, Anisimov related his initial response to this sight: "The great monument was a defenseless object that had endured a mercilessly crude transformation through the ignorance and superficiality of those who had surrounded it with a halo of surface grandeur and holy inviolability, not realizing the damage [their] overpaintings, additions, nail piercings, and mediocre touch-ups had caused."[81] Between 14 December 1918 and 5 April 1919, Grabar, Anisimov, and other specialists watched Chirikov clean this precious image.[82] In his 1922 lecture, Anisimov reviewed earlier scholars' evaluations of the icon and discussed the icon's multiple touch-ups as well as four major repairs dating back to 1237, when the panel was damaged during the Mongol conquest of Vladimir. These stages of the icon's transformation are depicted on a later diagram (fig. 7). Anisimov dated the earliest stratum to the eleventh century,[83] and he emphasized that this finding definitively disproved the legend that the image had been created by Saint Luke.[84] In addition, he argued that the dating of the earliest painted remnants proved that the panel was the original icon rather than a copy made in 1395, as several specialists, including Kondakov,[85] had concluded from examining the uncleaned image through its cover.[86]

It became very difficult to publish books on monuments of religious art and architecture after the revolution because the scarce supply of printing material was allocated first to political writings.[87] This explains Anisimov's inability to finish and publish several projects, including his monographs on Yaroslavl and Novgorod, as well as a series on Russia's best early icons and frescoes that he and Grabar had planned for 1928.[88] Already in 1923, Anisimov had written Kondakov that he was preparing a monograph on the original icon of the Vladimir Mother of God but had no hope of getting it published in the Soviet Union.[89] In desperation, he used a "special channel" in Moscow's foreign community to send his manuscript to Leonid Beliaev, Kondakov's former student and then editor for the Seminarium Kondakovianum in Prague.[90] Because he considered Anisimov to be "the best specialist presently working in Russian icon painting,"[91] Beliaev was delighted to publish the monograph. Russian and abridged English editions of the monograph were issued in 1928;[92] by an extraordinary coincidence, they appeared almost simultaneously with the Soviet publication of Anisimov's 1922 lecture on the restoration of the same icon, a work that he dedicated to the memory of Kondakov, who had died three years earlier in Prague. In addition to being the first scholar to judge the icon's artistic merits on the basis of the cleaned image (pl. 1), Anisimov integrated pre- and postrevolutionary scholarship into a comprehensive study of this ancient image's historical, political, and religious significance. The icon's portraitlike depictions, distinctive facial types of Mother and Child, keen religious resonance of the facial expressions, strong modeling, and restrained color convinced Anisimov that the panel reflected Macedonian Renaissance rather than Italo-Cretan influences, as other previous scholars, including Kondakov, had speculated.[93]

In the first decade of the twentieth century, leading icon scholars were convinced that Byzantine influences began to be overtaken by distinctively Russian elements no earlier than the fourteenth to fifteenth centuries.[94] Postrevolutionary revelations provided a strong impetus for reevaluating these estimates. In 1923, Anisimov wrote to Kondakov, "The discovery of Old Russian art has been the single area in which Russia has made genuine progress in these years since the revolution."[95] Those revelations provided the foundation for his last major work, the first real reconsideration of icon painting from the pre-Mongol period.[96] This 1928 article traces the evolution of cross-influences between monumental and panel painting in Rus, beginning with the twelfth-century Ustiug Annunciation. Countering earlier scholarly analyses, Anisimov argued that Russian elements were already discernible in thirteenth-century Novgorod images. Giving several examples to back up his argument, such as the Novgorodian icon of Saint John Climacus with Saints George and Blaise, Anisimov argued that the rounded faces, juxtaposition of clear, bright colors, straight compositional lines, and flattening of the figures characteristic of these images all indicate a Russian divergence from the Byzantine icon-painting canon.[97]

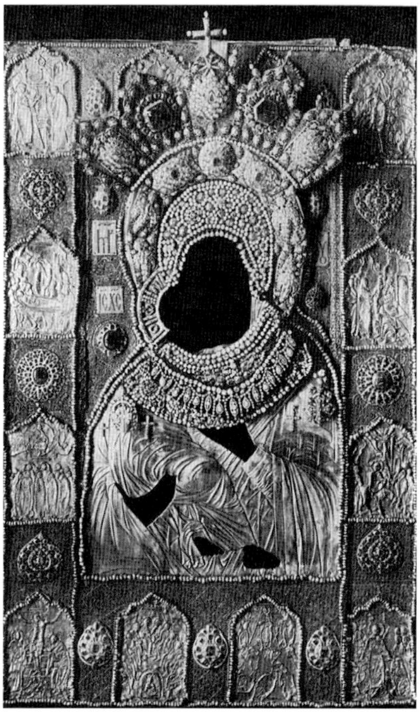

FIG. 6 Gold cover for the Vladimir Mother of God, 1410–31. Armory Palace, Moscow. Reproduced from Igor' Grabar', *O drevnerusskom iskusstve* (Moscow: Nauka, 1966).

In addition to valuing the historical and artistic significance of Russia's icons, Anisimov also acknowledged their central place in the lives of Orthodox believers. As a TsGRM colleague reported under interrogation in 1930, Anisimov "did not take an active part in the struggle against religion and refused to denounce the veneration of icons, removing them from churches only with permission from the believers."[98] After he was appointed director of the Division of Religious Antiquities at the State Historical Museum in 1921, he created the museum's

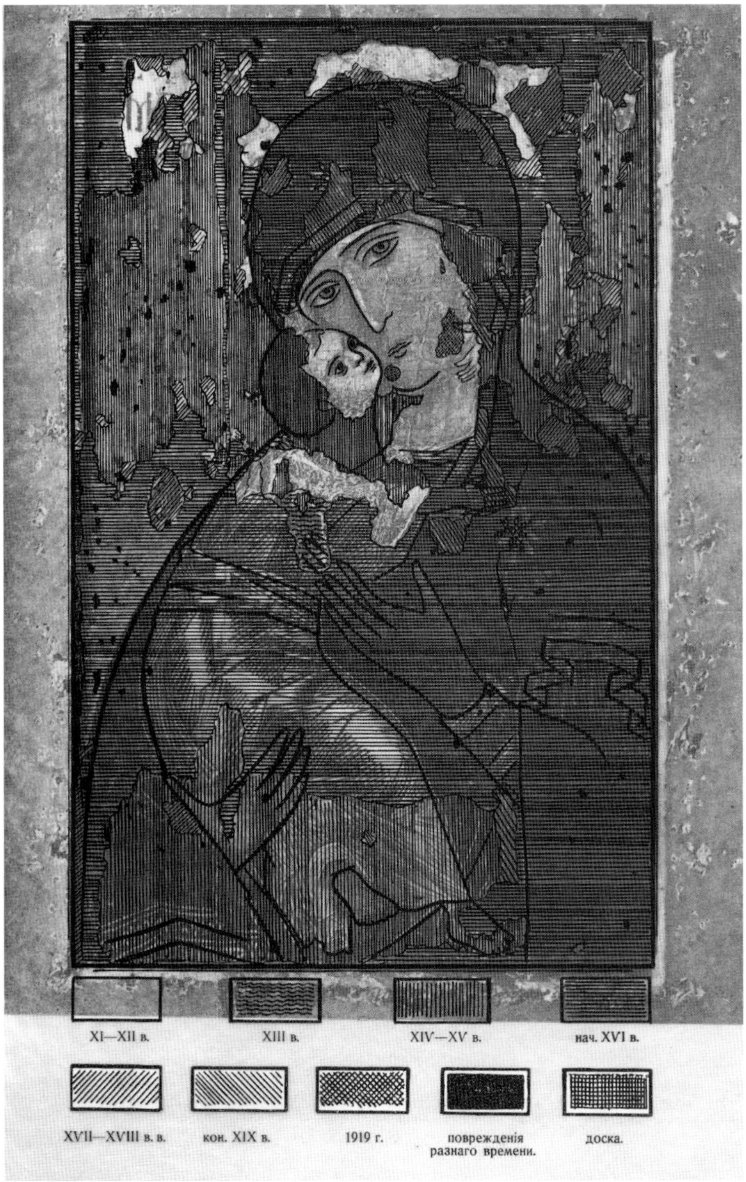

FIG. 7 Diagram of repairs and touch-ups of the Vladimir Mother of God. Reproduced from A. I. Anisimov, *Our Lady of Vladimir,* trans. N. G. Yaschwill and T. N. Rodzianko (Prague: Seminarium Kondakovianium, 1928).

first restoration workshop and the nation's first Department of Religious Customs.[99] He later claimed to have added twenty thousand objects to the collection.[100] As one of the Museum Fund sites,[101] the State Historical Museum held a great number of the country's most valuable icons, including the original Vladimir Mother of God, in addition to an enormous collection of ecclesiastical applied art. In 1926, Anisimov selected many of these objects for an innovative show, which he chose to call an "Exhibition of Monuments of Old Russian Icon Painting [*ikonopisi*]," eschewing the more politically correct term "painting" (*zhivopis'*). Instead of displaying icons according to their styles and epochs, Anisimov arranged the icons in settings illustrative of their integral roles in the everyday life and faith of Orthodox Russians. In the exhibition catalog, Anisimov sympathetically and apolitically explained the church and folk traditions that shaped this relationship, reflecting his belief that "Old Russian icon painting is no different than an illustrated history of the Russians' religious system of belief and moral philosophy. The icon itself is an abstract presentation of the religious and moral ideals of the Russian people."[102]

In the latter part of the 1920s, the status and cultural significance of old icons as well as that of icon specialists themselves were undergoing profound change. Xenophobia, militant atheism, and anti-intellectualism converged during this period to spawn the Soviet "Cultural Revolution," namely, an assault on the bourgeois intelligentsia and the cultural establishment by young Communist militants.[103] In 1927, Sergei Tretiakov fired the new revolution's opening salvo:

> All for combat!
> Force is best.
> A bullet to the brain
> Of Basil the Blest.
> Smash all the icons
> And the signs they have made.
> Explode the Iverskaya [Chapel
>   and icon]
> With a hand grenade![104]

The cultural militants first targeted the "bourgeois hegemony" of predominantly non-Party intellectuals educated before the revolution.[105] The description fit many icon specialists, who were doubly endangered because religion was also under attack. Ironically, this campaign targeted several of the most gifted specialists after they had just helped to tout Soviet achievements in scientific restoration during an unprecedented international exhibition of Russian icons.

Celebrating the eighth anniversary of Soviet restoration activity in 1926, Grabar exclaimed, "If a competition were held in Europe [today] to find the best restoration methods, those now being used at the TsGRM would be recognized as less harmful and more scientifically based than those of any other country."[106] Partially to prove this assertion, that same year Grabar began planning a traveling foreign exhibition of icons that had been restored and copied by Soviet specialists.[107] As it traveled from Vienna through Germany and on to London and America between 1929 and 1932, this exhibition publicized both Soviet restoration skills and the state's support for cultural preservation. As Wendy Salmond points out, Grabar additionally hoped to create an international market for Russian icons, making them a source of much-needed Western currency.[108] This aspect of the exhibition disturbed many Soviet specialists.[109] Having selected most of the icons for the exhibition as well as many of those intended for sale,[110] Anisimov himself experienced conflicting emotions. He initially felt proud that the exhibited icons would display "genuinely Russian art to the world" and was delighted at the possibility that the displayed images might link émigré Russians with their homeland.[111] However, he later expressed concern about "the ultimate fate of the icons" he had helped to send abroad, hoping that they would fall "into good hands" and would not, under any circumstances, be "rendered 'stateless.'"[112] In addition to taking an active role in organizing the exhibition, Anisimov introduced Soviet advances in icon scholarship and restoration to the readers of French and German journals.[113] In a catalog for the London exhibition, he also wrote a survey of the Russian icon's stylistic "flowering and decay." In Anisimov's view, the icon's unique balance of color, rhythmic line, and composition, epitomized by Rublev in the early fifteenth century, was gradually undermined by increasingly mannerist elements in the 1500s and, a century later, by the importation of realistic space and body volume from the West. This stylistic "decay" was completed by the use of distracting decorative and precious covers, a trend that reached its peak in the eighteenth and nineteenth centuries.[114]

As Grabar had hoped, the exhibition was enormously successful in showcasing the great skills of Soviet scholars and restorers. In the London catalog, for example, the English art historian Martin Conway proclaimed, "There does not exist anywhere a staff of artists so experienced in dealing with damaged and repainted panels as is employed in the Kremlin hospital for damaged works of art."[115] Yet two months before the exhibition opened in Berlin in 1929, Anisimov became the first and most prominent icon specialist to come under attack back in Moscow. The erstwhile scientific director became a target for the militants, whom he viewed as being "former members of the 'Black Hundreds' painted red" who were striving to destroy "the nation's still surviving remnants of general European and Russian culture."[116]

Anisimov's ordeal began on 7 December 1928, when *Izvestiia* announced his dismissal from the Scientific-Research Institute of Archeology and Art History (NIIAiI) and the Russian Association of Scientific-Research Institutions of Social Sciences (RANION). *Izvestiia*'s readers were informed that NIIAiI's board of directors had taken this step because Anisimov had committed an act they considered to be "inconsistent with the rank of a true member of the institute" when he permitted his monograph on the Vladimir Mother of God to be published by an émigré organization.[117] The Seminarium Kondakovianum revealed its "anti-Soviet" position in the unsigned foreword and introduction to the English and Russian editions of the monograph, respectively. The English foreword acknowledged that the Seminarium Kondakovianum had received financial support from the Czech Foreign Office and the "former Count V. N. Kokovtsev," the late tsar's Minister of Finance (1904–14), while the author of the Russian version noted that Anisimov and other Soviet scholars were having difficulty publishing their work at home. *Izvestiia* responded to this charge by pointing out that the Soviet state did not "prevent the publication of true scientific research" in Western countries that were not "hostile to the USSR."[118] In addition, Anisimov was reminded that many of his scholarly works, including his recently published "History of the Vladimir Icon in the Light of Restoration," were already in print in the Soviet Union. When asked by a colleague about his monograph's "counter-revolutionary foreword," he answered that it had been printed without his knowledge, and that in any case he could not simply dissociate himself from the Prague institute's staff: "These are respectable people!"[119] Despite the vociferous protests he lodged against the charges, his dismissal was not rescinded.

In early February 1929, Anisimov and thirty-six coworkers lost their positions at the Historical Museum, where the Department of Religious Customs was liquidated.[120] The foreign publication of his monograph contributed to his dismissal there as well. Museum authorities charged Anisimov with sending museum materials to émigré and foreign scholars without authorization (these included forty-five photos provided for Kondakov's use in *The Russian Icon*). The museum further claimed that he had exported valuable art for exhibition and sale abroad without proper documentation—a charge he vehemently denied, asserting that he, Grabar, and the director, E. I. Silin, had verified the legality of the exports. The All-Russian Art Institute (VKhIN, the forerunner of today's Institute of Arts) used the Historical Museum's charges to justify Anisimov's firing from that institution as well.[121] Following these dismissals, Anisimov lamented the abysmal state of the cultural environment in the Soviet Union in a letter to Beliaev: "The stupidity, primitivism, and malice of the Party are joined by the baseness, treachery, and servility of non-Party members, [creating] an atmosphere lacking even one atom of spiritual oxygen and fit only for the survival of degenerates."[122]

Back in 1926, Maximilian Voloshin had inscribed his watercolor portrait of Anisimov "with love and gratitude" to his subject for having "discovered the miracle of the Vladimir Mother of God for me."[123] Anisimov's difficulties three years later inspired Voloshin to write a poem about this icon, which he dedicated to the scholar on 26 March 1929. Voloshin describes the icon's dual roles as witness to the centuries of suffering endured by the Russians and as spiritual comforter during their tribulations. The poem ends with the image of "The Mother of Vladimir" (*Matushka Vladimirskaia*) offering an unnamed sufferer [Anisimov] a golden key to her heavenly dwelling in exchange for the rusty one that unlocks "our sorrowful fate" in this life.[124]

Little is known about Anisimov's life during the remainder of 1929 until June 1930, when he wrote his last two extant articles, both of which remained unpublished until 1983. His analysis of Pskov icons, discussed above, was written on 15 June 1930. On 30 June, he wrote about a triptych icon that the State Antiquariat had acquired from the collection of M. P. Botkin. In the latter article, Anisimov asserted that the panels did not originate in the thirteenth or fourteenth century, as Botkin thought, but had been created later by a Byzantine painter under the influence of the Italian Renaissance and closer in time to the papacy of Paul III (1534–49), who had received the triptych as a gift.[125]

By the late summer of 1930, Anisimov had been expelled from all institutions and agencies except the TsGRM, which found itself under increasing attack. He lost his position there that September and was finally arrested on 7 October by the State Political Directorate (OGPU). He would later complain to his OGPU interrogators that his replacement as TsGRM's scientific director lacked the scientific and educational qualifications required for the position. Explaining that a restoration workshop "is like a medical clinic where monuments are cured," he noted the absurdity of requiring the doctor "be a Marxist rather than an idealist in order to know how to treat patients."[126]

His arrest was followed by the secret police's "Anisimovshchina" campaign,[127] which eventually ensnared nearly all his close colleagues at the TsGRM.[128] In 1959, documents were found in an OGPU archive accusing the TsGRM of harboring an anti-Soviet group, "the All-People's Union for the Battle to Revive a Free Russia." Among the named conspirators were Grabar, Yukin, Levinson, Chirikov, and V. N. Zasypkin. Several were charged with belonging to "Anisimov's family," deliberately damaging frescoes, and "creating a system of professional secrets." Yukin was specifically accused of defending and supporting Anisimov's "ideology." Faced with accusations of espionage, vandalism, and other crimes, the TsGRM was closed in 1934.[129] Its inventory and surviving specialists were shifted to the Tretiakov Gallery, which had neither the space nor the resources to handle this transfer (the Vladimir icon was dropped and damaged during the process).[130] By then, icons had been redefined as "feudal art," and every person pictured in the 1923 photograph of commission members had been arrested, except for Suslov and Ostroukhov, who were deceased, and Grabar, who had already retired and returned to painting.[131]

Anisimov's interrogation began on 9 October and continued into the next month. During his interrogation, Anisimov wrote "protocols"[132] detailing his background, political views, domestic and foreign contacts,[133] and scientific perspectives. In addition to evoking the oppressive atmosphere of the time, these documents vividly illuminate the naïveté, idealism, and professional indignation of "one of the true guardians of Russian art."[134] Describing himself as a "Liberal Democrat" and idealist, Anisimov asserted that he had left the Kadets shortly after joining it in 1917 because he had "neither the interest nor the aptitude for politics." He confessed to playing the roles of a "pseudo-socialist" and "pseudo-Marxist" so that he could work in state institutions, where his only desire was to have "a piece of bread and the opportunity to work with art from an artistic [rather than a political] approach." Socialism is not bad as "an ultimate ideal," Anisimov explained, "if only it could be achieved with less repressive measures than those currently employed by the Soviet state" and if only the state would permit scholarly thought, in all its manifestations, the same freedom one found in France. Anisimov assured his interrogators that his lack of political orientation did not indicate that he did not love his country: "I would never give a foreigner anything that could be used against my country."[135] He defended even his sexual orientation in an outspoken manner, expressing his admiration for the manner in which Western Europeans dealt with homosexuality, and enlightening his interrogators with "a well-reasoned lecture" on the subject.[136]

On 23 January 1931, Anisimov was sentenced to ten years in camp. His crimes included having had extensive contacts with émigrés and foreigners, scorning state authority by allowing a foreign, anti-Soviet institute to publish his monograph, and gathering "valuable, extensive information" on "political points" from a group of "idealist–anti-Marxist" scholars to share with foreign agents in Moscow and émigrés. His belongings were confiscated, including his extensive icon collection,[137] and on 11 February 1931 he was sent to Kem. He was transferred from there to the Solovetsky Islands, where he immediately started cataloging and restoring icons and frescoes in the Solovetsky Monastery. The energy and passion he devoted to this work as well as his intellectual acuity deeply impressed his young cellmate, Dmitry Likhachev. In 1995, the renowned medievalist recalled that he had greatly appreciated his colleague's occasional lectures on Old Russian art. Anisimov even read Voloshin's poem to Likhachev at the end of a lecture on the Vladimir Mother of God.[138] Likhachev reports that a visiting Moscow commission later denounced the monastery's icon collection as "religious propaganda." After shutting down the monastery's museum, the visitors smashed an especially valuable fifteenth-century icon in Anisimov's presence, causing him to suffer an attack of angina.[139] In 1932, Anisimov was transferred to the White Sea–Baltic Canal Camp (BelBaltLag) in Karelia, where he could neither lecture nor restore icons. The harsh climate and conditions failed to temper his spirit, however, and he soon earned a reputation as a troublemaker there. According to an undated camp report, "[Anisimov] is systematically occupied with agitation and openly expresses his dissatisfaction with Soviet authority. [He] refuses to participate in communal work. This is very harmful [because] he has enormous authority among the prisoners." In June 1936, the same report notes that Anisimov had called the Russian people "idiots and slaves" and expressed admiration for Germany because of its reputation for being "an orderly place." During a discussion of Soviet literature in May 1937, Anisimov was further heard to say, "As a professor of the arts, I am perturbed, from the depths of my soul, knowing that [Soviet authorities] are killing young talent. [Because] the Stalinist reign prevails, mercenary, unskilled people and exceptional liars enforce the barbaric orders of the Bolsheviks."[140]

On 26 August 1937, at the height of the Great Terror, Anisimov was sentenced to death on the charges that he was a "glaring monarchist, fascist sympathizer, and slanderer of Soviet literature and art."[141] Unfortunately, Trotskaya and her husband, Lev, had been expelled by then, making it impossible for her to rescue Anisimov, as she had done nearly two decades earlier. His second death sentence was carried out a week later on 2 September.[142]

The state cleared Anisimov of all charges when he was officially rehabilitated in 1989. Vzdornov had already begun restoring Anisimov's scholarly reputation six years earlier. In the 1990s, Kyzlasova began cutting through the "historiography of the 'cult of Grabar'" to expand and extend the recognition of this remarkable scholar into the new millennium.[143] Anisimov had realized the importance of his work back in 1923, when he wrote Kondakov, "The more I come into contact with newly discovered monuments, the more moral satisfaction I receive, and I realize that this sometimes dangerous and grueling work has not been in vain."[144] His record of achievements bears this out. Not only did his work advance icon restoration and research during a turbulent period of cultural revolution, but it also has grown in significance, outliving the regime that destroyed him.

NOTES TO CHAPTER 4

1. A. I. Anisimov, "Raskrytie pamiatnikov drevnerusskoi zhivopisi," *Izvestiia Obshchestva arkheologii, istorii i etnografii pri Kazanskom universitete* 30, no. 3 (1920): 268; repr. in Anisimov, *O drevnerusskom iskusstve (Sbornik statei)*, ed. G. I. Vzdornov (Moscow: Sovetskii khudozhnik, 1983), 82. Citations below are to the 1983 edition.

2. G. I. Vzdornov, "'I zdes' i v vechnosti': pis'mo A. F. Loseva k N. M. Tarabukinu (15 ianvaria 1956 goda), *Kontekst: Literaturno-teoreticheskie issledovaniia* (1992): 192.

3. G. I. Vzdornov, "Aleksandr Ivanovich Anisimov (1877–1932)," *Sovetskoe iskusstvoznanie* 82, no. 2 (1984): 297–320. See also G. I. Vzdornov, "Aleksandr Ivanovich Anisimov," in *Restavratsiia i nauka. Ocherki po istorii otkrytiia i izucheniia drevnerusskoi zhivopisi* (Moscow: Indrik, 2006), 139–50.

4. I. L. Kyzlasova, *Aleksandr Ivanovich Anisimov (1877–1937)* (Moscow: Izdatel'svto Moskovskogo gosudarstvennogo gornogo universiteta, 2000).

5. Ibid., 37.

6. Anisimov, "Raskrytie," 100.

7. See especially G. I. Vzdornov, *Istoriia otkrytiia i izucheniia russkoi srednevekovoi zhivopisi. XIX vek* (Moscow: Iskusstvo, 1986).

8. Oleg Tarasov describes the work of these *ofeni-starinshchiki* in *Icon and Devotion: Sacred Spaces in Imperial Russia* (London: Reaktion, 2002), 55–57.

9. Vzdornov, "Anisimov," 298. Trubetskoy was president and Anisimov the secretary of the university's student association. See Anisimov, "Kniaz' Trubetskoi i moskovskoe studentchestvo," in *Voprosy filosofii i psikhologii* 16, nos. 1–2 (1916): 145–96.

10. Pavel Muratov, "Vokrug ikon," *Vozrozhdenie* (Paris), 28 January 1933, 21.

11. Anisimov, "Istoriko-arkheologicheskaia vystavka novgorodskogo obshchestva liubitelei drevnosti," *Novgorodskaia zhizn'*, 22 April–3 May 1910, 1–2, and 16 May 1910, 1–2. Muratov, "Vokrug ikon," 21.

12. See Anisimov, *Katalog vystavki XV Vserossiiskogo arkheologicheskogo s"ezda v Novgorode,* otdel 2 (tserkovnyi), Novgorod, 1911; *Dopolnenie k katalogu vystavki XV Vserossiiskogo arkheologicheskogo s"ezda v Novgorode,* otdel 2 (tserkovnyi), Novgorod, 1911; "Novgorod. XV arkheologicheskii s"ezd," *Russkaia khudozhestvennaia letopis'* (supplement to *Apollon*), no. 12 (1911): 191–94; and "Tserkovnaia starina na vystavke XV arkheologicheskogo s"ezda v Novgorode," *Starye gody* (February 1912): 4.

13. He gathered four hundred objects for the museum. Vzdornov, "Anisimov," 298.

14. His publications from this time include: "Restavratsiia fresok tserkvi Feodora Stratilata v Novgorode," *Starye gody* (February 1911): 43–52; "Restavratsiia ikonostasa tserkvi Spasa na Boru," *Russkie vedomosti,* no. 24 (February 1912): 4; "Sud'by khudozhestvennoi stariny v Rossii," *Russkie vedomosti,* no. 109 (13 May 1912): 6, and no. 114 (19 May 1912): 4; "Novootkrytie freski Novgoroda," *Starye gody* (December 1913): 50–55; and "Ikona Varlaama Khutynskogo v Novgorodskom eparkhial'nom drevnekhranilishche," *Trudy Novgorodskogo tserkovno-arkheologicheskogo obshchestva* 1 (1914): 148–67.

15. Like icon collectors Nikolai Likhachev, Stepan Riabushinsky, and Ilya Ostroukhov, Anisimov had his icons cleaned with no touch-ups. Vzdornov, *O drevnerusskom iskusstve,* 435n.

16. Vzdornov, *Restavratsiia i nauka,* 57.

17. Anisimov, "O sud'be starykh ikon v Rossii," *Trudy Vserossiiskogo s"ezda khudozhnikov. Dekabr' 1911–ianvar' 1912* (Petrograd, 1914), 155.

18. Ibid., 156.

19. Kondakov, Alexander Rostislavov, and Pavel Siuzor all spoke on the state's obligation to establish legal protection of antiquities, followed by an open discussion of the problem. G. Gabilev, "Khronika: Vserossiiskii s"ezd khudozhnikov," *Starye gody* (January 1912): 54.

20. V. N. Lazarev, *Russkaia srednovekovaia zhivopis'* (Moscow: Nauka, 1970), 7.

21. Nikolai Punin, "Vystavka drevne-russkogo iskusstva

(ustroennaia Moskovskim Arkheologicheskim Institutom imeni Imp. Nikolaia II)," *Apollon,* no. 5 (1913): 40. Sergei Makovskii, "Vvedenie," *Russkaia ikona,* no. 1 (1914): 6–7.

22. These earlier studies include: D. A. Rovinskii, "Istoriia russkikh shkol ikonopisaniia do kontsa XVII veka," *Zapiski imp. Russkogo arkheologicheskogo obshchestva* 8 (1856): 1–196; and F. I. Buslaev, "Obshchie poniatiia o russkoi ikonopisi," in *Drevnerusskaia literatura i pravoslavnoe iskusstvo* (1866; repr., St. Petersburg: Izdatel'stvo Russkogo Khristianskogo gumanitarnogo instituta, "Liga-Plius," 2001), 36–186.

23. Vzdornov addresses this generational conflict in *Restavratsiia i nauka,* 23–28, and in "Otkrytie drevnerusskoi zhivopisi. Dorevoliutsionnyi period," *Khudozhestvennoe nasledie. Khranenie, issledovanie, restavratsiia* 10 (1985): 24–39.

24. Muratov, "Blizhaishchie zadachi v dele izucheniia ikonopisi," *Russkaia ikona,* no. 1 (1914): 8.

25. N. M. Shchekotov, "Ikonopis' kak iskusstvo. Po povodu sobraniia ikon I. S. Ostroukhova i S. P. Riabushinskogo," *Russkaia ikona,* no. 1 (1914): 142.

26. Anisimov, "Etiudy o novgorodskoi ikonopisi: Zadacha etiudov: 1. 'Moliashchiesia novgorodtsy,'" *Sofiia,* no. 3 (1914): 9–28, and "Etiudy o novgorodskoi ikonopisi: 2. 'Chudo ot ikony Bogoroditsy,'" *Sofiia,* no. 5 (1914): 5–21. Citations below for both refer to the reprints in *O drevnerusskom iskusstve,* 11–59.

27. Buslaev, "Obshchie poniatiia," 14; Animisov, "Etiudy o novgorodskoi ikonopisi," 12–13.

28. Anisimov, "Etiudy o novgorodskoi ikonopisi," 35. Leonid Matsulevich criticized Anisimov's attack on Buslaev's "old-fashioned opinions." See L. A. Matsulevich, "Iz istorii russkoi nauki ob iskusstve, otvet N. Shchekotovu," *Russkaia ikona,* no. 2 (1914): 143–44.

29. Anisimov, review of *O proiskhozhdenii drevnerusskoi ikonopisi,* by G. Pavlutskii, *Starye gody* (November 1915): 37.

30. Nikolai Pavlovich Kondakov, *The Russian Icon,* trans. Ellis H. Minns (Oxford: Clarendon Press, 1927), 7.

31. On 13 December 1910, Anisimov wrote Kondakov, "Your moral support and ideological direction are especially dear to me." Quoted in Kyzlasova, *Anisimov,* 19. On 11 July 1923 Anisimov wrote Kondakov in Prague, "Although our hearts are separated, they beat in unison . . . [both] striving for the cultural success of the motherland and its national greatness." Anisimov, *O drevnerusskom iskusstve,* 23.

32. N. P. Kondakov, review of *Freski Ferapontova monastyria 1911,* by Vasilii T. Georgievskii, *Otchet o piat'desiat' piatom prisuzhdenii nagrad gr. Uvarova,* 1.

33. Kyzlasova, *Anisimov,* 21.

34. N. G. Porfiridov, *Novgorod 1917–1941, Vospominaniia* (Leningrad: Lenizdat, 1987), 179.

35. This portrait was first published in V. E. Lebedeva, *Boris Mikhailovich Kustodiev* (Moscow: Akademiia nauk SSSR, 1966), 188. For a discussion of this portrait, see also I. L. Kyzlasova, "Novoe ob Aleksandre Anisimove, po materialam ego perepiski s Borisom Kustodievym (1919–1926 gody)," *Iskusstvo khristianskogo mira* 7 (2000): 442–44; and Evgenii Klimov, "Vstrechi," *Novoe Russkoe Slovo* 5 (June 1977): 9.

36. "Ischezaiushchii Novgorod," *Rech',* 20 June 1916: 4; and "Unichtozhenie drevnego Novgoroda," *Apollon,* nos. 6–7 (1916): 76–82. Citations for the latter refer to the reprint in Anisimov, *O drevenerusskom iskusstve,* 63–79.

37. Quoted in Anisimov, "Unichtozhenie," 79.

38. Quoted in Nikolai Sukhanov, *Zapiski o revoliutsii,* vol. 2 (Berlin: A. I. Grzhebin, 1922), 160–61.

39. "Khudozhestvennaia letopis': Revoliutsiia i iskusstvo," *Apollon,* nos. 6–7 (1917): 70–71.

40. See Igor' Grabar', "Zadachi Kollegii po delam muzeev i okhrany pamiatnikov iskusstva i stariny," in *Igor' E. Grabar', O drevnerusskom iskusstve,* ed. O. I. Podobedova (1918; repr., Moscow: Nauka, 1966), 263–68. See also P. A. Semechkin, "Otdel po delam museev i okhrany pamiatnikov iskusstva i stariny Narkomprosa RSFSR. Izmeneniia v sostave tsentral'nykh restavratsionnykh organizatsii v 1918–1934," *Grabarevskie chteniia* 5 (2002): 52–63.

41. Over the next five years, Lenin would sign thirty-two decrees dealing with the preservation of monuments and museum holdings. See V. I. Lenin, *O* *literature i iskusstve,* 4th ed. (Moscow: Khudozhestvennaia literatura, 1969).

42. Private, museum, and church collections were either evaluated on site or channeled into the new Fund, established under the 1918 decree, "O registratsii, prieme na uchet i okhrane pamiatnikov iskusstva i stariny." See S. I. Gorelova, "Muzeinyi fond v pervye gody sovetskoi vlasti (1917–1925)," *Khudozhestvennoe Nasledie* 13 (1990): 203–16. Sometimes Fund icons were pawned, used to pay workers, sold to antique dealers, or even burned. See I. Kyzlasova, "History of the Collections of Greek Icons in Moscow," in *Post-Byzantine Painting: Icons of the 15th–18th Centuries,* ed. L. M. Evseeva (Athens: Domos, 1995), 30.

43. G. I. Vzdornov, "Komissiia po sokhraneniiu i raskrytiiu pamiatnikov drevnei zhivopisi v Rossii 1918–1924," *Sovetskoe iskusstvoznanie,* no. 2 (1980): 306–30. See also M. Roslavskii, "Problema vozrozhdeniia otechestvennoi restavratsii v deiatel'nosti Komissii po sokhraneniiu i raskrytiiu pamiatnikov drevnerusskoi zhivopisi. 1918," *Grabarevskie chteniia* 5 (2002): 40–51.

44. S. I. Gorelova, "Iz istorii restavratsii v SSSR (1918–1923)," *Khudozhestvennoe nasledie* 3 (1977): 193.

45. A. N. Krylova, "I. E. Grabar' i okhrana pamiatnikov. Chetyre etapa ego zhizni: svobodnyi chelovek, svobodnyi khudozhnik, obshchestvennyi deiatel', gosudarstvennyi sluzhashchii," *Grabarevskie chteniia* 5 (2002): 10–19.

46. Included were *ikonniki* Evgeny Briagin and Alexei and Alexander Tiulin and the scholars Pavel Muratov, Alexei Grishchenko, Vasily Georgievsky, Nikolai Shchekotov, and Nikolai Protasov.

47. G. I. Vzdornov, "Neizdannaia stat'ia A. I. Anisimova o G. O. Chirikove," *Voprosy iskusstvoznaniia,* no. 1 (1994): 408. Anisimov wrote the article in 1923 to mark Chirikov's twenty-five years as an icon specialist.

48. Quoted in Kyzlasova, *Anisimov,* 62.

49. Ibid., 26.

50. After Grabar's death in 1960, V. N. Lazarev wrote, "Almost always [Grabar's] personal interests [regarding artistic-cultural issues] coincided with those of the state. Therefore, when he undertook some enterprise and carried it out with inspiration, the state always benefited greatly from it." "Igor' Emmanuilovich Grabar': Nekrolog," *Vestnik mirovoi kul'tury* 4 (1960): 157.

51. Evgraf Konchin, "'Rzhavyi kliuch' Aleksandra Anisimova," *Sovetskaia kul'tura,* 29 June 1989, 6.

52. Anisimov described Grabar as a "charlatan," "a dog in the manger," and "a Khlestiakov of science." Quoted in *Anisimov,* 26, 29, 43. In contrast, the director claimed to have "never witnessed any squabbles, friction, or even simple unfriendliness" in the TsGRM's "work collective, where all specialists focused upon friendly execution of work with genuine enthusiasm." I. E. Grabar', *Moia zhizn'* (Moscow: Iskusstvo, 1937), 282.

53. Some colleagues criticized Anisimov for concentrating exclusively on discovering and cleaning a few ancient icons while dozens of others remained at risk on church property. Vzdornov, "Komissiia," 315. Countess Praskovia Uvarova organized nine All-Russian Archeological Congresses, including those in Novgorod and Pskov, where she and Anisimov clashed seriously. After emigrating, she wrote to Kondakov on 8 June 1921 complaining that, while Anisimov might reveal a few precious icons, his impulsiveness was liable to damage many more. Vzdornov, *Istoriia,* 108.

54. Anisimov, "Raskrytie," 94–96.

55. N. A. Okolovich, *Otchet Gosudarstvennogo Russkogo Muzeia, 1923–1925* (Leningrad, 1925), 19.

56. The first central workshop was located in the Holy Synod's former Kremlin office until 1921, when the commission moved across the river to the Moscow Archeological Society's former headquarters in the seventeenth-century house of Averky Kirillov. Vzdornov, "Komissiia," 395n. On the Petrograd workshop, see S. I. Gorelova, "Istoriia restavratsionnykh masterskikh Gosudarstvennogo Russkogo Muzeia, 1917–1941," *Khudozhestvennoe nasledie* 5 (1979): 139–82. Conflict between Petrograd and Moscow specialists over control of the Novgorod workshop forced Anisimov to close it only two months after he opened it in January 1919. On this conflict, see Vzdornov, "Komissiia," 314; Anisimov, "Raskrytie," 92; N. G.

Porfirov, "Pis'mo iz Novgoroda," *Dela i dni,* vol. 1 (Petrograd, 1920), 253–54. On the Vladimir and Yaroslavl workshops, see Anisimov, "Raskrytie," 88–89; Anisimov, "Dokladnaia zapiska o restavratsionnykh rabotakh vo Vladimire i Bogoliubove v 1918 gody," *Ferapontovskii sbornik* VII (Moscow: Indrik, 2006): 301–3. On the Vologda workshop, see G. I. Vzdornov, *Iz istorii restavratsii drevnerusskoi zhivopisi. Perepiska I. V. Fedyshina (1924–1936)* (Moscow: Vsesoiuznaia tsentral'naia nauchno-issledovatel'skaia laboratoriia po konservatsii i restavratsii muzeinykh khudozhestvennykh tsennostei, 1975), 4. On the Trinity Lavra of Saint Sergius workshop, see Anisimov, "Raskrytie," 90; Vzdornov, "Komissiia," 310–11; Mikhail Gusev, *Revoliutsiia i tserkvi,* nos. 3–4 (1920): 74–76. On the Pskov workshop, see Anisimov, "Raboty po raskrytiiu pamiatnikov zhivopisi drevnego Pskova," written in 1930 and first published in *O drevnerusskom iskusstve,* 357–64.

57. For the craft and significance of icon fittings, see Wendy R. Salmond, "The Art of the Oklad," *The Post, Hillwood Museum* 3 (1996): 5–15.

58. The institute was founded in 1920 as an independent scientific-research institution under the oversight of the Russian Academy of the History of Material Culture. *Khudozhestvennaia zhizn'* 2 (1920): 11–12; Vzdornov, "Anisimov," 306. See I. L. Kyzlasova, "O Moskovskom institute istoriko-khudozhestvennykh izyskanii i muzeevedeniia (1920-nachalo 1921 g.)," *Zabelinskie nauchnye chteniia. Istoricheskii Muzei-Entsiklopediia Otechestvennoi Istorii i Kul'tury (2000)* (Moscow: Gosudarstvennyi istoricheskii muzei, 2001), 518–35.

59. On Anisimov's positions at VKhUTEMAS and Yaroslavl University, see Vzdornov, "Anisimov," 307, 314. In 1923, Anisimov complained to Kondakov that it was "real moral torture" to deal with unprepared students in Moscow State University's "polluted, cluttered, and neglected" atmosphere. Quoted in Kyzlasova, *Anisimov,* 23.

60. Anisimov explains the project in "Vyiasnenie poniatii o priamoi i kosvennoi datakh," written in 1920 but first published in Anisimov, *O drevnerusskom iskusstve,* 134–41.

61. Vzdornov, "Anisimov," 302.

62. Anisimov mentions this discovery in "Raskrytie," 89.

63. Vzdornov, ed., *O drevnerusskom iskusstve,* 441n25; Anisimov, "Domongol'skii period drevnerusskoi zhivopisi," in *O drevnerusskom iskusstve,* 334–35.

64. Anisimov reported on his work there in 1920 in "Pis'mo iz Iaroslavlia," *Khudozhestvennaia zhizn',* no. 1 (January–February 1920): 16–17.

65. V. V. Igoshev, "Uchastie A. I. Anisimova v iaroslavskoi komissii po iz"iatiiu tserkovnykh tsennostei," *Khudozhestvennoe nasledie* 16 (1995): 90–95.

66. Anisimov, "Doklad uchenogo eksperta otdela muzeev Glavnauk Narkomprosa RSFSR A. I. Anisimova vo Vserossiiskuiu restavratsionnuiu komissiiu," *Iaroslavskii arkhiv: istoriko-kraevedcheskii sbornik* (Moscow and St. Peterburg: Atheneum-Feniks, 1996), 242–47.

67. Anisimov, *Restavratsiia drevnei russkoi zhivopisi v Iaroslavle* (Moscow: TsGRM, 1926).

68. Vzdornov, *O drevnerusskom iskusstve,* 445n3.

69. "Raboty po raskrytiiu pamiatnikov ikonopisi drevnego Pskova," first published in Anisimov, *O drevnerusskom iskusstve,* 356–64.

70. N. I. Trotskaia, "Muzeinoe stroitel'stvo i revoliutsiia," *Nauka i iskusstvo,* no. 1 (1926): 46.

71. Vzdornov, "'Byt' zdes' tiazhelyi krest . . .': Iz perepiski A. I. Anisimova i V. T. Georgievskogo s I. E. Grabarem (1918–1919)," *Pamiatniki otechestva* 30 (1993): 92.

72. Quoted in Evgraf Konchin, "'Rzhavyi kliuch,'" 6. Anisimov was also arrested in Ekaterinburg in 1921 but was freed before serving his sentence of six months' forced labor.

73. First published in Kyzlasova, *Anisimov,* 3.

74. In 1905, V. P. Gurianov removed the thick, sticky darkened layer of varnish and touched up several areas of the icon. In 1918, Chirikov cleaned the faces, and V. A. Tiulin and I. I. Suslov uncovered the rest of the image. See V. I. Antonovna, *Gos. Tret'iakovskaia Galereia, Katalog drevnerusskoi zhivopisi XI-nachala XVIII vv.,* vol. 1 (Moscow: Iskusstvo, 1963), 288.

75. Anisimov, "Nauchnaia restavratsiia i rublevskii vopros," in *O drevnerusskom iskusstve,* 105–34. See also Robert Bird's chapter in this volume for a discussion of this icon's significance for film director Andrei Tarkovsky.

76. G. Zhidkov, "Dva doklada A. I. Anisimova," *Sredi kollektsionerov,* no. 9 (1922): 65–67. Anisimov, "Istoriia Vladimirskoi ikony v svete restavratsii," *Institut arkheologii i iskusstvoznaniia. Trudy sektsii iskusstvoznaniia* 2 (Moscow, 1928): 93–107. Citations for the second lecture refer to the reprint in *Bogomater' Vladimirskaia: k 600-letiiu Sreteniia ikony Bogomateri Vladimirskoi v Moskve 25 avgusta (8 sentiabria) 1395. Sbornik/katalog,* ed. E. K. Guseva et al. (Moscow: Avangard, 1995), 67–75.

77. This approximate date is based upon the Hypatian and Laurentian Chronicles. See Anisimov, "Vladimirskaia ikona Bozhiei Materi," in *Bogomater' Vladimirskaia,* 44.

78. Anisimov, "Raskrytie," 94.

79. Anisimov, "Istoriia," 69.

80. Ibid., 70.

81. Ibid.

82. Every step of the revelation was recorded in a daily diary. See "Dnevnik rabot po raskrytiiu ikony Vladimirskoi Bogomateri," in *Bogomater' Vladimirskaia,* 26–39.

83. Anisimov, "Istoriia," 73. Anisimov wrote to Kondakov that the icon was painted no later than "the very beginning of the twelfth century," however. Kyzlasova, *Anisimov,* 30. In 1925, V. N. Lazarev and M. V. Alpatov dated the panel to the mid-twelfth century. "Ein byzantinisches Tafelwerk aus der Komnenenepoche," *Jahrbuch der preussishchen Kunstsammlungen* 46 (1925): 140–55. This later date is commonly accepted now.

84. He named nineteenth-century scholars I. M. Snegirev and I. P. Sakharov as propagators of that legend and specifically scolded Alexander Uspensky for passing it along on the basis of Gurianov's tracings. Anisimov, "Istoriia," 67–68.

85. Ibid., 69. Anisimov mentions in the published lecture that Kondakov had written him from Prague, expressing interest in his analysis of the Vladimir Mother of God. See letter, 8 August 1923, quoted in Kyzlasova, *Anisimov,* 32.

86. Anisimov's 20 May lecture was critiqued four months later by the St. Petersburg contingent of icon specialists, who continued to voice their rivalry with their Moscow colleagues at a meeting of the Russian Academy of the History of Material Culture in Petrograd. Among other objections, Nikolai Likhachev argued that there was no proof that the Vladimir Mother of God had been saved from the 1237 Mongol looting and fire in Vladimir's Dormition Cathedral. Thus the current image could well be a copy made at that time. Iu. A. Piatnitskii, "Doklad N. P. Likhacheva 'Ob ikone Vladimirskoi Bozhiei Materi,'" *Vspomogatel'nye istoricheskie distsipliny* 26 (1998): 65.

87. Georgievskii to Kondakov, 15 February 1923, in Vzdornov, *Istoriia,* 191.

88. Vzdornov, "Anisimov," 308–9.

89. Kyzlasova, *Anisimov,* 30–31.

90. Ibid., 36. He used this channel for other correspondence as well.

91. Beliaev, "Vystavka russkikh ikon," *Sbornik statei po arkheologii i vizantinovedeniiu,* vol. 3 (Prague: Seminarium Kondakovianum, 1929), 309.

92. Anisimov, *Vladimirskaia ikona Bozhiei Materi,* and *Our Lady of Vladimir,* trans. N. G. Yaschwill and T. N. Rodzianko (Prague: Seminarium Kondakovianum, 1928). The Russian version appears in Anisimov, *Bogomater' Vladimirskaia,* 40–66.

93. Anisimov, *Our Lady,* 29.

94. For example, see P. P. Muratov, "Russkaia zhivopis' do serediny XVII veka," in *Do-Petrovskaia epokha,* vol. 1 of *Istoriia russkogo zhivopisi,* ed. Igor' Grabar' (Moscow: I. Knebel', 1914), 5–450.

95. Kyzlasova, *Anisimov,* 23–24.

96. "Domongol'skii period drevnerusskoi zhivopisi," in *Voprosi restavratsii,* vol. 2 (Moscow: TsGRM, 1928), 102–82. Citations refer to the reprint in Anisimov, *O drevnerusskom iskusstve,* 275–350.

97. Anisimov, "Domongol'skii," 347.

98. Nikolai Levinson, quoted in Kyzlasova, *Anisimov,* 78.

99. A. N. Kheturov, "Istoriia sozdaniia i razvitiia otdela nauchnoi restavratsii G.I.M.," *Restavratsiia muzeinykh tsennostei: Trudy Gosudarstvennogo Istoricheskogo Muzeia,* no. 107 (1999): 127. See also I. L.

Kyzlasova, "Iz istorii otdela drevnerusskoi zhivopisi: A. I. Anisimov i O. N. Bubnova," *Trudy Gosudarstvennogo Istoricheskogo Muzeia* 107 (2004): 244–51.

100. Kyzlsova, *Anisimov,* 65.

101. I. L. Kyzlasova, *Russkaia ikona XIV–XVI vekov. Gosudarstvennyi Istoricheskii Muzei* (Leningrad: Avrora, 1988), 7–8.

102. Anisimov, *Putevoditel' po vystavke pamiatnikov drevnerusskoi ikonopisi* (Moscow: Krasnyi Proletarii, 1926), 9.

103. Later scholars would blame the militants for their "nihilistic tendencies." See S. I. Gorelova, "Istoriia restavratsionnykh masterskikh," 139; D. A. Ravikovich, "Okhrana pamiatnikov istorii i kul'tury v RSFSR (1917–1967)," *Trudy nauchno-issledovatel'skogo instituta museevedeniia i okhrany pamiatnikov istorii i kul'tury* 22 (1970): 65; and V. N. Lazarev, "Introduction," in K. Kornilovich, *Okno v minuvshee* (Leningrad: Iskusstvo, 1968), 3.

104. Quoted and translated by Richard Stites, "Iconoclastic Currents in the Russian Revolution: Destroying and Preserving the Past," in *Bolshevik Culture,* ed. Abbot Gleason, Peter Kenez, and Richard Stites (Bloomington: Indiana University Press, 1985), 17.

105. See Sheila Fitzpatrick, "Cultural Revolution as Class War," in *Cultural Revolution in Russia, 1928–1931,* ed. Sheila Fitzpatrick (Bloomington: Indiana University Press, Midland Book Edition, 1984), 8–40.

106. Grabar', "Restavratsiia u nas i na Zapade," *Nauka i iskusstvo,* no. 1 (Moscow: TsGRM, 1926): 92.

107. Letter to Georgii Vernadskii in Prague, 12 December 1926, in *Igor' E. Grabar': Pis'ma 1917–1941,* ed. T. P. Kazhdan (Moscow: Nauka, 1977), 158–59.

108. See Wendy Salmond's chapter in this volume.

109. Architectural historian Pyotr Baranovsky wrote to Fedyshin, a curator of the Vologda Museum, about the Moscow rumor that Gostorg was more interested in selling Russian art abroad than elevating its international status. *Perepiska,* 85. Fedyshin unsuccessfully attempted to hide three fifteenth-century icons from Gostorg agents when they came for them. *Perepiska I. V. Fedyshina,* 101, 105.

110. On 1 July 1929, Anisimov wrote to Fedyshin asking whether he might want to free up space in the Vologda museum's icon inventory by selling "redundant" icons to Gostorg. *Perepiska I. V. Fedyshina,* 88–89.

111. Letter to Beliaev, quoted in Kyzlasova, *Anisimov,* 53.

112. Quoted in Dmitry S. Likhachev, *Reflections on the Russian Soul* (New York: Central European University Press, 1999), 126.

113. Anisimov's articles include "Les anciennes icônes et leur contribution à l'histoire de la peinture russe," in *Fondation E. Piot. Monuments et mémoires publiés par l'Académie des Inscriptions et Belles-Lettres,* vol. 30 (Paris, 1929), 155–65; "Die altrussisches Ikonenmalerei (Anlässlich der Austellung von Denkmälern altrussischer Malerei)," *Ost-Europa* 4 (April–May 1929): 445–40; "L'exposition des anciennes icônes russes, *Gazette des Beaux-Arts, Chroniques des Arts et de la Curiosité* (February 1930): 11; "La peinture russe du XVI siècle (Théophane le Grec)," *Gazette des Beaux-Arts* (March 1930): 18–177; "La peinture d'icônes en Russie," *Formes* 4 (1930): 11–14.

114. Anisimov, "Russian Icon-Painting: Its Bloom, Over-Refinement and Decay," in *Masterpieces of Russian Painting,* ed. Michael Farbman (London: Europa, 1930), 61–91.

115. Martin Conway, "The History of Russian Icon-Painting," in *Masterpieces of Russian Painting,* ed. Michael Farbman, 18.

116. Letter to Beliaev, 31 May 1928, in Kyzlasova, *Anisimov,* 44.

117. "Souchastie prof. A. I. Anisimova v emigrantskom zhurnale," *Izvestiia,* 7 December 1928, 6.

118. Ibid.

119. Quoted in Kyzlasova, *Anisimov,* 78–79.

120. For details surrounding his arrest, see Kyzlasova, *Anisimov,* 48–52, 67.

121. Ibid., 33, 48, 52.

122. Ibid., 52.

123. Konchin, "'Rzhavyi kliuch,'" 6.

124. The complete poem was first published in Kyzlasova, *Anisimov,* 81–84.

125. Anisimov, "Triptykh papy Pavla III," in *O drevnerusskom iskusstve,* 365–80.

126. Kyzlasova, *Anisimov,* 68.

127. "Vypiska iz protokola zasedaniia Komissii po chistke apparata Tsentral'nykh gosudarstvennykh restavratsionnykh masterskikh 9 aprelia 1931," quoted in Vzdornov, *Istoriia,* 353.

128. Kyzlasova, *Anisimov,* 73.

129. For a full account of these events, see Vzdornov, *Istoriia,* 291–374.

130. Gorelova, "Restavratsionnoe delo v Gosudarstvennoi Tret'iakovskoi galerii: 1934–1944," *Khudozhestvennoe nasledie* 1 (1975): 6; I. A. Kochetov, "Drevnie kopii ikony Bogomater' Vladimirskaia," *Drevniaia Rus',* no. 3 (2003): 49.

131. Grabar left the TsGRM in 1930 to accompany the traveling exhibition before retiring. Grabar', *Moia zhizn',* 280.

132. His written reports, excerpts from his interrogations, and his OGPU records were first published in Kyzlasova, *Anisimov,* 57–79, and Vzdornov, *Istoriia,* 324–44.

133. They included art historians Fanina Halle in Austria, Martin Winkler in Germany, and Thomas Whittemore in the United States, in addition to the German journalist Franz Schiffer and Léon Kiffer, the French trade attaché in Moscow.

134. Konchin, "'Rzhavyi kliuch.'"

135. All quotations in Kyzlasova, *Anisimov,* 62, 63, 70, 74.

136. Ibid., 75.

137. Ibid., 76–77. At the request of Narkompros, the OGPU confiscated his first-rate collection of icons and ecclesiastical textiles, along with his library. An inventory taken on 20 October 1930 listed eighty-nine Russian, Greek, and Italian icons, leaves of Holy Doors, a statue of Saint Nicholas, and liturgical embroidery. His collection of textiles was transferred to the State Historical Museum and the Kremlin Armory. In December 2007, Irina Kyzlasova informed me that more than one hundred of Anisimov's icons are in the Tretiakov Gallery's collection.

138. Likhachev, *Reflections,* 125–27.

139. Ibid., 126.

140. "UFSB po Respublike Kareliia. Sledstvennoe delo A. I. Anisimova. P-133792, sheets 1–6," in Kyzlasova, *Anisimov,* 79–80.

141. Ibid., 80.

142. "Postanovlenie Troiki NKVD Karel'skoi ASSR ot 26 avgusta s.g. na Z/k Anisimova Aleksandra Ivanovicha, 1877 goda rozhdeniia privedeno v ispolnenie 2 sentiabria 1937 goda v 23 chasa 30 minut," in Kyzlasova, *Anisimov,* 79, 80.

143. Kyzlasova argues that it was impossible to establish an objective evaluation of the roles of Kondakov, Georgievsky, and Anisimov "under the conditions of the decades-long predominance of the cult of Grabar in historiography." Kyzlasova, *Anisimov,* 17.

144. Letter to Kondakov, 21 August 1923, quoted in Kyzlasova, *Anisimov,* 29.

JOHN-PAUL HIMKA

5

MOMENTS IN THE HISTORY OF AN ICON COLLECTION

THE NATIONAL MUSEUM IN LVIV, 1905–2005

This chapter surveys the history of an important icon collection in a historically disturbed part of Eastern Europe over the course of the last hundred years. It differs from most of the other contributions in this volume in that it deals with Russia only obliquely. Lviv (also known as Lemberg or Lwów) was the capital city of the Austrian crownland of Galicia. Before Austria took it in 1772, it had belonged to the Polish-Lithuanian Commonwealth. The city was founded by the Rus Prince Danylo of Galicia-Volhynia in the mid-thirteenth century. Lviv was never under Russian rule except for a brief period of occupation during World War I. After the war, Ukrainians and Poles fought over it, and the Poles won. Lviv remained a part of Poland from 1918 until 1939, when the Red Army took it, as agreed upon in the secret protocols to the Nazi-Soviet Non-Aggression Pact. In 1940, it was formally incorporated into the Ukrainian Soviet Socialist Republic. Nazi Germany turned on its former ally in 1941 and occupied Lviv until 1944, when the Soviets took it back. In 1991, Ukraine declared independence from the Soviet Union, and Lviv became part of the independent Ukrainian state.

The Carpathian mountain region south of Lviv had an exceptionally vibrant and distinctive tradition of icon painting, remnants of which still survive today. The Eastern Christians of both Lviv and the

I wish to thank the Ukrainian Studies Fund for paying for my travel to participate in the conference "The Icon and Modernity" and the Social Sciences and Humanities Research Council of Canada for supporting the research on which this article is based. I also would like to thank Robert Klymasz, who read an earlier draft, made valuable suggestions, and provided me with additional sources.

Carpathian region were Orthodox in religion until about 1700, when they accepted union with the Catholic Church, while retaining their own rituals and sacral culture. Since 1774, the former Orthodox of this region (and Transylvania) have been known as Greek Catholics. Most of the icons in the collection of the National Museum in Lviv derive from this Carpathian tradition. Icons began to be painted in monasteries in the mountain localities in the fourteenth and fifteenth centuries. These icons were informed by the general Byzantine and post-Byzantine tradition, but particularly important in their development were the iconographies elaborated in Novgorod and Pskov and, to a lesser extent, in Moldavia. Since the Carpathian region constituted the westernmost extension of the East Slavic Rus settlement, its iconography was early influenced by Gothic and other Western art. Over time, fewer monks and increasing numbers of craftsmen engaged in the painting of icons, with the mid-seventeenth century constituting the caesura between a more monastic and a more popular phase. Although North Rus influences were strong in the fifteenth century, the icons of the Carpathians lost touch with the Russian tradition thereafter. If icons have a nationality, then the icons in the National Museum in Lviv are not Russian icons, but Ukrainian icons.[1] The Lviv collection is the single largest repository of the products of the Carpathian iconographic tradition.

The icons in the Lviv collection were painted in an environment of animal husbandry, monasteries, Tatar raids, and serfdom. They were collected in an era of trains, nationalism, and Communism. They were produced in small wooden monasteries and in small towns in the foothills. They were collected in what was for this part of Europe a big city. Lviv's population was almost 130,000 in 1910 and is nearly 800,000 today. The vicissitudes of Lviv's recent history and the impact of new attitudes on the National Museum's icon collection reflect the interplay of art and nation in modernity.

HALCYON DAYS UNDER EMPEROR FRANZ JOSEPH, 1905–1914

The origins of the National Museum lie in the twilight years of Austria-Hungary. The museum's founder was the Greek Catholic metropolitan of Halych and archbishop of Lviv, Andrei Sheptytsky. Metropolitan Andrei had been born into an aristocratic Roman Catholic, Polish family but returned to the Greek Catholic Church of his ancestors and adopted the Ukrainian nationality; or, as they said in the early twentieth century, the Ruthenian nationality. As a scion of the upper elite, he had toured Western Europe and studied its art firsthand. He had a finely educated aesthetic sense,[2] a love of the visual arts, and great wealth. As head of the Greek Catholic Church from 1900 until his death in 1944, he was a magnanimous patron of the arts, sacral and secular.[3] His most generous donation was the National Museum with its rich collection of icons.

Sheptytsky began to purchase old icons long before the museum came into existence. As a novice at the Basilian monastery in Dobromyl in 1888, he had frequently visited the nearby village of Poliana, where the wooden church contained magnificent icons from the fifteenth and sixteenth centuries. Years later, however, he took some novices to the church to show them the icons and was horrified to discover that the villagers were about to burn them. They had built a new brick church, and they were knocking down the old one and disposing of its icons in the prescribed manner. In fact, the destruction of old icons in this region was immense at the end of the nineteenth century. The Ruthenian national movement had been urging the peasants to build new churches out of brick and stone to replace their wooden structures and to adorn them with new images painted by professionally trained artists. In the case of Poliana, however, Sheptytsky bought some of the icons and saved them. These were later to form the nucleus of the National Museum's collection.[4] Today icons from this purchase are on permanent display: the Raising of Lazarus (fig. 8), the Entry into Jerusalem, the Descent into Hades (pl. 3), and the Descent of the Holy Spirit, all from the sixteenth century. In his memoirs, which recount the incidents in Poliana, the metropolitan cannot remember exactly when he made his purchase, but suspects it was while he was bishop of Stanyslaviv, that is, in 1899–1900.

At the time Sheptytsky bought these icons, they were little understood and little appreciated. In his memoirs, he recalls his first trip to Kyiv in 1886 or 1887. He had visited the museum of the Spiritual Academy, which possessed "a beautiful, though not very large" collection of icons. The custos of the museum, Nikolai Petrov, a historian of great erudition, said to him: "No one knows if there are any differences among these icons, or styles, or features of a certain school, because no one so far has done any research on them." As Sheptytsky recalled, until the 1890s the dominant idea was that art had to be realistic, so it was difficult to appreciate the old icons.[5]

The art historian Mykhailo Dragan, who helped build the National Museum's collection, complained that, with very few exceptions, priests had no appreciation whatsoever for the icons. They treated them as scrap: they were stored in the bell tower, burned for fuel, or nailed to the outside of the church; they were used to make a tetrapod or closet or to patch broken windows and holes.[6] The director of the museum noted that old icons were also used to make altars and bell-tower steps.[7] Of course, the profanation of centuries-old icons as building material preserved them for posterity, while the pious act of burning them did not. Art historians, at least, can be grateful for the sacrilege.

Metropolitan Andrei's approach to the icons was primarily aesthetic rather than spiritual. He understood them as, in the first place, works of art. His memoirs open with a scene from Merezhkovsky's historical novel *Leonardo da Vinci* (1902), in which the artist visits the workshop of an icon painter in Rome who came as part of a Muscovite legation to the pope. Leonardo examines the icon with intense curiosity but, it seems, without the slightest recognition that the icon was an object of the same art of which he himself was a master. In the metropolitan's view, Merezhkovsky erred here: Leonardo was too sensitive an artist not to have appreciated the artistic quality of icons.

For this cultivated twentieth-century bishop, the aesthetic emotions produced by icons perhaps even accounted for why they were often considered miraculous:

> In general the icon was considered rather a genre of applied art, something like an Easter egg [*pysanka*], of interest perhaps, of value perhaps, but not an image, not a picture. I think, though, that not only I, but everyone else, has felt and feels some enchantment in all these works of the hieratic arts of the East. In my opinion, they work on human nature in such a way that sometimes instantaneously physical tremors of emotion run through a person from head to foot upon looking at a work of art, an icon. At such times someone might even ascribe to the old icon a wonder-working or even magical power. In fact these mysterious bodily

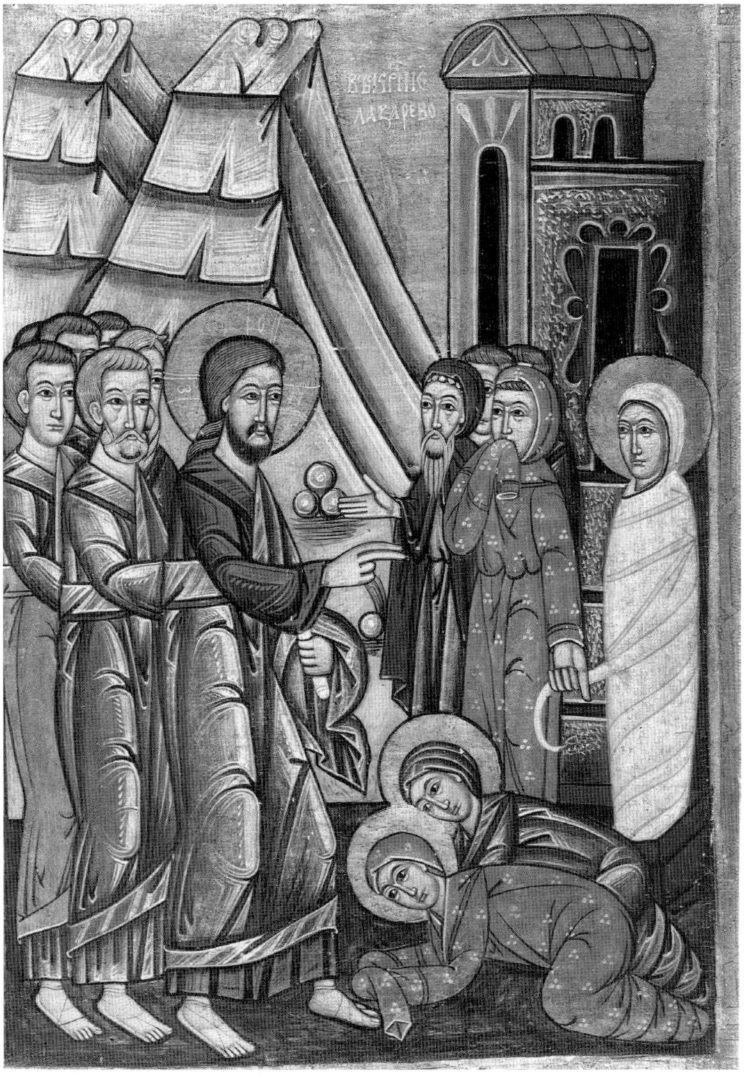

FIG. 8 Raising of Lazarus, Poliana, sixteenth century. Reproduced from Hryhorii Lohvyn, Lada Miliaieva, and Vira Svientsits'ka, eds., *Ukrains'kyi seredn'ovichnyi zhyvopys* (Kiev: Mystetstvo, 1976), LXXXVI.

> tremors, this physical emotion of the organism, is probably the result of a natural reaction to beauty, which unconsciously envelops the person.

These emotions are similar to love, he continues, and this love in the heart makes it difficult, or even impossible, to become a disinterested expert on icons.[8]

As the metropolitan's collection grew, he decided to use it as the basis for establishing a museum. It was formally initiated on 23 February 1905 and was originally named the Church Museum.[9] The metropolitan made an inspired choice of director in the young Ilarion Svientsitsky, who had studied in Lviv, St. Petersburg, and Vienna. The premises of the museum at first were a converted five-room carriage house within the complex of the metropolitan residence.[10] In 1907, the metropolitan bought another building for the museum from the Polish artist Jan Styka,[11] and in July 1911 he bought a two-story building, which remains in the museum's possession to this day (42 Drahomanov St.). During the first decade of the museum's existence, the metropolitan donated a small fortune in money (350,000 crowns) as well as 3,400 of the 16,500 items then in its collection.[12] In the year of its founding, 1905, the museum initiated systematic expeditions to the Ukrainian countryside to acquire icons.[13]

In July–August 1911, the museum was renamed the National Museum. At this point, the museum was still involved exclusively in collecting, not exhibiting, but as of 13 December 1913 it was opened to the public.[15] In connection with this, in 1913 Svientsitsky published the first guidebook, with photos of some of the displays.[16] Among the visitors to the museum in 1914 was the British historian Robert Seton-Watson.[17]

ICON ACQUISITIONS, 1905–1919

Year(s)	Number of Icons Acquired
1905–07	445
1908	282
1909	544
1910	68
1911	130
1912	185
1913	190
1914	127
1915–17	4
1918	197
1919	4
Total	2,176

Source: Ilarion Svientsits'kyi, *Pro muzei ta muzeinytstvo (narysy i zamitky)* (Lviv: Z drukarni "Dila," 1920), 76–77.[14]

Behind the scenes, work had begun on the restoration of the icons in the museum's collection. The most prominent artist hired for this purpose was Mykhailo Boichuk, who worked for the museum in 1913–14.[18] Boichuk, who had studied in Kraków, Munich, Vienna, and Paris, resided mainly in Kyiv after the war broke out and later went on to become one of the key figures in twentieth-century Ukrainian art as the leader of the Monumentalists in the Ukrainian Soviet Socialist Republic. The aesthetic program of his movement made much use of the old Ukrainian icons he knew so well. His story does not have a happy ending. Boichuk was arrested in the mid-1930s as an "agent of the Vatican" and shot; his paintings and frescoes were systematically destroyed.[19]

The first years of the National Museum's existence, before the eruption of World War I, were peaceful, a time of systematic accumulation and development. Only one incident marred this idyll. On 12 April 1908, a Ukrainian student, Myroslav Sichynsky, shot dead the viceroy of Galicia, the Polish count Andrzej Potocki. The Poles of Lviv, who at this time constituted the majority of the city's inhabitants, were enraged. On the day after the assassination, an angry mob marched through the city vandalizing Ukrainian institutions, and a few windows in the National Museum were broken as a result.[20]

WAR AND RUSSIAN OCCUPATION, 1914–1918

Not long after World War I broke out, Russian forces occupied Lviv. The Russian administration combated the Ukrainian movement, and this had repercussions for the National Museum. Its founder, Sheptytsky, was arrested on 19 September 1914 and exiled to the interior of Russia. He was unable to return to Lviv until 10 September 1917.[21] The museum's director, Svientsitsky, was arrested on 17 February 1915, released on 14 March, then exiled to Kyiv in June. He was unable to return to Lviv until 28 March 1918. With both the founder and director absent, the museum was endangered. Fortunately, a number of individuals rallied to protect it, with a particularly prominent role being played by Anna Pavlyk, once a famous radical activist. They formed a curatorium in June 1915. While in exile, Svientsitsky corresponded with the curatorium about how to preserve the museum. At one point he urged them to collect antiquities because lately Jews had been buying them up.[22]

The war years did bring some good fortune to the museum, however. The church in Bohorodchany, which possessed a splendid baroque iconostasis painted by Yov Kondzelevych and originally installed in the Maniava Skete, burned down in 1916 as a result of artillery fire. However, the Austrians were able to save the iconostasis and ship it for safekeeping to Vienna. Later it was transferred to the National Museum in Lviv, a very significant acquisition (pl. 4).[23]

Among the visitors to the museum in 1915 was the Russian liberal Pyotr Struve.[24]

A UKRAINIAN MUSEUM IN POLAND, 1918–1939

With the collapse of Austria-Hungary and the denouement of the war, Poles and Ukrainians clashed over Galicia. On 1 November 1918, the Ukrainians declared Galicia to be part of the West Ukrainian National Republic, with its capital in Lviv. Since the Poles were still numerically dominant in the city, however, they managed to expel the Ukrainians after a few weeks. The war continued in the rest of Galicia until June 1919, when the Ukrainian Galician Army was defeated.

During the course of hostilities, on 23 November 1918, the museum building was badly damaged by artillery fire, but Ukrainians in the United States sent money for repairs.[25] Also during the Polish-Ukrainian War, the museum was searched eight times for weapons. The intrusion of armed, angry soldiers into the museum exposed the staff and the director's family to serious peril.

Although the director was still occasionally harassed in the mid-1920s, the interwar period saw the return of systematic work in the museum.[26] In fact, from time to time the Polish government allotted funds to the museum.[27]

It was at this time that collection analysis and icon scholarship took a few steps forward. The two most important publications of those years were both the work of Svientsitsky: a book titled *The Iconography of Galician Ukraine in the Fifteenth and Sixteenth Centuries*[28] and an album of photographs of icons in the museum's collection (in black and white, of course).[29] The 1928 monograph on iconography remains the best piece of icon scholarship to come out of the museum. Five issues of a museum yearbook also appeared (1934–38).

The restoration of icons continued. An experienced restorer from Kyiv, Volodymyr Peshchansky, was hired by the museum in 1922–26. A talented local painter, Yaroslava Muzyka, began restoring icons in 1926;[30] she spent the spring and summer of 1928 improving her knowledge of restoration in Kyiv, Moscow, Leningrad, and Novgorod.[31] Visitors to the museum in 1928 included the Soviet consul in Lviv, Yury Lapchynsky, and the Ukrainian opera diva Salomea Krusceniski.[32]

Some insight into the mood and attitudes at the museum can be gleaned from an article that appeared in the 1938 issue of its yearbook. It showed how impressed foreign visitors were with the icon collection. A couple from Oxford was fascinated by the icons because of the "unique beauty of the rhythm of their draftsmanship and color." A performer from New York studied the costume and gestures in the icons in preparation for singing the folk songs of various nations. A few years previously the chief conservator of France and his wife, accompanied by the conservator of Lviv palatinate (*województwo*), visited the collection. The Frenchman declared that "he had discovered a great world of original beauty unknown to him before." In 1937, two Parisian artists spent several days with the icons sketching "the treasures of the living source of truly great art." The author of the article concluded from these examples: "Foreign experts on world art teach us to value the monuments and works of the Galician land at the same level as the artistic works of Western Europe."[33]

WORLD WAR II, 1939–1945

On 1 September 1939, Nazi Germany invaded Poland from the West. The initial panic of the Polish authorities resulted in trouble for the museum. The director's daughter, Vira Svientsitska, who was also on staff in the museum, was arrested by the Poles on the very day of the German attack. (In 1934–36, she had already spent a year and a half in prison for involvement with the Organization of Ukrainian Nationalists.)[34] That same night soldiers searched the museum, abducted its guard, and shot a dog. In the ensuing days, bombs shattered windows in the museum.

On 17 September, the Red Army invaded from the East, and Lviv was soon to become a part of Soviet Ukraine. The National Museum then ceased to be an independent entity, being merged with the newly formed Lviv Art Gallery. Svientsitsky resisted some of the new authorities' orders, such as to remove the statue of the museum's founder that stood in the square in front of the museum. Svientsitsky was therefore fired as director on 7 March 1941 and replaced soon thereafter by a certain A. Ch. Bakhmatov. Svientsitsky continued to work at the museum, however. Although the Communists were redesigning the museum to emphasize realism, the icon collection was not particularly threatened in these years. In fact, work began then on the restoration of the Bohorodchany iconostasis.

The German attack on the Soviet Union on 22 June 1941 resulted in Svientsitsky's reinstatement as director a week later. The museum continued to function under German rule,[35] visited by Germans and Ukrainians alike. The restoration of the Bohorodchany iconostasis continued, and the restoration of the Zhovkva iconostasis of Ivan Rutkovych began. Yaroslava Muzyka was again taking a leading part in this work. In the fall of 1943, as the Red Army advanced westward, some Ukrainians argued that the museum's collection should be evacuated west to save it from the Bolsheviks. Svientsitsky, however, opposed this, and his view prevailed.

Windows once more broke in the museum as Soviet bombs fell on Lviv on 9 April 1944. The Red Army returned in July, and on the 28th of that month Svientsitsky was reconfirmed by the Soviets as director. On 1 November 1944, the founder of the museum, Metropolitan Andrei Sheptytsky, "fell asleep in the Lord"—he was to be written out of the Soviet version of the museum's history in any case.[36] The National Museum was formally reopened in 1945 under a new name, the Lviv State Museum of Ukrainian Art (later the "State" was dropped). This time the museum was not merged with the Lviv Art Gallery.[37]

A SOVIET INSTITUTION, 1945–1991

Svientsitsky, who spoke his mind rather frankly, was to remain an intractable personality for the Soviets. For example, at a meeting in October 1945 with a Moscow representative of the All-Union Architecture Committee, he complained that wages for scholarly workers in Lviv were so low that they could not carry on with their work: "You eastern people are used to this kind of life, but we can't live this way. We know what scholarly work is and we want to have real compensation for it, enough so that we can continue to perform our work. We can't work naked and hungry and live in the little boxes that you live in."[38] Svientsitsky also kept on staff several members of the Organization of Ukrainian Nationalists, including his own daughter Vira and the restorer Yaroslava Muzyka, even though at this time a civil war still raged between the Soviet authorities and the armed nationalist underground. He also resisted taking on Communist Party and Komsomol members.[39] As a result, in 1947–50 the political police arrested a number of museum workers, including Vira Svientsitska, who was arrested on 3 November 1948 and did not return from the Gulag until August 1956.[40] The inevitable came on 25 November 1952, when Svientsitsky was replaced as director by Viacheslav Semiarchuk. Fortunately, Semiarchuk turned out to be a decent man, protective of the icons. Svientsitsky did not long survive his removal: he passed away on 18 September 1956 at the age of eighty.[41]

During this turbulent period, thousands of publications and works of art in the museum's collection were deliberately destroyed or stolen by the deputy director, Vasyl Liubchyk. In the main, the works affected were ideologically problematic, but not all of them, since a search revealed that Liubchyk had pilfered a Tiepolo and a number of rare books. He was prosecuted in 1957 but never punished.[42] Liubchyk did not take or harm any icons, but in early August 1952 a member of a Party commission advised the museum "to burn this church junk."[43]

In February 1953, the entire icon collection was moved across town to an Armenian cathedral, which the Soviet authorities had closed down. The move had been planned since at least April 1952. Although the cathedral was damp, it was better protected from the extremes of heat and cold than the museum building itself, and the entire icon collection was preserved intact.[44]

Vira Svientsitska returned from the camps to Lviv not long before her father's death. Director Semiarchuk hired her back, and she remained on staff until her own death on 21 May 1991.[45] During this time she was the most prolific scholar there. She put forward a view of the icons as folk productions that expressed the Ukrainian people's longing for national and social liberation. During the perestroika period, the patriotism in her interpretation of iconography grew even more pronounced. For example, in a 1990 book on the Lviv icon collection titled *The Heritage of the Ages,* she wrote: "By the masterpieces it created, the Ukrainian people testified to the greatness of its indomitable spirit, the high level of culture inherited from its ancestors, and the inexhaustible potential force of its creative genius."[46] She never seems to have thought about the icons as sacral art, and their theological significance did not figure in her writings, not even in those published in the early 1990s. In her book on Ivan Rutkovych, published in 1966, she wrote: "In the course of the seventeenth century, the icon gradually lost the meaning of a certain hieratic-mystical and abstract symbol, removed from life, and took on the characteristics of a realistic depiction filled with humanism." She liked Rutkovych because "he introduced into his religious compositions with traditional and new themes not only elements of portraiture, landscape, and scenes of daily life, but also social and patriotic motifs, thus enriching the means of artistic expression."[47] Her interpretation of icons suited the tastes of both Communists and nationalists.

In the Soviet Union and its successor states, there has been a long-standing conflict between museum workers and Christian believers. Our museum was also involved in this. It took advantage of Nikita Khrushchev's antireligious campaign in 1960 to lobby for state aid in preserving artifacts from congregations, generally by removing them from churches. The museum's petition was signed by the director at that time, Ivan Katrushenko, by the scholarly secretary Kh. Sanotska, and by Vira Svientsitska.

> It is well known that many valuable monuments of old Ukrainian art are located in cult buildings. It is not always possible to transfer them for

> preservation to the museum. Meanwhile the proprietors, concerned about "the splendor of the church," "restore" without supervision the painting and carving of prominent masters of the past, ruining beyond repair, almost before our eyes, original and very valuable works, often with dates and authorial signatures. . . . The Lviv State Museum of Ukrainian Art requests support in this endeavor and cooperation in taking measures to preserve particular monuments undamaged on site, or transfer them for permanent safekeeping to the museum.[48]

In the "times of stagnation" that followed Khrushchev, the museum soldiered along as a Soviet institution without much of note occurring. The situation changed when Gorbachev's glasnost and perestroika finally began to affect Ukraine in 1989, which was later than elsewhere in the Soviet Union. A sign of the times was that on 17 July 1990 the museum returned to its former name, the National Museum in Lviv.[49]

A NATIONAL MUSEUM IN INDEPENDENT UKRAINE, 1991–2005

On 24 August 1991, Ukraine declared itself an independent state, with major consequences for the icon collection. For one thing, less than a week later, on 30 August, the Lviv provincial authorities gave the National Museum the building of the former Lenin Museum. With the additional space, the museum was able to expand the number of icons on display. The section "Ukrainian Art of the Twelfth Through Eighteenth Centuries," conceived by Oleh Sydor, curator for Old Ukrainian art, occupied about half the galleries on two floors. It officially opened on 14 May 1999.[50]

Intellectual work on the icons intensified. Beginning in 1996, the museum sponsored an annual conference on Ukrainian sacral art.[51] It put on special exhibitions as well: icons of the Bohorodchany iconostasis (1995), of the Prylbychi iconostasis (which Sheptytsky knew from his childhood in that village) (1997), of the Passion (1998), of the Nativity of Christ (2000),[52] and of the Last Judgment (2001) (fig. 9).[53] Oleh Sydor worked on cataloging the icon collection, publishing some portions of the catalog in the revived yearbook of the National Museum.[54] An album of icons in the collection was also published in 1998 by the director at that time, Vasyl Otkovych, and the photographer Vasyl Pylypiuk.[55] Unfortunately, the publication left much to be desired in terms of both content and quality of illustrations.[56]

The National Museum has received some high-profile visitors since independence. A summit of European presidents was held in Lviv in May 1999, and nine heads of state visited the museum at that time. Earlier, on 17 November 1997, Hillary Clinton and Liudmyla Kuchma, the first ladies of America and Ukraine, not only toured the museum, but reportedly "took part directly in the restoration of the icon Old Testament Trinity" from the Bohorodchany iconostasis![57]

Yet by no means has independence been an unmixed blessing. Certain long-standing problems remain unsolved. Even in the Soviet period, scholars, foreign and Ukrainian alike, complained about the lack of access to the museum's holdings; little

FIG. 9 Last Judgment, Vovche, sixteenth century, detail.

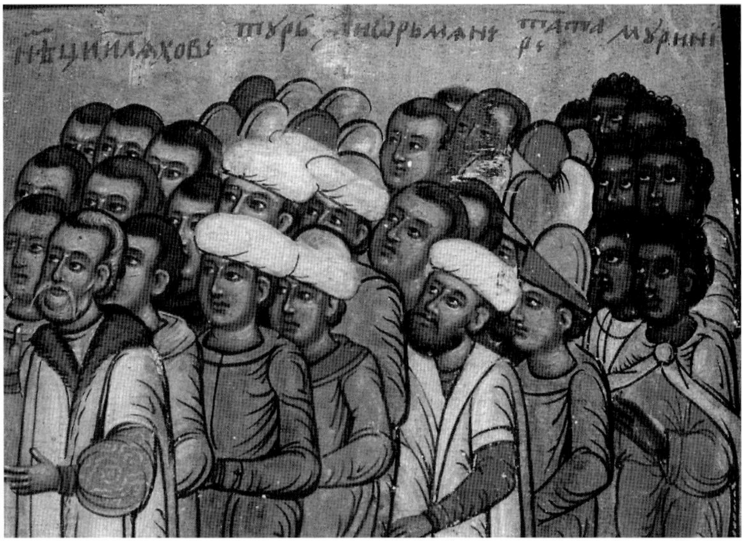

has changed for researchers since independence. The revived yearbook of the museum, an extremely valuable publication for everyone interested in these icons, cannot be purchased; the director gives it personally to fortunate recipients. No issue has appeared since 2001.

The museum does not have the resources to heat the building on Freedom (formerly Lenin) Prospect adequately in the winter. Visitors to the Last Judgment exhibition in December 2001 had to wear overcoats inside the building. What effect freezing temperatures have on five-hundred-year-old egg tempera and linden boards is hard to say. Perhaps the icons felt as if they were back in their unheated mountain churches.

The fall of Communism also changed the status of the Armenian cathedral, where the bulk of the icon collection had been stored for half a century. The Armenian community in Lviv successfully petitioned to have the cathedral reopened and restored to them, and the icons had to be moved. The Armenians gave money for a new structure in which to house the icons. Critics, however, say that the transfer is proving to be disastrous for the icons. They had been in a damp environment in the Armenian cathedral, but were moved at the end of 2002 to the dry environment of the new building. According to a newspaper article titled "A Coffin for Icons," the icons started to swell within two weeks of the move, and twenty of the icons were in critical condition. The curator of the collection, Oleh Sydor, resigned in protest. Since the whole affair became a public scandal, the director of the National Museum, Myroslav Otkovych, the brother of his predecessor, was transferred to other work.[58] By 2005, the issue of the transfer and possible deterioration of the icons had disappeared from the press. (Although that year saw a strike of the National Museum's staff, this had nothing to do with the icons.)

The most important development in recent years is that Sydor's successor as curator of the icon collection, Maria

Helytovych, has published excellent catalogs of two icon genres in the collection: the Mother of God "with praises" and the Savior in Glory.[59]

CONCLUSION

At the beginning of the century surveyed in this account, some people began to see icons anew. Attitudes toward icons were affected by the same shift of aesthetic paradigm that allowed taste to transcend the metanarratives of Western art, permitted the appreciation of African and "primitive" art, and precipitated the first works of abstract sculpture. They were now perceived not so much as instruments of salvation but as works of art. Perhaps this was just a translation of their sacrality into the worldview of modernity; art had become more sacred than religion in the modern outlook. For the traditional believers who worshiped something other than art, however, icons were a connection with the divine. And just like the mezuzah on the doorframe of Jewish houses, icons could lose their efficacy through physical deterioration. So when icons were old and dirty, covered with smudges from lamp oil, candle smoke, and incense, believers cast them into rivers, buried them in the earth, stored them in the belfries, or consigned them to bonfires.

People who saw in the new way, such as Metropolitan Andrei Sheptytsky, could not bear to see the new sacrality of art profaned in this way. Moreover, they saw in these images of the Savior, of the saints, and of the Mother of God something else that had become very sacred—the nation. The icons were embodiments of ancient national culture. They needed to be placed in national institutions, and where these were lacking they needed to be created. The good metropolitan, as we have seen, funded a National Museum in which to house the icons he had saved from believers as yet insufficiently infused with the modern spirit of nationality and art appreciation.

And so the icons were transferred from their natural habitat in the churches of the Carpathian region to the museum in the local capital city. Each icon, instead of fitting into the elaborate program of a village church, where they were arranged according to sacred history and geography, were now hung in the exhibit halls chronologically, completely divorced from a context of traditional worship and theology.

A museum is but a building in a city, and it experiences in its own way the history that transpires around it. The front passed over Lviv several times in each of the two world wars. After each war, Lviv was also caught in conditions of civil war (the Polish-Ukrainian war of 1918–19 and the anti-Soviet nationalist insurgency of 1944–50). The museum's founder, director, and staff were all at some point imprisoned and exiled. Extremist nationalists as well as Communists occupied leading posts in the museum at different times, and sometimes at the same time. Communism was, of course, a powerful manifestation of modernity in this part of the world. Fortunately for the icons, the Communists also saw them as the metropolitan did—as old works of art and repositories of national culture.

To me, the embodiment of all that transpired was Vira Svientsitska, the daughter of the National Museum's first and longest-serving director. Imprisoned by both the Poles and the Soviets for her

Ukrainian nationalism, she later made a brilliant career in the Soviet-era museum and art history establishment. She had no interest at all in religion and instead worked out a discourse about icons that stressed social and national liberation, a discourse that could serve nationalists and Communists equally well. Unlike many others in cultural institutions across Ukraine, she made the transition from Soviet power to independence easily. And it was just as easily that the former Lenin Museum became the new National Museum with its superb collection of Carpathian icons.

In 1976, I was in a department store in what was then called Leningrad. I was shocked to find a corner there with a statue of Lenin, adorned with flowers and inscribed with the following words: *Lenin i nyne zhivee vsekh zhivykh*—"Even today Lenin is more alive than anyone alive." It seemed so incongruously religious to me. In that same year, I visited the Lenin Museum in Lviv. Portraits and posters of the Great Lenin hung on every wall. Today on those same walls one finds Saint George, Jesus Christ, Saint Peter, and the Mother of God. Before there were scenes of the speech at the Finland Station and the storming of the Winter Palace; now these have been replaced by the Transfiguration and the Last Judgment. Much has changed. Or not.

NOTES TO CHAPTER 5

1. John-Paul Himka, *Last Judgment Iconography in the Carpathians* (Toronto: University of Toronto Press, 2009).

2. His closest collaborator in the work of the museum described the metropolitan as follows: "Himself an aesthete-connoisseur of the fine arts, even with an artistic talent for drawing, Metropolitan Andrei Sheptytsky looked at all the remnants of our cultural-national life from the point of view of art and style in connection with church ritual and folk tradition." Ilarion Svientsits'kyi, *Pro muzei ta muzeinytstvo (narysy i zamitky)* (Lviv: Z drukarni "Dila," 1920), 25.

3. See Myroslava M. Mudrak, "Sheptyts'kyi as Patron of the Arts," in *Morality and Reality: The Life and Times of Andrei Sheptyts'kyi,* ed. Paul R. Magocsi (Edmonton: Canadian Institute of Ukrainian Studies, University of Alberta, 1989), 289–311.

4. Andrei Sheptyts'kyi, "Moi spomyny pro predmet muzeinykh zbirok," in *Dvaitsiat'piat'-littia Natsional'noho Muzeiu u L'vovi,* ed. I. Svientsitskyi (Lviv: Naukova fundatsiia halyts'koho mytropolyta Andreia Sheptyts'koho, 1930), 3. For an analysis of the Poliana icons, see Mariia Helytovych, "Ansambl' ikon tserkvy Pokrovu Bohorodytsi v Poliani poblyzu Dobromylia ta pam"iatky ioho kola," in *Zachodnioukraińska sztuka cerkiewna: Dzieła—twórcy—ośrodki—techniki: Materiały z międzynarodowej konferencji naukowej 10–11 maja 2003 roku,* ed. Jarosław Giemza (Łańcut: Muzeum-Zamek w Łańcucie, 2003), 83–105.

5. Sheptyts'kyi, "Moi spomyny," 1.

6. Mykhailo Dragan, "Z pratsi v muzeiu i dlia n'oho," in Svientsits'kyi, *Dvaitsiat'piat'-littia Natsional'noho Muzeiu,* 41.

7. I. Svientsits'kyi, *Ikonopys' halyts'koi Ukrainy XV–XVI. vikiv,* Zbirky Natsional'noho muzeiu u L'vovi (Lviv, 1928), 2.

8. Sheptyts'kyi, "Moi spomyny," 1.

9. I. Sventsitskii, *Natsional'nii [sic] Muzei vo L'vove (1905–1915),* Otdel'nyi ottisk iz No 31 [1915] Neofitsial'noi chasti "L'vovskogo Vestnika" (Lviv, 1915), 1.

10. Mudrak, "Sheptyts'kyi as Patron of the Arts," 290.

11. Mykola Batih, "Bili storinky v istorii Natsional'noho Muzeiu u L'vovi," *Litopys Natsional'noho Muzeiu u L'vovi,* no. 1 (6) (2000): 7. There is a somewhat different chronology in Mudrak, "Sheptyts'kyi as Patron of the Arts," 290.

12. Sventsitskii, *Natsional'nii Muzei vo L'vove,* 2–3. On discrepant information and difficulties in establishing the extent of the metropolitan's largesse, see Mudrak, "Sheptyts'kyi as Patron of the Arts," 303n20.

13. Zoriana Lyl'o, "Natsional'nyi muzei u L'vovi: stanovlennia ta formuvannia zbirok," in Jarosław Giemza, ed., *Zachodnioukraińska sztuka cerkiewna,* pt. 2: *Materiały z międzynarodowej konferencji naukowej Łańcut-Kotań 17–18 kwietnia 2004 roku* (Łańcut: Muzeum-Zamek w Łańcucie, 2004), 214.

14. Writing in this same publication, Svientsitsky states that the icon collection comprised "about 1,200 numbers." Svientsits'kyi, *Pro muzei ta muzeinytstvo,* 26. I am not sure how to explain the discrepancy between this statement and the total I received after adding up all the icons acquired in 1905–19. Perhaps some inventory numbers included more than one item, or perhaps certain acquisitions were not eventually incorporated into the museum collection.

15. "Litopys rozvytku Natsional'noho Muzeiu," in Svientsits'kyi, *Dvaitsiat'piat'-littia Natsional'noho Muzeiu,* 69–70.

16. Ilarion Svientsits'kyi, *Iliustrovanyi providnyk po Natsional'nim Muzeievi u L'vovi* (Zhovkva: Pechatnia Vasylyian, 1913).

17. "Vyznachni hosti muzeiu," in Svientsits'kyi, *Dvaitsiat'piat'-littia Natsional'noho Muzeiu,* 78–79.

18. Svientsits'kyi, *Ikonopys' halyts'koi Ukrainy,* 3. On other restorers in this period, see Lyl'o, "Natsional'nyi muzei u L'vovi," 214.

19. Volodymyr Kubijovyč and Danylo Husar Struk, eds., *Encyclopedia of Ukraine,* 5 vols. (Toronto: University of Toronto Press, 1984–93), s.v. "Boichuk, Mykhailo" (by S. Hordynsky); Myroslav Shkandrij, *Modernists, Marxists, and the Nation: The*

Ukrainian Literary Discussion of the 1920s (Edmonton: Canadian Institute of Ukrainian Studies Press, University of Alberta, 1992), 163–68.

20. "Litopys rozvytku Natsional'noho Muzeiu."

21. *Tsars'kyi viazen' 1914–1917* (Lviv: Nakladom Komitetu "Zhyvoho Pamiatnyka," 1918).

22. Batih, "Bili storinky," 8–11.

23. Ibid., 10.

24. "Vyznachni hosti muzeiu."

25. Ilarion Svientsits'kyi, "XXV. lit diial'nosty Natsional'noho Muzeiu," in Svientsits'kyi, *Dvaitsiat'piat'-littia Natsional'noho Muzeiu u L'vovi,* 13. "Litopys rozvytku Natsional'noho Muzeiu."

26. Batih, "Bili storinky," 11.

27. Lyl'o, "Natsional'nyi muzei u L'vovi," 222, 226.

28. Svientsits'kyi, *Ikonopys' halyts'koi Ukrainy.*

29. Ilarion Svientsitskyi-Sviatyts'kyi [*sic*], *Ikony halyts'koi Ukrainy XV–XVI. vikiv,* Zbirky Natsional'noho muzeiu u L'vovi (Lviv, 1929).

30. Svientsits'kyi, *Ikonopys' halyts'koi Ukrainy,* 3.

31. I. Svientsits'kyi, "Zvit upravy Natsional'noho Muzeiu za 1928 rik. Zahal'nyi stan u XXV-mu rokovi diial'nosty," *Kanadys'kyi ukrainets* (Winnipeg), 1 May 1929.

32. Ibid., 8 May 1949.

33. (ia. v.), "Z muzeinykh problem: iak slid dyvytysia na vystavy tvoriv mystetstva," *Litopys Natsional'noho Muzeiu* (1938): 10. See also Lyl'o, "Natsional'nyi muzei u L'vovi," 221–25.

34. Solomiia Diakiv, ed., *Lysty Mytropolyta Andreia Sheptyts'koho do Ilariona Sventsits'koho. Z arkhivu Natsional'noho muzeiu u L'vovi* (Lviv: NVF "Ukrains'ki tekhnolohii," 2005), 21–22.

35. Some documents indicate that the museum was closed throughout the German occupation: Tamara Halaichak et al., eds., *Kul'turne zhyttia v Ukraini. Zakhidni zemli. Dokumenty i materialy,* 3 vols. (Kiev: Naukova dumka, 1995–), 1:136, 1:151. However, the museum diary that Batih relied upon, "Bili storinky," tells a different story altogether.

36. See, for example, H. D. Iakushchenko and Ia. I. Nanovs'kyi, *L'vivs'kyi muzei ukrains'koho mystetstva. Zhyvopys, skul'ptura, hrafika* (Kiev: Mystetstvo, 1975).

37. Batih, "Bili storinky," 13–17.

38. Halaichak, *Kul'turne zhyttia v Ukraini,* 1:292–93; see also 1:511.

39. Batih, "Bili storinky," 17–18.

40. Ibid., 22. Mykola Batih, "Bili storinky v istorii Natsional'noho Muzeiu u L'vovi 1952–1962 rr.," *Litopys Natsional'noho Muzeiu u L'vovi,* no. 2 (7) (2001): 15.

41. Batih, "Bili storinky," 27.

42. Halaichak, *Kul'turne zhyttia v Ukraini,* 1:673–74, 2:251–53, 2:285, 2:504–6, 2:566–67. See also Batih, "Bili storinky," 23–26.

43. Batih, "Bili storinky," 26. Batih, "Bili storinky . . . 1952–1962," 7.

44. Batih, "Bili storinky . . . 1952–1962," 7–9. A more negative characterization of the conditions in the Armenian cathedral can be found in Myroslav Otkovych, "Problemy muzeinoho zberihania tvoriv ikonopysu," in *Zachodnioukraińska sztuka cerkiewna,* pt. 2: *Materiały z międzynarodowej konferencji naukowej Łańcut-Kotań 17–18 kwietnia 2004 roku,* ed. Giemza, 539.

45. Batih, "Bili storinky . . . 1952–1962," 15. Kubijovyč and Struk, *Encyclopedia of Ukraine,* s.v. "Svientsits'ka, Vira."

46. V. I. Svientsits'ka and O. F. Sydor, *Spadshchyna vikiv. Ukrains'ke maliarstvo XIV–XVIII, stolit' u muzeinykh kolektsiiakh L'vova* (Lviv: Kameniar, 1990), 10.

47. Vira Svientsits'ka, *Ivan Rutkovych i stanovlennia realizmu v ukrains'komu maliarstvi XVII st.* (Kiev: Naukova dumka, 1966), 12, 58.

48. Halaichak, *Kul'turne zhyttia v Ukraini,* 2:467–68.

49. Tetiana Lupii, "Khronika 1991–1999 rokiv," *Litopys Natsional'noho Muzeiu u L'vovi,* no. 1 (6) (2000): 59.

50. Ibid., 59, 74.

51. Ibid., 66, 73.

52. Ibid., 64, 71, 73, 75.

53. I flew to Lviv to see this last exhibition myself.

54. Oleh Sydor, "Ikony maistriv Oleksiia i Dymytriia v kolektsii Natsional'noho muzeiu u L'vovi. Z materialiv do zvedenoho kataloha zbirok NML," *Litopys Natsional'noho muzeiu u L'vovi,* no. 1 (6) (2000): 89–152. Oleh Sydor, "Reiestr ikon Strashnoho Sudu v kolektsii NML," *Litopys Natsional'noho muzeiu u L'vovi,* no. 2 (7) (2001): 90–96.

55. V. P. Otkovych and V. Pylyp"iuk, *Ukrains'ka ikona XIV–XVIII st., Zbirky Natsional'noho muzeiu u L'vovi* (Lviv, 1998).

56. John-Paul Himka, "Episodes in the Historiography of the Ukrainian Icon," *Journal of Ukrainian Studies* 29 (Summer–Winter 2004): 156–57.

57. Lupii, "Khronika 1991–1999 rokiv," 71–72, 76.

58. Viktoriia Sadova, "Truna dlia ikon," *Arhument-hazeta,* 23 January 2003.

59. Mariia Helytovych, *Bohorodytsia z Dytiam i pokhvaloiu. Ikony kolektsii Natsional'no muzeiu* (Lviv: Svichado, 2005); idem, *Ukrains'ki ikony "Spas u Slavi"* (Lviv: Vydavnytstvo "Drukars'ki kunshty," Natsional'nyi muzei u L'vovi, 2005). I have reviewed the latter in *Journal of Ukainian Studies* 31 (Summer–Winter 2006): 240–42.

WENDY R. SALMOND

6

HOW AMERICA DISCOVERED RUSSIAN ICONS

THE SOVIET LOAN EXHIBITION OF 1930–1932

On 14 October 1930, the first exhibition of Russian icons ever to take place in the United States opened at the Museum of Fine Arts in Boston. Over the next nineteen months it traveled to nine venues across the country, introducing the American public to a form of medieval painting virtually unknown outside Russia.[1] Billed as the "Union of Soviet Socialist Republics Loan Exhibition," its avowed goal was to share with the outside world the full story of Russian icon painting's evolution from the twelfth to the nineteenth centuries, thereby adding a vital missing chapter to the history of medieval art.

The exhibition's organizers sent abroad some of the oldest and most significant icons then in Soviet collections. They included the twelfth-century Saint Nicholas from the Monastery of the Holy Spirit in Novgorod; the thirteenth-century Saint John with Saint George and Saint Blaise from Novgorod; three icons by the fifteenth-century master Andrei Rublev from the iconostasis of Vladimir's Dormition Cathedral; and Dionysius's two great icons of Saint Kirill Belozersky from the late sixteenth century. But it was the story of how such icons were rescued from neglect and restored to their original state that made the exhibition a major cultural event of the early Depression era. Interwoven with the scholarly, objective history of stylistic evolution was a dramatic contemporary saga of discovery and liberation. Photos of the exhibition as it was installed at the Cleveland Museum of Art show how emphatically the marks of scientific conservation were left visible on the surfaces of key icons, a constant reminder of their journey from a dark, soot-encrusted past to a light-filled present of radiant color (fig. 10).

The metaphor of restoration was not lost on the American public. It did much to resolve the paradox of an atheist, iconoclastic government protecting and promoting the art of a religion that it was determined to exterminate. Here, it seemed, was a revolutionary regime that genuinely cared about cultural patrimony, rescuing art treasures of universal significance from a church whose clergy had neither taken adequate care of them nor allowed others to do so. In liberating icons from the clutches of religion, the Soviets reclaimed them as great works of art that transcended the narrow confines of ritual and superstition.

Even as it promoted the universality of the icon and the striking modernity of its "significant form," however, the exhibition quietly pursued a second agenda: to create a market demand for icons in the bourgeois West. Long before the Cold War made such tactics commonplace, these secularized icons were pulled into the Soviet Union's ideological battle with the West, and the story of the icon's salvation became one of the regime's most effective publicity stunts. That the Soviets' venture failed, at least as initially conceived, may be deduced from the conspicuous absence of important Russian icons from the great majority of American museums and private collections. Instead, a very different sort of icon captured the imagination of private collectors, icons of relatively recent date whose value lay in their secular aura of human tragedy and imperial splendor.

SOVIET PLANS AND PREPARATIONS

Although its organizers downplayed the fact, the Soviet loan exhibition was essentially a prerevolutionary idea. A thriving market for icons had developed in Russia in the decade leading up to World War I. This coincided with a new culture of concern for national heritage that highlighted the role of conservation, expressly opposing it to the "vandalisms" of the Orthodox Church.[2] The "discovery" of the icon by collectors,

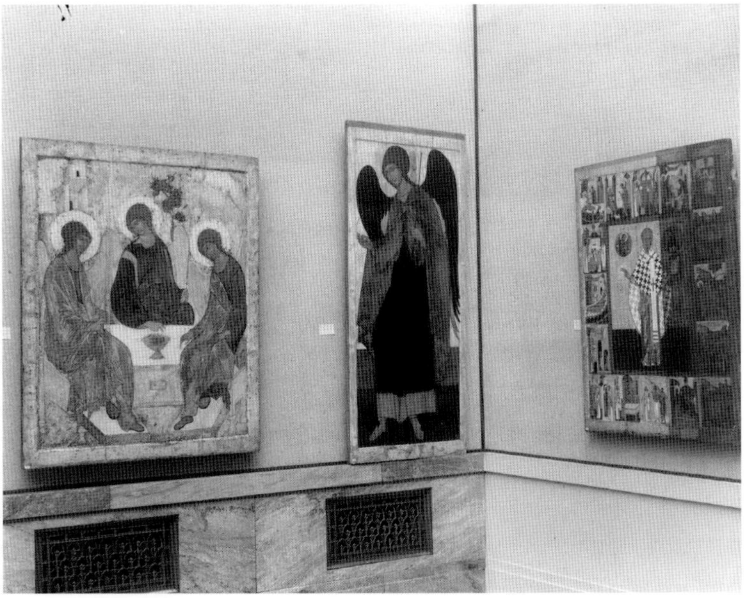

FIG. 10 View of the Soviet Loan Exhibition at the Cleveland Museum of Art, showing a copy of Andrei Rublev's icon of the Old Testament Trinity, a deesis icon of the Archangel Gabriel, and a partially cleaned vita icon of Saint Nicholas. Archives, Cleveland Museum of Art, Records of the Registrar's Office: Gallery View Photographs, Gallery 9 [Gallery 220], Russian Icons, 18 February–20 March 1932.

aesthetes, and scholars owed much to the skills of a cadre of master icon painters, who used the secrets of their craft to return ancient icons to their original state by removing layers of darkened varnish and overpainting. The extraordinary beauty of the paintings brought about a fundamental reassessment of early Russian art, a process that reached its high point in the exhibition of icons from private collections held in Moscow in 1913.[3] "Before three or four years have passed," it was predicted, "Europe will be thinking of a similar exhibition, and Russian icon painting will become an honored guest in Western museums."[4]

These hopes for international recognition of Russia's greatest cultural asset were dashed by the outbreak of war in 1914 and the disruption that followed the 1917 Revolution. When the collecting and restoration of icons started up again, in 1918, it was in a very different world. With the decree on the Separation of Church and State (1918), the Orthodox Church was stripped of its legal claim to the rich storehouses of its churches and monasteries. Throughout the Civil War period monasteries were liquidated, churches demolished or converted to secular purposes, and private property abolished. The result was a flood of confiscated and displaced icons.

As the icon's natural habitat disappeared, opportunities for its scholarly study blossomed.[5] Once off-limits to profane contact, the church's oldest and most venerated icons were now accessible to scientific study. Under the leadership of Igor Grabar and Alexander Anisimov, the Commission on the Restoration of Works of Art and Antiquities (from 1924, the Central State Restoration Workshops)[6] performed heroic acts of rescue and preservation under the most adverse conditions. Driven by the urgency of saving unique works from destruction, but also by the thrill of the hunt, the commission launched a series of expeditions searching in particular for icons of the pre-Mongol period and works by the elusive and legendary Andrei Rublev.[7] Even miracle-working icons were subjected to intense scrutiny by a team of restorers led by Grigory Chirikov (all of them active in the prerevolutionary collecting boom) and closely supervised by Grabar and Anisimov. The commission used X-rays, insisted on scrupulous photo documentation, and outlawed the dubious restoration practices (so-called antiquarian restoration) of the prerevolutionary period. In the course of the 1920s, the boundaries of icon history expanded and shifted in response to their discoveries. A series of exhibitions featuring newly restored icons was held in Moscow, followed by an exhibition of fresco facsimiles in Berlin in 1926.[8] The workshops' pioneering work attracted the admiring attention of the European scholarly community through its journal, *Questions of Restoration (Voprosy restavratsii)* (1926–28), and members' contributions to international journals.

But in early 1928, official cultural policy shifted drastically. On 23 January, the decree "On Measures to Intensify the Export and Realization of Antiques and Works of Art" was issued, orchestrated to coincide with the start of the First Five-Year Plan. Henceforth, the Soviet functionaries in Gostorg (the state trade organization) and Antikvariat (its Head Office for Buying and Realizing Antiquarian Objects, created in 1925) were to exercise exclusive control over the selling and export of art and antiques. The foreign currency raised went to fund Soviet industry.[9] Although such sales had been occurring sporadically since 1921, a period of unprecedented cultural "dumping" now began, paralleling the dumping of Soviet wood pulp and grain on the international market. In such a climate, even icons were potentially realizable cultural assets, and Gostorg was already making plans to market them.

It was at this point that Igor Grabar, director of the Central Restoration Workshops, intervened.[10] Disgusted by the Soviet authorities' inept handling of the international art market (large quantities of museum-quality art were being sold at bargain prices), fearing the heavy-handed tactics they might bring to selling icons, but also eager to promote his workshops' achievements, Grabar sent Gostorg a proposal for selling icons abroad, drawing on the supply-and-demand principles of the capitalist art market: "Experience shows that all major turnovers of specific groups of works of art have invariably been prepared for ahead of time by the appropriate commercial circles, by orchestrating a series of measures geared toward creating a demand and introducing some sort of 'fashion.' If Narkomtorg [the People's Commissariat of Trade] wants to make a big business out of icons, it must quickly start puffing up 'the Russian icon' and creating a fashion for it."[11] Grabar's strategy was to arrange a traveling exhibition complete with the scholarly apparatus of catalog, articles, and lectures, its purpose to celebrate "our achievements in the field of restoration." Only in this manner could a demand be created, proper prices established, and a long-term market assured. "After such a triumphal march across Europe," Grabar argued in another memo, "prices for Russian icons will increase tenfold."[12] To satisfy Gostorg's demand for immediate profits and to offset any expenses, he also proposed that a proportion of the icons exhibited would be auctioned off at the close of the exhibition.

Gostorg approved, and the exhibition was rapidly organized, drawing on the collections of museums in Moscow, Leningrad, and the provinces, on recently restored icons still in the restoration workshops, and on the vast reserves in state storerooms.[13] Grabar was very clear about the parameters of the selection. This was to be a purely *Soviet* enterprise, including none of the great works from prerevolutionary collections. Against the wishes of his colleagues, who feared the icons would never return from abroad, Grabar insisted on including critical early works of the twelfth, thirteenth, and fourteenth centuries without which, he argued, the full history of icons could scarcely be understood.[14] Where vital works were too fragile to travel, such as the twelfth-century Vladimir Mother of God (pl. 1) and Rublev's *Old Testament Trinity* (pl. 2), exact copies were to be made by the workshop staff.[15] Particular care was taken not to include works confiscated from private collections that could become the subject of lawsuits with émigrés. Also excluded were especially venerated, miracle-working icons that might rouse the ire of the Orthodox abroad. The result was an exhibition in which some of the newly discovered jewels of Russian icon painting rubbed shoulders with what émigré writer Vladimir Weidle described as a handful of copies and "a whole set of second-class icons."[16] In addition, a stock of more commonplace icons was selected, cleaned, and appraised in preparation for the foreign market.

The itinerary evolved in fits and starts, expanding as the success of the exhibition became assured. From February through May 1929, it toured five cities in Germany, the first country to recognize the Soviet government and the hub of Soviet efforts to sell large quantities of Russian art abroad.[17] After a month in Vienna, the exhibition moved on to the Victoria and Albert Museum in London, where thirty thousand visitors saw it in six weeks. A splendid catalog was published with essays by Sir Martin Conway and art historian Roger Fry.[18]

Staff from the restoration workshops in Moscow accompanied the exhibition, giving lectures and demonstrations. They were also charged with negotiating prices and selling, although there is no evidence that they were successful in securing actual sales.[19] Ultimately, Antikvariat abandoned the idea of direct sales for fear of negative publicity, and the exhibition became exclusively promotional.[20] By the time it arrived in the United States, Americans were quite categorically informed that "none of the paintings are for sale, the significance of the Exhibition being in that it introduces to the Western world a branch of art produced by a culture different from our own, yet springing from the same parent stem—the art of Byzantium in the twelfth century."[21]

With the late addition of the United States to the exhibition's itinerary, Grabar hoped to see vindicated his personal conviction that the United States was the most fertile ground on which to build a commercial icon market. In 1924, he had accompanied an exhibition of contemporary Russian art to New York and had come away with the impression that "in contrast to the meager European market, America presents a quite sufficient demand for the work of Russian artists."[22] He had specifically noted that "the best-selling are the 'Russian goods,' everything that in the American imagination is 'very Russian,' and particularly religious things."[23] Moreover, he knew that American collectors had dominated the international art market over the past three decades.[24] In April 1929, he reported to Antikvariat from the exhibition's Cologne venue: "More than once people approached me to ask whether it was possible to buy in Moscow anything remotely equal to the icons being shown here, and also whether it was possible to buy copies. To the first question we answered that in Moscow one can buy first-class icons. . . . I propose that the only country where they will be able to be liquidated is the United States of America and perhaps Paris."[25]

AMERICAN RECEPTION AND PERCEPTION

When the crates containing the icons arrived in Boston, in August 1930, the American public was very much a tabula rasa on which to inscribe a new Soviet history of icons. "It is not altogether unreasonable that the word 'icon' should summon a mental image of something very dim and esthetically rather dull," wrote one journalist.[26] In prerevolutionary times, an American's encounter with icons was generally "limited to those small metal-bound panels with perforations for showing the painted figures underneath"—in other words, the mass-produced icons that populated the visual landscape of late imperial Russia.[27] Anyone wishing to read up on the subject could consult a meager handful of recent publications by the émigré scholars Nikodim Kondakov and Pavel Muratov, but these were already outmoded, since they depended on information and collections formed before the revolution. Those intrepid individuals who made the pilgrimage to the Soviet Union were almost certain to come across icons for sale in markets or on the street, and they often bought them as souvenirs. But with no icons in American museums to educate their taste and little information available in English, these occasional collectors were babes in the woods when buying these misleading and ambiguous images.[28]

Yet while they knew next to nothing about Russian icons, Americans were fascinated by every aspect of life in the young Soviet Union, and the media offered a steady stream of information and commentary. Coverage was especially heavy throughout 1930. The campaign for establishing diplomatic relations between the United States and the Soviet Union was being vigorously fought in the Senate, a scandal on the dumping of lumber and pulp had just broken, and reports of slave labor ("a murderous harvest soaked with human blood," to quote Representative Hamilton Fish) were rife.[29] But the most emotionally charged item of news on Russia was the Soviet government's war on religion, which had reached a crescendo that spring. The U.S. press gave daily bulletins on the closing of churches, the persecution of clergy and believers, and the demonstrative destruction of icons. On 2 February 1930, Pope Pius XI launched a "holy crusade against the Soviet Union." Prayer meetings were held in New York's Cathedral of Saint John the Divine and Saint Patrick's Cathedral as a "protest against the religious persecutions in Soviet Russia." In March, the American Committee on Religious Rights and Minorities issued a report that "religious persecution appears to prevail in Russia on a scale unprecedented in modern times." It was in this climate that the exhibition opened in Boston that October and would continue to operate over the next two years. Thus in 1931, the Cathedral of Christ the Savior, Moscow's largest church, was demolished, while the "war on Easter" produced "great bonfires in which sacred articles are burned, torchlight processions, mock-religious carnivals with floats ridiculing sacred customs."[30] In 1932, the final year of the exhibition, the Alexander Svirsky Monastery was turned into the Soviet Union's largest colony for prostitutes and beggars, Leningrad's Kazan Cathedral on Nevsky Prospect reopened as the Museum of the History of Religion and Atheism, and mass arrests of clergy began nationwide.

The discrepancy between the Soviet regime's iconoclastic campaign of destruction and its sudden sponsorship of icons was an inevitable theme in press coverage of the exhibition. On the whole, though, the trend was to isolate the aesthetic value of the exhibition from the ethical and political complications. As an article in *International*

Studio blithely put it, "The critics who condemn [the icon exhibition] are divided into two camps: those deprecating the sacrilege of removing holy objects from the churches, and the opponents of intercourse with an unrecognized government. Nobody bothers much about either dissenting faction."[31] A note in *Commonweal* summed up the argument of the exhibition's supporters in these terms: "If it is art, it doesn't matter in the least who wrought it, or who instigated it or even who stole it."[32] Whatever the experts, the pious, and the patriotic might say against it, the exhibition "was for the average gallery goer an experience and a revelation. . . . Here, for those jaded with western painting, were virgin fields."[33]

The public profile of the icons very quickly shifted from that of booty confiscated by an impious regime to that of cultural ambassadors, functioning not unlike the model prisons and hydroelectric dams that formed the itinerary for thousands of tourists then flocking to Soviet Russia. Reviewers repeatedly pointed out the regime's commitment to the preservation of cultural patrimony, even as the demolition of churches and the forced sales of art abroad continued unabated. Especially effective was the way in which the church became the villain of the piece, while the Soviet state figured as the icon's rescuer from certain destruction. In his brief introductory essay to the catalog, Grabar described the damage caused to masterpieces of "early Russian painting" (a term increasingly preferred to "icon") by those who used them. He conjured up "a flat damp country" where icons were placed in "somber, unheated, badly ventilated churches," and wrote of sensational finds like Rublev's iconostasis from the Dormition Cathedral in Vladimir, left by clergy to molder in an outbuilding. This theme of clerical neglect had been widespread before the revolution, but now it acquired ideological urgency as a further nail in the coffin of the Orthodox Church's credibility. Even those disturbed by current events took the long view that "when the perspective of years has robbed the antireligious and confiscatory action of the Soviet regime of its unfortunate contemporary significance, the world of art and culture will be thankful for the work that it has accomplished."[34]

The drama of this rescue story was further intensified by the genuinely thrilling story of how Russian conservators had developed pioneering techniques for stripping off layers of smoke-darkened varnish and later overpainting to reveal the original layer beneath in all its unsuspected brilliance of color and beauty of line. In establishing Soviet ownership of these "reborn" icons, it was consistently stressed that "icons restored before 1917 are not represented in the exhibition," even though the same restorers were responsible for icons cleaned before and after the revolution.[35] Only in the workshops of the Central Restoration Workshops were modern techniques like X-ray used. A new scientific purism was adopted, with inpainting and retouching officially outlawed.[36]

The rhetoric of science's triumph over superstition that permeated the exhibition was especially critical during 1930–32, when the Soviet campaign against religion was reaching unprecedented extremes. Some of the most sensational press photos of 1930–31 showed peasants making bonfires of their icons, young members of the League of the Militant Godless tearing metal covers off icons, and laughing Red Army men carting icons and church fixtures out of the Simonov Monastery shortly before its demolition. The exhibition, by contrast, seemed to offer an acceptable aesthetic rationale for these acts of iconoclasm. As one reporter wrote, "Russia is not always as bad as she is painted. Not long since the world was scandalized at the pictured representation of frenzied peasants making bonfires of icons, stripped from churches henceforth to be devoted to secular purposes. That little of artistic value perished in these fires is to be presumed from the care given to fine examples of this religious art now gathered into museums."[37] The exhibition's secondary message was thus conveyed in the form of an art history lesson: whatever they might mean within the confines of Orthodoxy, once freed from their religious function, icons could legitimately be subjected to rigorous culling. The vast majority was good for nothing and, as the catalog made clear, this applied to virtually all icons produced from 1800 onward, the period of "decay." One or two of these late icons were included in the exhibition as pointed illustrations of the aesthetic decline of the post-Petrine era.

The achievements of Soviet science, the exhibition implied, made possible a new way of seeing icons, without which they could not hope to enter the universal history of art. The exhibition became "another of those dramatic triumphs of aesthetic revaluation that our modern eclecticism has made possible."[38] Lee Simonson, the young New York theater designer who worked as Moscow's go-between in bringing the exhibition to the United States, was an impassioned spokesman for the Russian icon's relevance:

> Modern painting for the last century has been struggling to free itself from the transparent glazes and the underlying chiaroscuro of the Renaissance, trying to achieve what we have come to recognize as "pure color" and to organize that color so that it will convey forms without losing any of its color value by interposing the veils of cast light and shadow. To some critics the goal has been approximated by the paintings of Henri Matisse, to others by the frescoes of Diego Rivera. To me at least it has never been more completely achieved than in many of these Russian icons of three or four centuries ago. For that reason I venture to believe that they will ultimately prove to be a source of inspiration to modern painters and eventually exert a profound influence on the development of modern art.[39]

The obstacle to aesthetic appreciation that the dematerialized otherworldliness of Russian icons presented to a Western audience attuned to Renaissance painting could be removed if they were thought of as powerful visual experiences, above all as pure color. No one better described the inevitability of partial understanding—of form's primacy over content and function—than the English critic Roger Fry, who had written in the London catalog the previous year:

> I have no idea of what this passion for the most abstract religious ideas—ideas

> altogether withdrawn from the common world of human life and nature—can have implied to those who felt them. In this sense I find Russian art far more remote than the Byzantine art out of which it came. . . . There is a certain satisfaction in noting that, coming to this art as we do without previous knowledge, without traditional references and predilections, we almost immediately pick out those pictures which Russians have always held in most esteem. . . . [E]ven those who find it impossible, however dimly, to conceive the mental atmosphere of a medieval Russian artist, can meet him on the common ground of his splendid decorative inventions and his unforgettable harmonies of colour.[40]

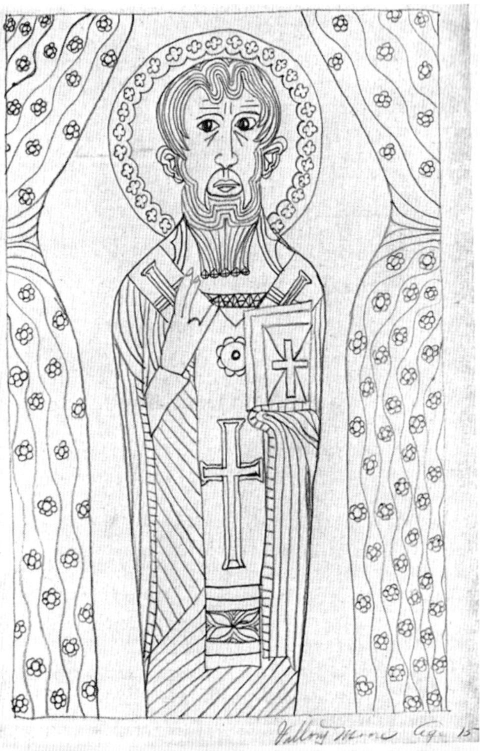

FIG. 11 Drawing by fifteen-year-old Vallory Moore, inspired by the thirteenth-century icon of Saint John Climacus with Saint George and Saint Blaise in the Soviet Loan Exhibition at the Worcester Art Museum, March–April 1931. Reproduced from the Bulletin of the Worcester Art Museum 22, no. 2 (July 1931): 30. Courtesy of the Worcester Art Museum.

A vivid demonstration that the icons awakened a responsive aesthetic chord was their incorporation, at the Worcester Museum of Art, into the museum's child-education program (fig. 11). The Educational Department used the loan icons to initiate children into the nature of creativity, situating them within the contemporary debate on the nature of primitivism. The project's premise was that, "because of its clarity and definition, primitive art is more easily understood by the child than the subtle art of a highly developed culture. . . . It is allied in inspiration and in execution with his own work and therefore stimulates him to create instead of to reproduce."[41]

On a number of levels, then, the exhibition had prepared the ground for the brisk sales that were presumably to follow. While initial plans to sell the icons straight out of the exhibition had to be reluctantly shelved, potential American consumers had been given their first basic lesson in the aesthetic and historical significance of Russian icons.

THE FORMATION OF AMERICAN ICON COLLECTING

Measured by any standard, the exhibition was one of the blockbusters of the early Depression era. The directors of some of America's most prestigious museums scrambled to secure the show for their institutions in response to the quite unanticipated public interest. Extensive and enthusiastic press coverage was accompanied by a flurry of publications in the scholarly press. Meanwhile, back in Moscow and Leningrad, stockpiles of icons set aside for export awaited their buyers.

Customers for icons did indeed emerge in the United States in the wake of the traveling exhibition, but not for the icons that Grabar might have chosen. Only the collection acquired in 1935 by Pittsburgh businessman George Hann could legitimately be described as "important," in that it reflected in microcosm the sweep of the icon's long history as first presented in the traveling exhibition.[42] The unique Hann collection aside, the collecting of icons in the United States turned away from the kinds of serious early icons promoted through the loan exhibition in favor of the late icons it explicitly marginalized.

There is no doubt that the impact of the Depression on the American art market made it extremely difficult for icons to compete for scarce resources with more tried and true forms of art, such as Old Master painting and French eighteenth-century furniture. Despite the exhibition's glowing reviews and excellent attendance figures, no American museum took advantage of the opportunity to actively add important early icons to its collection. When, for instance, at the end of 1931 Count B. Musin-Pushkin offered the director of the Brooklyn Museum both an exhibition of icons and an entire collection for purchase, he was told that he was unlikely to "succeed," because "interest in ikons is confined to such a small number that the chances of sale would be very slight."[43] (This was in marked contrast to the exhibition of Byzantine art held in Paris in 1931, at the close of which a large number of items changed hands.)[44]

Those Americans who did buy icons in the 1930s were attracted to a very different sort of icon, for very different reasons. Almost without exception, they were late icons of the seventeenth, eighteenth, and nineteenth centuries. During "the great tourist invasion" of 1929–30, the legal export of icons as souvenirs was heavily promoted. At the behest of the trade organs, the Soviet Union's new tourist industry, headed by Intourist, actively encouraged visitors to buy liberally in the Torgsin ("Trade with Foreigners") and commission shops. Travelers' anecdotes remind us how ubiquitous such commercial outlets were in the 1930s and how icons acquired there were generally seen as souvenirs or curios.

In addition to icons purchased in the Soviet Union, the effort to create a market on American soil proved decisive for the formation of American icon collections and public attitudes toward icons. Working through intermediaries, the Soviets devised "sale-exhibitions" as a mechanism for liquidating on the American market the personal effects of the imperial family, confiscated from their residences at Tsarskoe Selo, Gatchina, the Anichkov Palace, and the Winter Palace. In January 1931, the Wallace H. Day Galleries at 16 East 60th Street in New York held an exhibition of decorative arts from the Hermitage Palace, the contents of which were sold off after a short delay when Grand Duchesses Ksenia and Olga sued (unsuccessfully) to prevent the sale. The sale included icons, for the most part small nineteenth-century devotional icons embellished with silver covers, and the purchasers, so it was reported, were mainly women looking for *objets* to decorate their homes.

Then in early 1932, just as the official loan exhibition of icons was moving on to the Cleveland Museum of Art, entrepreneur Armand Hammer and his brother Victor launched the first of their celebrated department-store sales of Russian imperial art at Scruggs-Vandoort-Barney in St. Louis. The previous March, the Hammers had begun marketing "Fine Russian Icons and Relics from Royal Russia" out of their L'Ermitage Galleries at 3 East 52nd Street. The new enterprise involved a marketing strategy that Armand Hammer would later recall with cynical relish: "I promoted the hell out of the sale by giving it a healthy dose of snob appeal. I ordered the printing of fancy price tags embossed with the Imperial Romanoff two-headed eagle crest and prepared an elaborate catalog that paid tribute to the 'skilled artisans devoted to the glory of the czar.' . . . Our success in St. Louis led to sales in eight other stores, culminating in a huge sale at Lord & Taylor in New York."

Repeating his initial success at department stores across the country (three of the cities had also been hosts to the traveling exhibition),[45] Hammer targeted a particular kind of American collector for the art entrusted to him, including late icons: women (some wealthy but not always so) who found special significance in owning something that had once belonged to the murdered Romanov family. Aesthetically distinct from earlier icons, whose monumental simplicity had elicited comparisons with the modernist aesthetic, they were part of an inventory that included Fabergé *objets de vertu*, ecclesiastic vestments, and the table linens of the imperial family. Many of the icons that passed through the Hammer brothers' hands, and those of their main American competitor, Alexander Shaffer, in the 1930s, were accompanied by parchment testimonials asserting that they were from the private apartments at Tsarskoe Selo, the Winter Palace, and Gatchina.[46] Icons now in the Detroit Institute of Arts, the Metropolitan Museum of Art, the Rochester Memorial Art Gallery, and many private collections were acquired in this way.[47] Following the department-store sales, the Hammers established Hammer Galleries in New York, which was "fed by a continuing stream of art objects from Moscow . . . a collection of Hammer family and Soviet-owned merchandise."[48]

The Hammers were under no illusions about the aesthetic value of their stock, marketing them not as works of Russian painting, but as "a collection of memorabilia, freighted with human interest and drawn together by a thread of lasting significance." As the Hammers' sales brochure for 1935 put it, "To possess even one of these relics is to own a bit of the world's history, to have at hand tangible evidence of the rise and fall of a great Empire. . . . And too, there is romance in bringing into our homes these various beautiful objects that once delighted the eyes of monarchs, that furnished an imperial background for the young Grand Dukes and Duchesses of far away mysterious Russia."[49] As for the icons, they were to serve as decorative notes in the domestic interior, helping "to consecrate a quiet corner for a few minutes' rest in the season's busy rush."

In the slick sales patter of the Hammers' Depression-era marketing, these icons came to the end of a long journey of transformation. Stripped of their original liturgical function, they acquired a new identity, joining the assortment of imperial possessions that could be used in the American home, "either for décor, to embellish the cabinets of your own collections, or for actual use in the routine of everyday living."[50] Their appraised value had little to do with their intrinsic properties as paintings, still less with their devotional function, and everything to do with the associations the viewer brought with him or her. The intense gleam of small silver and enamel *oklads,* often arranged in symmetrical clusters on the wall, created an aesthetic that is still closely associated with Russian icons in the United States. The "startling modernism" of the great church icons seemed very far away.

CONCLUSION

Much to the relief of Russia's museum community, the icons in the loan exhibition returned home intact at the conclusion of the American tour, although not always to the institutions that had loaned them. In 1934, the Central State Restoration Workshops were purged and closed down, and many of its staff members repressed and imprisoned, including Anisimov and Chirikov.[51] Thereafter, the workshops' functions and collection were transferred to the State Tretiakov Gallery.

In the United States, although the traveling exhibition had been a great public relations success, it had signally failed to produce a systematic and informed market base. The few American icon collections that emerged in its wake are to this day considered of minor importance (full of "tourist junk," one writer observed).[52] The exhibition had expressly driven home the point that, by 1700, icon painting was in decline, a determination that was to remain in effect until the disintegration of the Soviet Union. The Hammers' cheap marketing ploys, with their department-store environment and emphasis on icons as decorative touches within a contemporary décor, above all the perceived "decadence" and tinselly surface effects of the icons themselves, so far removed from the "pure painting" and transcendent effects of Golden Age icons—all played a part in situating American collections at the very bottom of an emerging aesthetic hierarchy that answered the expectations of Western modernist aesthetics and Soviet scientific materialism alike. Rhetorically, the exhibition established the uneasy and unequal coexistence of two sorts of icon, one rare and desirable, the other plentiful and despised. Moreover, the emphasis on the problems of attribution and dating—which resulted from Orthodoxy's liturgical practices (repainting, copying)—made potential buyers wary of investing heavily in important icons and contributed to the resistance of American museums to collecting and displaying Russian icons. The complicated legacy of this early experiment in Soviet cultural diplomacy affects the perception of icons in the United States to the present day.

NOTES TO CHAPTER 6

1. After two months at the Museum of Fine Arts in Boston (14 October–14 December 1930), the exhibition traveled to the Metropolitan Museum of Art in New York (13 January–23 February 1931); the Worcester Museum of Fine Arts (March–April); the Rochester Memorial Art Gallery (opened 1 May); the De Young Memorial Art Museum, San Francisco (1 July–31 August); the Saint Paul Art Center in Minnesota (9 October–9 November); the Art Institute of Chicago (22 December–17 January 1932); the Cleveland Museum of Art (18 February–20 March); and the Cincinnati Art Museum (April).

2. See particularly the journals *Mir iskusstva* (1898–1904) and *Starye gody* (1907–16) for expressions of the intelligentsia's hostile attitude toward the clergy.

3. *Vystavka drevne-russkogo iskusstva ustroennaia v 1913 godu v oznamenovanie chestvovaniia 300-letiia tsarstvovaniia Doma Romanovykh. Imperatorskii Moskovskii arkheologicheskii institut imeni Imperatora Nikolaia II* (Moscow: [Institut], 1913).

4. Pavel Muratov [review], *Starye gody* (April 1913): 31.

5. "By the mid-1920s icons had disappeared from public buildings and remained, according to data for Moscow, in only 76 percent of workers' homes. In 1925 . . . this figure was reduced to 59 percent." N. B. Lebina, *Povsednevnaia zhizn' sovetskogo goroda: Normy i anomalii 1920/1930 godov* (St. Petersburg: Zhurnal 'Neva'; Letnii Sad, 1999), 133.

6. The commission was part of the Collegium on Museum Affairs and Preservation of Works of Art and Antiques (1918–24).

7. On the theme of Rublev, see Lindsey Hughes, "Inventing Andrei: Soviet and Post-Soviet Views of Andrei Rublev and His Trinity Icon," *Slavonica* 9, no. 2 (2003): 83–90.

8. Byzantisch-russische Monumentalmalerei.

9. *Sud'by muzeinykh kollektsii: Materialy VI Tsarskosel'skoi nauchnoi konferentsii* (St. Petersburg: Tsarskoe Selo, 2000), 130. On the phenomenon of the Soviet sales of art and antiques in the interwar period, see Nikolas Il'in and Natal'ia Semenova, *Prodannye sokrovishcha Rossii* (Moscow: Trilistnik, 2000); Waltraud Bayer, ed., *Verkaufte Kultur: Die sowjetischen Kunst- und Antiquitätenexporte, 1919–1938* (Frankfurt am Main: Peter Lang, 2001); and Anne Odom and Wendy R. Salmond, eds., *Treasures into Tractors: The Selling of Russia's Cultural Heritage, 1918–1938* (Washington, D.C.: Hillwood Museum and Gardens, 2009).

10. Grabar's role in organizing the exhibition is unclear. Anisimov complained that it was essentially he who organized it, while Grabar got to accompany it and "make an 'international' career for himself." See I. L. Kyzlasova, *Istoriia otechestvennoi nauki ob iskusstve Vyzantii i Drevnei Rusi 1920–1930 gody: Po materialam arkhivov.* (Moscow: Izdatel'stvo Akademii gornikh nauk, 2000), 289. However, the actual idea and the political clout to realize it seem to have been Grabar's. In March 1927, Anatoly Lunacharsky had agreed to a similar proposal by Grabar for sending an icon exhibition to Frankfurt (Manuscript Division, State Tretiakov Gallery, henceforth OR GTG, f. 106, 16761, line 1). Presumably, Lunacharsky's waning authority prompted Grabar to renew his campaign: in August 1928, he wrote to the Gostorg administration (OR GTG, f. 106, ed. kh. 527) before sending the memo to A. Ginzburg, head of Antikvariat, which is published in his collected letters (see note 11 below). In a letter to Glavnauka of January 1929, however, he disavowed his own role, writing that the exhibition was "formed on the initiative of Gostorg, which conceived the entire exhibition" (OR GTG, f. 106, ed. kh. 529, line 1).

11. Letter from Grabar to A. M. Ginzburg, 20 September 1938, in *Igor' Grabar' Pis'ma 1917–1941* (Moscow: Nauka, 1977), 179.

12. OR GTG, f. 106, 527.

13. The provenance of the icons in the exhibition was as follows: Central Restoration Workshops (26), Antikvariat (13), Novgorod Museum (9), State Historical Museum (13), Tretiakov Gallery (13), Russian Museum (6), Vologda and the Trinity Lavra of

Saint Sergius (8 each), Vladimir Museum (5), Yaroslavl (4), Arkhangel, Pskov, and Donskoy Monastery Museums (2 each), and one each from Tver, Rostov, and Aleksandrov Monastery Museum.

14. See Grabar's letter to Glavnauka dated 14–15 January 1929, in which he complains about the decision by Glavnauka's Expert Commission to exclude certain works from the exhibition (OR GTG, f. 106, 529). The catalog of the traveling exhibition shows that Grabar won the argument.

15. The copies were of the Vladimir Mother of God and Christ Not Made by Hands from the Dormition Cathedral in the Moscow Kremlin, Andrei Rublev's *Old Testament Trinity* from the Trinity Lavra of Saint Sergius, the Orant Mother of God from Yaroslavl, Dmitry Solunsky (from Dmitrov, head only), and the head of an archangel (from the State Historical Museum, the so-called Angel with the Golden Hair). Six fresco facsimiles from the church of Saint Peter in Yaroslavl were also sent but were not exhibited at the American venues.

16. V. Veidle, "Russkie ikony v Londone," *Vozrozhdenie* (Paris), 14 December 1929), 2. These lower-quality works were presumably originally selected as suitable for sale during the exhibition.

17. On the Soviet transactions with Berlin, see Bayer, *Verkaufte Kultur;* Iu. N. Zhukov, *Operatsiia Ermitazha (Opyt istoriko-arkhiv-nogo rassledovaniia)* (Moscow: Moskvitianin, 1993).

18. Michael Farbman, ed., *Masterpieces of Russian Painting* (London: A. Zwemmer, 1930). It was Roger Fry who first suggested that the Victoria and Albert Museum take the exhibition. In a 21 May 1929 letter to the director, E. R. D. MacLagan, he wrote: "It seems to me that it was likely to be of great interest to art historians if I suggested . . . that possibly you might find him [Farbman?] some place to show in and to some extent extend your protection and encouragement to it" (Victoria and Albert Museum Archives, VX.1929-006).

19. Accompanying the exhibition to Germany with restorer N. I. Briagin, Grabar was under constant pressure to produce sales. "Find out also what the chances are of selling things of first-class quality that are not in the exhibition. We can also make up collections," went one message from Antikvariat's head in Moscow, dispatched on 30 March 1929 (OR GTG, f. 106, op. 1, 3872, line 1). Ekaterina Dombrovskaya was the initial courier of the exhibition to London, but she was later replaced by Pavel Yukin. When interrogated by the OGPU in 1931, Yukin revealed that the icons in the London exhibition included fifteen high-priced icons earmarked for sale. Kyzlasova, *Istoriia otechestvennoi nauki,* 288, 351.

20. According to Kyzlasova, "The bureaucrats gave up the idea of selling works from the exhibition only after its sensational success." *Istoriia otechestvennoi nauki,* 288, 351.

21. "Early Icons in Boston Show," *Art News* 29 (4 October 1930): 30; *Literary Digest,* 6 December 1930, 18–19.

22. Russian State Archive of Literature and Art (henceforth RGALI), f. 2307, op. 10, ed. khr. 352, line 30.

23. Letter from Grabar to Moscow artists participating in the Exhibition of Russian Art in America, 18 March 1924, in *Grabar', Pis'ma 1917–41,* 120.

24. On the 1924 exhibition, see Marie Turbow Lampard, "Sergei Konenkov and the 'Russian Art Exhibition' of 1924," *Soviet Union/ Union sovietique,* 7, pts. 1–2 (1980): 70–88. On the American art market of this period, see Merle Secrest, *Duveen: A Life in Art* (New York: Alfred A. Knopf, 2004), and Gerald Reitlinger, *The Economics of Taste* (New York: Holt, Rinehart & Winston, 1964).

25. OR GTG, f. 106, 16771.

26. Edward Alden Jewell, "Marvel-ous Paintings: Flaming Colors Express Symbols of Northern Race—Slavic Love of Drama," *New York Times,* 18 January 1931.

27. Ralph Flint, "Russian Icons on View at the Metropolitan," *Art News* 29 (17 January 1931): 34.

28. An exception was the Kunz Collection at the Smithsonian Institution in Washington, D.C., but this was considered of purely ethnographic value. See Richard E. Ahlborn and Vera Beaver-Bricken, *Russian Copper Icons and Crosses from the Kunz Collection: Castings of Faith* (Washington, D.C.: Smithsonian Institution, 1991). Those wishing to read about icons in English prior to 1930 were limited to two scholarly monographs: Nikodim Kondakov, *The Russian Icon,* trans. Ellis Minns (Oxford: Clarendon Press, 1927), and Aleksandr Anisimov, *Our Lady of Vladimir,* trans. N. G. Yaschwill and T. N. Rodzianko (Prague: Seminarium Kondakovianum, 1928). For French speakers, Pavel Muratov was the acknowledged authority: *L'ancienne peinture russe,* trans. André Caffi (Rome: A. Stock, 1925); *Les Icones russes* (Paris: Éditions de la Pléiade, 1927).

29. On efforts in the U.S. Congress to counter Soviet dumping, see "Backs Embargo Bill as Soviet Dumping Spreads over World," *New York Times,* 24 September 1930, 1. For Fish's criticism of Soviet convict labor, see "Fish for Sending Agents," *New York Times,* 3 February 1931, 1.

30. Charles Phillips, "The Soviet Easter," *Commonweal,* 1 April 1931, 597.

31. "Notes of the Month," *International Studio,* February 1931, 49. The legal problem of American museums accepting an exhibition from an unrecognized government was solved when the American-Russian Institute for Cultural Relations with the Soviet Union assumed responsibility for the exhibition during its tour of the United States. The first branch of the ARI was created in New York in 1927 and by 1929 had spread to many other American cities. A major goal was to promote recognition of the Soviet government, but it was generally touted as "an adventure in international understanding. It is conceived in good will and dedicated to the promotion of cultural relations between the peoples of the Soviet Republics and the American public. It fosters mutual amity, world peace, and cultural unity." *The Art of Soviet Russia,* foreword by Fiske Kimball, introduction and catalog by Christian Brinton (New York: American Russian Institute, 1936). On the protests from émigré groups, see "Icon Exhibit Stirs Protest," *Art News* 29 (10 January 1931): 7; "Atheist Russia Lends the World Her Sacred Icons," *Literary Digest,* 6 December 1930, 18–19.

32. "Icons into Idols," *Commonweal,* 21 January 1931, 312.

33. "A Perspective View of the New York Season (1930–1931)," *Parnassus* 3 (May 1931): 9–10.

34. "Atheist Russia Lends the World Her Sacred Icons," 18.

35. Alexandre Anisimov, "L'Exposition des anciennes icones russes," *Gazette des beaux-arts,* 20 February 1930, 11. For an émigré perspective on the works excluded, see Veidle, "Russkie ikony v Londone," 2.

36. In practice, these uncompromising standards proved untenable, and by the late 1920s retouching was widely used.

37. "Atheist Russia Lends the World Her Sacred Icons," 18.

38. Flint, "Russian Icons on View at the Metropolitan," 34.

39. *Bulletin of the Metropolitan Museum of Art* 26 (January 1931): 6.

40. Roger Fry, "Russian Icon-Painting from a Western-European Point of View," in Farbman, ed., *Masterpieces of Russian Painting,* 56, 58.

41. "Art and the Child," *Bulletin of the Worcester Art Museum* 22 (July 1931): 29, 32.

42. For a complete catalog of the Hann collection, see *The George R. Hann Collection. Part One. Russian Icons. Ecclesiastical and Secular Works of Art. Embroidery, Silver, Porcelain, and Malachite,* Christie's (New York, 17–18 April 1980). On the details of its formation, see Salmond, "Russian Icons and American Money," 237–63.

43. Letter from William Henry Fox, director of the Brooklyn Museum, to Count Musin-Pushkin. Brooklyn Museum of Art Archives, Records of the Office of the Director (W. H. Fox, 1913–33).

44. I am grateful to Dr. Helen Evans of the Metropolitan Museum of Art for providing me with information on the sales from the Paris Exposition internationale d'art byzantin (28 May–9 July 1931).

45. From St. Louis, the stock went to Marshall Field's (Chicago), Bullocks Wilshire (Los Angeles), Halle's (Cleveland), the Emporium (San Francisco), B. Forman Co. (Rochester), Kaufmann's (Pittsburgh), Woodward & Lothrop (Washington, D.C.), and Lord & Taylor (New York).

46. Alexander Schaffer opened his own gallery, the Schaffer Collection of Russian Imperial Treasures, at Rockefeller Center in 1933.

47. Lillian Pratt bought her first icon at the Lord & Taylor exhibition in January 1933, and Mrs. James Sibley Watson purchased an icon of the Ascent of Elijah in his Fiery Chariot for $375 at B. Forman Co. That same year she gave the icon to the Rochester Memorial Art Gallery. The icon's provenance was given as the Winter Palace (33.1)

48. Carl Blumay with Henry Edwards, *The Dark Side of Power: The Real Armand Hammer* (New York: Simon & Schuster, 1992), 106.

49. Hammer Galleries, Inc., *Treasures from the Palaces of Old Russia* (New York, 1935).

50. *Treasures from the Palaces of Old Russia,* 1935.

51. On the fate of these men and others engaged in the study of medieval Russian culture in the 1930s, see Kyzlasova, *Istoriia otechestvennoi nauki.* On Anisimov in particular, see Shirley A. Glade's chapter in this volume.

52. Edward Jay Epstein, *Dossier: The Secret History of Armand Hammr* (New York: Carroll & Graf, 1999), 138.

PART III

INTERMEDIAL ICON

JEFFERSON J. A. GATRALL

7

POLENOV, MEREZHKOVSKY, AINALOV

ARCHEOLOGY OF THE CHRIST IMAGE

Images of Christ abound in Dmitry Merezhkovsky's historical trilogy *Christ and Antichrist*. In *Leonardo da Vinci* (1902), Merezhkovsky traces the Italian master's self-doubt during his painting of the Christ figure in *The Last Supper*, while in *Peter and Alexis* (1905), Old Believer icons lurk in the political and spiritual background of post-schism Russia. The most ancient images of Christ in the series nevertheless belong to the first novel, *Julian the Apostate* (1896), which is devoted to the storied life of its eponymous hero, the so-called last pagan emperor of Rome (r. 361–63) and author of the anti-Christian polemic *Against the Galileans*. In Merezhkovsky's rendition of the future emperor's childhood, a five-year-old Julian, under the supervision of his Christian tutor, visits a fourth-century Arian church east of Constantinople. During a service at this church, Merezhkovsky's impressionable young hero is struck by two sharply contrasting depictions of the figure who will become his lifelong nemesis:

> The boy looked upward at an enormous, semi-circular mosaic between the columns of an arch: it was an Arian image of Christ—the dark, menacing, emaciated face had a long, thin nose, austerely pursed lips, and a golden halo with a diadem like that of a Byzantine emperor. He blessed the world with his right hand, and in his left he held a book on which was written: "The world is yours. I am the light of the world." He sat on a magnificent throne, and a Roman emperor—Constantius, it seemed to Julian—kissed his feet.

Julian then looks down into "the semi-darkness" and encounters a very different Christ type on the bas-relief of a sarcophagus "from the first times of Christianity": "Among the [tomb's engravings] was the Good Shepherd carrying a sheep on his shoulders. . . . It was a joyful and simple barefooted youth, with a beardless face, humble and small, like the faces of poor peasants; he had a smile of quiet merriment. . . . The youth with the sheep on his shoulders gazed at Julian, at him alone, with a mysterious question. And Julian whispered the word he'd heard from [his tutor]: 'The Galilean'!"[1] Merezhkovsky's incorporation of these two images in *Julian the Apostate* exemplifies a broad interest in early Christian iconography on the part of traveling Western scholars and artists in the final decades of the nineteenth century. These secular pilgrims frequented numerous sacred sites throughout Italy and the Ottoman Empire, from the Roman catacombs to the temple ruins of Jerusalem, all of which offered a wealth of images and artifacts purportedly related to the person of Christ. An ethos of discovery pervaded this international trend as a whole, with the findings of professional archeologists quickly making their way into painting and works of fiction.

In this chapter, I examine what effects these twin forces of scholarly discovery and artistic appropriation had on the modern iconography of Christ by focusing on three key Russian figures: the painter Vasily Polenov, the novelist Merezhkovsky, and the archeologist Dmitry Ainalov. Within the context of their respective fields of cultural production, all three extended the nineteenth-century quest of the historical Jesus to a search for early examples of his likeness. This search involved a literal movement through space—Polenov traveled through Palestine, Merezhkovsky to Istanbul, and all three to Italy—as well as a figurative journey through time. For all three, ancient Christ images not only offered historical insights concerning the peoples who produced and venerated them; these images also furnished rich material for an archeologically informed makeover of Christ's perceived physical appearance. David Strauss and Ernest Renan, among other midcentury biblical scholars, had rewritten sacred Christian narrative along secular lines, giving birth to that most conspicuously modern of Christ types—the historical Jesus. Polenov, Merezhkovsky, and Ainalov in turn sifted through the surviving remnants of the earliest Christian art in search of a viable likeness of Christ for modernity.

In this revisionist project, iconography took precedence over aesthetics. Polenov, Merezhkovsky, and Ainalov here differed from their successors in the avant-garde.[2] In his seminal essay "Iconography and Iconology," Erwin Panofsky defines iconography as "that branch of the history of art which concerns itself with the subject matter or meaning of works or art, as opposed to their form." At its most basic level, the study of "iconography proper" depends on the ability to identify recurring image types.[3] For the boy Julian, as for so many exhibition visitors in fin-de-siècle Russia, a true likeness of Christ is one in which Christ can, in fact, be recognized. As many nineteenth-century scholars and artists were discovering, however, early Christ images generally failed to conform to long-familiar iconographic patterns. Indeed, the growing store of Christ images known to Western science challenged a pervasive belief that there existed a common, recognizable likeness, one that had maintained the integrity of its basic outline from one century to the next and despite regional variations in style. Such archeologists and art historians as Adolphe Napoléon Didron, Giovanni Battista de Rossi, and Nikodim Kondakov examined a diverse body of lost or neglected images from Rome, Istanbul, Mount Athos, and elsewhere, in the process raising scholarly and public awareness across Europe and Russia of the heterogeneous nature of early Christian iconography.

In an 1895 master's thesis on "mosaics of the IV and V centuries," Ainalov, then Kondakov's student, contributed directly to this international project of organizing the heterogeneous Christ images of late antiquity into a coherent, linear history of types. In a related manner, Merezhkovsky and Polenov looked to early Christ images not simply as artistic models to be imitated, in the manner of a *style byzantin,* but as ancient artifacts infused with potential historicity. In *Julian the Apostate,* Merezhkovsky exposes the equivocal testimony of early Christ images, while in published notes to *Christ and the Adulteress* (1887), Polenov explains how the latest archeological discoveries influenced his painting's innovative iconography. From the point of view of audiences, the stakes involved in the archeology of the Christ image were nevertheless highest not in print media—whether novels or monographs—but in the public space of the exhibition. More so than even churches, secular exhibitions represented the most direct forum for testing revisionist Christ images. For *Christ and the Adulteress* (1887), Polenov consulted a wide range of ancient artifacts in a quixotic attempt to reconstruct the physical appearance of the historical Jesus. Many Petersburg critics and exhibition visitors not only objected to Polenov's portrayal of Christ; they had difficulty even locating Christ on the canvas.

In short, the science of archeology, especially in conjunction with the medium of painting, offered new methods and contentious results to a question from the first centuries of Christianity: What had the earthly Jesus looked like? The answers that this question received are of less interest here than the texts and images that generated them. In order to assess what is at stake in the nineteenth-century archeology of the Christ image, an archeological approach is required, one that is interdisciplinary in scope and attuned to the discursive structures of its sources. To borrow Foucault's famous definition, such an "archeology" aims "to rediscover on what basis knowledge and theory become possible."[4] Even as nineteenth-century scholars, writers, and painters unearthed and reproduced ancient Christ images, their efforts, often in unintended ways, contributed to a modern rupture in the iconography of Christ, as new histories replaced outdated apocrypha and as the sacred and familiar gave way to the heterogeneous and estranged.

MEREZHKOVSKY AND THE TYPES OF CHRIST

The year 1896 stands out as a high point for the archeology of the Christ image in Russia. In addition to the publication of Merezhkovsky's *Julian the Apostate,* Russian archeologists and art historians organized an exhibition that year in Moscow devoted to the early history of the Christ image. Sponsored by the Society of Lovers of Art, this exhibition, the first ever in Russia consisting exclusively of pre-Renaissance Christian art,[5] featured medieval Russian icons as well as replicas and photographic reproductions of early Christian and Byzantine frescoes, mosaics, and sculptures. Among the members of the Society who participated in the exhibition were Vasily Polenov and Dmitry Ainalov. Polenov contributed three illustrations of sarcophagi from the Lateran museum in Rome to the exhibition's collection, while Ainalov delivered a public lecture to a standing-room-only audience on "Images of Christ in Christian Art." In fact, Ainalov had presented an earlier lecture at the Society in 1894, the subject of which furnished the title for the exhibition two years later: "The Types of Christ."[6]

This title seems apt for an analysis of Merezhkovsky's novel, too. In the passage quoted above, the boy Julian confronts examples of two very different Christ types: an Arian mosaic of an enthroned Christ and a sarcophagus bas-relief of the Good Shepherd. The exhibition catalog, most likely written by Praskovia Uvarova, a leading figure in Russian archeological circles and the first female member of the Russian Academy of Sciences,[7] likewise grapples with the implications of such seemingly incommensurable Christ types. In the respective narratives that they construct around this same set of images, Merezhkovsky's novel and the exhibition catalog provide a telling study in contrast.

Through dozens of detailed descriptions, the catalog provides visitors with an up-to-date historiography of the earliest known types of Christ. At each step in this history, heterogeneity is carefully minimized. In a linear fashion, the catalog divides the exhibition's Roman and Byzantine numbers into three basic headings: "the ideal type," "the transition to the historical type," and "the historical type." Grouped together under the ideal type are more than a dozen copies of marble engravings from fourth- and fifth-century Roman sarcophagi. Aside from two examples of Christ as Orpheus, all the selected engravings depict the Good Shepherd. The exhibition thus marginalizes more overtly allegorical Christ types from the same period, such as the grapevine or the fish symbol. The catalog simply notes that such variations on the ideal type exist and accounts for their unfamiliar and "pagan" appearance on three grounds: first, early Christians refrained from depicting Christ directly out of fear of persecution from Roman authorities; second, Christian artists would in any case have begun with what they knew, namely, classical style and pagan subject matter; third, later Christian artists required "centuries" in order to forge "verisimilar representations" (*podobnye izobrazheniia*) of Christ. For these reasons, Christians of the first three centuries were "forced" to turn to "symbols and allegorical representations, which were easy for them to borrow from the Old Testament and from the antique models with which they were familiar."[8] In short, the ideal type was allegorical by default.

As the catalog notes, moreover, the ideal type developed "in the catacombs."[9] By the time of the Moscow exhibition, the Roman catacombs, if not always readily accessible to outside scholars, had enjoyed half a century as the epicenter in the archeology of the Christ image. In 1841, Giovanni Battista de

Rossi, generally regarded as the modern founder of "Christian archeology," began his pioneering excavation of Rome's neglected catacombs. Over the next few decades, de Rossi unearthed long-lost tombs of martyr-saints and contributed to deciphering the symbolic system of catacomb artwork.[10] In the wake of his discoveries, which were popularized across Europe through a spate of historical novels, including Henryk Sienkiewicz's *Quo Vadis* (1897),[11] the notion that the catacombs housed the most ancient surviving Christian art became widely accepted. The catacombs predated the establishment of Christianity as a state religion in the fourth century, while after the ninth most catacombs ceased to have visitors and fell into virtual oblivion. Christ images from the catacombs, as if sealed off from the vagaries of medieval apocrypha, thus became endowed with an aura of scientific authenticity upon their rediscovery. Some scholars even held out hope of discovering an actual portrait of the historical Jesus somewhere along the unexplored miles of "subterranean Rome" (*Roma sotterranea*). De Rossi himself was skeptical of this possibility. As he argues, anything resembling a set iconography for the "face of Christ" is "extremely rare among the most ancient paintings": "The reason for this appears to me to have been the prevalence of the symbolic system. We can thus assign no iconographic value to the figures of Christ resurrecting Lazarus, let alone those of the Good Shepherd."[12]

The catalog for the Moscow exhibition sides with leading Catholic archeologists in Rome in citing fear of persecution as a rationale for why early Christians were not more realistic in their art. Here Catholic and Orthodox scholars tended to differ from their Protestant colleagues in Germany and England, for whom the seeming absence of portraitlike depictions of Christ before the fourth century reflected a principled rejection of graven images among early Christians. The persecution defense for catacomb symbolism occurs in historical fiction as well. For example, in *Fabiola; or, The Church of the Catacombs* (1854), written by the Catholic cardinal and tractarian Nicholas Wiseman, a pious Roman grave-digger assures the novel's protagonists (as well as the reader) that "our Lord was represented under the symbol of Orpheus, to conceal His sacred representation from Gentile blasphemy and sacrilege."[13]

In Merezkovsky's *Julian the Apostate,* the bas-relief of the Good Shepherd that Julian sees on a "tomb" bears close parallels to the reproductions of catacomb sarcophagi from the Moscow exhibition. Merezhkovsky's fictional sarcophagus belongs to "the earliest Christian times"; moreover, it is older than its ecclesiastical setting, a fourth-century Arian church in Myrca on the outskirts of Caesarea Cappadocia in what is now central Turkey. According to one ancient authority, Julian and his brother helped build this church during their childhood exile from Constantinople.[14] From the fourth to tenth centuries, sarcophagi of martyr-saints from the Roman catacombs were in fact frequently relocated above ground to Byzantine-style cathedrals, where they were enshrined as relics. Concerning the beardless Good Shepherd of the catacombs in particular, the catalog explains that it represents a symbolic rendering of Christ based on a parable from John 10:11–18: "Its outstanding trait is youth, a sign of divinity."[15] In other words, the Good Shepherd in whom Julian recognizes the "Galilean" is not a portrait or likeness of the person Christ but an allegorical representation. Merezhkovsky himself plays on the irony of his young hero's partiality for a shepherd youth over any of the other Christ types on the same sarcophagus, which include "Orpheus, Moses, Jonah and the Whale, the Dove, and the Fish." All these types of Christ, Merezhkovsky explains, represent no more than "simple-hearted symbols of childlike belief" (*prostodushnye simvoly detskoi very*).[16]

Passing on to the fifth and sixth centuries and beyond, the catalog recounts to exhibition visitors the slow transition from the ideal to the historical type in early Christian art after the Peace of the Church in 317. In the era of the public, state-sponsored Christian art under Constantine I and his successors (with the singular exception of his grandson Julian), cathedral mosaics of an adult, bearded Christ began gradually to supplant the ideal type of the catacombs. According to the catalog, artists drew on various circulating legends about ancient portraits of Jesus as well as on speculation from Church Fathers about his physical appearance. In terms of nineteenth-century aesthetics, the historical type is thus more "realistic" than the ideal type. Crucially, this belated move toward realism enables the catalog to credit Byzantium (and implicitly the Orthodox faith) with the emergence of the first authentic likeness of Christ: "After the Christian faith was accepted publicly, and Emperor Constantine, breaking from the ancient traditions of pagan Rome, transferred his capital to the East, the faithful could hardly deny themselves the desire to have a true representation of the image of the Savior [*vernogo izobrazheniia lika* Spasitel'ia]."[17]

The exhibition included about two dozen reproductions of mosaics and frescoes from Rome, Ravenna, Istanbul, and elsewhere depicting the so-called historical type of Christ, including what must have served as the source for the menacing "Arian Christ" that the boy Julian views in Merezhkovsky's novel: the ninth-century Christ on the Throne located in the narthex of the church of Hagia Sophia in Istanbul (fig. 12). While traveling with his wife, Zinaida Gippius, through Italy and Greece in 1891, Merezhkovsky had made a special point of visiting the Hagia Sophia (then the mosque Ayasofya Camii).[18] Merezhkovsky's ekphrasis corresponds point by point with the catalog description of this mosaic, except that, in a creative anachronism, where the catalog identifies Justinian (r. 527–65) as the emperor receiving a blessing at Christ's feet, the boy Julian recognizes his uncle Constantius (r. 337–61), the man who murdered his father, usurped the throne, and sent him with his brother into exile in Asia Minor.[19]

Such superficial resemblances between *Julian the Apostate* and the exhibition catalog nevertheless do not conceal the gulf separating their diverging historical narratives about the same cultural artifact—the early Christ image. In the catalog, the image of Christ, moving beyond the paganism of the Roman catacombs, reaches the full maturity of realism only in Orthodox Byzantium.[20] In its attempt to maintain a linear historiography, the catalog further devises a middle category, "Transition to the Historical Type," for those problem images of Christ that, as late as the ninth century, preserved the symbolism peculiar to the ideal type in rendering the adult and portraitlike Christ of the historical type. By contrast, Merezhkovsky situates two incommensurable images of Christ from different historical periods in the same space, the Arian church of Julian's childhood. The pastoral symbolism of the Good Shepherd competes with the imperial iconography of an enthroned Christ, one whose halo bears an emperor's "diadem" and whose figure, in keeping with the doctrine of Arianism, appears more human than divine.[21] Moreover, Merezhkovsky interprets the purported rise of realist portraiture in Byzantine iconography in a very different sense than does the catalog. Thus the boy Julian does recognize one of the faces in the mosaic, but it is his uncle's in the guise of a supplicant; the enthroned Christ, by contrast, bears little resemblance to the Galilean shepherd of Julian's imagination. Concerning the same mosaic from Hagia Sophia, Fyodor Buslaev, in his landmark 1866 study of the Russian icon, had observed, "It is a curious testimony for the history of Eastern iconography that the artistry of icons did not preclude portrait representations of contemporary personalities."[22]

Julian the Apostate marks a significant but little-explored shift in the iconography of Christ in Russia at the end of the nineteenth century. In his novel, Merezhkovsky dramatizes the impossibility of recovering Christ's true likeness through the history of his images. The Manichean struggle

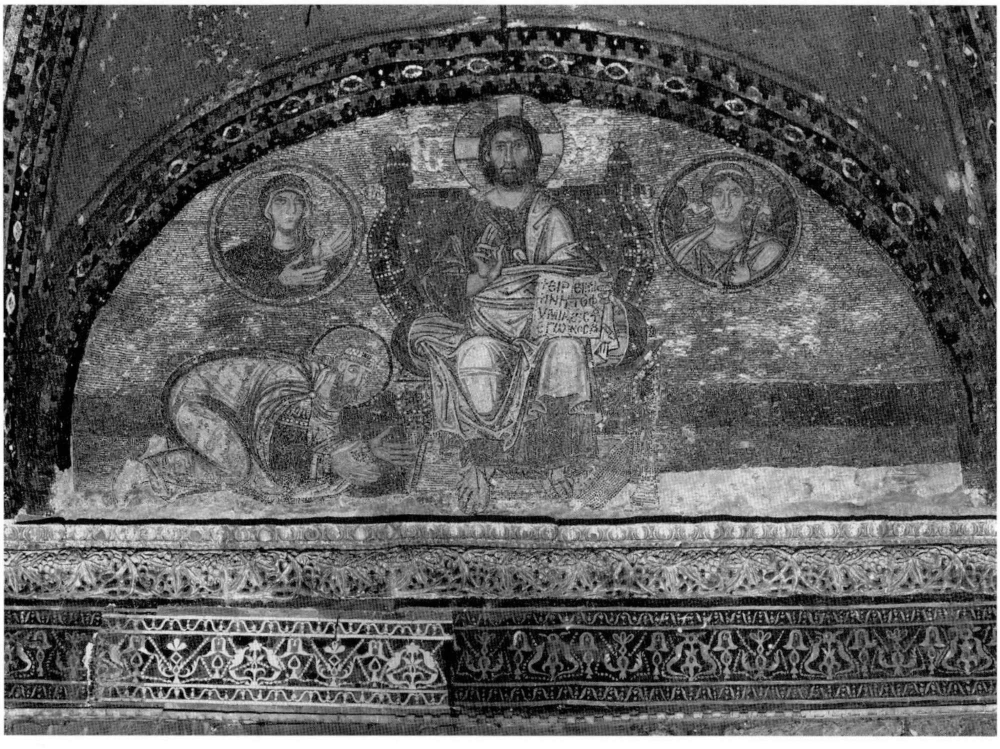

FIG. 12 Mosaic of Christ on the Throne. Church of Hagia Sophia, Istanbul.

between "Christ and Antichrist," the trilogy's title and overarching theme, manifests itself even within the most ancient Christian art. More than three hundred years separate the boy Julian from the boy Jesus. What remains in the absence of the original is not a faithful copy of Christ's true likeness; on the contrary, the Good Shepherd, no less than the enthroned Christ, represents only one of its multiplying simulacra.

The irrevocable heterogeneity of the Christ image persists even in the Russian setting of *Peter and Alexis,* the concluding novel of Merezhkovsky's trilogy. Not unlike the late imperial compendium icon, in which Mother of God icons are arranged according to regional and national types,[23] the rise of nationalized Christ types represents a major trend in modern iconography. In Leskov's "At the Edge of the World" (1876), for example, the narrator states his preference for the "image" or "countenance" of Christ on Russian icons—literally, his *lik,* a Church Slavonic term—over the polished "face" (*litso*) on Renaissance paintings: "Our folk art understood the external features of Christ's representation [*Khristovo izobrazhenie*] . . . and came closer to the truth of the internal traits of his character."[24] Like Dostoevsky[25] before him, Leskov insists on the authenticity and continuity of the Russian Christ even as he acknowledges the existence of rival types from the West. For Merezhkovsky, by contrast, heterogeneity is a permanent condition of the Christ image, whether in Julian's Constantinople, Leonardo da Vinci's Italy, or Peter the Great's Russia. In the trilogy's epilogue, "The Christ to Come," false Christs, each leading their own doomsday cult, proliferate across the eighteenth-century Russian countryside. The protagonist of the epilogue, having made contact with one such cult, poses the troubling question of how there can be so "many Christs." To borrow the provocative reply he receives, for the eponymous Christ of Merezhkovsky's trilogy, "The spirit is one, but the flesh is many."[26]

AINALOV AND THE HISTORICAL TYPE

The historical type occupied a pivotal position in the nineteenth-century archeology of the Christ image. What the historical type lacked in antiquity it made up for in its subsequent continuity. For the average visitor at the 1896 Moscow exhibition, the historical type was immediately recognizable as Christ in a way that catacomb renderings were not. As the catalog puts it, the historical type gave rise to the likeness of Christ that would be "accepted by the whole Christian world."[27]

Modern archeology had even developed an explanatory model—what can be termed the copy theory of the icon—to help account for the perceived stability of Christ's likeness over the centuries. In 1839, the French archeologist Adolphe Napoléon Didron was granted permission to enter the reclusive Orthodox monasteries at Mount Athos in northern Greece, where he discovered, or rather was shown, an eighteenth-century icon painter's manual. In his introduction to this text, which he published in French translation in 1845, Didron argues that the Eastern icon—unlike Renaissance paintings, which use human models—represents the copy of a copy produced with the aid of church-sanctioned manuals: "In Greece the artist is the slave of the theologian; his work, which will be copied by his successors, copies the paintings of those before him."[28] In contrast to the catalog of the Moscow exhibition, Didron emphasized that the likeness of Christ, especially in the West, revealed significant variation at every stage of its history, from the catacombs to the Renaissance and beyond. In a chapter on "the history of the Christ image" from his influential two-volume *L'Iconographie chrétienne: Histoire de Dieu* (1843), Didron draws on a wealth of historical examples to challenge the "false" opinion that there ever was a "unique type" of Christ.[29] His publication of the Mount Athos manual two years later nevertheless added fresh support to this long-standing belief; from medieval Byzantium to modern Orthodoxy, icon-painting manuals had worked to promote, even enforce, iconographic homogeneity.

In Russia, Didron's copy theory was readily adapted to suit local needs (even if the archeologist himself came under harsh criticism at times).[30] The earliest icon painters in Russia had been Greek, and by the twelfth century Novgorod had its own copy of the *mandylion*, a perfect likeness of Christ "not made by human hands" (*nerukotvornyi*). The medieval Russian icon, after the sixteenth century, had become somewhat naturalized under the pressures of Western influence. Yet the face of Christ in a nineteenth-century Russian icon still conformed to the basic schema of the Byzantine *mandylion*, thanks in part to the continued use of *podlinniki*, or pattern books, in the icon-painting centers in the Vladimir province.

The more intractable problem nevertheless concerned not the posterity of the historical type but its obscure origins: When did the historical type first emerge, and what connection, if any, did its belated emergence have with the supposed physical appearance of the earthly Jesus? Kondakov, Buslaev's student, briefly broached these questions in his 1876 *The History of Byzantine Art and Iconography*. Kondakov, examining miniatures from Greek manuscripts, describes the rise of the historical type in the fourth and fifth centuries as a "Renaissance of antique art on Byzantine soil," a period in which an "ancient naturalism" emerged as a "result of vacillation, of a truthful search for a historically real type of Christ." In particular, early portraitists of Christ consulted interpretations of his physical appearance from the Church Fathers. These anonymous artists "vacillated" inasmuch as the Church Fathers disagreed among themselves. Thus Christ is often illustrated in manuscripts of the period with a long face, with "long hair falling on his shoulders, black as tar, as well as with a short black beard." Yet even within the same manuscript, Christ could also be depicted as a "youth" with "blond or curly red hair" and "with or without a beard." Kondakov analyzes the "vacillation" of one Byzantine miniaturist in terms that could be extended to Polenov and other modern painters of the historical Jesus: "It's understandable that this artist has submitted to the contemporary and sufficiently naive demands of naturalism, albeit not of an absolute naturalism; or rather, he strove to be naturalist within the limits of a given type."[31]

In his published master's thesis *Mosaics of the IV and V Centuries* (1895), Ainalov went further in speculating on the origins of the historical type. Ainalov had already established a name for himself in archeological circles for his work on four icon panels originally from Mount Sinai, which had for decades remained in the private collection of Bishop Porfiry Uspensky. After Uspensky's death in 1890, Kondakov and two students, Ainalov and Nikolai Petrov, dated these four works to the sixth and seventh century, making them the oldest-known icon panels in existence. The tsarist government capitalized on this serendipitous discovery of ancient Byzantine icons on Russian soil by supporting the establishment of the Russian Archeological Institute in Istanbul in 1894.[32] A few years later, Ainalov's *The Hellenistic Origins of Byzantine Art* (1900) helped revolutionize the study of early Christian art. In this monograph, Ainalov argues that the first Christian art emerged in such Hellenistic centers as Alexandria, Antioch, and Asia Minor, not in Rome and its catacombs.

In preparation for his earlier master's thesis, Ainalov in 1892–93 nevertheless traveled to sites in central Italy, which remained more accessible than those in the Ottoman Empire. In his thesis, Ainalov challenged a common assumption—one espoused by the author of the exhibition catalog—that the oldest instance of the historical type originated in the catacombs of Callixtus, the extensive networks of which de Rossi had made famous half a century earlier. Several Christ images from catacombs in or near the Callixtus network vied for this distinction in the nineteenth century; the catalog prefers a certain "sixth-century mosaic" portraying Christ's face in profile.[33] As this late date suggests, the catalog tacitly acknowledges the widespread view that portraitlike depictions of Christ in the catacombs, especially mosaics, represent additions introduced after the Peace of the Church.

In his own search for the origins of the historical type, Ainalov, passing over the catacombs, instead argues for the precedence of a fourth-century mosaic from the mausoleum of Saint Costanza. This mausoleum, which Constantine I built for his sister, houses a mosaic in which Christ stands on a cloud with Peter and Paul on either side. The attractive and youthful Christ has "yellow . . . parted hair," an "oval face," a "beard parted at his chin," and "blue, almond-shaped" eyes (fig. 13). Going against the tide of such nineteenth-century painters as Polenov, who sought to counteract the Europeanized Christ of the Renaissance by darkening, within very narrow limits, both his complexion and hair, Ainalov thus identifies a blond-haired, blue-eyed Christ as the "first known historical type."[34] As he remarked to the Society of Lovers of Art in 1894, the dark-skinned "Byzantine type"—such as the enthroned Christ in Merezhkovsky's novel—appeared later and reflected merely "the influence of the ethnological peculiarities of the peoples of the East."[35]

In support of his choice, Ainalov argues that the Saint Costanza mosaic represents a historical type—not an ideal type, as had been previously thought—precisely inasmuch as it corresponds to the verbal portrait of Christ found in Lentulus's "Letter to the Roman Senate." In this apocryphal letter, which dates possibly to the thirteenth century, Lentulus, Pontius Pilate's supposed successor, describes Christ as "a man of stature middling tall . . . with a reverend countenance": "In those days there ap-

FIG. 13 Mosaic of Christ. Mausoleum of Saint Costanza, Rome.

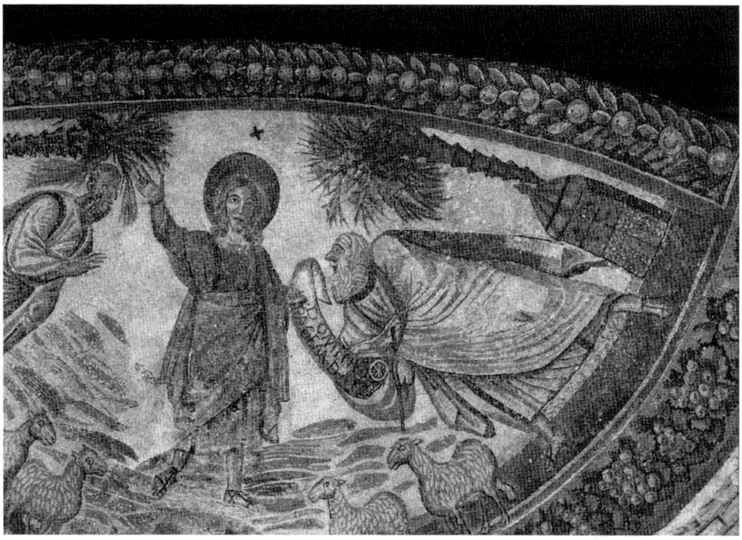

peared, and there still is, a man of great power named Jesus Christ . . . having hair of the hue of an unripe hazel-nut and smooth almost down to his ears . . . having a parting at the middle of the head according to the fashion of the Nazarenes . . . having a full beard of the colour of his hair, not long, but a little forked at the chin."[36] In Ainalov's view, the mosaic of Christ from the mausoleum of Saint Costanza, other than lacking a "copious" beard, closely resembles the description of Christ in Lentulus's letter, right down to his Nazarene-style hair. Unwilling to let the matter rest there, Ainalov further lends Lentulus's letter its own quasi-historical claim to authenticity with the following provocative suggestion: "If we remember that the images of Abgar, Veronica, and Nicodemus arose precisely in the East, then we will have to admit that the Nazarene type of Christ also came to Europe from the East and traveled alongside these legends."[37] While the earliest extant variants of Lentulus's letter are written in Latin, the language of the Roman Church, the Nazarene type, Ainalov argues, ultimately derives from Eastern antecedents. The Easternness of the Byzantine type is a mere parochialism, an effect of local influences; the Eastern roots of the Nazarene type, by contrast, have a historical basis.

Ainalov alludes here to three other legendary images: Abgar's cloth, Veronica's veil, and Nicodemus's shroud. These images—or rather the competing relics in Eastern and Western Christendom that purport to be their originals, including the Vatican Veronica and the Shroud of Turin—are inseparable from the legends surrounding them. Passed down orally and through apocryphal texts, each legend narrates a different story in which the outline of Christ's face becomes miraculously imprinted on a piece of cloth, whether the canvas of a painter whom King Abgar of Edessa dispatches to Christ (pl. 4), the veil that Veronica gives Christ on his way to the cross, or the shroud that Nicodemus buys for his burial. These legends not only underwrite the truth claims of each image tradition; as the folklorist Wilhelm Grimm argued in an 1841 article,[38] the legends likely predated the existence of any actual images.

For Ainalov, then, the origins of the historical type lay in apocryphal legends of the True Face. Ainalov singles out Lentulus's letter because, unlike the other three legends, it provides a detailed textual description of Christ's physical appearance. Within the context of Ainalov's evolving research, his suggestion of an Eastern origin for the historical type anticipates the revolution he would soon bring about in Byzantine studies with *The Hellenistic Origins of Byzantine Art* (1900). Within the context of nineteenth-century biblical scholarship, his relocation of the blond-haired, blue-eyed "Nazarene type" to the East reflects a small but growing trend to build a scientific rationale for a pure-race Aryan Jesus, a figure that assumed extreme form in later Nazi theology.[39]

Yet at another level, Ainalov, for all his erudition, seems motivated here and throughout his analysis of the Saint Costanza mosaic by a certain unexpressed desire—one lurking in the subtext of the exhibition catalog as well—that early images of Christ should somehow be faithful portraits of the historical Jesus. Legends on the origin of the Christ image could no longer be accepted at face value in the modern science of archeology.[40] In a secular update of Christian apocrypha, Ainalov instead reconceptualized these circulating legends as source materials for truth-seeking Byzantine artists. Such nineteenth-century artists as Polenov, drawing on the modern methods of source criticism, were indeed using these same legends in this manner. In *Mosaics of the IV and V Centuries,* Ainalov privileges East over West, the historical "Nazarene type" over the parochial Byzantine type, as well as popular legends over learned disputes among the Church Fathers. The mosaic of Christ from the mausoleum of Saint Costanza may represent a derivative portrait from an apocryphal tale, but then for the Russian Byzantinist both image and text arose in the East, where the historical Jesus once lived and where the traces of his likeness are scattered closer than anywhere else to the origin.

POLENOV AND THE HISTORICAL JESUS

Paintings of the historical Jesus, a modern Christ type, generated controversies in one city after another across Europe and the United States throughout the second half of the nineteenth century. In the wake of the midcentury rise of realism, the staple subject matter of historical painting—Christian and Greco-Roman events and legends (*historia*) belonging to the Great Time of an absolute past—became increasingly *historicized.* In this broader realist trend, the emphasis in paintings of Christ shifted from the monumentalizing of sacred narrative toward the project of historical reconstruction, with results that frequently proved jarring for audiences. Noteworthy (and often notorious) examples include William Holman Hunt's *Finding of the Saviour in the Temple* (1860), Mihály Munkácsy's *Le Christ devant Pilate* (1881), Vasily Vereshchagin's *Execution on a Roman Cross* (1887), and James Tissot's gouache cycle *La Vie de Notre Seigneur Jésus-Christ* (1896). In Russia, Vasily Polenov was among a number of painters, including Ivan Kramskoy and Nikolai Ge, who chose to unveil realist interpretations of the Christ image at exhibitions of the Itinerants (*Peredvizhniki*), a group that had broken from the St. Petersburg Academy in 1870 in part because of its valorization of a prerealist historical style.[41]

Although working independently, each of the above painters contributed to the development of a realist iconography for the historical Jesus. In hindsight, this body of paintings, especially given the realist assumptions underpinning their elaborate historical constructions, may no longer appear persuasive. At least until the 1890s, the very concept of the historical Jesus nevertheless remained highly contentious. In the doctrine of mainstream churches across Christendom, the earthly Jesus is also the eternal God; Jesus, in his human nature, could perform miracles or rise from the dead at a specific historical juncture precisely because, in his divine nature as Christ, he was, is, and always will be. As Albert Schweitzer argues, this doctrine of Christ's dual nature, established at the fourth-century Council of Chalcedon, "had first to be shattered before men could once more go out in quest of the historical Jesus, before they could even grasp the thought of His existence."[42] The historical Jesus is not simply earthly. In David Strauss's *Leben Jesu* (1835) and Renan's *Vie de Jésus* (1863), Jesus, precisely in becoming historical, is consigned to the spatiotemporal limits of first-century, Roman-occupied Palestine. In the process, his divinity, while not explicitly denied, is placed outside the limits of historiography as a science. The situation was similar in realist historical painting. In Russia, the scandal of historicizing the earthly Jesus indeed fell disproportionately to painters, beginning with Alexander Ivanov's *Appearance of Christ to the People* (1857). Russian censors of foreign print media worked tirelessly, if ultimately in vain, to bar the historical Jesus from entering the country. Renan and Strauss were banned, as was discussion of their works in the press.[43] It was thus frequently left to painters of the "Ivanov-Strauss-Renan school," as one character calls them in *Anna Karenina*,[44] to assume the leading role in introducing the Russian public to the figure of the historical Jesus.

As in the case of biblical scholarship, moreover, realist approaches to traditional Christian iconography developed largely in secular environments. Within Russian Orthodoxy, Polenov, it should be noted in passing, belonged to a separate group of painters, led by Viktor Vasnetsov, who worked to build and decorate churches in neo-Byzantine style. In 1881–82, for example, Polenov painted the iconostasis for Vasnetsov's Byzantine-inspired Church of the Savior Not Made by Hands at Abramtsevo. Yet outside the walls of the church, the reception of his *Christ and the Adulteress* (pl. 10), first shown at the fifteenth exhibition of the Peredvizhniki in St. Petersburg in 1887, exemplifies the high stakes surrounding secular paintings of the historical Jesus in Russia. In light of recurring controversies occasioned by such works as Nikolai Ge's *Last Supper* (1863) and Ivan Kramskoy's *Christ in the Wilderness* (1872), Polenov's painting initially met official resistance. The censor rejected Polenov's proposed title—*Who of You Is Without Sin?*—in favor of the traditional and more heavy-handed *Christ and the Adulteress* (*Khristos i greshnitsa,* literally,

"Christ and the Sinner"). Shortly after the opening of the exhibition the painting was ordered taken down. Days later, however, in a private viewing, it was purchased by no less a patron of the arts than Alexander III. Thus unlike Vereshchagin's *Execution on a Roman Cross* (1887) or Ge's *What Is Truth?* (1890), both of which were scandalizing polite society in traveling exhibitions abroad at almost the same time, Polenov's *Christ and the Adulteress* did not suffer the fate of being banned from public exhibition inside Russia.

Following the tsar's intervention, which protected Polenov from the kinds of ad hominem attacks to which his predecessors had been subject, his painting prompted an unusually substantive critical debate. In his own words, Polenov intended to depict "Christ as he was in reality" (*kak on byl v deistvitel'nosti*): "I wanted to search out historical truth . . . to represent my subject as close to reality as possible, whatever that reality had been."[45] What distinguishes *Christ and the Adulteress* from most other Russian paintings of the historical Jesus is not the novelty of Polenov's intentions but the exhaustiveness of his method. In *Christ and the Adulteress,* Polenov's hyperrealist attention to historical detail extended from the archeology of Jerusalem, especially Herod's temple, to the ethnography of ancient Jewish society. Of particular relevance here as well was his extensive research into early Christian and Byzantine art. The resulting painting represents a comprehensive realist revision of the traditional iconography of the Adulteress in the temple from the eighth chapter of John.[46]

By the 1880s, the minimal requirement for painters attempting to represent "Christ as he was in reality" was a pilgrimage to Palestine, then part of the Ottoman province of Syria.[47] In the decades following Napoleon's 1799 Palestinian campaign, large numbers of Western travelers, for the first time since the Crusades, were in a position to visit the "Holy Land"—a place that, despite its modern, predominantly Arab inhabitants, remained steeped in biblical times for pilgrims, tourists, artists, and scholars alike.[48] Not all biblical sites were easily located, however. In the Western rediscovery of Palestine, the work of Edward Robinson, a pioneer of "biblical archeology," deserves special mention. Through modern excavation techniques and the etymological analysis of contemporary Arabic place-names, Robinson, in 1838 and again in 1852, located and described long-lost biblical sites across Palestine.[49] For later artist-pilgrims such as Polenov, Robinson and his followers had literally remapped the terrain over which the historical Jesus had once walked. Polenov traveled twice to Jerusalem and elsewhere in Palestine, the first time in 1881–82 in preparation for the painting *Christ and the Adulteress,* the second in 1899 in conjunction with continuing work on the roughly five dozen paintings of his full cycle, *From the Life of Christ* (1882–1909).[50] After preparing dozens of sketches at biblical locations during his first visit to Palestine, Polenov headed to Rome, where he spent the winter months of 1883 drawing individual character studies of Jewish models. By 1885, still two years before the painting itself was completed, so many preparatory sketches from Rome and Palestine had accumulated that Polenov took the unusual step of displaying them in St. Petersburg at the thirteenth exhibition of the Peredvizhniki.[51]

In order to demonstrate the meticulous care with which he had resurrected "the era of the gospels," Polenov donated his ample notes on *Christ and the Adulteress* to the critic Alexander Sobolev, who published a sixty-page brochure to coincide with the painting's exhibition in 1887.[52] For the temple itself, Polenov consulted the work of contemporary archeologists, especially Melchior de Vögüé's celebrated 1864 monograph, *Le Temple de Jérusalem,* which the artist ordered specially from abroad.[53] In the final painting, Polenov even added loose rocks here and there to indicate that the temple, begun by Herod the Great in 19 BCE, would still have been under construction during Jesus' lifetime. Polenov's chosen setting for the encounter between Christ and the Adulteress—the outer gates of the Court of the Gentiles—further illustrates the intricate layers of his revisionist iconography. Combining the roles of ethnographer and exegete, Polenov justified his unorthodox decision to stage the episode outside the temple along three lines: first, Christ's ethnically diverse followers would not have been permitted inside; second, Mosaic law would have likewise forbidden the presence of a woman, let alone an adulteress, in the temple's inner court; lastly, Christ must have been in the floorless outer courtyard, since John records that he wrote "on the earth with his finger."[54] As a finishing touch to his portrayal of the Court of the Gentiles, Polenov included twin Greek tablets on the temple gates warning Gentiles from entering on pain of death. The fragment of one such tablet had, in fact, been discovered by Clermont Ganneau during an archeological excavation of the temple sixteen years earlier.[55]

Needless to say, critics were not slow to note excesses in Polenov's peculiarly syncretic historical realism. In response to Sobolev, the critic I. I. Kristi wrote an article-length pamphlet of his own, "Historical Truth in Painting: Apropos a Painting by Polenov." Kristi criticized, among other things, Polenov's decision to include such superfluous figures as Simon of Cyrene (mounted on a horse on the lower right) and the Pharisee Gamaliel (descending from the steps of the temple).[56] Moreover, for all his signature mastery in depicting Palestinian landscape, Polenov strangely relocates the Mount of Olives so that it appears, in a picturesque flourish, behind the temple in the background. With complete candor, Polenov admits in his published notes that, in reality, the mountain would not be visible from the painting's vantage point.[57] Lastly, it is curious that Polenov lavishes so much attention on a gospel scene widely regarded at the time as apocryphal in biblical historiography. Even Renan, who accorded more historicity to the Gospel of John than did most of his German colleagues, writes that "the account of the women taken in adultery . . . gives room for grave critical doubts."[58]

Polenov's revisionism in *Christ and the Adulteress* extended as well to a speculative reconstruction of the physical appearance of the historical Jesus. As both supporters and detractors of Polenov noted, the figure of Christ is not readily recognized among the crowd on the painting's left side. The writer Vladimir Korolenko, one of Polenov's defenders, provides a vivid account of his own first impression: "At first glance it's as if you don't notice the main figure in the painting; you feel already a certain indefinable uneasiness. Who's that person sitting on the rock lit by the sun? Is it possible that it's . . . Christ? Yes, you're convinced, with a feeling akin to disenchantment, this figure is him—precisely this strong, muscular, deeply sunburned wandering Eastern preacher."[59] As Sobolev argues, in having "to seek" for the figure of Christ at all, the viewer experiences a sense of "foreboding" about what will be found: "You find Him, but it's as if it's not He."[60]

To soften the blow of such defamiliarization, Polenov incorporated several small details to help guide his viewers to the painting's main figure. First, borrowing a telltale sign from the end of the episode of the Adulteress in the temple, Polenov portrays Christ already bending over, as if intending to write on the ground, even as the Pharisees first approach. Second, Christ is the only seated figure on the left fully illuminated by sunlight. Lastly, by a peculiar omission, Christ is also the only figure in the entire painting not wearing some form of head covering. In fact, Christ's white cap was removed by the anxious artist—seemingly at the insistence of his horrified mother—just days before the opening exhibition.[61] Sobolev considered this last-minute omission an "error" that should be rectified.[62] The white cap did return to its place on Christ's head the following year in Polenov's *On the Tiberias (Gennesaret) Lake* (1888), after which it would remain a fixed iconographic detail in the cycle *From the Life of Christ.*

Polenov's concessions to convention in *Christ and the Adulteress* underscore a dilemma common to any attempt at iconographic revision: a Christ not recognizable as such is no longer Christ. In his pamphlet, Kristi succinctly summarizes the conservative position on Polenov's Christ image: "All these citations from Mr. Sobolev . . . do not give the artist the right to offer a representation with which we are not familiar."[63] Noncanonical iconography could even be interpreted as a form of pictorial blasphemy. As one concerned viewer of "shaky Orthodox convictions" wrote to Polenov in a letter, "You deliberately depart from the traditional type, without any explanation . . . or apology . . . so that you needlessly insult the religious feelings of the enormous majority of your viewers."[64]

In contrast, proponents of realist depictions of the historical Jesus tended to associate iconographic revision with scientific progress in such fields as archeology and ethnography. As Vasily Vereshchagin wrote in an outspoken defense of his own Palestinian sketches, "Yes, it's the complete truth: we are different from [the Old Masters] in many respects; we think differently, we are more daring in our synthesizing of facts about the past, present, and future."[65] The soft-spoken Polenov responded to a charge of "nihilism" from one outraged viewer in a similar, if less confrontational, manner: "Without a doubt, [my portrayal] is not canonical, as Roman or Byzantine artists came to represent him, especially inasmuch as he would have worn the Jewish or Galilean clothes of the common people. Precise depictions of Jewish dress from that time have not survived, but there have nevertheless come down to us certain details through both archeology and ethnography that give the possibility of recovering with reasonable certainty the external appearance of that epoch."[66]

Ancient images from the Mediterranean and the Middle East occupy a central place among Polenov's evidence on the possible appearance of the historical Jesus. In terms of Christ's attire, Polenov's acknowledged sources are highly eclectic: Christ's long white tunic derives from the bas-relief of an ancient Assyrian palace; his cloak is modern Egyptian; his outer garment, belt, shoes, and walking stick are borrowed from this same bas-relief as well as from the garb of the contemporary inhabitants of Palestine; and the contentious white cotton cap, or *keffiyeh,* in Arabic, comes in part from the bas-relief of a catacomb found in the church of Santa Maria Maggiore in Rome, in part from the observed dress of modern Arabs, and in part from circumstantial evidence involving the harsh climate of ancient Palestine.[67]

As even this cursory summary of Polenov's sources reveals, his reconstruction of the likeness of the historical Jesus does not rest on the sturdiest of foundations. In terms of the Assyrian bas-relief cited above, for instance, Polenov refers in his notes not to the original archeological research on the palaces of Nineveh by Paul-Émile Botta but to the derivative work of an English Egyptologist named Joseph Bonomi, who sought to correlate Botta's findings with the Old Testament. The image in question shows the torture of slaves after an Assyrian conquest in the sixth century BCE. Bonomi speculates that these slaves are "Palestinians," or rather "Samaritans," from the time of the Jewish captivity in Babylon; Shadrach, Meshach, and Abednego, when they were cast into the "fiery furnace," would conceivably have been dressed in the same manner.[68] Polenov has Christ wear the same Samaritan-style long white tunic. In other words, he draws on an Assyrian bas-relief from the sixth century "before Christ" to approximate what the historical Jesus might have worn in first-century Jerusalem.

By way of contrast, Polenov's justification for covering Christ's head with a white cap is based in part on an image a thousand years and thousands of miles removed from the palaces of Nineveh, namely, a bas-relief on a sarcophagus located in the fifth-century church of Maria Maggiore in Rome. This sarcophagus had been originally housed in the second-century Crypt of Lucina from the catacombs of Callixtus. In his notes, Polenov refers to a reproduction of this bas-relief—which indeed does present a number of figures wearing head covering—from an illustration in Buslaev's *General Remarks on Russian Icon Painting* (1866). As with his use of Bonomi's research, Polenov is concerned at least as much with Buslaev's interpretation as with the reproduced image itself. Buslaev expresses praise for its "excellent execution" as well as for the "naturalism" of its "real portraits."[69] Lending a historicist twist to Buslaev's naturalist gloss, Polenov writes in response to the same bas-relief that "when Jewish figures started to be given more typical traits on Christian sarcophagi in

Rome, they began to be represented in caps."[70] In other words, Polenov follows here the same logic that the catalog for the 1896 Moscow exhibition applies to the historical type: it requires centuries for Christian artists in Rome to work out how to depict first-century Jewish figures in Jerusalem in a realistic manner.

As his references to contemporary Palestinian and Egyptian dress indicate, moreover, Polenov has a habit of conflating modern Arabs and ancient Jews. This habit—one he shares with most of his modern sources—reflects among the most tenacious clichés of nineteenth-century travel literature on Palestine: the immutability of the East. For Western travelers seeking to reimagine the events of biblical history in as vivid a manner as possible, it was generally necessary to ignore the eighteen intervening centuries after the Roman dispersal of the Jews in 70 C.E. The French artist James Tissot, who produced hundreds of gouache biblical illustrations during the 1890s, even felt a sense of urgency as the pristine topography of biblical Palestine became endangered by the march of Western progress: "The [existing] data . . . in these days of the invasion of the engineer and the railway [will] disappear before the irresistible impulse of the aggressive modern spirit."[71] Polenov himself was more circumspect in generalizations of this sort than many Western travelers. Yet his ostensibly scholarly project of gauging possible correlations between ancient Jewish and modern Arabic dress is inevitably prejudiced toward a desired identity between past and present, without which barriers to historical reconstruction would be greatly compounded. (In a related manner, Polenov took issue with Renan's suggestion that the geography of modern Palestine was not now what it had been in the era of the gospels.)[72] Almost by default, Polenov's archeology of the Christ image ends up reifying an Orientalist ethnography.

Polenov's efforts to ground his portrayal of Christ's face in early Christian iconography encounter a rather different, and more original, set of problems. As Polenov writes in his notes to Sobolev, "Christians of the first centuries did not have any conception of what the face of Christ looked like in reality."[73] Polenov runs through a long list of ancient sources on Christ's supposed physical appearance, including the views of Augustine, Tertullian, Justin the Martyr, Clement of Alexandria, Celsius, and Gregory of Nyssa. Polenov here is actually paraphrasing, without attribution, Buslaev's study of icon painting. Significantly, Polenov, like Buslaev, ends his list with Origen's equivocation that "there is no definable image of Christ, but he appears to each according to his own understanding."[74] Moreover, these interpretations of the Church Fathers, which Didron and Kondakov had analyzed as well, were based not on the gospels but on typological readings of two Old Testament verses: in Psalms 44:3, the king of Korah, an allegorical type, is called the "most beautiful son of Man," while in Isaiah 53:2, the "son of Man" is said to be without "form" or "beauty." As Polenov explains in a letter, the patristic literature on the appearance of Christ is "extremely conflicting": "One writes that [Christ] was physically almost a monster [*urodom*]; another, on the contrary, clothed him with a beautiful physical appearance."[75]

Faced with the same conflicting accounts, Nikolai Ge in *What Is Truth?* (pl. 11) found inspiration in the first and slightly earlier of these two patristic traditions. As Repin recounts, Ge intended to portray in his painting a Christ who, "in protest against the pagan ideal," assumed the "most humble and insignificant human image in order to demonstrate to people that what was important was the soul."[76] In *What Is Truth?* Ge presents what even Tolstoy, his biggest defender, termed an "exceptionally unattractive" Christ.[77] Short, wispy-haired, pursed-lipped, and steely-eyed, Ge's Christ has no peer in nineteenth-century Russian religious painting. The furor that *What Is Truth?* provoked at the eighteenth exhibition of the Peredvizhniki in 1890 exceeded in intensity even the controversy surrounding Ge's own *Last Supper* nearly three decades earlier. Alexander III could barely contain his disgust in ordering *What Is Truth?* removed from the exhibition, calling the picture "repulsive."[78]

Polenov settled on a less-provocative course. Given the absence of reliable early portraits of Christ, he defends the creativity of the artist in his published notes. Indeed, he employs a traditional Russian folk figure—a slow-moving wanderer (*strannik*) with a walking stick—to create a genuinely novel iconographic type amid the proliferating Christs of late nineteenth-century painting. In terms of the archeology of the Christ image, however, Polenov works to smooth over the differences between various contradictory traditions in the patristic literature, portraying a Christ neither excessively tall nor excessively short, neither black-haired nor blond, neither beautiful nor ugly, with a face darkened as much by wind and sun as from the fact of his Eastern ethnicity. The same can be said of Polenov's approach to modern disputes as well. Thus Polenov appears to have drawn on the theories of Frederic Farrar, an English clergyman and biblical scholar who, in an influential equivocation of his own, viewed the historical Jesus as part Jewish and part Greek.[79] Rather than falling on one side or the other in these debates, both ancient and modern, Polenov's uncannily unassuming Christ—one so still and expressionless that he disappears in crowds, fades into landscapes—emerges as the synthesis of his own avatars.

For all his iconographic hedging, Polenov, via Sobolev's text, does identify specific models for his portrayal of Christ's face. His student Konstantin Korovin had briefly posed for an initial sketch.[80] Yet even while using a living model—a legacy of the Renaissance—Polenov was guided by two ancient images: "The type of Christ in the present picture . . . was derived partly from a Greek manuscript by Euthymius Zigaben, located in the Vatican library and published by D'Agincourt, and partly from an ancient fresco from the end of the second century, which has long ceased to exist but which has been preserved in an etching by Bosio. . . . [This etching is] an early example of a representation of Christ close to that Eastern type which would later become unchanging."[81] Polenov thus selects two examples that are related, in different ways, to Byzantine iconography. The miniature in question derives from Zigaben's twelfth-century *Dogmatica Panoplia,* the illustrations of which are reproduced in Seroux D'Agincourt's *Histoire de l'art* (1823) (fig. 14).[82] As in the first image that the boy

Julian sees in Merezhkovsky's novel, Christ is seated on a throne, from which he blesses a reigning emperor, in this case Alexius I Comnenus (r. 1081–1118). With an elongated face and short parted hair and beard, the face of Christ in this Greek miniature reflects the distinctive features of the *mandylion*. In the first instance, then, Polenov returns to a thoroughly Orthodox example from a Greek manuscript. Such a return to the supposed origin is characteristic of iconographic reform, not least inside the church. Here Polenov is a modern Nikon, the seventeenth-century Moscow patriarch who sought to correct the iconography of Christ by revisiting Greek models. Polenov's Byzantine-inflected iconography is at once newer and older than the Renaissance-inspired academic norms for depicting Christ that were defended with such intransigence by his conservative critics.

Polenov's second model derives from the archeology of the Roman catacombs. In his 1632 treatise *Roma sotterranea*, Antonio Bosio, the first modern excavator of the catacombs, included a sketch of a medallion fresco of Christ from the ceiling of a cubiculum in what he thought were the catacombs of Callixtus (fig. 15). More than two hundred years later, de Rossi, Bosio's self-styled heir, relocated and remapped this cubiculum, placing it instead in the nearby catacombs of Domitilla. The fresco itself was nearly indecipherable, however, due in part to a fire a few decades earlier. In retrospect, it is difficult to reconstruct what exactly Bosio (or rather his illustrators) might have seen in the original fresco.[83] In any case, by the time that de Rossi began work in the catacombs of Domitilla in the 1850s, Bosio's sketch had taken on a life of its own. Thus a woodcut of Bosio's sketch appeared in the 1851 English translation of Franz Kügler's authoritative *Handbook of the History of Painting* (1837). The German art historian argued that the fresco represented the first portrait-style depiction of Christ.[84] From Kügler's translated text Bosio's sketch made its way into guidebooks on Italy. Writing in 1879, J. Spencer Northcote and William Robert Brownlow, British colleagues of de Rossi, observes how often visitors to Rome were disappointed in not being able to find the original fresco: "[They] seek it where it is not to be found, in the Cemetery of Callixtus. It really exists in the Cemetery of Domitilla. . . . [The painting is] at present terribly defaced, and some of its distinctive features are almost obliterated."[85]

In Russia, Bosio's sketch was shown at the 1896 Exhibition of the Types of Christ in Moscow. The catalog, which still identifies the fresco with the catacombs of Callixtus, lists it as a historical type but refrains from hazarding a guess as to its antiquity. As for Polenov, he cites a gloss on Bosio's sketch from the Russian archeologist Alexei von Friken's four-volume *The Roman Catacombs and Monuments of Early Christian Art* (1872–85): "The oval, slightly elongated face of the Savior has here a serious, though slightly melancholy expression; the thin short beard, the mustache down, the hair parted in the middle of the head and falling on the shoulders."[86]

No less important than the iconographic details of Bosio's sketch are the intertwining narratives of continuity that authenticate it. Bosio's sketch portrays a bearded, adult Christ—not a shepherd youth—from a cubiculum that predates the Peace of the

Church. Polenov, who conflates the age of the fresco with that of the cubiculum, dates both to "the end of the second century." In other words, for Polenov, the fresco comes tantalizingly close to bridging the gap between the death of the historical Jesus and the delayed emergence of the historical type. The smaller this gap, the greater the possibility that some sense of what the historical Jesus had actually looked like might have somehow been passed on. Polenov nevertheless leaves this last logical step more implied than spoken. At the same time, Bosio's sketch struck many catacomb observers as potentially authentic portraiture not simply because of its presumed antiquity but inasmuch as it appeared to harmonize with canonical—that is, much later—iconographic norms. Polenov and others tended to cover over an otherwise intractable problem of origins with elaborate narratives linking extant images and texts. Kügler and Friken both comment on the compelling similarities between Bosio's sketch and Lentulus's letter, the same text portrait that Ainalov compares with the mosaic from the mausoleum of Saint Costanza. In short, Bosio's sketch becomes, as it were, Janus-faced: on the one hand, it looks backward to the historical Jesus

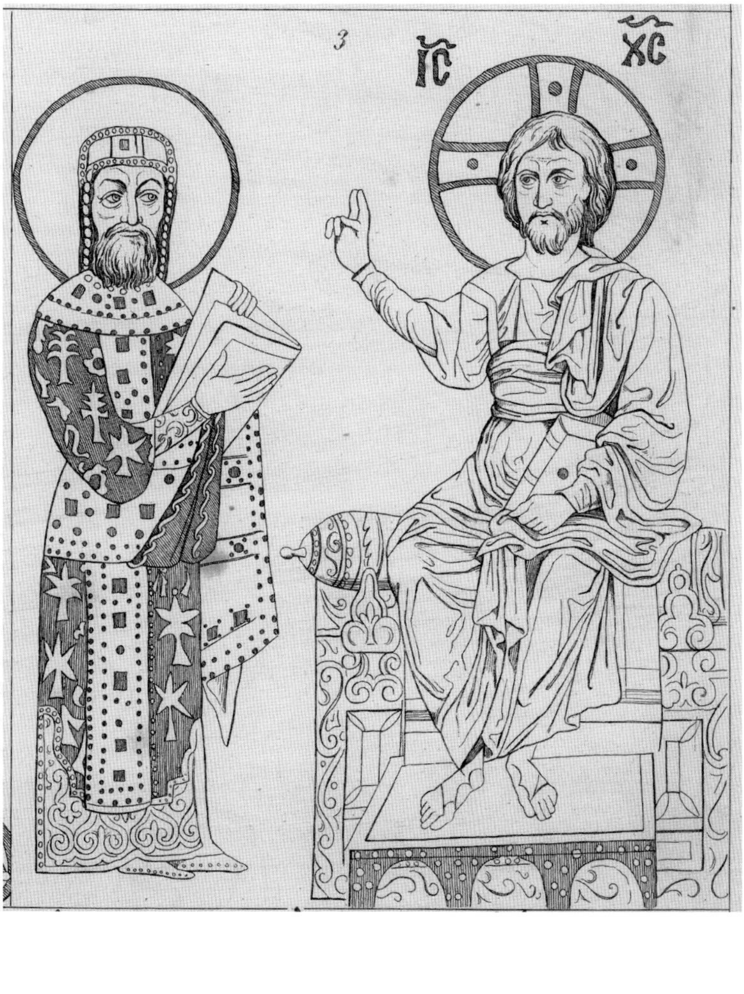

FIG. 14 Christ Blessing Alexis I, Greek miniature, twelfth century. Reproduced from *Sammlung der vorzüglichsten Denkmaeler der Malerei vorzugsweise in Italien vom IV. bis zum XVI. jahrhundert, gesammelt und zusammengestellt durch J.B.L.G. Seroux d'Agincourt.* A. Ferd. von Quast (Frankfurt: G. W. Mettenius, 1840). Tablet LVIII. Avery Architectural and Fine Arts Library, Columbia University, New York.

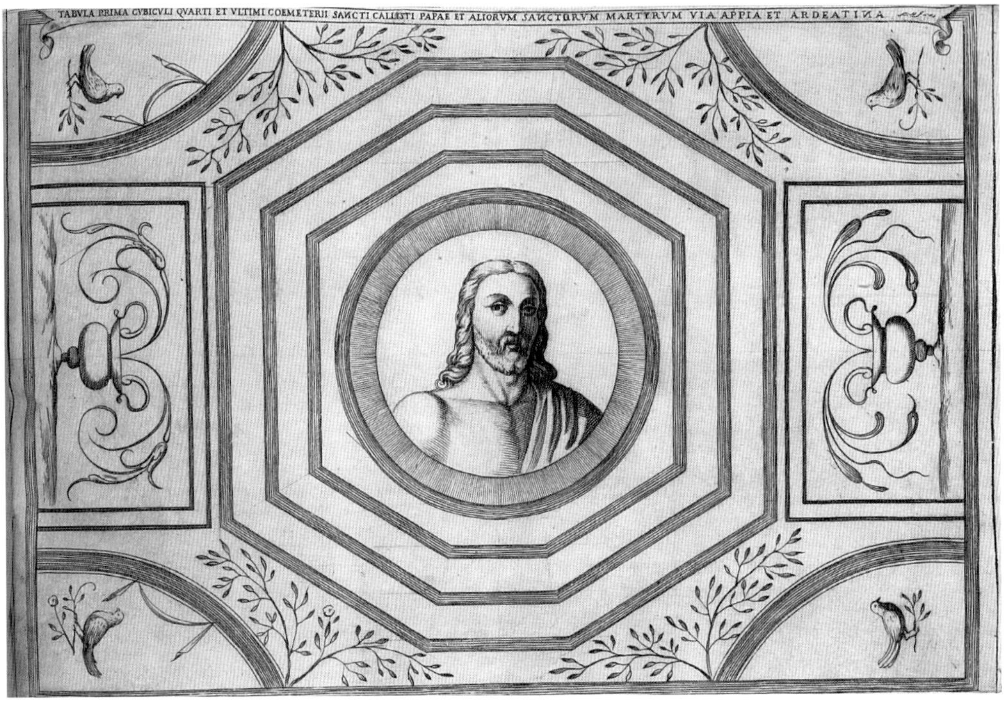

FIG. 15 Catacomb ceiling image in Antonio Bosio's *Roma sotterranea: Opera postvma* (Rome, 1632), book III, chapter XXIII, folio 253. Collection of the New-York Historical Society.

through the lens of a catacomb image almost apostolic in its antiquity; on the other, it looks forward, in Polenov's words, to that "Eastern type which would later become unchanging."

This first narrative of continuity is further reinforced by the fresco's conspicuous fate. The fresco survived long enough for Bosio to unearth it near the turn of the seventeenth century but not for de Rossi to rediscover it unscathed in the nineteenth. In *Christ and the Adulteress,* Polenov thus models his Christ not on an ancient original but on a line of relatively recent copies that run from Bosio to Kügler to Friken. In this sense, he pushes his own Christ image, however tenuous its claim to historicity may be, toward that peculiar realism of the Orthodox icon, a realism not of the mirror but of the copy.[87]

In the archeology of the Christ image, this catacomb fresco of Christ emerges as a sort of modern equivalent of an icon's prototype. Bosio's sketch of this fresco in turn functions not unlike the legends of Veronica's veil, Nicodemus's shroud, or Abgar's cloth. The last legend is particularly relevant. Abgar's cloth, purportedly an imprint made during Christ's lifetime, was "rediscovered" in Edessa in the sixth century. In 944, it was removed to Constantinople, while in 1204 it disappeared after Crusaders sacked the city. Yet even in its absence, the Holy Cloth continued to serve as the sanctioned prototype for Byzantine (and later Russian) portrait icons of Christ.

The legend of Bosio's sketch follows a similar narrative arc of discovery, loss, and preservation. Here the supposed prototype, a fresco from a second-century catacomb, belongs to a time not far removed from the very days when the apostles Peter and Paul walked the streets of Rome. As if sealed away in a time capsule, this image remained virtually unknown and untouched until Bosio's literally groundbreaking discovery. Modern science, not the medieval church, wrote the supporting narratives for Bosio's sketch. Indeed, these narratives, well into the twentieth century,[88] ensured that the sketch would long outlive the destruction of the original fresco. Like Abgar's cloth, this defaced fresco, if more through the wishful supplement of words than any correspondence between images, has been preserved for posterity only through its copies, not least that of Polenov's own itinerant Christ.

CONCLUSION

From the vantage point of the present, it is difficult to appreciate how defamiliarizing noncanonical Christ images could be for nineteenth-century audiences, whether they were confronted with catacomb sarcophagi at the Moscow Exhibition on the Types of Christ or modernized portraits of the historical Jesus at exhibitions of the *peredvizhniki*. Among Polenov's many detractors, few understood the consequences of audience resistance to iconographic revision better than did Lev Tolstoy. In a remarkable letter to Pavel Tretiakov in defense of Ge's *What Is Art?* Tolstoy surveys attempts in Europe and Russia at forging a viable, modern iconography for Christ, one that does not falsely deify him and yet does not offend viewers either: "Catholic art predominantly portrayed saints, the Madonna, and Christ as gods [*kak bogi*]. Such it was until recent times, when there arose attempts to portray [Christ] as a historical figure. But it is hardly feasible to portray as a historical figure a person [*litso*] who has been acknowledged for centuries, and is still acknowledged by millions, as God." For Tolstoy, neither direct provocation nor a sentimental bringing of Christ "down to earth" provides a "way out" of this iconographic double bind. Yet neither does seeking to "avoid the controversy altogether," which he accuses Polenov of doing in *Christ and the Adulteress*.[89]

A more generous reading of Polenov's intentions would be that he sought to alter only what was necessary in moving from the Christ image of mainstream Christianity—a variable likeness that nevertheless remained recognizable across a range of contemporary traditions, from Western academies to Russian icon-painting guilds—toward a secular iconography of the historical Jesus. Yet as in biblical historiography over the same period, the historical Jesus proved elusive in nineteenth-century painting, a figure constructed far more from the threads of speculative narrative than from whatever scant empirical evidence was available to artists. In 1908, surveying more than a century of scholarship, Albert Schweitzer concluded that "there is nothing more negative than the result of the critical study of the life of Jesus."[90] In giving visual form to the historical Jesus, painters likewise challenged a familiar and relatively uniform likeness without being able to promise a new unity in its place.

Even as Polenov acknowledged the limits of his method, he worked tirelessly in the hope that his image of the historical Jesus might nonetheless persuade audiences. In this sense, he shared a longing for a true and faithful likeness with Ainalov and, through the characters of his novels, with Merezhkovsky. In *Julian the Apostate,* Merezhkovsky returns to the fourth century and encounters a multitude of image types, none of which captures whole Christ's true likeness and yet all of which carry some potential trace of his original presence. Polenov and Ainalov, by contrast, sift through examples of the historical type in an effort to bridge the daunting gap between the death of the historical Jesus and the earliest surviving remnants of his afterimages. That the artist and scholar settle on disparate models—a fourth-century mosaic and a "second-century" catacomb fresco, a blond-haired Nazarene type and a dark-haired Byzantine one—belies their attempts to establish a common origin. Taken as a whole, the nineteenth-century archeology of the Christ image undermined not only the origin myths of the True Face but also the narratives of a unified, enduring likeness. Here Merezhkovsky's novel, in its irreducible heterogeneity, anticipates better the fate of Christ's image into the twentieth century and beyond. In their different archeological projects, and despite very different intentions, Merezhkovsky, Polenov, and Ainalov each gave new life to manifold Christ types from the first centuries of the Christian faith and, in so doing, contributed to the fracturing of the Christ image in modernity.

NOTES TO CHAPTER 7

1. D. S. Merezhkovskii, *Smert' bogov (Iulian Otstupnik),* in *Khristos i Antikhrist: Trilogiia,* 4 vols. (1896–1905; repr., Moscow: Kniga, 1989), 1:25–26. All translations from Russian are mine. For a somewhat dated English translation, see Dmitri Mérejkowski, *The Death of the Gods,* trans. Herbert Trench (New York: Putnam, 1901), pt. I, chap. 4, 34–35.

2. For avant-garde poets, see Sarah Pratt's chapter in this volume. See Shirley A. Glade's chapter as well on the shift from an iconographic focus to an aesthetic one in early twentieth-century icon scholarship.

3. Erwin Panofsky, "Iconography and Iconology: An Introduction to the Study of Renaissance Art," in *Meaning in the Visual Arts* (Chicago: University of Chicago Press, 1982), 26, 28.

4. Michel Foucault, *The Order of Things: An Archaeology of the Human Sciences,* trans. Alan Sheridan (New York: Vintage Books, 1970), xxi, xxii.

5. For a brief discussion of this exhibition, see G. I. Vzdornov, *Istoriia otkrytiia i izucheniia russkoi srednevekovoi zhivopisi. XIX vek* (Moscow: Iskusstvo, 1986), 209.

6. Dmitrii Vasil'evich Ainalov, "O tipakh Khrista vo vremeni nachala khristianstva i v epokhu Vozrozhdeniia," *Trudy pervogo s"ezda russkikh khudozhnikov i liubitelei khudozhestv v 1894-om godu* (Moscow: I. N. Kushnerev, 1900), 49–52.

7. *Katalog vystavki tipov Khrista* (Moscow: Tipografiia A. I. Mamontova, 1896). Uvarova's name appears at the end of the catalog but not on the title page. More than a hundred items from her personal collection were shown at the exhibition.

8. Ibid., 5, 6. Italics in the original.

9. Ibid., 5.

10. For synopses of the discoveries made in the catacombs from the Renaissance onward, see Robert W. Gaston, "British Travellers and Scholars in the Roman Catacombs 1450–1900," *Journal of the Warburg and Courtauld Institutes* 46 (1983): 144–65; J. Stevenson, *The Catacombs: Rediscovered Monuments of Early Christianity* (London: Thames and Hudson, 1978), 45–54.

11. On the catacomb novel as a genre, see Michel Durand, "Les Héros des Cimetières souterrains, ou le mythe victorien des Catacombes," *Cahiers Victoriens & Edouardiens* 23 (1986): 17–34; Vicent A. Lankewish, "Love Among the Ruins: The Catacombs, the Closet, and the Victorian 'Early Christian' Novel," *Victorian Literature and Culture* 28, no. 2 (2000): 239–73.

12. De Rossi, *La Roma sotterranea cristiana,* 3 vols. (Rome: Cromolitografia pontificia, 1864–77), 2:359–60.

13. Nicholas Wiseman, *Fabiola; or, the Church of the Catacombs* (London: Burns & Oates, 1854), 159.

14. Sozomen, in *The Ecclesiastical History of Sozomen: Comprising a History of the Church from A.D. 324 to A.D. 440,* trans. Edward Walford (London: Bohn, 1855), bk. v, chap. 2, 201–5. The church has not survived.

15. *Katalog vystavki tipov Khrista,* 9.

16. Merezhkovsky, *Iulian Otstupnik,* 26.

17. *Katalog vystavki tipov Khrista,* 6.

18. Z. N. Gippius-Merezhkovskaia, "Dmitrii Merezhkovskii: Roman vospominaniia," in *14 dekabria. Dmitrii Merezhkovskii: Roman vospominaniia,* ed. O. N. Mikhailov (Moscow: Moskovskii rabochii, 1990), 325–28. The Hagia Sophia (Greek) or Ayasofya (Turkish) is now a museum.

19. This mosaic is listed as item 46 in the catalog. *Katalog vystavki tipov Khrista,* 21. Twentieth-century Byzantinists tended to identify the kneeling figure with later emperors, perhaps Leo VI (r. 886–912). See Thomas Whittemore, *The Mosaics of Saint Sophia at Istanbul: Preliminary Report of the First Year's Work: The Mosaics of the Narthex* (Paris: John Johnson at the Oxford University Press for the Byzantine Institute, 1933), 18.

20. *Katalog vystavki tipov Khrista,* 6.

21. Arius (c. 250–336), whose widespread teachings were deemed heretical at the first council of Nicea (325), argued that

Jesus, the "only-begotten," was a created being, and thus not eternal or "unbegotten," like God the Father.

22. F. I. Buslaev, "Obshchie poniatiia o russkoi ikonopisi," in *Drevnerusskaia literatura i pravoslavnoe iskusstvo* (1866; repr., St. Petersburg: Izdatel'stvo Russkogo Khristianskogo gumanitarnogo instituta, "Liga-Plius," 2001), 36–186: 97. Buslaev dates this mosaic between the eighth and tenth centuries.

23. See Elena Boeck's chapter in this volume.

24. N. S. Leskov, "Na kraiu sveta," in *Sobranie sochinenii,* 6 vols., ed. L. Anninskii (1873; repr., Moscow: Ekran, 1993), 4:394, 395.

25. In Dostoevsky, see especially Prince Myshkin's contrast between "our Christ" and the "distorted Christ" of the Roman Catholic Church. F. M. Dostoevsky, *The Idiot,* pt. 4, chap. 7.

26. Merezhkovskii, "Epilog: Khristos Griadushchii," in *Khristos i Antikhrist,* 4:245.

27. *Katalog vystavki tipov Khrista,* 6, 19.

28. Adolphe Napoléon Didron, *Manuel d'iconographie chrétienne grecque et latine, par Denys de Fourna,* trans. Paul Durand (New York: Franklin, 1963), xi; quoted in Hans Belting, *Likeness and Presence: A History of the Image Before the Era of Art,* trans. Edmund Jephcott (Chicago: University of Chicago Press, 1994), 17.

29. Adolphe Napoléon Didron, *Iconographie chrétienne: Histoire de Dieu* (Paris: Imprimerie royale, 1843), 245.

30. On the connection between Didron and Russian scholarship on the icon, see Belting, *Likeness and Presence,* 17–21; F. I. Buslaev, "Russkoe iskusstvo v otsenke frantsuzskogo uchenogo," *Kriticheskoe obozrenie,* 1879, no. 2, 1–20; no. 5, 1–24.

31. N. P. Kondakov, *Istoriia vizantiiskogo iskusstva i ikonografii po miniatiuram grecheskikh rukopisei* (Odessa: Ul'rikh i Shul'tse, 1876), 73, 75.

32. For an account of this discovery, see G. I. Vzdornov, *Istoriia otkrytiia i izucheniia russkoi srednevekovoi zhivopisi,* 183–86. The panels were lost during World War II. For Byzantine scholarship in nineteenth-century Russia, see also W. Eugene Kleinbauer, *Early Christian and Byzantine Architecture: An Annotated Bibliography and Historiography* (Boston: G. K. Hall, 1992), lxxxi–xcv.

33. The catalog, which does not include illustrations, provides insufficient textual detail to identity this exhibition item with complete certainty. The catalog is possibly referring to a much-disputed illustration of Christ in profile from Thomas Heaphy's *The Likeness of Christ: Being an Inquiry into the Verisimilitude of the Received Likeness of Our Blessed Lord,* ed. Wyke Bayliss (London: Bogue, 1880), plate VIII.

34. D. V. Ainalov, *Mozaiki IV i V vekov* (St. Petersburg: Balashev, 1895), 22–30: 25.

35. Ainalov, "O tipakh Khrista," 49.

36. "Letter of Lentulus," *The Apocryphal New Testament,* ed. J. K. Elliott (Oxford: Clarendon Press, 1993), 542–43; Ainalov, "Mozaiki IV i V vekov," 25–26.

37. Ainalov, "Mozaiki IV i V vekov," 28.

38. Wilhelm Grimm, "Die Sage vom Ursprung der Christusbilder," *Deutsche Akademie der Wissenschaften zu Berlin. Philologische und historische Abhandlungen der Königlichen Akademie der Wissenschaften zu Berlin* 27 (1842): 121–75.

39. On the subject of nineteenth-century racialized Christ types, see Jefferson J. A. Gatrall, "The Color of His Hair: Literary Portraits of the Historical Jesus," *Novel: A Forum on Fiction* 42, no. 1 (2009): 109–30.

40. See, for example, Ernst von Dobschütz's near-contemporaneous *Christusbilder: Untersuchungen zur christliches Legende,* 3 vols. (Leipzig: J. C. Hinrichs'sche, 1899), 1:v-viii.

41. For nineteenth-century realist representations of Christ, including paintings of the historical Jesus, see Elena Petrova, "Zemnaia zhizn' Iisusa Khrista v russkom izobrazitel'nom iskusstve," *Iisus Khristos v khristianskom iskusstve i kul'ture XIV–XX veka* (St. Petersburg: Palace Editions, 2000), 21–33; Michael Paul Driskel, *Representing Belief: Religion, Art, and Society in Nineteenth-Century France* (University Park: Pennsylvania State University Press, 1992); and Friedrich Gross, *Jesus, Luther und der Papst im Bilderkampf 1871 bis 1918: Zur Malereigeschichte der Kaiserzeit* (Marburg: Jonas, 1989).

42. Albert Schweitzer, *The Quest of the Historical Jesus,* trans. W. Montgomery (1908; repr., Mineola, N.Y.: Dover, 2005), 3.

43. For Russian censorship of biblical scholarship, see Marianna Tax Choldin, *A Fence Around the Empire: Russian Censorship of Western Ideas Under the Tsars* (Durham: Duke University Press, 1985), 68–70, 175–98.

44. L. N. Tolstoi, *Anna Karenina,* pt. 5, chap. 9.

45. V. D. Polenov, letter to A. A. Goriainova, 22 March 1897, in *Vasilii Dmitrievich Polenov. Pis'ma, dnevniki, vospominaniia,* ed. E. V. Sakharova (Moscow: Iskusstvo, 1950), 300.

46. E. V. Paston, *Vasilii Dmitrievich Polenov* (St. Petersburg: Khudozhnik RSFSR, 1991), 65.

47. For Russian painters traveling to Palestine, see *Sviataia zemlia v russkom iskusstve: Katalog,* ed. L. I. Evleva (Moscow: Gosudarstvennaia Tret'iakovskaia galeriia, 2001).

48. For nineteenth-century French and British travel to Palestine, see especially Edward Said, *Orientalism* (New York: Vintage, 1979), 166–97.

49. E. Robinson and E. Smith, *Biblical Researches in Palestine, Mount Sinai, and Arabia Petraea: A Journal of Travels in the Year 1838,* 3 vols. (Boston: Crocker & Brewster, 1841).

50. Polenov included *Christ and the Adulteress* in the full cycle. In 1909, he displayed fifty-eight paintings at an exhibition in St. Petersburg; sixty-four paintings were shown shortly thereafter in Moscow and Tver. Paston, *Vasilii Dmitrievich Polenov,* 94.

51. Ibid., 65.

52. A. Sobolev, *Evangel'skaia epokha v kartine V. D. Polenova 'Khristos i greshnitsa': Opyt khudozhestvennoi kritiki i poiasnenie kartiny* (Moscow: Tipografiia A. I. Mamontova, 1887).

53. Marquis de Melchior Vögué, *Le Temple de Jérusalem: Monographie du Haram-ech-Chérif, suivie d'un essai sur la topographie de la Ville-sainte* (Paris: Noblet, 1864).

54. Sobolev, *Evangel'skaia epokha v kartine V. D. Polenova,* 32–37.

55. Jack Finegan, *The Archeology of the New Testament: The Life of Jesus and the Beginning of the Early Church* (Princeton: Princeton University Press, 1992), 197.

56. I. I. Kristi, *Istoricheskaia pravda v iskusstve: Po povodu kartiny Polenova* (Moscow: M. Katkov, 1887), 5.

57. Sobolev, *Evangel'skaia epokha v kartine V. D. Polenova,* 19.

58. Ernest Renan, *The Life of Jesus* (1863; repr., Boston: Little, Brown, 1903), 443.

59. V. G. Korolenko, quoted in O. A. Liaskovskaia, *V. D. Polenov: 1844–1927* (Moscow: Izdanie G. T. T., 1946), 31–32.

60. Sobolev, *Evangel'skaia epokha v kartine V. D. Polenova,* 38.

61. T. V. Iurova, *Vasilii Dmitrievich Polenov* (Moscow: Iskusstvo, 1961), 76.

62. Sobolev, *Evangel'skaia epokha v kartine V. D. Polenova,* 36

63. Kristi, *Istoricheskaia pravda v iskusstve,* 16.

64. S. S. Abamelek-Lazarev, letter to Polenov, 12 January 1887, in *Vasilii Dmitrievich Polenov,* 219.

65. Vasilii Vasil'evich Vereshchagin, "Realizm," in *V. V. Vereshchagin: Povesti, ocherki, vospominaniia* (Moscow: Sovetskaia Rossiia, 1990), 196. This tract first appeared in English translation in New York in 1891.

66. Polenov, letter to Goriainova, in *Vasilii Dmitrievich Polenov,* 300.

67. Sobolev, *Evangel'skaia epokha v kartine V. D. Polenova,* 45, 46, 50, 51, 59.

68. Joseph Bonomi, *Nineveh and Its Palaces: The Discoveries of Botta and Layard Applied to the Elucidation of Holy Writ* (London: George Bell and Sons, 1878), 197.

69. Buslaev, *Obshchie poniatiia o russkoi ikonopisi,* 90, 168.

70. Sobolev, *Evangel'skaia epokha v kartine V. D. Polenova,* 59.

71. Quoted in Ian Thompson, "Tissot as a Religious Artist," in *James Tissot,* ed. Krystyna Matyjaszkiewicz (New York: Abbeville Press, 1984), 91.

72. Liaskovskaia, *V. D. Polenov,* 27.

73. Sobolev, *Evangel'skaia epokha v kartine V. D. Polenova,* 42.

74. Buslaev, "Obshchie poniatiia o russkoi ikonopisi," 92–93; Sobolev, *Evangel'skaia epokha v kartine V. D. Polenova,* 39–40.

75. Polenov, letter to Goriainova, in *Vasilii Dmitrievich Polenov,* 300.

76. Il'ia Emifovich Repin, "Nikolai N. Ge i nashi pretenzii k iskusstvu," *Niva,* no. 11 (1894): 540.

77. L. N. Tolstoi, letter to N. N. Ge, 5 November 1893, in *Nikolai Nikolaevich Ge: Pis'ma, stat'i, kritika, vospominaniia sovremennikov,* ed. N. Iu. Zograf (Moscow: Iskusstvo, 1978), 184.

78. Quoted in Zograf, ed., *Nikolai Nikolaevich Ge,* 346n17.

79. Frederic W. Farrar, *Life of Christ,* 2 vols. (London: Dutton, [1877]), 1:313. On the Greco-Jewish Jesus, see Gatrall, "The Color of His Hair," 116–23.

80. Konstantin Korovin, *Konstantin Korovin vospominaet . . .* , ed. I. S. Zil'bershtein and V. A. Samkov (Moscow: Izobrazitel'noe iskusstvo, 1990), 98.

81. Sobolev, *Evangel'skaia epokha v kartine V. D. Polenova,* 41.

82. J. B. L. G. Seroux D'Agincourt, *Histoire de l'art par les monuments, depuis sa décadence au IVe siècle jusqu'à son renouvellement au XIVe,* 6 vols. (Paris: Treuttel, 1832).

83. As Francis Haskell points out, Bosio and his colleagues "inevitably had often to rely for their researches on pen-and-ink drawings made for them by a series of copyists." These drawings tended to be of weak quality and reflected less the "style of the originals" than what copyists "expected—and, no doubt, hoped—to see." Haskell, *History and Its Images: Art and the Interpretation of the Past* (New Haven: Yale University Press, 1995), 102–10: 107. On the issue of how illustrations from Bosio's manuscript have been used, and misused, as visual evidence in Christian archeology, see also Simon Ditchfield, "Text Before Trowel: Antonio Bosio's *Roma Sotterranea* Revisited," *Studies in Church History* 33 (1997): 343–60: 356–60; Peter Burke, "Images as Evidence in Seventeenth-Century Europe," *Journal of the History of Ideas* 64, no. 2 (2003): 273–96: 281–82.

84. F. Kügler, *The Schools of Painting in Italy,* part 1 of *Kugler's Handbook of Painting,* ed. Charles L. Eastlake, trans. Margaret Hutton (London: Murray, 1851), 15–16.

85. J. Spencer Northcote and W. R. Brownlow, *Roma Sotterranea; or, An Account of the Roman Catacombs Especially of the Cemetery of St. Callixtus; comp. from the works of commendatore de Rossi,* 2 vols. (London: Longmans, 1879), 2:218–19.

86. A. fon-Friken, *Rimskie katakomby i pamiatniki pervonachal'nogo khristianskogo iskusstva,* 4 vols. (Moscow: Izdatel'stvo K. T. Soldatenkova, 1872–85), 3:136; Sobolev, *Evangel'skaia epokha v kartine V. D. Polenova,* 41–42.

87. On the realism of the Orthodox icon, see Leonid Ouspensky, *Theology of the Icon,* 2 vols., trans. Anthony Gythiel (Crestwood, N.Y.: St. Vladimir's Seminary, 1992), 1:167–70.

88. See, for example, C. C. Dobson, *The Face of Christ: Earliest Likenesses from the Catacombs* (Milwaukee: Morehouse, 1933), 73–78.

89. L. N. Tolstoi, letter to S. M. Tret'iakov, July 1890, in *L. N. Tolstoi i khudozhniki: Tolstoi ob iskusstve: pis'ma, dnevniki, vospominaniia,* ed. I. A. Brodskii (Moscow:Iskusstvo, 1978), 98.

90. Schweitzer, *The Quest of the Historical Jesus,* 396.

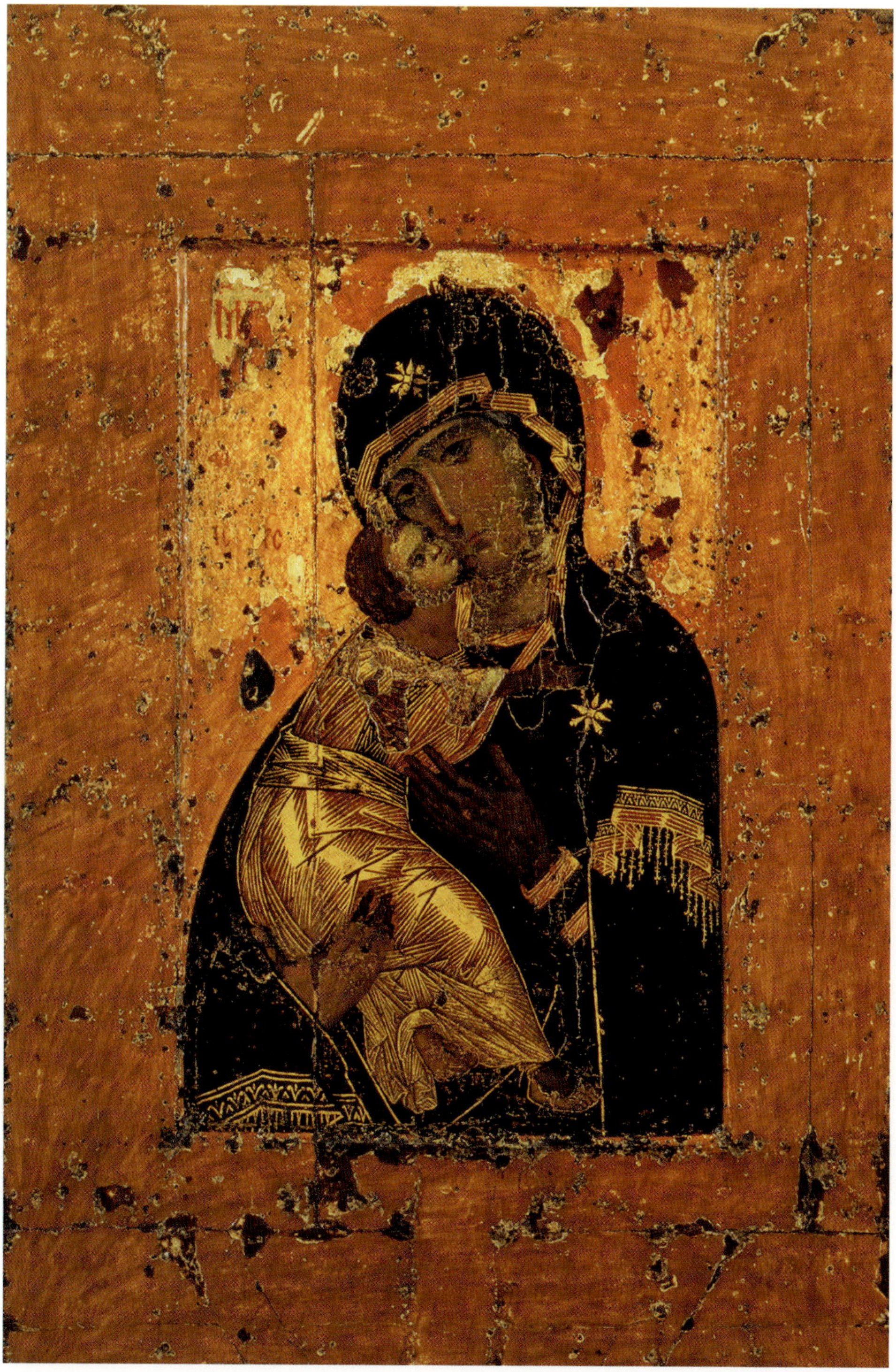

PLATE 1 The Vladimir Mother of God, Byzantine, twelfth century, tempera on wood. State Tretiakov Gallery, Moscow.

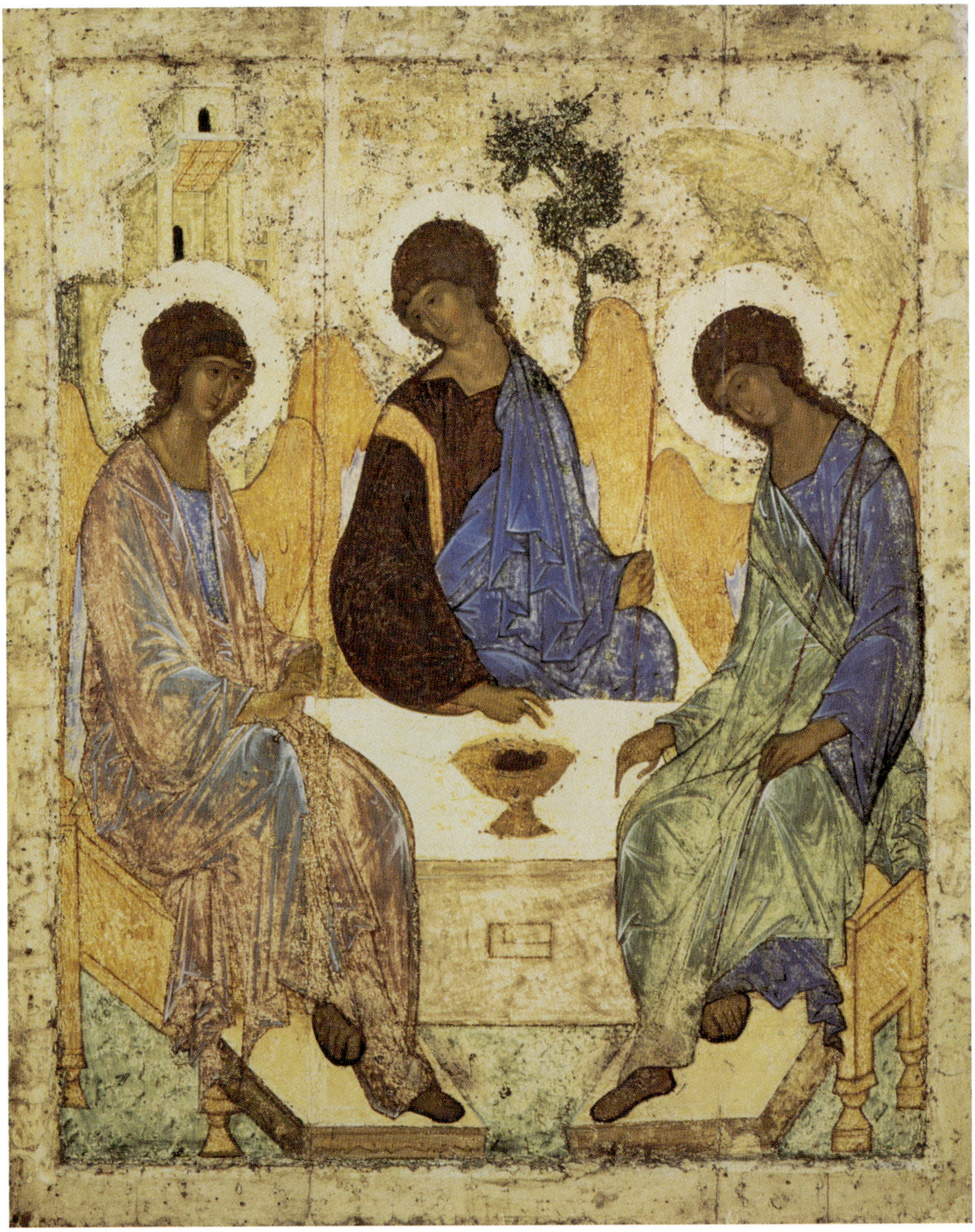

PLATE 2 Andrei Rublev, *Old Testament Trinity,* c. 1410, tempera on wood. State Tretiakov Gallery, Moscow.

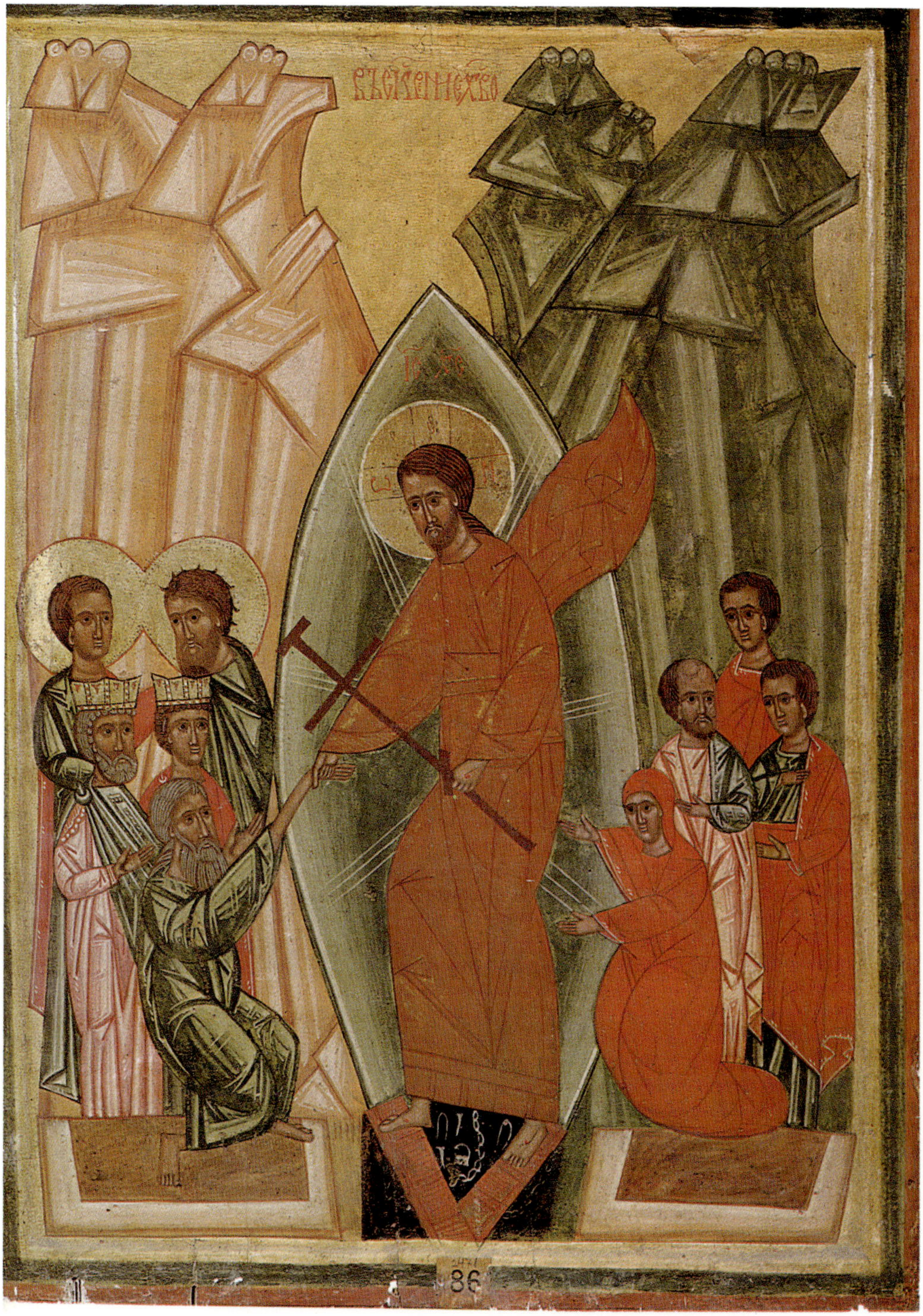

PLATE 3 Descent into Hades, Poliana, sixteenth century. Reproduced from Hryhorii Lohvyn, Lada Miliaieva, and Vira Svientsits'ka, eds., *Ukrains'kyi seredn'ovichnyi zhyvopys* (Kiev: Mystetstvo, 1976), XXXVIII.

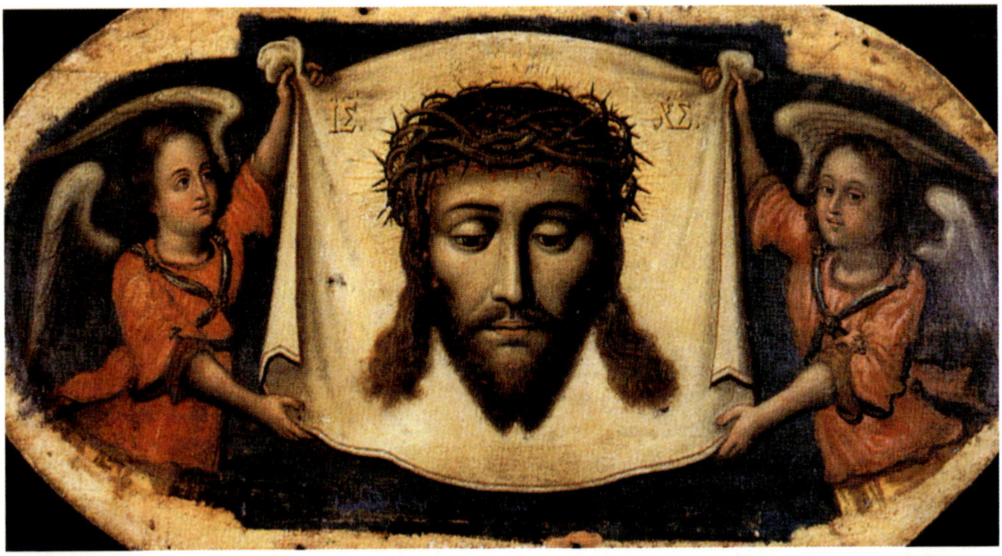

PLATE 4 Icon of the Holy Face, Bohorodchany iconostasis. Reproduced from Volodymyr Ovsiichuk, *Ukrains'ke maliarstvo X–XVIII stolit'. Problemy kol'oru* (Lviv: Instytut narodoznavstva Natsional'noi akademii nauk Ukrainy, 1996), 396.

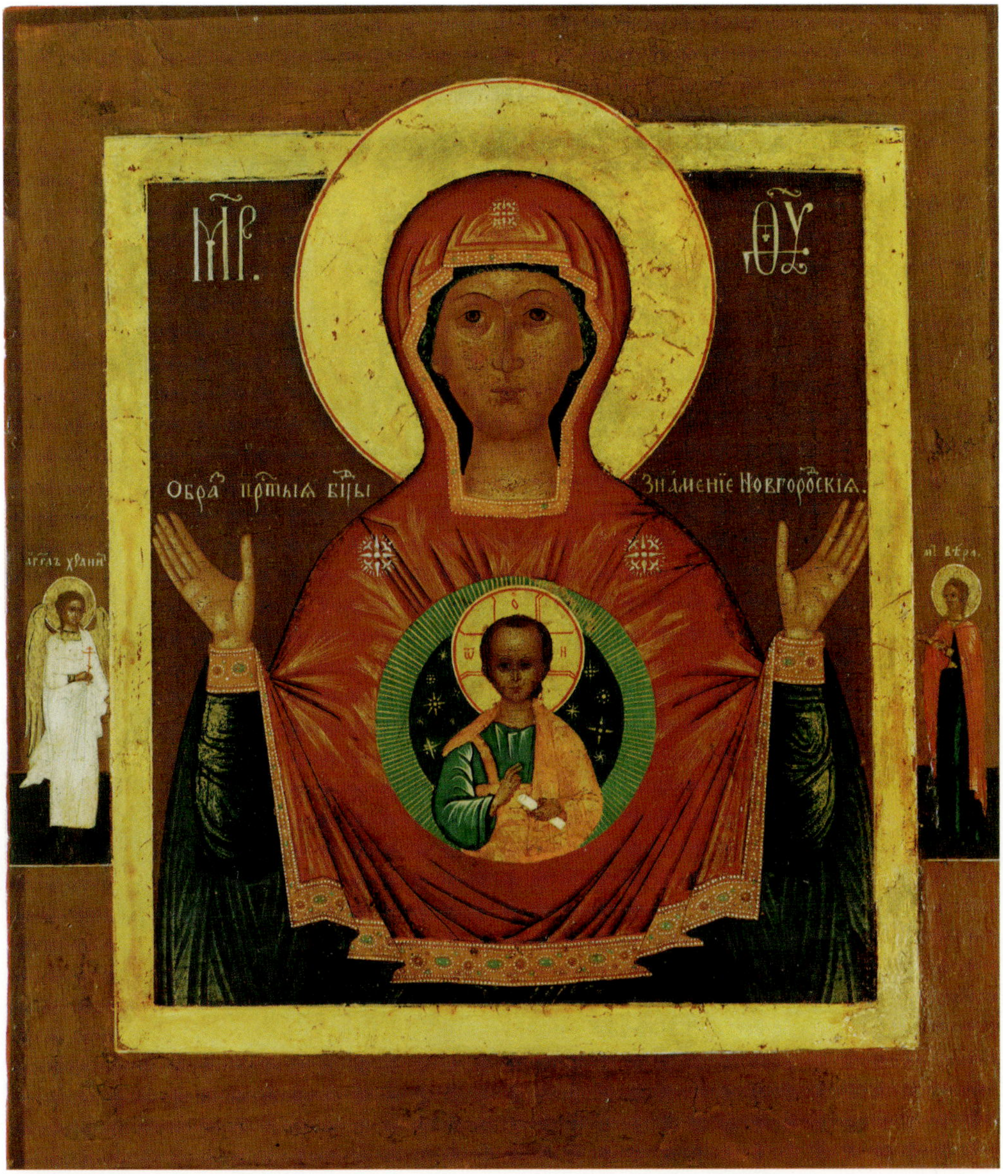

PLATE 5 Orant Virgin, 1850. Museum of Russian Icons, Clinton, Massachusetts.

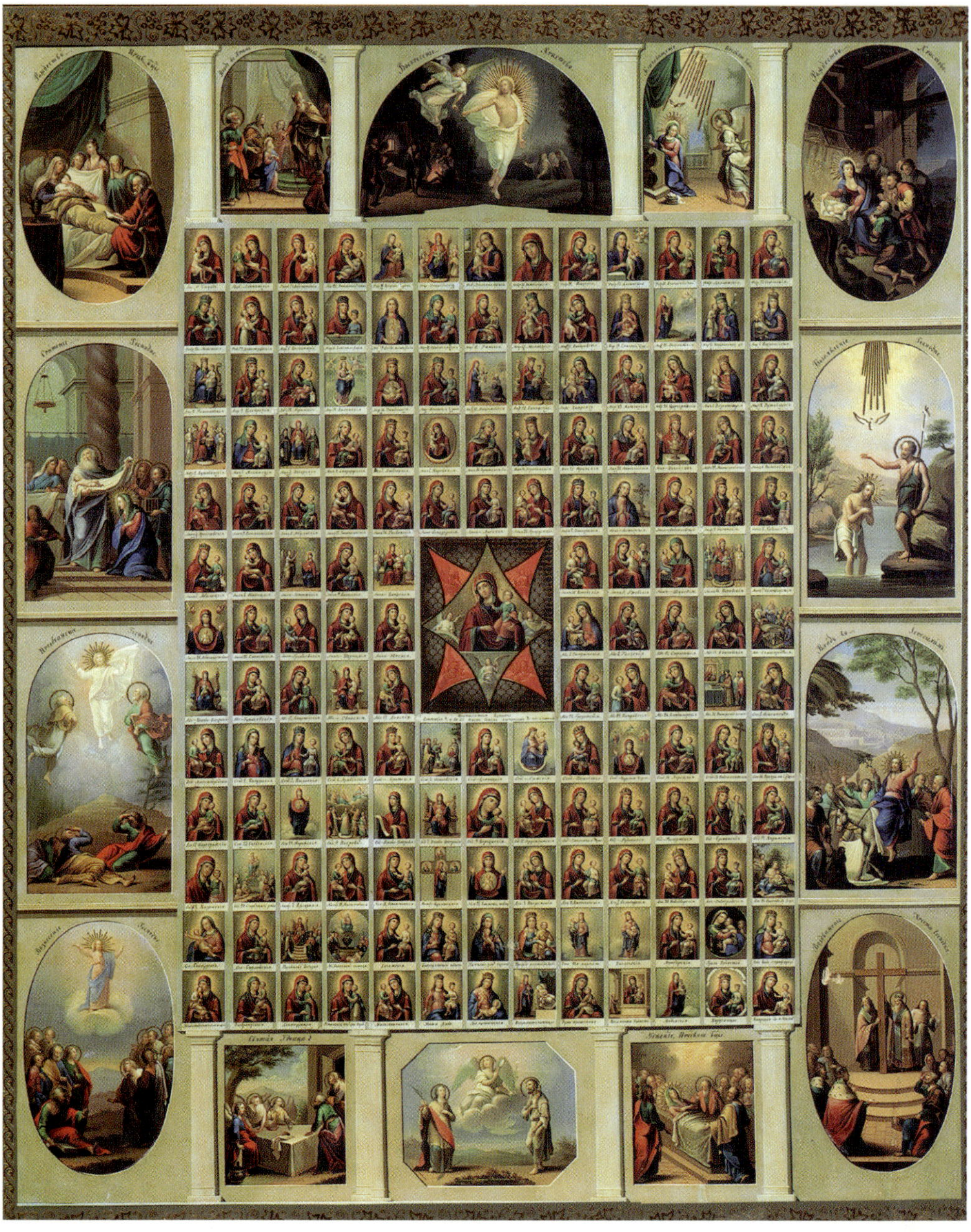

PLATE 6 Compendium icon of the Virgin, nineteenth century. Modern copy.

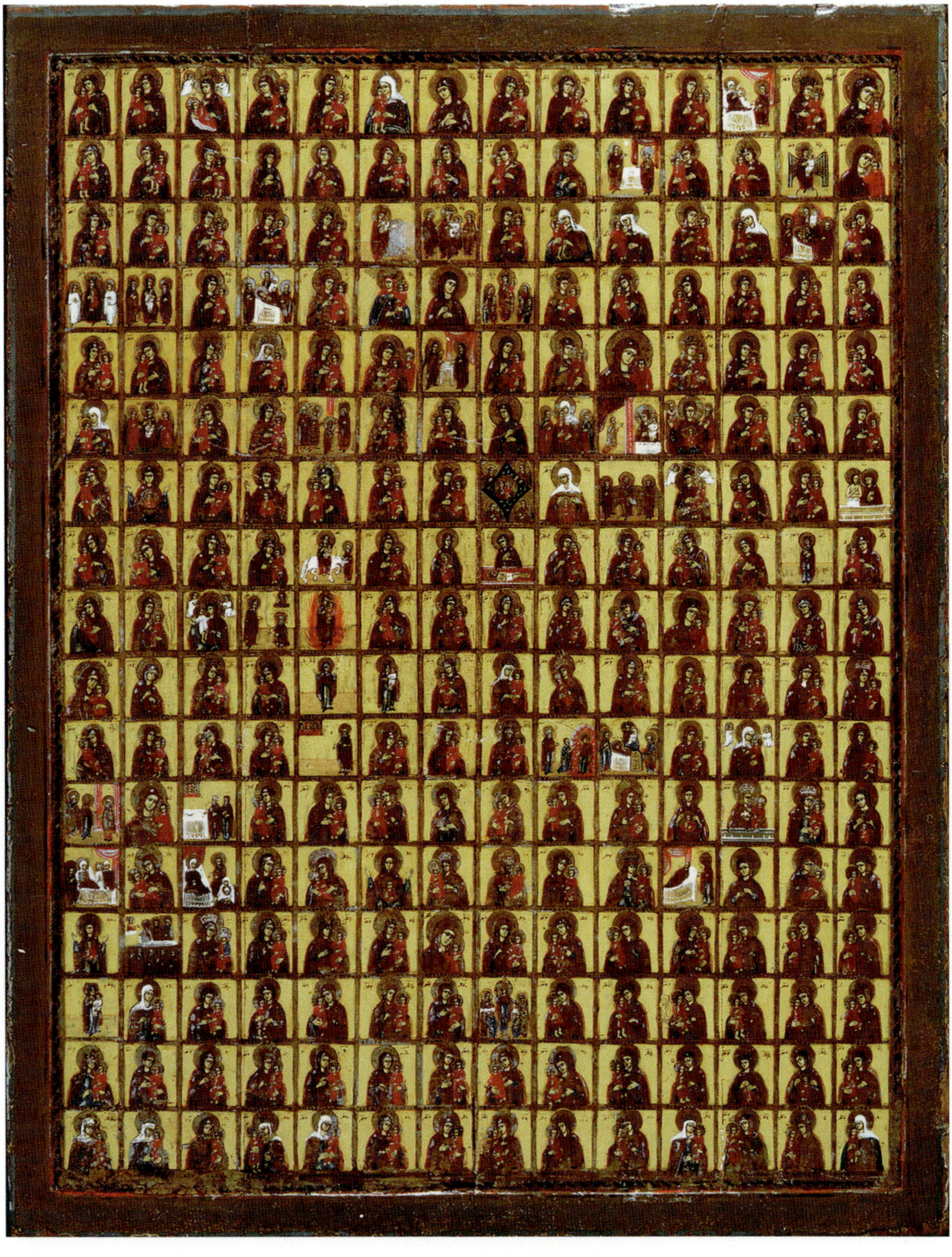

PLATE 7 Miraculous icons of the Mother of God, Kholui (Vladimir), late nineteenth–early twentieth century, tempera on wood. Intesa Sanpaolo Collection, Gallerie di Palazzo Leoni Montanari, Vicenza.

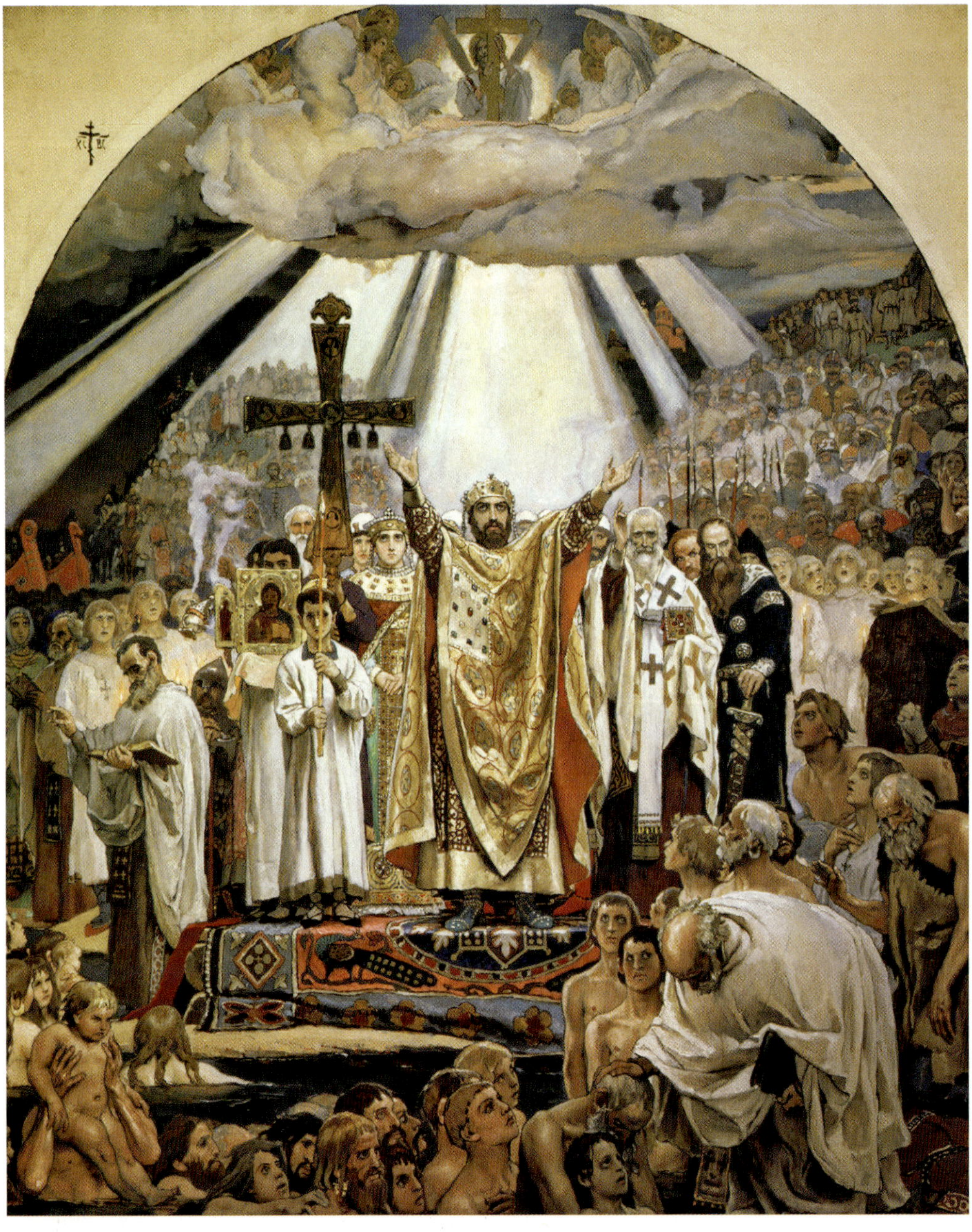

PLATE 8 Viktor Vasnetsov, *Baptism of Rus,* sketch for the Saint Vladimir Cathedral in Kiev, 1885–96, oil on canvas. State Tretiakov Gallery, Moscow.

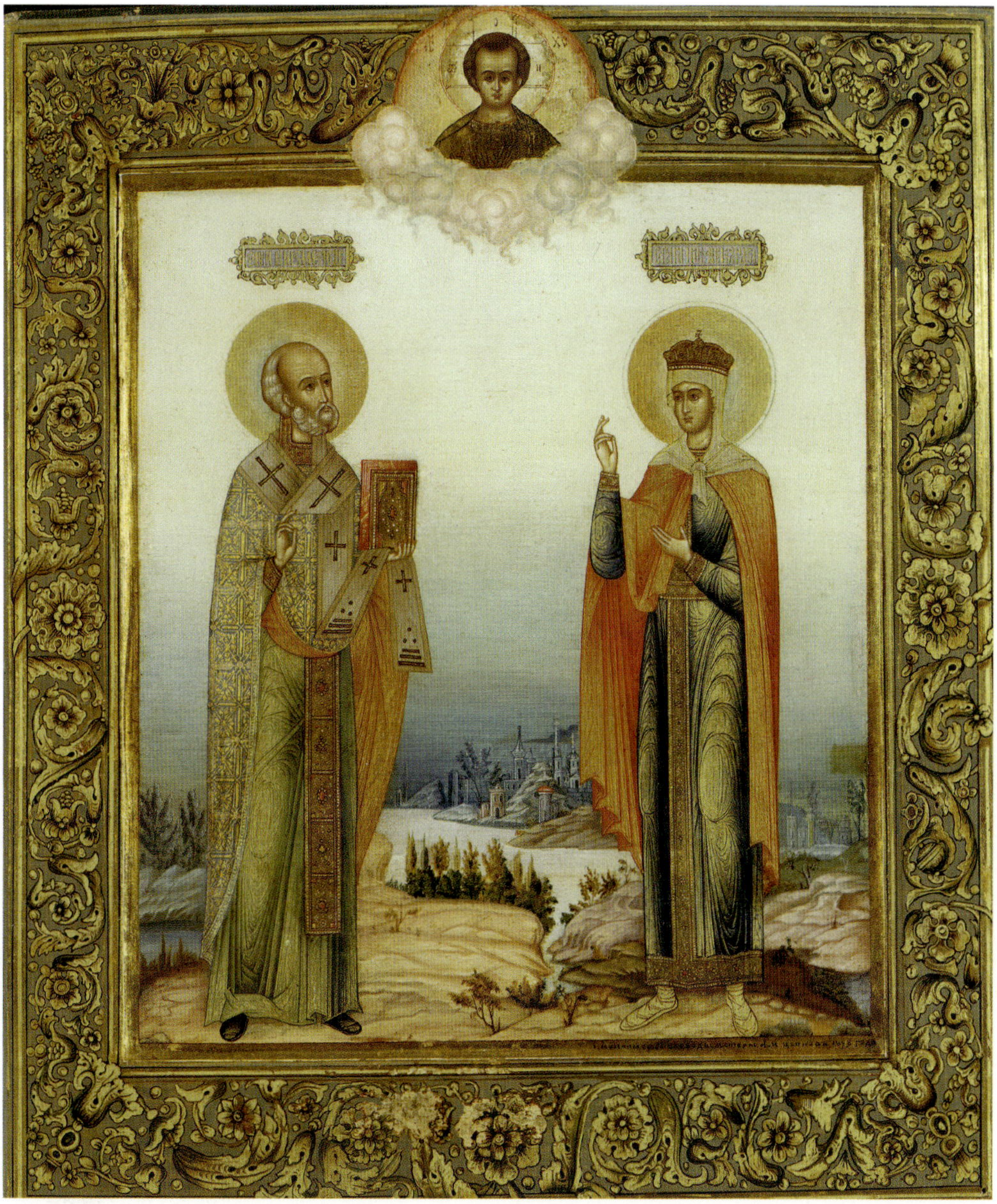

PLATE 9 Alexander Tsepkov, *Saint Nicholas the Miracle Worker and Saint Tsarina Alexandra,* 1898, tempera on wood. State Hermitage Museum, St. Petersburg.

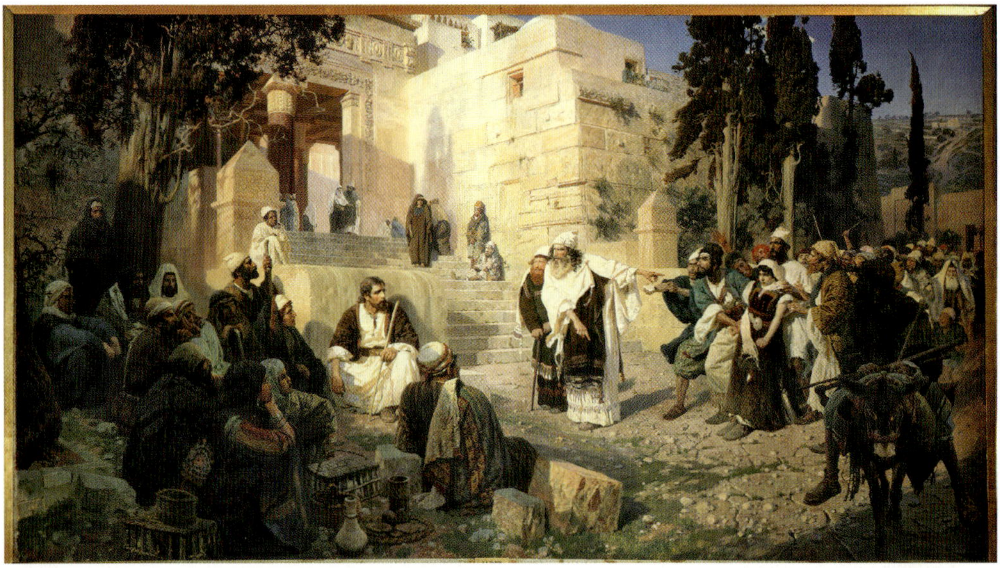

PLATE 10 Vasily Polenov, *Christ and the Adulteress,* 1886, oil on canvas. State Russian Museum, St. Petersburg.

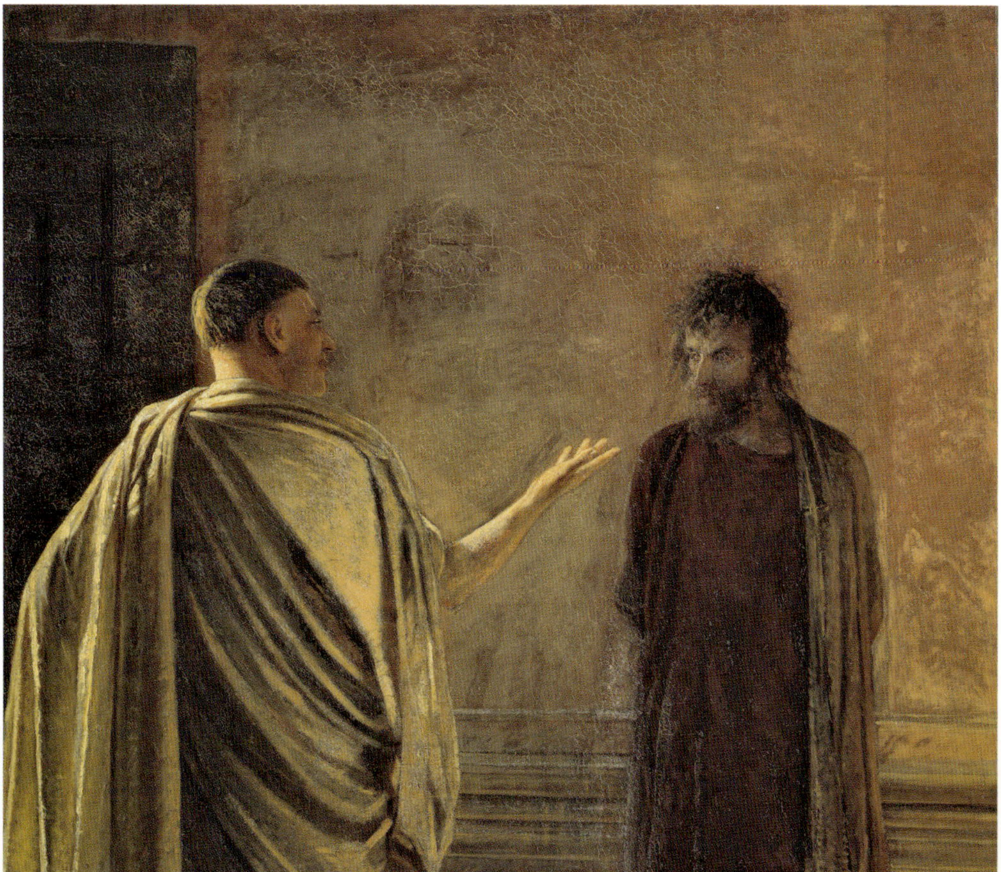

PLATE 11 Nikolai Ge, *What Is Truth?* 1890, oil on canvas. State Tretiakov Gallery, Moscow.

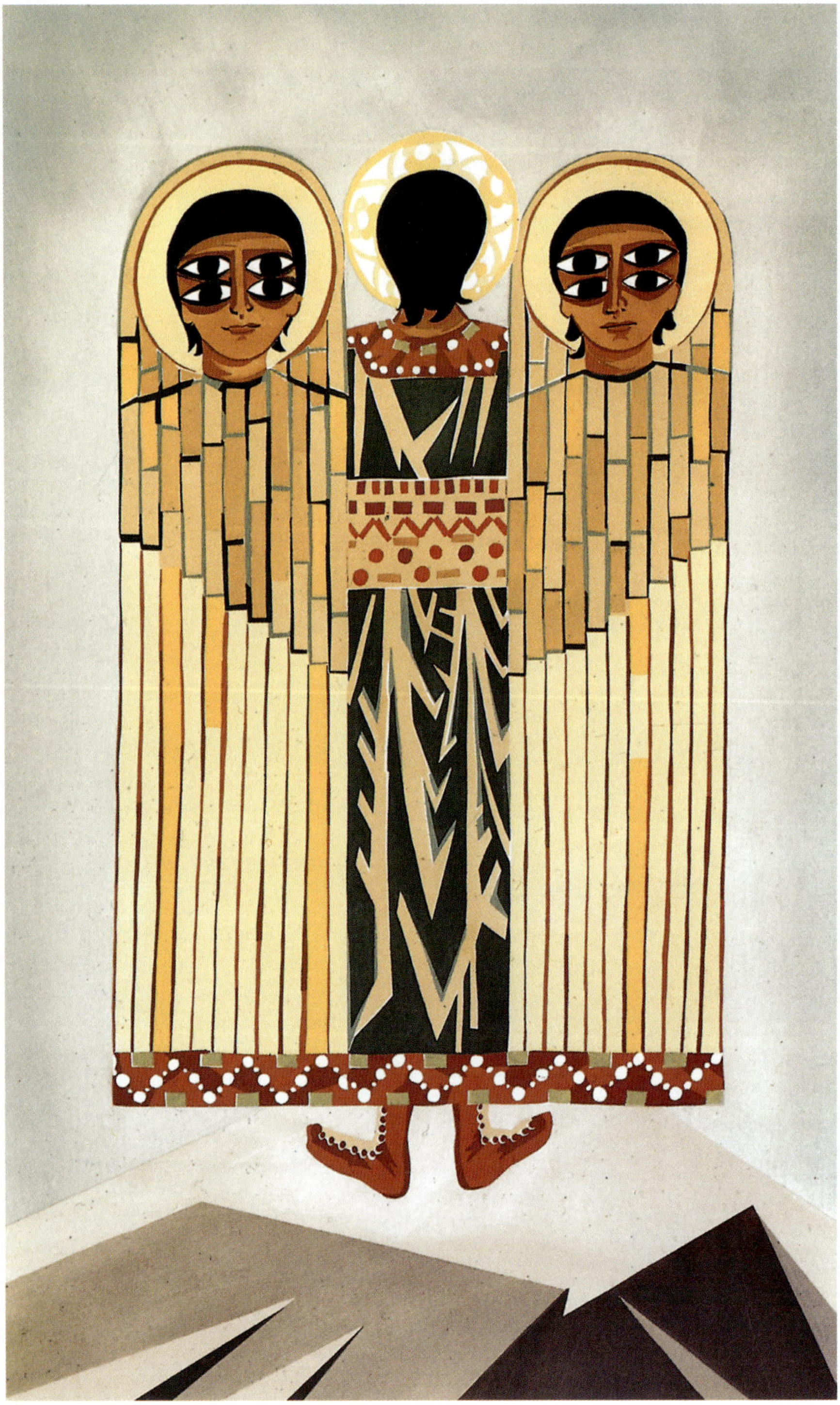

PLATE 12 Natalia Goncharova, costume sketch for an angel from the ballet *Liturgy,* 1915, watercolor on paper. Central Theatrical Museum, Moscow. © 2008 Artists Rights Society (ARS), New York/ADAGP, Paris.

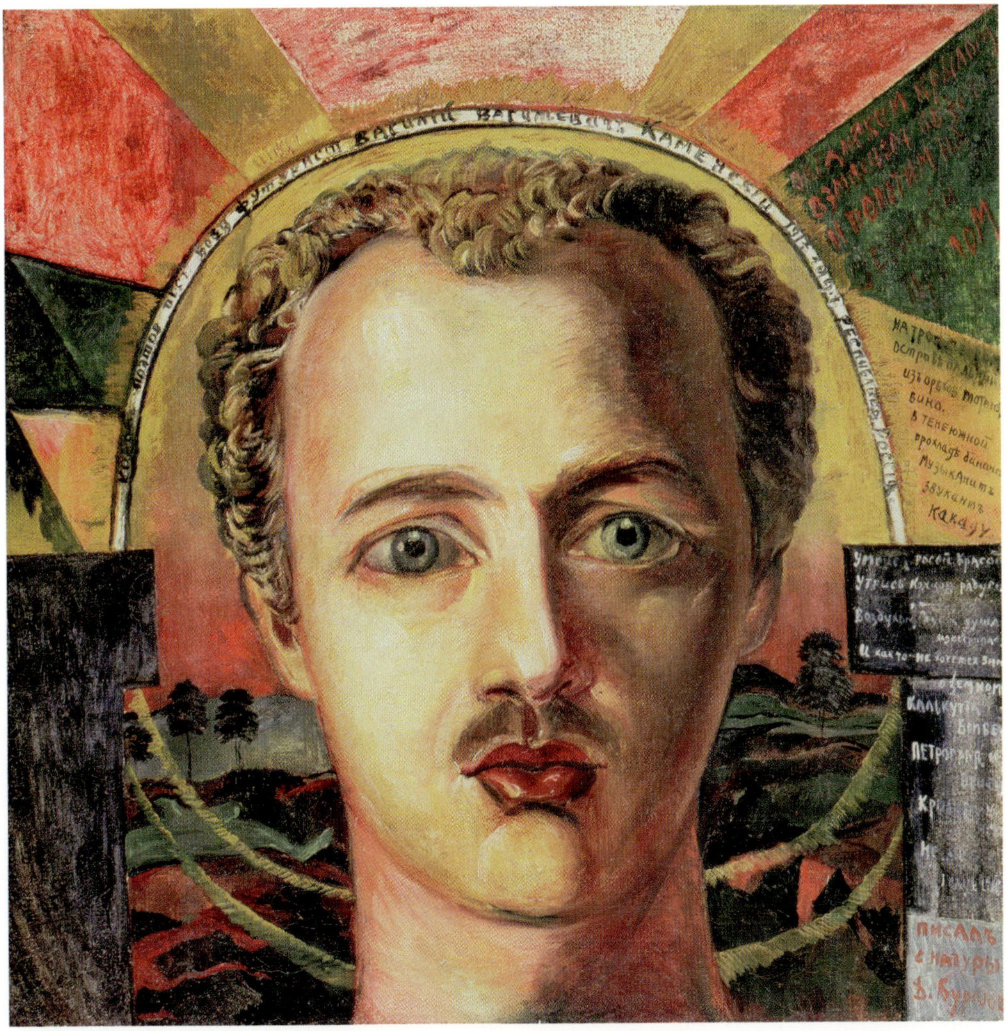

PLATE 13 David Burliuk, *Portrait of Vasily Kamensky,* 1917, oil on canvas. State Russian Museum, St. Petersburg.

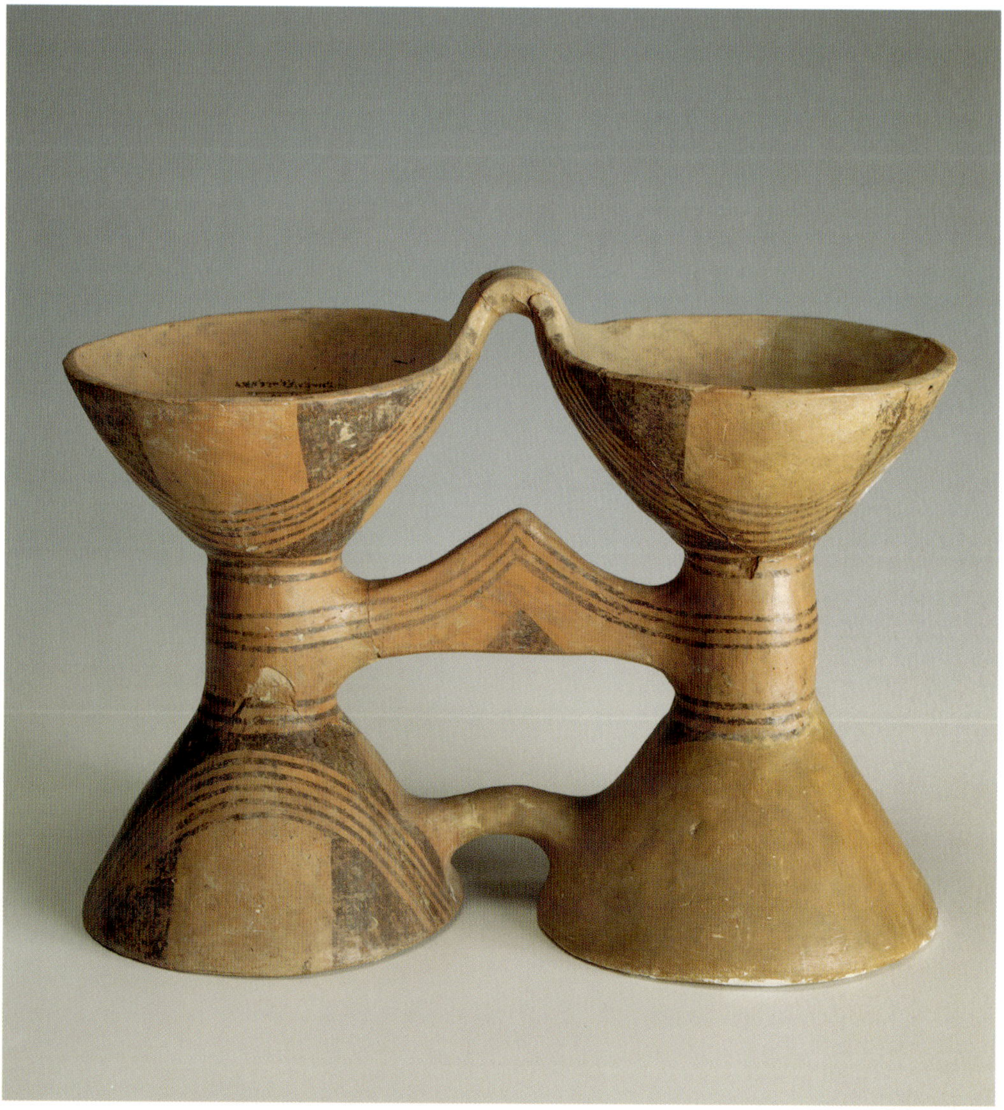

PLATE 14 Binocular-shaped vessel, Tripolye Culture, Dniester Area, Chernovtsy Region, the Village of Polivanov-Yar, Russia (now Ukraine), second half of the fourth millennium BCE, clay. State Hermitage Museum, St. Petersburg.

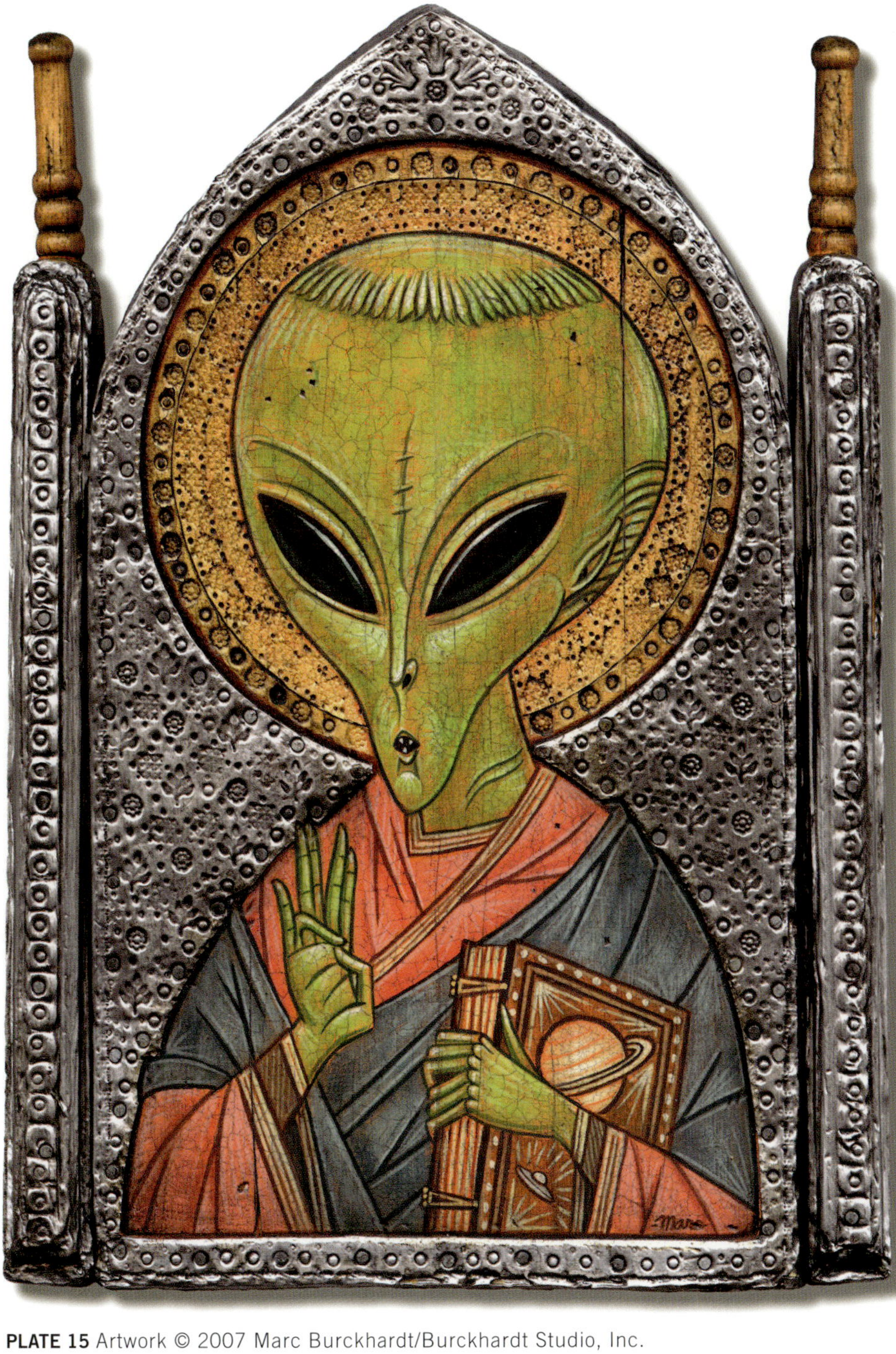

PLATE 15 Artwork © 2007 Marc Burckhardt/Burckhardt Studio, Inc.

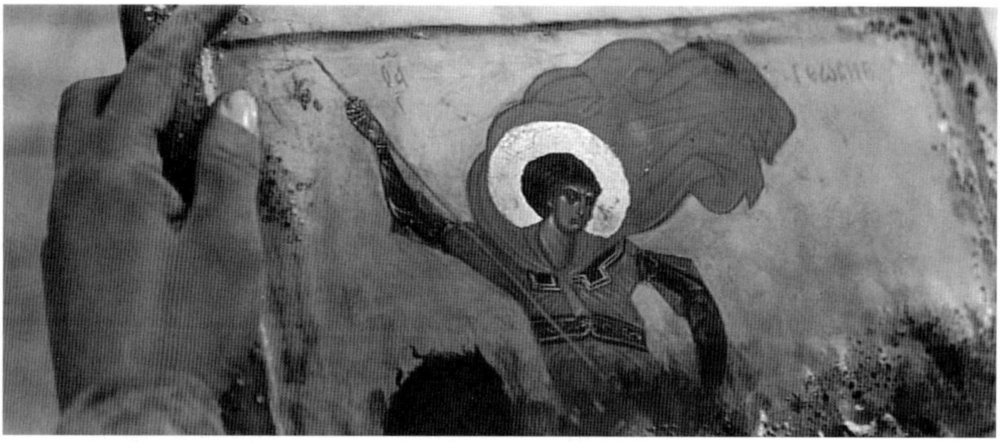

PLATE 16 Icon of Saint George in *Andrei Rublev,* dir. Andrei Tarkovsky (1966/1969).

8

AVANT-GARDE POETS AND IMAGINED ICONS

Never will I cease honoring the matter which wrought my salvation! . . . I salute . . . matter with reverence, because God has filled it with His grace and power. Through it my salvation has come to me.

We use all our senses to produce worthy images. . . . What the book is to the literate, the image is to the illiterate. Just as words speak to the ear, so the image speaks to the sight; it brings us understanding.

—JOHN OF DAMASCUS, ON THE DIVINE IMAGES

SEMIOTICS AND THE TRIUMPH OF ORTHODOXY

"To those who mock and profane the holy images . . . Anathema!" proclaims the service of the Triumph of Orthodoxy celebrated on the first Sunday of Lent: "We confess and proclaim our salvation in word and image."[1] The liturgy for the day honors the eternal memory of those who "substantiate their spoken words with writings and their deeds with *representations,* for the propagation and affirmation of the truth by *word and image.*"[2] The Triumph of Orthodoxy was the triumph of the icon itself—the acknowledgment of the full theological and liturgical significance of the holy image and its direct relation to the Incarnation of Christ. Vera Shevzov elaborates the changing liturgical context of the Triumph of Orthodoxy in her chapter in this volume, providing a rich framework for the semiotically oriented discussion here. But what *is*

I would like to express my thanks to John Bowlt, Richard Meyer, Oleg Minin, Thomas Seifrid, and Alexander Zholkovsky in the Literary, Visual, and Material Culture Initiative at the University of Southern California for inspiration and help with this chapter.

an image, or icon? What is meant by representation? The Church Fathers grappled with these questions during the iconoclastic controversy of the eighth and ninth centuries. In the twentieth and twenty-first centuries, their work has come to prefigure key aspects of semiotic theory, the theory and practice of the Russian avant-garde, and even postmodern theories of the nature of art and the artist, including corollary discussions of the concept of "originality."[3] My argument here is that the Church Fathers were semioticians *avant la lettre,* and that they are still the unrecognized forefathers of the avant-garde. The evidence for this connection is provided by "imagined icons"—images that gradually emerge as visual impulses from within the relevant texts, in this case poems by the Russian twentieth-century poets Vladimir Mayakovsky, Velimir Khlebnikov, and Nikolai Zabolotsky. The imagined icons contribute more than a simple visual effect: they provide key elements of the philosophical, ideological, and theological foundations of the poems, the poet's own literarily or politically revolutionary attitudes notwithstanding.

Given the backward-looking nature of the icon and the thoroughgoing anachronisms of the Orthodox Church, we would expect the icon to be among the first objects cast overboard from the Steamship of Modernity. And yet, the artistic avant-garde unabashedly exploited the vocabulary of the icon, as can be seen in the works of Filonov, Larionov, Goncharova, Petrov-Vodkin, and Malevich, among others. What, then, was the relationship of the literary avant-garde to the icon? There is still much to be done in answer to this question.

Outside the Slavic-Byzantine sphere, virtually all semiotic conceptions of the icon rest in one way or another on the work of the nineteenth- and early twentieth-century scholar Charles Sanders Peirce.[4] Peirce taught briefly at Johns Hopkins and Harvard, and contributed to the fields of astronomy, geology, physics, history of science, pragmatic philosophy, and semiotics. He died almost unknown to the philosophical world.[5] It has been said that Peirce anticipates Derrida's critique of the binary relation between signifier and signified, and that, like Derrida, he "can induce a feeling resembling cognitive vertigo, because his triadic thinking generates more consequences than one can readily take into account."[6]

Vertiginous or not, Peirce's double triadic system recalls some aspects of the Orthodox theology of the icon. Peirce's initial triad involves the *object,* the *interpretant,* and the *sign.* This reflects Peirce's premise that we, as interpretants, do have direct experience of reality, of the object, but are unable to think or process our knowledge without signs. Peirce then provides a second triad, this one breaking down the concept of the sign into *symbol, index,* and *icon.* According to Peirce, the symbol is an arbitrary connection, such as a national language, and because of its arbitrariness it partakes of the "thirdness" of the triad. The index, for its part, exists as a sign in closer existential relation to the object, as a symptom relates to an illness or as a weather vane relates to the wind, and so reflects "secondness" within the triad of signs. The icon reflects "firstness" within the triad because it represents an object by actually sharing certain properties with it, or duplicating properties by which the object is organized.[7] The religious icon is a Peircean icon that shares properties or organizational principles with the "object" it represents—the Person, Face, or Visage (*Litso*) of a holy figure. In so doing, the icon creates a communicative link, or communion, between the divinity of the holy figure and the supplicant. Peirce further asserts that the icon points to the prelinguistic real objects of perception, thereby anticipating Lacan's notion of the "imaginary," a spectrum of visual images that precedes the acquisition of language, but that also coexists with language; as well as Lacan's contention that there is no sign that is not determined by a previous sign, so that all thought partakes of, and contributes to, an infinite process of knowing and communicating.[8]

In a parallel sense, Orthodox theologians argue that a person experiences God's world directly, but that various sets of signs—the Old and New Testaments, the writings of the Church Fathers, and religious icons—are essential for a full grasp of this reality, as well as for one's ability to communicate it to others. The religious icon thus relies on a set of triadic relations much like the ones Peirce outlined, with the holy figure as the object, the viewer as the interpretant, and the icon as the sign. As a visual "imaginary," the religious icon does not depend on language. And much as Peirce's icon is part of an infinite process of knowing, the religious icon likewise brings the viewer into the realm of Great Time, time that has no beginning and no end.

The poems treated in this chapter share the striking ability to expand triadic relations between *object, interpretant,* and *sign* from the realm of the *literary* to the realm of the *visual.* They contain a virtual visual image that lies partially hidden beneath layers of writing. The "object" of the triad remains the same holy figure throughout, but the "sign" changes from the "thirdness" of the Peircean *symbol,* which is to say language, to the "firstness" of the *icon.* In similar fashion, the "interpretant" begins as a *reader* but is gradually transformed into a *viewer* or *supplicant.*

We know that Russian poets sometimes wrote about icons. We assume that Lermontov mentally positioned himself in front of an icon of the Theotokos when he wrote "I, Mother of God, now with a prayer" (*Ia, mater' Bozhiia, nyne s molitvoiu*).[9] We assume that Mayakovsky envisioned himself in front of an icon of Christ when, in "A Few Words About Myself" (*Neskol'ko slov obo mne samom*), he wrote that Christ "escaped from his icon."[10] And we assume that Zabolotsky envisioned an icon both when he called on Saint Paraskeva Piatnitsa for aid in the last two stanzas of his early poem "The Bathers" (*Kupal'shchiki*) and when, some twenty years later, he wrote about the holy family's "Flight into Egypt" (*Begstvo v Egipet*).[11] But what we are interested in here is something more complex. It is not poems about icons, or poems as prayers. Rather, our focus is poems that expand the triadic relation from the realm of the literary to the realm of the visual. What we will see is that Mayakovsky, the literary *enfant terrible* of the Russian Revolution, creates an imagined icon that enlarges his portrayal of himself, while Khlebnikov and Zabolotsky create imagined icons that not only relate to the themes of the given poems but also are icons about icons; they circle back to the theology and semiotics of the icon itself.

VLADIMIR MAYAKOVSKY: THE KING OF LIGHT BULBS

The first example is an excerpt from the prologue of Mayakovsky's *Vladimir Mayakovsky: A Tragedy* (*Vladimir Maiakovskii: Tragediia*). The play was published in 1913 and is marked by the pronounced struggle with God that characterized certain periods in Mayakovsky's career. The tragedy itself is replete with "disturbed echoes of New Testament phrases," and the narrator, "Vladimir Mayakovsky," plays the role of an urban savior amid Futurist industrial squalor.[12] When he says,

> Come unto me,
> all ye who ripped the silence,
> ye who howled
> because the nooses of noon were too
> tight![13]
>
> [Придите все ко мне,
> кто рвал молчание
> кто выл
> оттого, что петли полдней туги,—]

he is paraphrasing Christ's words in Matthew, "Come unto me, all ye that labor and are heavy laden, and I will give you rest" (11:28). In Russian and Slavonic translations of the gospels, this passage even has a proto-Soviet ring: "Pridite ko mne vse truzhdaiushchiesia" (not quite *trudiashchiesia,* or "laborers," but close).[14]

When Mayakovsky continues a few lines further on,

> I shall merely touch your heads with
> my fingers,
> and you will grow lips
> for enormous kisses,
> and a tongue,
> native to all peoples.
>
> [Я вам только голову пальцами
> трону,
> и у вас
> вырастут губы
> для огромных поцелуев
> и язык,
> родной всем народам.]

he recalls the healing laying on of hands that occurs repeatedly in the New Testament, as well as the more comprehensive message of love and understanding (if not "enormous kisses") among nations, and the concept of speaking in tongues, the divine language of the Pentecost. The passage also suggests the angel's words to the shepherds at the Nativity: "Behold, I bring you good tidings of great joy, which shall be to all people (*vsem liudiam*)" (Luke 2:19).[15]

It is through the tragedy's portrayal of Vladimir Mayakovsky as urban savior, along with the marked juxtaposition of light and darkness, that the imaginary icons emerge—in this case, icons of the Descent into Hades, Christ Pantocrator, and the Ascension. In the first five lines of the excerpt, Mayakovsky brags of his fearless hatred of daylight, and affirms his role in the nightlife of the city.

> With swollen fingers spouting reddish
> hairs,

The sun has caressed you with a gadfly's
persistence:
in your souls, a slave has been kissed to
death.
I, undaunted,
have borne my hatred for sunlight
through the centuries,
my soul stretched taut as the nerves of
a wire.
I am the King of Light Bulbs!

[Пухлыми пальцами в рыжих
волосиках
солнце изласкало вас с
назойливостью овода—
В ваших душах выцелован раб.
Я, бесстрашный,
ненависть к дневным лучам понес в
веках;
И с душой натянутой, как нервы
про́вода,
Я—царь ламп!]

Conflating Christ's role as the "King of the Jews" with his assertion, "I am the light of the world," Mayakovsky asserts, "I am the King of Light Bulbs." He operates not by means of daylight, but by means of a special light that shines when it is dark, "the light that shineth in the darkness" (John 8:12). Representations on icons likewise function not on the basis of ordinary daylight, but on the basis of divine light, which abolishes shadows, and sometimes takes the form of a mandorla, halo, circle, or half-sphere around a holy figure, or rays of light emanating from the figure.[16] And, of course, the notion of superseding daylight with electric light bulbs also provides a handy prefiguring of the Leninist slogan "Communism = Soviet power + electrification."

The role of light is an important aspect of the icon of the Descent into Hades (pl. 3), which exists as a barely hidden layer beneath Mayakovsky's text. Hell as represented on icons is not the fiery furnace of the Western tradition, but rather a dark, gaping abyss that has never been penetrated by divine light. Christ, in his ultimate act of humility, descends into Hell ("harrows Hell") to rescue the damned, whose tortured existence within the abyss parallels the horrors portrayed by Hieronymus Bosch. In order to emphasize the triumph of divine light over the darkness of Hell, Christ is portrayed in "a radiant halo . . . often spangled with stars round the outer edge and pierced with rays issuing from Him. His garments . . . are a golden-yellow hue, made luminous throughout by thick golden rays."[17] Appearing as the King of Light Bulbs in the dark and hellish city, amid the lame, blind, criminal, and downtrodden, Mayakovsky casts himself as an urbanized and updated Christ on an imagined icon of the Descent into Hades.

The last segment of the excerpt combines images of manure and Karenina-like suicide not only with the gentlemanly lexicon of what Lydia Ginzburg defines as the nineteenth-century "school of harmonious precision,"[18] but also with imaginary icons of Christ Pantocrator and the Ascension of Christ.

Then I, limping with my shabby little
soul,
shall go off to my throne

with the starry holes in the worn-out
dome.
I'll lie down,
radiant,
in clothing of languor,
on a soft couch of genuine manure;
and quietly,
kissing the knees of the crossties,
the wheel of a locomotive will embrace
my neck.

[А я, прихрамывая душонкой,
уйду к моему трону
с дырами звезд по истертым сводам.
Лягу,
светлый,
в одеждах из лени
на мягкое ложе из настоящего
навоза,
и тихим,
целующим шпал колени,
обнимет мне шею колесо паровоза.]

Leaving out the manure and the homicidal locomotive as essential forms of Mayakovskian flailing and thrashing, we see that the hero, Mayakovsky, departs from the people in order to ascend to a throne with stars in a dome. He characterizes himself as *svetlyi*—"bright" or "holy"; he reclines on a soft bed and wears the clothing of languor—possibly the loose clothing of the Byzantine period; and he is surrounded or embraced by a wheel and stars. He has presented us with icons of Christ Pantocrator, often painted inside domes, as in the Church of the Savior on Blood (*Spas na krovi*) in St. Petersburg, and the Ascension of Christ. In the end, Mayakovsky creates an imagined mixed-media artwork, a palimpsest, that relies on the theological and semiotic triad of the holy personage or *object,* the supplicant or *interpretant,* and, in the meaning of both Charles Sanders Peirce and the Church Fathers, an *icon.* It is these imagined icons that make Mayakovsky's representation of his own reality complete—and that make him the King of Light Bulbs.

VELIMIR KHLEBNIKOV: THE KING OF TIME

Unlike Mayakovsky, Khlebnikov does not wrestle with God. Rather, he incorporates Orthodox elements in a panoply of cultural influences—from paganism, to Cubo-Futurism, to the mathematical theories of Lobachevsky, to the poetry of Walt Whitman. Anything was fodder for Khlebnikov's omnivorous imagination.[19] As the son of an ornithologist, Khlebnikov shaped his skills of perception in the countryside. He was not a city boy, and he arrived in St. Petersburg with a "rich and keenly developed way of seeing the world that was vastly different from the views of the literary establishment in the capital."[20] A sense of rural *ostranenie* or "defamiliarization" induced by the gap between the countryside and the teeming urban setting of Petrograd would also mark Zabolotsky when he arrived in the same city some years later. Both of these newly urban poets demonstrated an unsentimental relation to nature, a country boy's yearning for serious knowledge, naive fearlessness in the face of radical thinking, and elements of the religious upbringing typical of the countryside, where icons in various settings—not just at church, but at home and at school—were simply part of life.

Khlebnikov's defamiliarized vision gave him a natural affinity for Cubo-Futurism, in which, to quote Roman Jakobson, "everything is based on relationship and interaction, between parts and wholes, between color and shape, between the representation and represented."[21] Continuing this thought, Krystyna Pomorska writes that in Khlebnikov's poetry, "we have the Cubist theory of relativity applied to the visual arts. . . . According to its rules, the concept of space in paintings underwent profound changes. It became relativity in the sense that objects were situated in free perspective with respect to one another, were displaced against the principles of traditional perspective."[22] The distortion of traditional perspective here discussed in connection with Cubism applies equally well to icons. Consider Florensky's notion of "reverse perspective," reflecting the viewer's participation in the triadic function of the icon, or the notion of "isometric perspective," reflecting the fact that the icon painter "did not work on the basis of observation of nature, but represented objects as he knew them," the main concern being "to bring out the essence of things."[23]

For Khlebnikov, with his pronounced distrust of human reason, it was a short step from Orthodoxy to Cubo-Futurism in terms of the function and structure of art. As Ouspensky writes, "The icon sometimes uses irregular and shocking forms, just as holiness sometimes tolerates extreme forms which seem like madness in the eyes of the world, such as the holiness of the fools in Christ." He continues with a citation from a self-proclaimed fool in Christ: "They say that I am mad . . . but without madness, one does not enter into the Kingdom of God. . . . To live according to the Gospel one must be mad. As long as men are reasonable and of sober mind, the Kingdom of God will not come on earth."[24]

Khlebnikov, the self-proclaimed King of Time, was both an artist-visionary and, in his own way, an unorthodox Orthodox holy fool. One biographer, acknowledging the peculiarities of Khlebnikov's character, and knowing his background as an amateur ornithologist, described him as a bird: "With his habit of standing on one leg, his attentive gaze, with his propensity for sudden flights, for breaking away from spaces and flights into the future, he, more than anything, resembled a long-legged, thoughtful bird."[25] Within this context—the context of ornithology, Cubo-Futurism, and icons—Khlebnikov's well-known but mystifying poem "Bobeobi sang the lips" (*Bobeobi pelis' guby*) begins to make sense—but not too much sense, of course. The first issue is what the poem means literally, given its mixed lexicon of Russian and *zaum* or transrational language:

> Bobeobi sang the lips.
> Veeomi sang the eyes.
> Pieeo sang the eyebrows.
> Lieeei sang the countenance.
> Gzi-gzi-gzeo sang the chain.
> Thus on a linen cloth of some kind of
>   correspondences
> Beyond [all] dimension lived the Face.[26]
>
> [Бобэоби пелись губы.
> Вээоми пелись взоры.
> Пиээо пелись брови.
> Лиэээй пелся облик.
> Гзи-гзи-гзэо пелась цепь.
> Так на холсте каких-то соответствий
> Вне протяжения жило Лицо.][27]

This is not the well-known Khlebnikovian type of *zaum* based on Slavic roots and used, for example, in "Incantation by Laughter" (*Zakliatie smekhom*). As Pomorska notes, "What strikes us here first of all is that the vocables . . . not only do not have any meaning in the Russian language code, but their construction is alien to Russian phonology." Pomorska then argues that the *zaum* constitutes sound-images or *zvukoobrazy,* with *bobeobi* phonetically prefiguring *guby* (lips); *veeomi* prefiguring *vzory* (eyes, literally "gazes"), and *lieeei* prefiguring *oblik* (countenance) and *litso* (face).[28] This is certainly possible. Beyond the concept of the *zvukoobraz,* however, lies Khlebnikov's early experience recording birdcalls in the wild and its possible influence on his poetic lexicon. In his "Ornithological Observations in the Pavdinsk Province," published in *Nature and Hunting* (*Priroda i okhota*) in 1911, the poet transcribes birdcalls for the cuckoo, black woodpecker, hazel grouse, and nutcracker. The transcriptions themselves form little stories.

> The nutcracker often sits for a while with closed eyes after feeding, ruffling its feathers and evidently reveling in the sounds of its voice, as if recounting something of its impressions of the day in its own strange language: "pee-oo, pee-oo, pee-oo," it moans painfully and piteously; "pee-ee, pee-ee, pee-ee," it pipes in a delicate voice, like the cry of the hazel grouse; then insistently and intelligently, "knya, knya, knya"; then switches to muttering, "kya, kya, kya"; then trembling with intensity, almost as if it were angry, and ruffling its feathers, it makes a rude hoarse hiss.[29]

In one of his many poetic fragments, Khlebnikov creates another small story of birdcalls. This one bears phonetic resemblance to "Bobeobi," reproducing the calls made by birds of the taiga that somehow provide accompaniment to a forest divinity with unbound wavy hair and blue eyes. The divinity in turn holds and kisses an unidentified but clearly cherished child.

Whitethroat: beboteu-veviat'!
Brambling: t'zerti-edigredi!
Yellowhammer: kri-ti-ti-ti, tii!
Yellow-breasted bunting: v'or-ver-viru,
  s'ek, s'ek, s'ek!
Woodpecker: tpran', tpran', tpran' a-an'!
Green chiff-chaff: pryn', ptsireb, ptsireb!
    Ptsireb se, se, se!
Whitethroat: beboteu-veviat'!
Forest divinity (with unbound wavy
  hair, with blue eyes, cuddles a child):
But I know as long as I live
That there is wah, that there is yoohoo.
(Covers the head of the child
  with kisses.)
Whitethroat: beboteu-veviat'!

[Славка: беботэу-вевять!
Вьюрок: тьерти-едигреди!
Овсянка: кри-ти-ти-ти, тии!
Дубровник: вьор-вер-виру, сьек,
  сьек,сьек!
Дятел: тпрань, тпрань, тпрань, а-ань!
Пеночка зеленая: прынь, пцирэб,
  пциреб!
    Пциреб сэ, сэ, сэ!
Славка: беботэу-вевять!
песное божество (с распущенными
  волнистыми волосами, с

голубыми глазами, прижимает
ребенка.):
Но знаю я, пока живу,
Что есть уа, что есть ау.
(Покрывает поцелуями голову
ребенка.)
Славка: бeботэу-вевять!][30]

We already know that for Khlebnikov *zaum* was an attempt to reach a greater metaphysical truth. Here, the poem's title, "Wisdom in a Bird Trap" (*Mudrost' v silke*), and the mysterious, nurturing presence of the forest divinity reminiscent of Christ, or perhaps John the Baptist with his unruly hair, suggests such greater meaning. We see one of the sources of both the phonetics and the larger context of Khlebnikov's *zaum*.[31]

The poem "Bobeobi" likewise focuses on the interrelation of this world and a higher realm. The interrelation is reflected in a number of ways. In the area of lexicon, it is in the combination of: "everyday" Russian—*guby* (lips), *brovi* (eyebrows), *tsep'* (chain), *tak* (thus, so), *kholst* (linen cloth) and so on; elevated, archaic, abstract, or enigmatic Russian—*vzory* (gazes), *oblik* (countenance), *sootvetstviia* (correspondences), *protiazhenie* (dimension), *Litso* (Face), and the curious but recognizable verb *pet'sia* (to sing itself); and *zaum,* which by its very essence represents something beyond the "everyday." In terms of overall structure, the interrelation evolves from Khlebnikov's use of the Tiutchevian practice (which we will see again in Zabolotsky's poem) of putting forward a set of specifics in the main body of the poem, and then following this with a short concluding segment that raises the specifics and the poem as a whole into a higher metaphysical arena.[32]

In this case, the turn includes the evocation of an imagined icon, namely, the icon of Christ Not Made by Human Hands (*archeiropoietos* or, in Russian, *nerukotvornyi*), also known as the icon of the Holy Face or Holy Visage (pl. 4). In the East, the story of the icon centers on a certain King Abgar, a leper, who sent an emissary to paint a portrait of Christ. The emissary reported that he could not paint Christ "because of the indescribable glory of His face." Christ, however, gave the painter a piece of cloth with which he had dried his face, and on which miraculously appeared the image of his face—not made by human hands.[33] Indeed, Khlebnikov's invention of a reflexive form of the verb "to sing"—*pet'sia,* "to sing oneself"—suggests exactly this lack of human intervention in the composition of the face. Each feature "sings itself," or brings itself into being.

The icon is remarkable not only because of the story of its origin, but because of its singular image: not a biblical scene, not the depiction of a historical event, but simply Christ's face—Christ's face with neither neck, nor shoulders, nor any other type of visual context. The whole meaning of the icon lies in the combination of the striking individual features that constitute the Holy Face. When Leonid Ouspensky and Vladimir Lossky elucidate the meaning of this icon, they describe the image feature by feature in a manner reminiscent of Khlebnikov's poem, but with scholarly rather than poetic tools and goals.

They write (with my comments interjected in brackets):

> The regular features of the visage are rendered schematically: the beautiful line of the mouth [Khlebnikov's *guby*] has nothing of the carnal; the elongated and very straight nose forms, with the arched eyebrows [Khlebnikov's *brovi*], a pattern that recalls a palm tree. The grave and impassive expression of this visage [Khlebnikov's *oblik* and *Litso*] of the God-Man . . . is the impassivity of an absolutely pure human nature, which excludes sin, but remains open to all the sorrows of the fallen world. The large dilated eyes [Khlebnikov's *vzory*], turned toward the onlooker, have an attentive and saddened look, which seems to penetrate the depths of consciences, without overwhelming them.[34]

As Khlebnikov's poem moves toward its larger meaning, the key words themselves become broader in meaning, moving from the specific *guby, vzory, brovi,* to the more generalized *oblik* (countenance), then to *tsep'* (chain), which suggests both a material chain with its onomatopoetic jingling, and a metaphysical chain or linkage from this world to the next. The word *tak* (thus) signals the transition to the conclusion, the two concluding lines that sum up the forgoing series and that make the whole metaphysically greater than the sum of its parts. The movement toward abstraction continues with the concept of "correspondences" (*sootvetstviia*), and it reaches its climax with the revelation of "the Face" or "Person" (*Litso*), which lived beyond all dimensions or outside of space (*vne protiazheniia*).

Along with the abstract theological potential of this language, Khlebnikov provides an important concrete detail that leads to the emergence of the imagined icon: the word *kholst,* meaning "linen" or "canvas." To prevent splitting, a piece of loosely woven linen is glued to the board on which an icon is painted. Still more important, the icon of the Holy Face comes specifically from a story about the image of Christ's face transferred to a piece of linen, the Holy Cloth (*mandylion*). Indeed, the Feast of the Holy Face on 16 August is called the feast of "the image of Our Lord 'not made by human hands,' the image which is called the holy linen."[35] For all his paganism and cultural omnivorousness, Khlebnikov presents us with a poem based on an imagined icon that articulates a central tenet of Orthodox theology, namely, the significance and triadic function of the icon itself. For it is the icon of the Holy Face, along with the icon of the Triumph of Orthodoxy, that explicitly celebrates the linkage of the divine world and the human supplicant by means of an image of the Face and Person—*Litso*—of Christ.[36]

A descendent of the icon of the Holy Face can also be seen in the portrait of Vasily Kamensky by the Futurist artist David Burliuk (pl. 13). The discussions of Khlebnikov's Cubism by Jakobson and Pomorska could easily be applied to the portrait, which is sometimes said to be the inspiration for Khlebnikov's poem. This certainly could be true, but at the same time the portrait itself is clearly based on the icon of the Holy Face, complete with a halo, rays of divine light, and golden coloring.[37]

NIKOLAI ZABOLOTSKY: THE KING OF NOTHING IN PARTICULAR AND "WANNABE" SOVIET POET

The great paradox of Nikolai Zabolotsky's life was that he wanted nothing more than to be a poet, and to be a *Soviet* poet if that's what it took. But even after he returned from camp rehabilitated, his attempts at being a Soviet poet were undercut by his roots in the avant-garde and the cultural defamiliarization created by his upbringing in the countryside—an upbringing that included Orthodoxy. Some of his late poems are simply shallow, and we are not concerned with those. But those of his later poems that display artistic and intellectual depth inevitably reach down to these non-Soviet roots—and, not incidentally, link him to Khlebnikov, whom he greatly admired.[38] The poem "I do not seek harmony in nature" (*Ia ne ishchu garmonii v prirode*) is one of these. It is not one of the flagrantly avant-garde poems that earned him a term in a Soviet labor camp, but a poem apparently linked to the "revolutionary" values of the Soviet state. Zabolotsky positioned it as the opening work in the first collection of verse he published after he returned from camp, blatantly out of the chronological order in the volume overall. Given this obvious sign of importance, it is not surprising that Yury Lotman goes so far as to call it "Zabolotsky's poetic manifesto."[39]

> I do not seek harmony in nature.
> Neither at the base of the cliffs nor in
> the clear arc of the heavens
> Alas, have I discerned
> The rational harmony of first
> principles.
>
> How willful is her dark universe!
> In the fierce singing of the winds,
> My heart does not hear true
> consonance,
> My soul does not sense harmonious
> voices.
>
> But at the quiet hour of an autumn
> sunset,
> When the wind falls silent in the
> distance,
> When, surrounded by a weak glow,
> Blind night goes down to the river,
>
> When the darkened water
> Tired by turbulent motion
> And uselessly heavy labor
> Becomes quiet in the troubled
> half-sleep of exhaustion,
>
> When the vast world of contradictions
> Sates itself with fruitless play—
> It is as if the archetype of human pain
> Rises up from the abyss of the waters
> before me.
>
> And at this hour mournful nature
> Lies around sighing heavily,
> And the untamed freedom in which
> evil is inseparable from good
> Is not dear to her.
>
> And she dreams of the sparkling shaft
> of the turbine,
> And the measured sound of rational
> labor,
> And the singing of smokestacks and the
> glow of a dam,

And power lines filled with current.

Thus, falling asleep in her bed,
The insane but loving mother
Harbors the lofty universe of the child
within her
In order to catch sight of the sun
together with her son.

И пенье труб, и зарево плотины,
И налитые током провода.

Так, засыпая на своей кровати,
Безумная, но любящая мать
Таит в себе высокий мир дитяти,
Чтоб вместе с сыном солнце
увидать.]

[Я не ищу гармонии в природе.
Разумной соразмерности начал
Ни в недрах скал, ни в ясном
небосводе
Я до сих пор, увы, не различал.

Как своенравен мир ее дремучий!
В ожесточенном пении ветров
Не слышит сердце правильных
созвучий,
Душа не чует стройных голосов.

Но в тихий час осеннего заката,
Когда умолкнет ветер вдалеке,
Когда сияньем немощным объята,
Слепая ночь опустится к реке,

Когда, устав от буйного движенья,
От бесполезно тяжкого труда,
В тревожном полусне изнеможенья
Затихнет потемневшая вода,

Когда огромный мир противоречий
Насытится бесплодною игрой, –
Как бы прообраз боли человечьей
Из бездны вод встает передо мной.

И в этот час печальная природа
Лежит вокруг, вздыхая тяжело,
И не мила ей дикая свобода,
Где от добра не отделимо зло,

И снится ей блестящий вал
турбины,
И мерный звук разумного труда,

What is the essence of Zabolotsky's poetic manifesto? A first reading suggests that it is the manifesto of the Soviet poet Zabolotsky wanted to be. Such a reading of stanzas 1–6 suggests that nature, left to her own devices, is not harmonious, but blind, exhausted, full of contradictions, and incapable of separating good from evil. In the penultimate stanza, Soviet Man steps in, as nature dreams images that could be a poster for Soviet industrialization: turbine shafts, smokestacks, and hydroelectric power (fig. 16). In the closing stanza, nature, characterized as an irrational but loving mother, embodies past, present, and future, as she falls asleep, harboring the lofty universe of her child—presumably Soviet Man—within her, in order to catch sight of the sun together with her son.

But Zabolotsky's most politically correct verse is also the most vulnerable to subversion.[40] The stanza seems to imply that Mother Nature should learn from Soviet Man, thereby becoming harmonious and rational. And yet, rationalism, for Zabolotsky, is a double-edged sword. Too much reason is constraining, and a certain amount of mindlessness serves the free-flowing intuition of greater truth.[41] It is the poem's depiction of a universalized, loving, but "insane" (*bezumnaia,* literally "mindless") mother—the mother of a son who

FIG. 16 Nikolai Troshin, Dnieper Hydroelectric Station, photomontage. Reproduced from *L'URSS en construction* (*USSR in Construction,* French edition), no. 3 (1934). Private Collection / Archives Charmet.

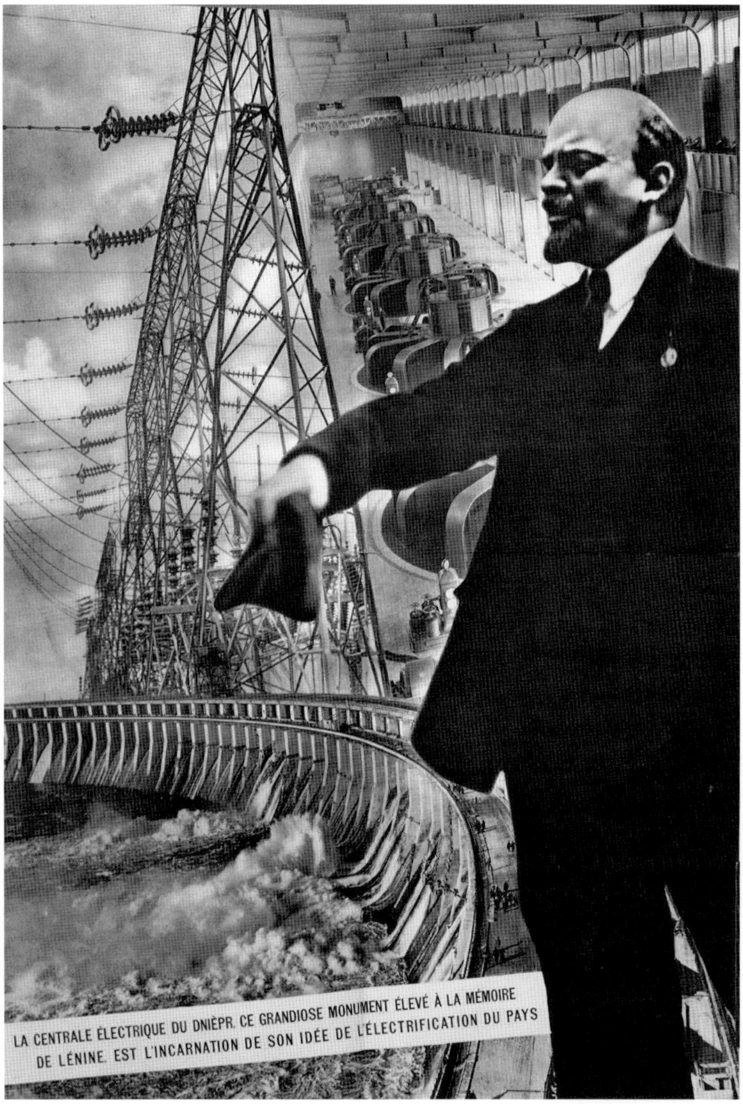

will lead her to enlightenment—that signals the presence of religious imagery. This is an image of Mother Nature, but it is also an image of the Theotokos or Mother of God, who in Orthodox terms is the Mother of Christ as well as the "universal Mother, the Mother of all humankind."[42] The Theotokos links the physical and metaphysical aspects of the universe, guarantees the physical aspect of Christ's dual nature, and, as we might say, "always already" links the past to the future.[43] She assures the fact of the Incarnation that leads to the validation of the icon itself as a material representation. Finally, like Zabolotsky's "mindless but loving" Mother Nature, who is unable to grasp the full significance of the world she carries within her, the Theotokos cannot fully understand her son's utterances, but, according to the Gospel of Luke, keeps "all these things, pondering them in her heart" (Luke 2:19).[44]

Zabolotsky portrays Mother Nature's effort at understanding the "things" she keeps and ponders in her heart, in terms of "catching sight of the sun together with her son." Prayers celebrating the Theotokos repeatedly make reference to the "sun" of enlightenment brought through her son, Jesus Christ. The prayer celebrating the Nativity of the Theotokos begins, "Thy birth, O Theotokos . . . hath declared joy to all the universe: for from thee arose the Sun of Righteousness, Christ our God," while the prayer on the Presentation of Christ at the Temple begins, "Rejoice, O Theotokos . . . for from thee hath arisen the Sun of Righteousness, Christ our God, who doth give light to those in darkness."[45]

With these conceptual parallels as a basis, the first imaginary icon emerges, the icon of Our Lady of the Sign (pl. 5). This is an icon on which the Theotokos can be said to "harbor the lofty universe of the child within her," and it is typically placed near the top center of the iconostasis in Russian Orthodox churches. The young Zabolotsky would have seen variants of it time and time again during his formative years.[46] On such icons, the Theotokos is portrayed with raised hands (Orant), and an image of the Christ Child is superimposed in a *clipeus* or *mandorla* on the upper portion of her torso.[47] She is "pregnant" both literally and figuratively, because she always and eternally links this world to the world to come.

Another imagined icon emerges in connection with the notion of the mother falling asleep, the icon of the Dormition (*Uspenie*). The Theotokos is portrayed on her deathbed, "having fallen asleep in the Lord"—*usopshaia,* in Russian. The mother in Zabolotsky's poem is not dead, but she is "falling asleep"—*zasypaia,* a word based on the same root as *usopshaia.* Each mother is accompanied by her son, but on the icon of the Dormition there is a reversal of maternal and filial roles: Christ now holds the figure of a child, which represents his mother's soul waiting to be taken up to heaven, there to encounter the full light of God's radiance—or, to cast it again in Zabolotsky's terms, "in order to catch sight of the sun together with her son."

This, then, is the conclusion of the poem designated to set the proper tone for the first collection of verse published by Zabolotsky after his return from camp—a mixed-media palimpsest that undercuts its own "Soviet" meaning. As an effort at Soviet rehabilitation, it both succeeds and fails. The images of the smokestacks, dams, and transmission lines are impressive and very "Soviet," but they are ultimately overpowered by the image of Mother Nature *cum* Theotokos. The image of rational Soviet Man is overshadowed by the image of Christ. And with the help of the imagined icons as both signifiers and signified, as both medium and message, the Soviet insistence on rational reconstruction of nature is overshadowed by the Triumph of Orthodoxy. The Church Fathers, Charles Sanders Peirce, and the poets of the Russian avant-garde make exceptionally strange bedfellows. In the end, though, they all live in the same place—the realm of Great Time, where past is future and future is past, and where this is known and shown not just through the Word, but through the icon.

NOTES TO CHAPTER 8

1. See Leonid Ouspensky, *Theology of the Icon,* 2 vols., trans. Anthony Gythiel (Crestwood, N.Y.: St. Vladimir's Seminary Press, 1992), 1:165n.

2. Italics added. Ouspensky, *Theology of the Icon,* 1:151–52, 164–65.

3. See, for example, Kaja Silverman, *The Subject of Semiotics* (New York: Oxford University Press, 1983); Donald Kuspit, *The Cult of the Avant-Garde Artist* (Cambridge: Cambridge University Press, 1994); Rosalind Krauss, *The Originality of the Avant-Garde and Other Modernist Myths* (Cambridge, Mass.: MIT Press, 1990).

4. In the Russian context, see Boris Uspensky, *A Poetics of Composition: The Structure of the Artistic Text and Typology of a Compositional Form* (Berkeley and Los Angeles: University of California Press, 1973); Uspensky, *The Semiotics of the Russian Icon,* PdR Press Publications in Semiotics of Art 3, ed. Stephen Ruby (Lisse: Peter de Ridder Press, 1976); V. D. Likhacheva, "Svoeobrazie kompozitsii drevnerusskikh ikon," in *Khudozhestvennoe nasledie drevnei Rossii i sovremennost',* ed. V. D. Likhacheva and D. S. Likhachev (Leningrad: Nauka, 1971).

5. Edward C. Moore and Richard S. Robin, eds., *From Time and Chance to Consciousness: Studies in the Metaphysics of Charles Peirce* (Oxford: Berg, 1994); and *Studies in the Philosophy of Charles Sanders Peirce* (Amherst: University of Massachusetts Press, 1964).

6. Leroy F. Searle, "Peirce, Charles Sanders," in *The Johns Hopkins Guide to Literary Theory and Criticism,* ed. Michael Groden and Martin Kreiswirth (Baltimore: Johns Hopkins University Press, 1994), 559.

7. See Silverman, *The Subject of Semiotics,* 14, 16, 19; Ludwig Nagl, "The Ambivalent Status of Reality in K. O. Apel's 'Transcendental-Pragmatic' Reconstruction of Peirce's Semiotic," in Moore, *From Time and Chance to Consciousness,* 60. In his "Prolegomena to an Apology for Pragmatism," Peirce writes: "An analysis of the essence of a sign, (stretching that word to its widest limits, as *anything which, being determined by an object, determines an interpretation to determination, through it, by the same object*), leads to a proof that every sign is determined by its object, either first, by partaking in the characters of the object, when I call the thing an *Icon;* secondly, by being really and in its individual existence connected with the individual object, when I call the sign an *Index;* thirdly, by more or less approximate certainty that it will be interpreted as denoting the object, in consequence of a habit (which term I use as including a natural disposition), when I call the sign a *Symbol.*" Charles Sanders Peirce, *Collected Papers of Charles Sanders Peirce,* vol. 4 (Cambridge, Mass.: Harvard University Press, 1906), par. 531.

8. See Nagl, "The Ambivalent Status of Reality," 60; Silverman, *The Subject of Semiotics,* 21; John F. Boler, "Habits of Thought," in Moore, *Studies in the Philosophy of Charles Sanders Peirce,* 386–87.

9. "Molitva," in M. Lermontov, *Stikhotvoreniia. Poemy. Maskarad. Geroi nashego vremeni* (Moscow: Khudozhestvennaia literatura, 1972), 134.

10. V. V. Maiakovskii, *Izbrannye proizvedeniia,* Biblioteka poeta, 2 vols. (Moscow: Sovetskii pisatel', 1963), 1:76–77. Translation adapted from Vladimir Mayakovsky, *The Complete Plays of Vladimir Mayakovsky,* trans. Guy Daniels (New York: Simon & Schuster, 1968), 21–22. See also Edward J. Brown, *Mayakovsky: A Poet in the Revolution* (Princeton: Princeton University Press, 1973), 87–88.

11. "Kupal'shchiki" and "Begstvo v Egipet," in N. Zabolotskii, *Polnoe sobranie stikhotvorenii i poem,* Novaia biblioteka poeta (St. Petersburg: Akademicheskii proekt, 2002), 94, 256. See also Sarah Pratt, *Nikolai Zabolotsky: Enigma and Cultural Paradigm* (Evanston, Ill.: Northwestern University Press, 2000), 26–28.

12. See Brown, *Mayakovsky,*_ 86–88, 93–96. See also Juliette R. Stapanian, *Mayakovsky's Cubo-Futurist Vision* (Houston: Rice University Press, 1986), 45–48, 157–70.

13. Maiakovskii, *Izbrannye proizvedeniia,* 1:133–35. Translation adapted from Mayakovsky, *The Complete Plays,* 21–22.

14. KJV; Russian Synodal Version; *The New Testament in Slavonic,* BFBS, 1959. One can also hear echoes of the inscribed speech on the Statue of Liberty, which, like Mayakovsky, promises to protect the oppressed and provide light leading to a better future: "Give me your tired, your poor, / Your huddled masses yearning to breathe free, / The wretched refuse of your teeming shore. / Send these, the homeless, tempest-tossed, to me, / I lift my lamp beside the golden door!" Emma Lazarus, "The New Colossus," in *Emma Lazarus: Selections from Her Poetry and Prose,* ed. Morris U. Schappes (New York: Cooperative Book League, 1944), 40–41.

15. KJV; The Russian Synodal Version reads: "Ne boites': ia vozveshchaiu vam velikuiu radost', kotoraia budet vsem liudiam." The Slavonic is similar.

16. See Ouspensky, *Theology of the Icon,* 1:159.

17. Leonid Ouspensky and Vladimir Lossky, *The Meaning of Icons,* trans. G. E. H. Palmer and E. Kadloubovsky (Crestwood, N.Y.: St. Vladimir's Seminary Press, 1982), 187–88. See also Vladimir Lossky, *The Image and Likeness of God* (Crestwood, N.Y.: St. Vladimir's Seminary Press, 1985), 31–32, 42.

18. The words "languor" (*len'*), "soft" (*miagkii*), "couch" (*lozhe*), "quietly" (*tikhim*), and "will embrace" (*obnimet*) can be seen as typical of the School of Harmonious Precision, given a very different context and authorial intention, however. See Lidiia Ginzburg, *O lirike* (Leningrad: Sovetskii pisatel', 1964).

19. Most of the basic biographical information about Khlebnikov used here comes from Nikolai Stepanov, *Velimir Khlebnikov* (Moscow: Sovetskii pisatel', 1975); and Charlotte Douglas, "Introduction" and "Kindred Spirits," in Velimir Khlebnikov, *Collected Works,* vol. 1, trans. Paul Schmidt, ed. Charlotte Douglas (Cambridge, Mass.: Harvard University Press, 1987), 3–34, 165–94.

20. Douglas, "Introduction," 12.

21. Roman Jakobson, quoted in Krystyna Pomorska, *Russian Formalist Theory and Its Poetic Ambiance* (The Hague: Mouton, 1968), 20. See also Stepanov, *Khlebnikov,* 31–33.

22. Pomorska, *Russian Formalist Theory,* 99.

23. Egon Sendler, *The Icon: Image of the Invisible: Elements of Theology, Aesthetics, and Technique,* trans. Steven Bigham (Redondo Beach, Calif.: Oakwood Publications, 1988), 119, 142–43. Pavel Florenskii, "Obratnaia perspektiva" and "Ikonostas," in *Sobranie sochinenii,* vol. 1, ed. N. A. Struve (Paris: YMCA Press, 1985), 117, 193–96. See also D. S. Likhachev, *Poetika drevnerusskoi literatury* (Moscow: Nauka, 1979); Likhacheva and Likhachev, *Khudozhestvennoe nasledie drevnei Rossii i sovremennost'.*

24. Ouspensky, *Theology of the Icon,* 1:191–92.

25. Quoted in Stepanov, *Khlebnikov,* 34.

26. My translation. See also the translation in Vladimir Markov and Merrill Sparks, eds., *Modern Russian Poetry* (Indianapolis: Bobbs-Merrill, 1966), 329.

27. Velimir Khlebnikov, *Sobranie sochinenii,* 3 vols. (St. Petersburg: Akademicheskii proekt, 2001), 1:111.

28. Pomorska, *Russian Formalist Theory,* 98.

29. Khlebnikov, quoted in Douglas, "Introduction," 7; see also "Ornithological Observations in the Pavdinsk Province," in Velimir Khlebnikov, *Collected Works,* 201–22.

30. Khlebnikov, *Sobranie sochinenii,* 178–79. For examples of Khlebnikov's *zaum* based on other languages, rather than birdcalls, see Stepanov, *Khlebnikov,* 137.

31. Stepanov, *Khlebnikov,* 134. With a slightly different interpretation of the *zaum* terms *ya* (here translated as a baby's cry "wah!") and *ay* (which Russian speakers use to signal each other from a distance, here translated as "yoohoo!"), the speech of the forest divinity could also be translated in Christ-like biblical terms as follows: "But I know as long as I live that I am the alpha [first cry of a baby] and the omega [voice calling from the next world]." See Rev. 1:8.

32. See, for example, "In the stifling silence of the air" (*V dushnom vozdukha molchan'e*), "The earth's countenance is still forlorn" (*Eshche zemli pechalen vid*), "Look, on the river's expanse" (*Smotri, kak na rechnom prostore*), "The sun shines, the waters sparkle" (*Siiaet solntse, vody bleshchut*), among others, in F. I. Tiutchev, *Lirika,* 2 vols. (Moscow: Nauka, 1965), 1:59, 83, 130, 152.

33. See Ouspensky, *Theology of the Icon,* 1:51–52 (including note 2), 69–72.

34. Ouspensky and Lossky, *The Meaning of Icons,* 72.

35. Ouspensky, *Theology of the Icon,* 1:53. In connection with the mention of "the image of the holy linen," it is interesting to speculate on the possible significance of a statement by Khlebnikov to his father, who had expressed concern about the intellectual respectability of aspects of his son's work. Khlebnikov writes: "I am convinced the day will come when you will be proud of me, for I will spread out a magic tablecloth (*kholst*) upon which will appear a spiritual feast for the whole of humanity." In this case, the linen is a tablecloth. Quoted in Douglas, "Introduction," 17.

36. Ouspensky, *Theology of the Icon,* 1:151.

37. My thanks to John Bowlt for bringing the portrait to my attention.

38. "Khlebnikov's birds" appear in Zabolotsky's "Vchera, o smerti razmyshliaia," and Khlebnikov himself appears moldering in his grave in "Torzhestvo zemledeliia" Zabolotskii, *Sobranie stikhotvorenii i poem.* See Darra Goldstein, *Nikolai Zabolotsky: Play for Mortal Stakes* (Cambridge: Cambridge University Press, 1993), 123–25, and Pratt, *Nikolai Zabolotsky,* 115–16, 156–58.

39. Iu. M. Lotman, *Struktura khudozhestvennogo teksta,* Brown University Slavic Reprint Series (Providence: Brown University Press, 1971), 274. For additional discussion of the poem, see Pratt, *Nikolai Zabolotsky,* 213–31.

40. One senses echoes, rather distant ones perhaps, of Tiutchev's poem "Nature is not what you think" (*Ne to, chto mnite vy, priroda*), in which the persona compares his imagined interlocutor to a deaf-mute who cannot hear the voice of Mother Nature because of his foolish and overly rationalistic turn of mind. But it is the parallel with Zabolotsky's own "The Creators of Roads" (*Tvortsy dorog*), specifically the powerful closing of the original third canto, that provides the strongest support. The canto leaves the reader with an image of nature—represented by the creatures of the earth that live in the tundra (*tvar' zemnaia*)—falling asleep and affirming the harmony that is seldom remembered by man.

41. See Pratt, *Nikolai Zabolotsky,* 159–65, chap. 4.

42. I am indebted to Lauren Leighton for suggesting the parallel with the Theotokos. See G. P. Fedotov, *The Russian Religious Mind,* 2 vols. (Cambridge, Mass.: Harvard University Press, 1946–66), 1:360–61.

43. Jaroslav Pelikan, *The Spirit of Eastern Christendom (600–1700),* vol. 2 of *The Christian Tradition: A History of the Development of Doctrine* (Chicago: University of Chicago Press, 1974), 226–27.

44. See Lossky, *The Image and Likeness of God,* 199–200.

45. *A Manual of Eastern Orthodox Prayers* (Crestwood, N.Y.: St. Vladimir's Seminary Press, 1991), 30, 32.

46. See Nikolai Zabolotskii, "Rannie gody," in *Izbrannye proizvedeniia,* 2 vols. (Moscow: Khudozhestvennaia literatura, 1972), 2:208–31; see also Pratt, *Nikolai Zabolotsky,* 23–29.

47. See Ouspensky and Lossky, *The Meaning of Icons,* 77; John Baggley, *The Doors of Perception: Icons and Their Spiritual Significance* (Crestwood, N.Y.: St. Vladimir's Seminary Press, 1988), 92; Ouspensky, *Theology of the Icon,* 1:276; Likhacheva, "Svoeobrazie kompozitsii drevnerusskikh ikon," fig. 7; Fedotov, *The Russian Religious Mind,* 2:359; André Grabar, *Christian Iconography: A Study of Its Origins* (Princeton: Princeton University Press, 1968), 128 and plates 304, 305; M. S. Alpatov, *Art Treasures of Russia* (New Yok: Harry N. Abrams, 1967), fig. 23.

PART IV

PROJECTIONS

DOUGLAS GREENFIELD

9

FLORENSKY AND THE BINOCULAR BODY

Take care of your eyes—you still very much need them.
—LETTER TO MIKHAIL FLORENSKY, 1936

BINOCULAR VESSELS

In 1913, Pavel Florensky published the essay "The Stratification of Aegean Culture," an analysis of the material culture of antiquity. Here he discerns the spirit of the Minoan age in the design and ornamentation of its pottery, clothing, jewelry, votive objects, and cult vessels. Florensky argues that artifacts allow us to detect the values of the culture and time in which they were made; artifacts are "reagents" (*reaktivy*) that render values visible. According to Florensky, fashion is "one of the most sensitive reagents for any culture." Reading decadence in the overrefinement of ladies' dress, he connects the Minoan age with his own. Cretan costume reveals spiritual decline; beneath it seethes "an agitation of the soul very like that with which the end of the nineteenth century is stamped" (fig. 17). The swelling bustles of the late Victorian era likewise "show the deformity of soul that developed in this dead age, weighed down by the censorship of positivism." The Cretans closely resemble us in "external forms," so it follows that they resemble us in "inner content" as well. We should ask ourselves, writes Florensky, "whether their worldview is really as far from our own as today's philistine supposes, naively regarding his century and his decade as the height of cultural progress."[1]

The question of progress, in particular technological development, is critical to understanding the paradoxical modernity of the Old Russian icon in Florensky's thought. In this chapter I will examine how Florensky's icon theology derives from his philosophy of technology. In the double logic of technological teleology and cyclical history, the icon is a tool whose time has come, again.

"The Stratification of Aegean Culture" illustrates Florensky's long interest in the

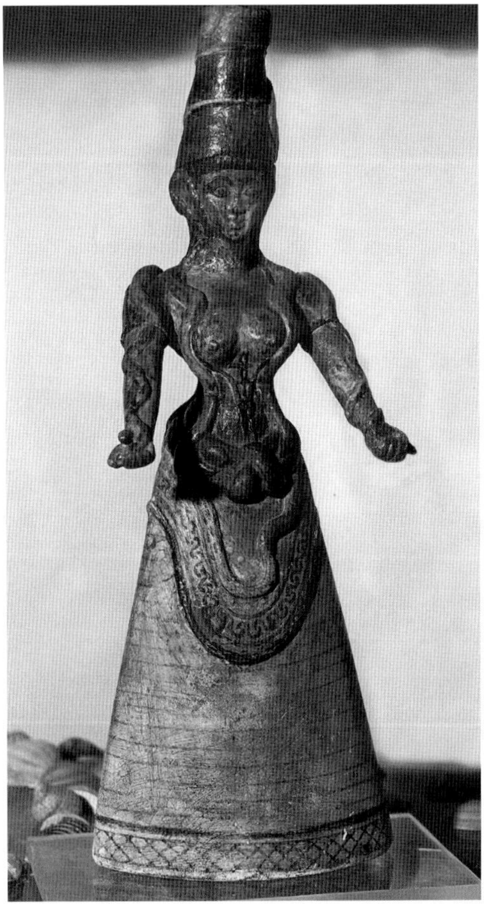

FIG. 17 Snake goddess, Minoan, clay. Archaeological Museum, Heraklion, Crete.

making and using of artifacts, a subject to which, in 1917, he devoted a series of lectures at the Moscow Theological Academy. In the first, "Homo Faber," Florensky follows Henri Bergson in defining man as a maker of tools. It is in toolmaking that man recognizes himself: "Reason," he writes, "is exteriorized in tools [*v orudiiakh*], and the tool is the material form of reason. . . . Reason is potential technology [*tekhnika*], and technology is actual reason."[2] He expanded the lectures for the planned volume *At the Watersheds of Thought: Features of a Concrete Metaphysics* (1917–22, pub. 1990). The phrase "concrete metaphysics" (*konkretnaia metafizika*) expresses Florensky's conviction that the orders of scientific and spiritual knowledge are inextricably linked. To this geologist, physicist, and priest, the ultimate purpose of science was to reflect a higher unity; scientific facts have a symbolic character, pointing beyond themselves to equally objective spiritual truths. Florensky's notion of artifacts as "reagents" demonstrates his belief that scientific and philosophical methods are compatible: the philosopher produces reactions to detect the soul of an age.

Florensky worked out his organic theory of technology in two lengthy essays in the volume: "The Extension of Our Senses" (*Prodolzhenie nashikh chuvstv*) and "Organ Projection" (*Organoproektsiia*). Theories of organ projection—the notion that tools are natural extensions of human limbs and senses—were widespread in the nineteenth century. In Germany, Ernst Kapp fired imaginations with his *Fundamentals of a Philosophy of Technology* (1877). Kapp proposed that tools, from the most primitive to the most complex, were extensions of human organs: the hammer and the lever extend and magnify the movement of the arm; clothing extends the shelter of the skin; the railroad extends the circulatory system; and the telegraph extends the nervous system. Kapp theorized that it was only through technology that humanity came to know itself in its depths. In forming our world we form ourselves. In Kapp's view, "The intrinsic relationship that arises between tools and organs, and one that is to be revealed and emphasized—although it is more one of unconscious discovery than of conscious invention—is that in the tool the human continually produces itself."[3] Critics nevertheless disputed Kapp's claim that *all* toolmaking was organ projection, raising a twofold question. First, are all of our organs projected in technology? And second, is every tool a projection of one of our organs? If we suppose an essential connection between tools and organs, quipped the positivist philosopher Ernst Mach, "precisely which organ is projected in a propeller, in a dynamo, in an interference refractometer?"[4]

Though he dismisses any facile solution to this complex problem, Florensky answers, yes, every organ has a corresponding tool, or someday will; and every tool has an organic prototype, whether we have found it yet or not. He states, "We know far from all the organs of our own body":

> Life may project a certain organ in technology before it becomes known to us anatomically, in us or even in other organisms, other living creatures, non-human ones. . . . If the study of organisms is a key to technical invention, then, conversely, we can regard technical inventions as a reagent for our *self-knowledge.* Technology can and should provide the stimulus to biology, and vice versa. In ourselves and in life generally we discover as yet unrealized technology; in technology, we discover as yet unstudied sides of life. The line of technology and the line of life run parallel, but the points at which they correspond may run ahead or lag behind one another. This is what lets us judge each of these lines *predictively,* at a greater distance than they are given to us in fact—the line of life in consciousness; the line of technology, in reality.[5]

Florensky offers the model of fish that possess specialized structures for generating electric fields. In the electric organs of eels, for example, we glimpse the possibility of making tools to extend latent electric organs of our own. Jules Verne's description of Captain Nemo's electric gun in *20,000 Leagues Under the Sea* is, he suggests, as much forecast as fiction. All tools have organs as their prototypes.

In the next essay in the series, "The Symbolism of Visions," Florensky deepens the connection between our technology and our selves. Both tools and organs, he emphasizes, have their source in the soul. From some metaphysical impulse toward self-realization, the divine image within us is expressed in successive layers of materiality; our soul is reflected in our bodily organs, which, in turn, are projected in our tools. Florensky calls this activity, which proceeds unconsciously, *symbolization.* "Understanding a *symbol-tool* [simvol-orudie]," he says, "means recognizing in it the ray of life that forms it, and detecting the connection between this symbol-tool and others."[6]

From bustle gowns to electric guns, "external forms" manifest "inner content," or, in other words, ethos and organs. The essay on the character of Aegean culture and the essays on technology are related by a mysterious object that Florensky describes toward the end of the former: an archeological find consisting of two bottomless cups on tall hollow conical bases, linked by crosspieces (pl. 14). He gives it a name: it is a "double vessel" or a "binocular-shaped vessel." Florensky has found, as he puts it, a name for a hitherto nameless object and, conversely, an object for a hitherto objectless name. That name, he says, denotes a sacred symbol, whose form the object resembles and to which it is a clue. This symbol, it turns out, is that of "doubling" (*udvoenie*), which indicates creative force. The symbol's artifactual expression is a vessel with the shape, to the minds of its modern discoverers, of binoculars, whence its name.[7] The proleptically binocular vessel probably interested Florensky because it illustrates his claim that life may project an organ in technology before it is known to science. To Florensky, this sacred utensil, a symbol-tool, would have appeared to predict important nineteenth-century discoveries in the physiology of binocular disparity—the fact that each eye sees a slightly different image. The organ projected in the binocular vessel is the eye now known to science—the eye whose distinct view only partially composes the unitary image we see.

Florensky assigns the vessel a ritual function in the cult of a female deity, where its plural sign presumably symbolized a fullness of creative potential. Yet as Florensky writes, "New influences drove the cult of Mother-Earth and her double vessels underground." In its banning and, Florensky is hopeful, in its rediscovery, the binocular vessel acts as a reagent. Artifacts enable us to detect history's spiritual strata, its alternating worldviews. The binocular vessel was lost in the depths of time because the new religion's "*point of view*," he adds with emphasis, had changed.[8] As we shall see, point of view is of great moment here. The reality of binocular vision is the very basis of Florensky's criticism of linear perspective in art.

BINOCULAR VISIONS

In the 1830s, the English physicist Charles Wheatstone successfully measured binocular parallax, or the degree to which the angle of the axis of each eye differed when focused on the same point. The human organism, he claimed, had the ability to synthesize retinal disparity into a unitary image. Wheatstone's research would lead him to patent, in 1838, the first stereoscope. The stereoscope is an apparatus with two eyepieces through which an observer views two photographs of the same scene taken at slightly different angles (fig. 18). These stereoscopic pictures are made by a single camera with two lenses set approximately two and a half inches apart—about the same distance as that between the eyes. Thus the left image corresponds to what the left eye would see, and the right image to the right eye. The stereoscope helps the observer to combine the two images, creating an effect of three-dimensional depth and solidity. It was one of a number of optical devices founded on the physiology of the observer, whose vision became an object of empirical and experimental research in the early nineteenth century. Popular entertainments such as the stereoscope, zoetrope, and kaleidoscope were based on the study of optical phenomena, such as binocular disparity, peripheral vision, retinal afterimages, and attention thresholds.

Florensky based his criticism of perspective on such phenomena,

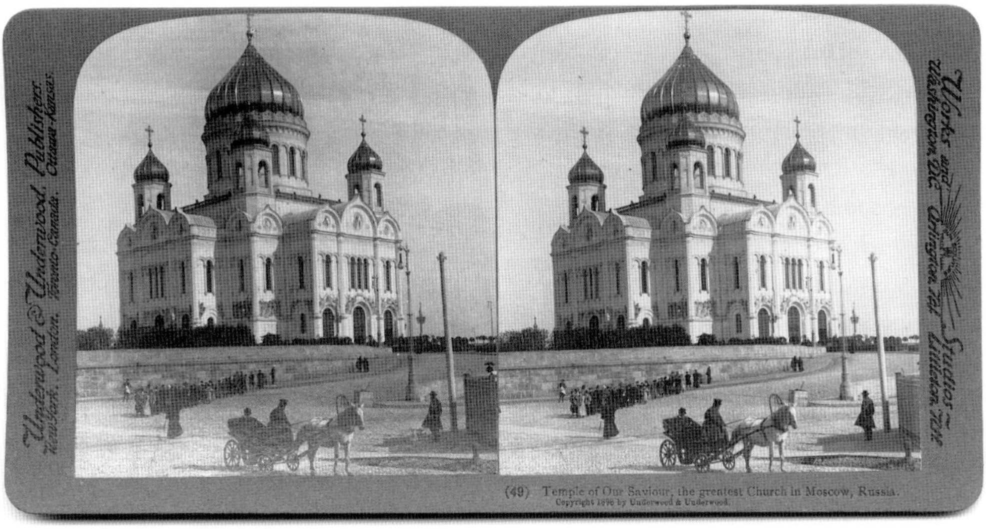

FIG. 18 Cathedral of Christ the Savior, Moscow, 1898, stereograph. Bequest of Donald W. Strickland, UCR/California Museum of Photography, University of California, Riverside.

particularly binocular disparity. As he argues in a 1922 essay, "[The single] 'point of view' in perspective is an attempt by the individual consciousness to tear itself away from reality, even away from its own reality—from the body, from the second eye."[9] In notes for a 1921 lecture, Florensky sketched two drawing devices from Albrecht Dürer's sixteenth-century study on perspective (fig. 19).[10] As these devices show, one-point perspective necessarily presumes a monocular view of the visible world. By contrast, Florensky takes sight to be an antinomy—the simultaneous affirmation of opposites, of A and not-A. In Florensky's logic, "All truth is antinomian, and all antinomian truths are but aspects of the one Truth."[11] So he insists, "We see with *two* eyes, not one, that is, from *two* points of view at once, not one as perspective projection requires. Therefore, the image we form during *real* sight is not the one abstractly posited in manuals on perspective but instead one that necessarily represents the combination of at least two separate, noncoincident perspectives."[12] Real sight comprises two contradictory but equally necessary points of view.

In his study of the historical construction of vision, Jonathan Crary explains how one drawing device, the camera obscura, functioned as a powerful epistemological model in the West for centuries.[13] The camera obscura is a device that operates on the optical principle that when light passes through a small hole into a dark interior, an inverted image will appear on a flat surface opposite the hole. Copying with the aid of a camera obscura—tracing and fixing its image on canvas—was widespread among astronomers and artists during the Renaissance and Enlightenment.

The camera obscura's aperture corresponds to a single, disembodied, mathematically definable vantage point on the world. For rationalist and empiricist thinkers, such as Descartes and Locke, the device stood as a philosophical metaphor for how reason corrects the uncertainties of human vision and the distorting or distracting effects of the other senses. Florensky treats the camera obscura, which facilitates perspective drawing, as a reagent for the worldview of Leonardo, Descartes, and Kant. Perspective, which imposes a grid on reality, is the "artistic equivalent" of the Renaissance. Renaissance logic is a logic of things, isolated entities with no intrinsic connection. Like perspective drawing, the Western tendency is toward "marking life with straight parallel lines [*razgraflenie zhizni*]": things never intersect.[14] Like the artist-perspectivist, who watches the world through the chink (*skvazhina*) of the camera obscura, Shakespeare is "not a creator but a person watching the world through a keyhole [*zamochnuiu skvazhinu*], a person who has no place in a worldview of his very own devising." His oeuvre, an encyclopedia of human feelings, characters, and situations, expresses the very essence of the Renaissance relation to life: the world is data to be fitted into general conceptions.[15] Florensky states that "the *spirit* of Renaissance thought, and the whole history of the Enlightenment is to a considerable extent occupied with a struggle with life, in order to smother it completely with a system of schemas."[16] He felt that the pernicious Renaissance spirit persisted to his day.[17]

In "Reverse Perspective" (1920), Florensky describes the camera obscura as a projection of the cyclopean eye of the artist-perspectivist; his eye is "not the organ of a living being, living in the world and laboring, but the glass lens of the camera obscura."[18] The organ of vision of a living being, we recall, is truly double. Therefore we should expect it to be projected in a technology like the stereoscope, whose reality effect is predicated on the very principle of disparity, on binocular vision. Unlike perspective, the stereoscope uses the idiosyncrasies of human vision—its plural points of view—to produce its depth effect.[19]

Florensky devotes the essay to proving that the presumed inferiority of the "reverse perspective" techniques of medieval icon painting—the disregard for vanishing points, the tendency of background figures

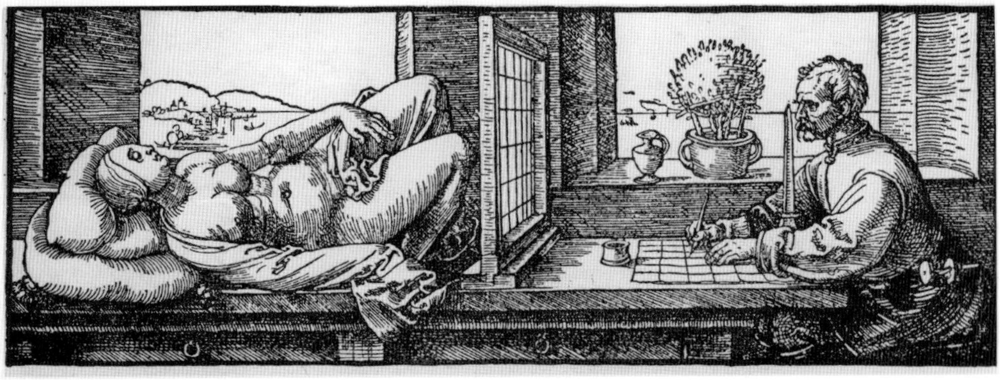

FIG. 19 Albrecht Dürer, *Man Drawing a Reclining Woman,* woodcut. Reproduced from *Underweysung der Messung* (Nuremberg, 1527).

to be larger than foreground figures—is in fact closer to natural perception than Renaissance perspective, the geometries of which have been inculcated into our minds. "A violent reeducation of human psychophysiology took place from the fifteenth to eighteenth centuries," he complains. "Perspective is foreign to humans because it is a conspiracy against natural perception: it requires you to see not that which is, but instead that which it is desired you see."[20] To Florensky's mind, to mediate perception is to deform it, and thereby to risk "the deformity of the soul." Florensky deemed modern man "half-blind" in his search for God; bred in a culture of schemas, his "spiritual sight" (*dukhovnoe zrenie*) is maimed.[21]

In this regard, Florensky's letters to his children from exile—lessons on a very broad range of topics—can be thought of as instruction in *de-educating* the senses. Writing to his son Vasily on the subject of binocular vision, Florensky shows how visual images are essentially antiperspective. He points out that we see with two eyes and that each eye projects light rays at its object, citing the ancient theory that the eye emanates as well as receives light rays (extramission).[22] Here, as elsewhere, Florensky follows Aristotle in stressing that the sense of sight is really an expansion of the sense of touch.[23] And he couches his explanation in the language of organ projection (*proektsiia, proektirovat'*) and sense extension (*rasshirenie*). Sight is *manual.* So, as Ernst Mach might have asked, in precisely which tool is the pair of eyes projected?

The icon would be a likely answer. Florensky's writings on the icon suggest that it is the projection of our plural organs of vision. The icon is a sort of sacred stereoscope, Orthodoxy's answer to the camera obscura. Although it appears to be antimimetic, only the Orthodox icon depicts reality objectively.[24] The scientific truth of binocular vision reflects Truth; binocularity's symbol-tool, in turn, is the icon. And half-blinded by perspective, modern man must prop up his vision by the icon, a "spiritual crutch."[25]

Florensky repeatedly describes the icon as a sort of primitive hand tool. The iconostasis, he writes, "breaks [*probivaet*] windows" in the visible world to the ultimate reality of the saints.[26] As I just noted, Florensky equates haptic and optic perception throughout his writings on aesthetics. Our pair of eyes is projected in a hand tool for suprasensible perception. To tweak slightly the title of James Billington's classic cultural history of Russia, the icon *is* the ax.[27] The notion that the icon "breaks windows" to an antiperspective, anti-Western world inverts Western perspective's primary trope, Alberti's window. In his influential treatise on linear perspective, *On Painting* (1435), the Italian architect and painter Leon Battista Alberti compared the canvas to an open window on reality. Florensky is also, I would argue, inverting the terms of Russia's most famous Westernizing myth, the founding of St. Petersburg as related in Alexander Pushkin's 1833 poem *The Bronze Horseman.* In the prologue to the poem, the Westernizing tsar Peter I stands and surveys the swamp and forest upon which he will lay the geometric and rectilinear grid of his capital city. Peter will open Russia to the West by constructing on this empty canvas. "Nature," Peter declares, "destines us here / To break a window to Europe [*V Evropu prorubit' okno*]."[28]

Western engineers and architects designed Peter's city according to the norms of classical perspective and symmetry. Indeed, St. Petersburg is a kind of Alberti's window, with its strict 2:1 or 4:1 ratios of street width to building height and its Western facades. It is as if this "tsar and lawgiver," as Florensky suggestively calls the artist-perspectivist, projected a map on the landscape from his detached, fixed vantage on the shore.[29] Like Peter, the perspectivist sees not living reality but a grid.[30] By contrast, Florensky's icon painter, wielding an icon-ax, breaks a window back to the Slavic East, to the City of God seen in Orthodox revelation. Like the binocular vessel, the rediscovery of which delighted Florensky, the icon's time has come again, along, he hoped, with the medieval worldview for which it is a reagent.

"MAKOVETS" REALISM / MEDIEVAL REALISM

Over against St. Petersburg, Florensky set the hill called Makovets, on which the Trinity Lavra of Saint Sergius near Moscow was founded, and for which Florensky's favorite group of writers and artists was named. Active in Moscow in the early 1920s, "Makovets" defined itself against the iconoclasm of the radical avant-garde. In Florensky's words, "'Makovets' must be a Makovets—the focus of the loftiness of Russian culture, from which the waters of creative work flow down in various directions. . . . 'Makovets' is not the geometric center, nor the arithmetic mean of various trends [*techenii,* literally, streams]; it is a living node from which threads extend." To be "Makovets" means to be integrative, organic. (The group first called itself "Art-Life.") The Makovets is a single (*edinyi*) "source" that waters all Russia; in their sincere love for the land and its people, the "Makovets" artists fight for the unity (*edinstvo*) of Russian culture, a unity destroyed by Peter's reforms, imposed from abroad. Like the medieval icon painters to whom, Florensky noted, they owe inspiration, the *makovchane* "break through [*probivat'sia*] to reality" in their art.[31] To Peter's city, by contrast, corresponds a lifeless art of illusion through perspective projection. The "geometric center" and "arithmetic mean of various trends [streams]"—to which Florensky opposed "Makovets"/Makovets—suggest St. Petersburg, which is crisscrossed by artificial waterways.

Florensky was the chief exponent of the realism embraced by the "Makovets" artists. He wrote a manifesto of sorts for the group ("On 'Makovets'") and a programmatic essay, "On Realism," for its journal *Makovets.* In the essay he contrasts realism with "illusionism," with art forms that confuse our preconception with reality. In this respect, formal differences aside, Renaissance linear perspective, with its goal of representing the third dimension, and Russian Suprematism, with its goal of representing the fourth, are equally false.

Florensky believed that all cultures regularly alternate between what he called medieval and Renaissance worldviews. Among medieval cultures, which are characterized by organicity, objectivity, concreteness, and cohesion, Florensky counted the Homeric Age, Hellenic culture, and Muscovy. The people of medieval cultures possess "unified vision"; they see the whole in the parts. Among Renaissance cultures, which are characterized by fragmentation, subjectivity, abstraction, and superficiality, Florensky counted the Minoan Age, the Archaic Age, and the European Renaissance, the decadent spirit of which persisted to his own day.

Artifacts reveal whether a culture is medieval or Renaissance in worldview. Products of medieval cultures evince the "most ancient . . . and patristic understanding of being as consisting of man and nature; neither can be added to, nor separated from, the other: this is the primeval, heavenly harmony of the inner and the outer."[32] Products of Renaissance cultures, by contrast, are marked by fragmentation. For example, Florensky detected spiritual decline in the prevailing division between portrait and landscape painting. Abstract concepts of genre reduce nature to an accessory in the first case; man to an accessory in the second. Florensky's primary example of an artifact that manifests an "integral worldview" was the Old Russian icon. He pointed to the fact that it took *two* masters to paint an icon: one to paint the face—the locus of our inner life; and one to paint the rest—the outer world (clothes, buildings, the outdoors) in which we realize ourselves.[33] This equal division of labor told Florensky that medieval Rus saw nature and man as a whole, not as *man* plus nature or *nature* plus man. Medieval art, likewise, privileged neither portrait nor landscape. "The spirit of medieval man," he states, "is the affirmation of reality within himself and without; hence his objectivity. Illusionism is characteristic of the subjectivity of modern man."[34]

The medieval mind apprehends reality as "organism."[35] This intuition of being, of the truth that I and not-I, subject and object, are interconnected, manifests itself in crafts that continue body and soul. "External forms," the products of culture, express "inner content."[36] The image of the triune God, simultaneously many and one, in which we are made, eyes and all, is expressed in what medieval cultures make.

The Old Russian icon and the binocular vessel ("so characteristic of the early Bronze Age")[37] are the arts of the "middle ages" of European history and of technological development, respectively. Their makers apprehended the "trans-subjective reality of being"[38]—and projected it. Uneducated, spontaneous *plural* vision—iconic, binocular, and stereoscopic—is objective because it proceeds directly from the antinomial truth of being, from the interrelation of things. Works of Naturalism and Suprematism, by contrast, are sheer abstraction. Modern man imposes purely subjective geometries on the world, and consequently he represents it in disintegrated parts.

Ultimately, an art that doubles nature (Naturalism) is as useless and lifeless as nonrepresentational art (Suprematism), which pictures things not of this world. Landscape painters and Suprematists, claimed Florensky, want not to represent things but instead to *re-create* them. They are makers of "machines, not artistic creations."[39] Florensky's repeated depiction of such works as machines (*mashiny*) is telling. The common notion is that the "tool" (*orudie*) facilitates manual work. In "Organ Projection," Florensky points out that the hand is the prototype of most tools, including optical instruments, since, as noted above, he regards sight as "touching with the retina."[40] A *machine* does not depend on the body, so does not reflect the soul. (Florensky never uses the word to denote organ projections.) In his memoirs, Florensky recalls having, from earliest childhood, a faculty of distinguishing handmade things from machine-made ones. Machine-made things aroused in the boy an instinctive loathing, almost bodily disgust. "Soulless and flat," they offended his feeling of the life force permeating everything else, not least handmade things.[41]

It turns out that "Makovets" realism is an art of organ projection. Among the artists of "Makovets," Florensky singled out for praise the puppeteer Nina Simonovich-Efimova.[42] In the preface he wrote to Simonovich-Efimova's book *Notes of a Puppeteer,* Florensky describes a show she gave at Sergiev Posad in 1922. In performance, the glove puppets appear to possess a mind of their own: "Putting the look of the puppet on their hands and letting the reason of the hand take on an independent face, [the puppeteers] free [the reason of the hand] from subordination [*podchineniia*] to the reason of the head, which becomes, conversely, an appendage of manual reason [*sluzhebnym organom ruchnogo*]." Florensky emphasizes that the puppet theater is not "illusionistic," does not aspire to be "like the real thing." On the contrary, the puppets "bring about a new reality *in fact.*" Like icons, which Florensky imagined as hand tools, the glove puppets break through the everyday, through the "error of life in all its aspects," to timeless truth. They open "a window on an eternally living childhood" within. Here and elsewhere Florensky identifies a return to childhood with entry to the Heavenly Kingdom, to a forgotten, but not lost, "primordial closeness with all being."[43] Childlike perception, he maintained, is true. In "Reverse Perspective," after detailing all the contrivance of Dürer's drawing devices, Florensky complains that "it has taken *more than five hundred years* of socialization to inure the eye and the hand to perspective; but without deliberate instruction neither the eye nor the hand of a child, or even of an adult, would submit [*podchiniaiutsia*] to this training and reckon with the rules of perspective."[44]

The glove puppet, a hand with eyes, is, like the icon, a symbol-tool that enables hand and eye (which Florensky equated) to unlearn their training. The icon facilitates our antiperspective, binocular vision; true knowledge of being takes place before the brain combines our plural points of view. Likewise the puppet subordinates abstract reason to the reason of the body. Through the puppet theater, we start to "see the lost Eden" of unity.[45]

Florensky's heroes of art and science, in particular Mozart, Goethe, Pushkin, and Michael Faraday (1791–1867), managed to resist the education of eye and hand in abstract schemas, remaining "children":

> The secret of genius is to preserve childhood—a childlike constitution—all your life. This is the constitution that affords genius the objective perception of the world; it is not centripetal perception but a kind of reverse perspective of the world, and therefore it is integral and real. The illusory can never be genius, no matter how brilliant it may be. For the essence of genius perception is penetration deep

> into things, whereas the essence of the illusory is shutting oneself off from reality. The most typical geniuses—Mozart, Faraday, Pushkin—are children in their way.[46]

Florensky told his children to pay no heed to their poor punctuation, noting that Pushkin was careless about his commas. Write what comes out, he urged. In punctuation, no less than in perception, "received rules . . . impart coldness and . . . kill warmth."[47] True art expresses spontaneous being. In "Reverse Perspective," he observes that children's drawings, like medieval icons, lack perspective: "Only with the loss of an immediate relation to the world do children lose reverse perspective and submit to a schema inculcated into them." The way children think and, it follows, the way they depict the world are akin to genius.[48]

What Florensky called "integral" or "childlike" cognition, the subject's apprehension of being, his "penetration" into things, is a feature of Russian religious philosophy. As Richard Gustafson notes, Florensky's epistemology is rooted in an Eastern Christian tradition that emphasizes an intuited reciprocity between the knower and the known. "Russian epistemology," explains Gustafson, "is grounded in moral and metaphysical total unity. It often assumes that the subject in the subject-object relationship is what Solovyov called the 'divine principle' within, and it wants to establish a relationship of equality and mutuality between the subject and object."[49] Against Western rationalist epistemology, which assumes the identity of a thing with itself, Russian thinkers posit a special cognitive faculty for transcending the self and uniting with objects of knowledge.[50]

Florensky's concept of organ projection or extension stems from his epistemology. Artifacts reflect ways of knowing: the medieval icon, like the medieval knowing subject, penetrates deep into things, opening windows on reality; the camera obscura, like the Kantian subject, is shut off from reality, of which it has only a keyhole view. Florensky's prediction that we will soon project embryonic electric organs suggests a hope of new subject-object relationships. Real knowledge, he stressed, "manifests the genuine extension [*rasshirennost'*] of the subject and the genuine uniting of his energy (in the terminology of the fourteenth century) with the energy of the reality being known."[51] The fourteenth-century vocabulary of "energies" Florensky employs is that of Saint Gregory Palamas (1296–1359), the great champion of the mystical tradition of Hesychasm. Over against the Western law of identity, Florensky set the Hesychast idea that a thing is simultaneously "essence" (Gk. *ousia*) and radiant "energy" (Gk. *energeia*). The "energy" is both equal and not equal to the "essence," and all entities can interrelate and even interpenetrate through their "energies" even as their "essences" remain intact.[52] Total unity comprises these reciprocal actions and relationships: "Everything is interconnected by secret bonds," affirmed Florensky. "The energies (*energii*) of things *flow into* other things, and each lives in all, and all in each."[53] By this antinomian logic, A and not-A, I and not-I, connect.

Artists and scientists of genius are "true realists" in their reciprocal, living relation to things.[54] They do not impose subjective schemas on the world. Children at heart, realists see things from plural points of view. Proponents of Naturalism, by contrast, see everything from the same viewpoint. Their abstract, passive relation to reality is organ-projected in a fixed-focus device: the snapshot camera. Echoing his criticism of the camera obscura, Florensky wrote that Naturalism "as little comprehends things as a photograph . . . and is as soulless as the glass lens of the camera."[55] Florensky scoffed at the French writer Émile Zola, the leading exponent of Naturalism in fiction: "Zola chases after reality with a Kodak—and doesn't catch a thing. Pushkin goes 'where the free mind leads' and is always true to reality; his images always feel solid [*plotnyi*] and full of life." Zola's snapshots of French society are "incorporeal [*besplotnye*] shadows, emptiness, abstract arguments." Various vices and virtues take the place of characters in his novels. "There's not a single living person—they're all schemas of abstract concepts." Like linear perspective, the *roman à thèse* reflects the subjectivism of modern man, who makes reality a prison house of disintegrated objects. Naturalism is no more than a passive photographic "fixing" (*zakreplenie*) of chance items; its reality is an illusion. Zola's descriptions make up no greater whole. For all their detail, Florensky said, they are "stage props." Like Shakespeare's inventory of the human condition, Zola's work is "a catalog, not a picture."[56]

In a 1935 letter from exile, Florensky excitedly tells his son Mikhail how to take a mushroom "photograph," that is, a spore print made by placing the cap, gills down, on a sheet of paper.[57] This living image, produced by the action of seeds, suggests an answer to the snapshot. A picture should bear the trace of the body. Accordingly, he regarded iconic, reverse perspective as the very "physiology of visual art."[58]

Florensky's essays on time and space in art help explain his notion of the failed poetic image as a photograph. He closely follows Bergson in rejecting the truth claims of chronophotographic analyses of motion (fig. 20).[59] Both reason that movement is synthesis and flux, and that the camera registers merely frozen moments, none of which have any relation to preceding or successive moments. An instantaneous photograph of a body has nothing in common with immediate perception. Our eye perceives things in time: we see one organ and then another. Sight spreads across an object; perception has a past and a future. Yet a snapshot puts everything in the same temporal rank. This simultaneity of organs or parts, this perpetual present, explains Florensky, is an illusion, not how or what we see. The isolated moment of the snapshot is equal only to itself. Snapshot photography expresses Western epistemology's deadening law of identity. An artistic representation, by contrast, is full of internal contradictions. Artists capture the essence of the whole by tracing a spatiotemporal path over an image. They unite successive moments of sight by anatomical and physical incongruity, with various organs and parts corresponding to various moments of perception. Thus the medieval icon, which depicts movement by "absurdly" combining front and side views of the body (in particular the chest and the back), is true to human perception.[60]

The Makovets, and the realism to which the hill lends its name, is an icon of

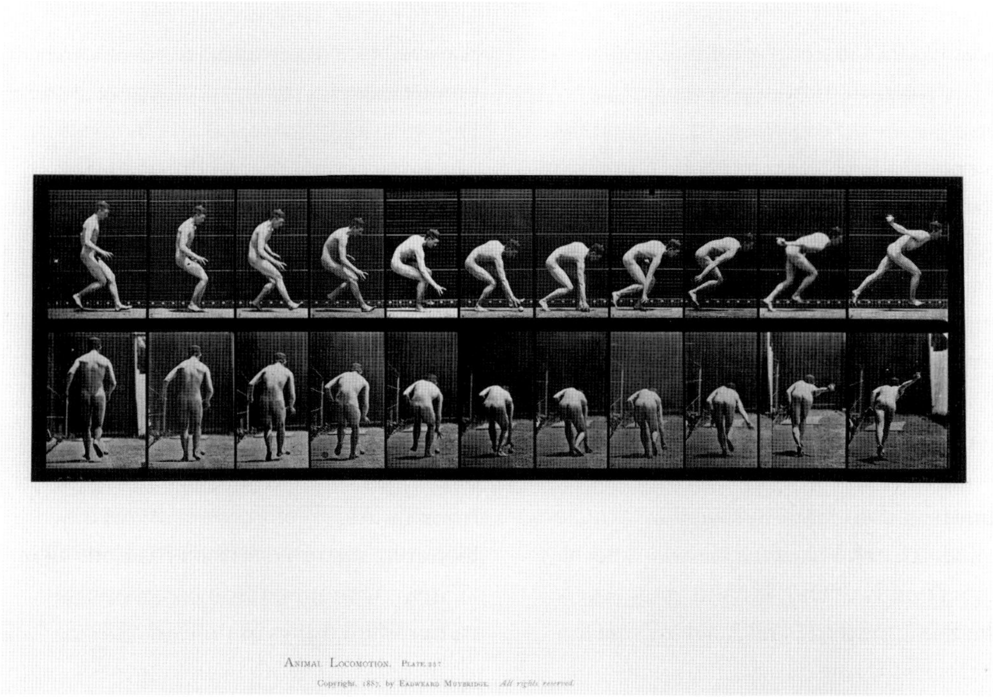

FIG. 20 Eadweard Muybridge, *Animal Locomotion: An Electro-Photographic Investigation of Consecutive Phases of Animal Movements. Commenced 1872–Completed 1885,* vol. I, *Men (Nude),* 1880s. Metropolitan Museum of Art, New York.

Russian culture, not a snapshot. The Trinity Lavra of Saint Sergius, founded on the hill, is "an artistic portrait of Russia in its integrity, in comparison with which every other place is no more than a photo." Like an icon, it faithfully renders its subject in movement. As an icon "comprises a diversity of impressions of a face," so the monastery unites all the aspects of Russian history to form a vital, "solid" whole. A snapshot, by contrast, registers only chance, disconnected moments.[61]

Florensky's work on the committee appointed to turn the monastery into a museum resulted in several of his most celebrated essays. In two essays of 1918, "The Trinity–St. Sergius Lavra and Russia" and "Church Ritual as Synthesis of the Arts," Florensky portrays Saint Sergius (1313–1392), the monastery's founder, as a Russian Prometheus. The lifetime of the saint, he explains, coincided with the last bloom of art and thought in Byzantium. Sergius lighted the flame of medieval Russian culture from the dying fire of Byzantium, which blazed with the "Promethean fire of Hellenism."[62] In Sergius, the Russian people "recognized itself, its cultural-historical place, its cultural mission" to be the torchbearer of Byzantium and thereby of ancient Greece.[63] Florensky affirms that Sergius set Russia and the world the example of creative activity in the building of the Holy Trinity Cathedral.[64]

Florensky believed the Trinity Lavra could be the nexus of a renewed medieval culture, and he fought to keep it intact in the revolution's iconoclastic early years.

Preserved as a community of artists and scholars, the monastery would "realize its high destiny to produce an integral culture, to re-create the integral spirit of antiquity, to reveal a new Hellas."[65] The "House of Saint Sergius," as Florensky calls the monastery, is an "experimental station and laboratory" for solving modern aesthetics' biggest problem, the creation of the total work of art.[66]

Florensky's essay "Organ Projection" builds toward the "tool of tools"—the house. The house is that "synthetic tool that unites in itself many tools and, in principle, all tools." In the same terms as he later describes the House of Saint Sergius as a synthetic portrait of all Russia, Florensky explains that the human body in its integrity is projected in the house. The house collects all of our tools and, as such, all of our parts.[67] The monastery is the *Gesamtkunstwerk* of which avant-garde artists only dreamed: church ritual harmonizes form, movement, light, sight, sound, and smell.[68]

PERMAFROST REALISM

In 1933, Florensky was accused of criminal conspiracy and condemned to ten years in prison camps. He was held first in Siberia and then at Solovetsky, the remote island monastery turned prison camp. He was executed in Leningrad in December 1937. Nearly 150 remarkable letters home bear witness to terrible privation, and to vast spiritual resources as well. One topic that connects the letters is discovery and invention—Florensky would pursue his scientific interests until his death. In Siberia, at the Skovorodino Experimental Permafrost Station, he did research on ice and permafrost, and, at Solovetsky, on the production of iodine and agar from seaweed. Florensky repeatedly compares his predicament on the infamous "archipelago" to that of the castaways on Jules Verne's *Mysterious Island,* the sequel to *20,000 Leagues Under the Sea.* In his research, Florensky is, like the castaways, compelled to invent all the tools he needs from scratch.[69] Reinvention is the theme of the letters in more ways than one. In his search for meaning and hope in exile, Florensky tried to make artistic sense of a milieu that often reduced him to despair. In a letter from his third month on the islands, Florensky pictures surroundings as accidental as a landscape painting, Suprematist composition, or snapshot:

> The local nature, despite views that can only be called beautiful and unusual, is alien to me: the sea is not a sea but something either mud-gray or black-gray; the stones were brought by glaciers, the hills were deposited here, composed of glacial debris. In general, nothing is native, everything arrived here from elsewhere, including the people. When you realize it, this accidental landscape depresses you, as if you've found yourself in an untidy room. The same is true of the people; all contacts with people are casual, superficial, and not determined by any kind of deep inner motives. Just as the crystalline rocks that compose the boulders are interesting in themselves, but become uninteresting in their isolation from their native layers, so the local people, significant in themselves . . . are uninteresting precisely because they have been brought from else-

where, and tomorrow will turn up somewhere else.[70]

I interpret the long poem that Florensky wrote in the camps as an effort to turn this abstract, "accidental landscape"—which mirrors the chaos of prison—into an icon. Florensky transforms permafrost, the poem's surprising, stated theme, into a new Trinity Lavra. "Oro" (1934–37) narrates the childhood of Oro, the last hope of the Orochons, a once-great people of Siberia. The Orochons practice both shamanism and Orthodoxy—a syncretism that fit the author's organicist thinking.[71] According to Florensky's outline of the unfinished poem, the boy is destined to become a great scientist and enlightener.[72] The future savior is christened Mikhail but nicknamed Oro, or "reindeer," the animal on which the Orochon ("reindeer breeders") base their economy and culture.[73] Florensky wrote the poem for his son Mikhail (Mik), in whom he placed great hopes,[74] naming him after his beloved Michael Faraday, the great British physicist and chemist. Florensky had been obsessed with Faraday since childhood.[75] He especially admired Faraday as a visual thinker, likening him to Goethe in his ability to think "not in abstract schemas . . . but in concrete images." Precisely because Faraday did not impose himself on reality, he was able to penetrate it, to see what others could not.[76] James Clerk Maxwell (1831–1879), who mathematically formulated the electric field theory proposed by Faraday, attested to his predecessor's holistic vision. In language that would please the Platonist Florensky, Maxwell writes that "Faraday, in his mind's eye . . . saw a medium where [the mathematicians] saw nothing but distance. . . . Faraday's methods . . . begin with the whole and arrive at the parts . . . while the ordinary mathematical methods were founded on the principle of beginning with the parts and building up the whole."[77] In one letter home, Florensky notes that Oro is a composite portrait of Mikhail and his namesake, among others. Like Faraday, Oro "thinks in images."[78] He is a modern culture hero and, in the cycle of time, a medieval one—a new Saint Sergius.

A shaman foretells that Oro will one day "apprehend the secret of permafrost,"[79] and on his advice his parents dedicate the child to the spirits of permafrost. Just as Sergius gave Russia the symbol of the Holy Trinity—the heavenly vision that had guided him since childhood[80]—Oro will reveal the mystery of "permafrost, a triple symbol."[81] Permafrost, whose "crystal cupola" emerges from the taiga moss,[82] is, like the Trinity Lavra, the repository of the "fire of Hellenism." Permafrost, Florensky says, conceals the "gold fire" of gold. Intact, permafrost is a creative force; when exploited for gain, it can turn destructive. He expands, "But the same goes for the soul. Permafrost covers up past bitterness, insults, and sad observations in the soul. There's no need to dig in the soul's depths. Permafrost courage [*Merzlotnaia bodrost'*] gives strength to cope with the destructive forces of chaos. Permafrost is Hellenism."[83]

Like his creator, Oro performs research at the Skovorodino Experimental Permafrost Station. Florensky saw the monastery, we recall, as an "experimental station and laboratory." The poem "Oro," he comments in one letter, is permeated by a "Hellenic understanding of life." Its hero is called—

like Sergius, Faraday, and Florensky himself—to discover and to invent in the spirit of the living unity of all that is: "Life isn't all fun and games. . . . But, knowing all this, you need to keep harmony in mind's eye and try to realize it. Oro goes through a series of hardships and trials, but goes through them to get stronger, to develop his worldview, so that he can perform a feat of science, so that he can take a new approach to nature—a new concrete-realistic understanding of the world to counteract the lifeless, the abstract, and the illusory."[84] Like a "Makovets" artist, puppeteer, or icon painter, Oro tries to "break through" (*probit'*) the permafrost "firmament" to reality.[85]

By a twist of fate, the study of ice and permafrost in the camps let Florensky realize an old metaphor for total unity: crystal. Ice crystal was one of Florensky's favorite images of harmony. Its orderly atomic structure was a standard by which he measured cultural products. In a 1904 essay, he contrasts pieces of glass, which solidifies without crystallization, to pieces of ice. On the surface, glass and ice appear the same, but in terms of molecular structure they are as different as an orchestra from the din of the marketplace. Ice is "music," "harmony, "efficiency," "organization." Glass is "chaos and disorder," "anarchy." Disconnected particles compose a piece of glass; there is no *whole*. A piece of ice, by contrast, comprises its particles. In ice, he explains, "every particle occupies its definite, intrinsic place in the *tissue* [tkani] of the whole, in the organization of the marvelous structure."[86]

Medieval culture heroes, yesterday and tomorrow, change the world by creating in the image of crystalline, permafrost perfection in which God created us. They do not master or colonize nature; that is, they do not impose their subjectivity on it. They apprehend in the empirical world the same reality within. Medieval artifacts are organ projections, which directly continue the self. The litmus test for medieval worldviews is whether an era's artifacts evince organicity, whether they are works of glass or works of ice, so to speak. It is a test Florensky applied to all human art, including—to return to bustle gowns—fashion. "Clothes," he observes in the 1921 essay *Iconostasis,* "are body parts." Like any artifact, they reveal the spirit of their age. Florensky compares the folds of garments on Old Russian icons with the folds on icons from modern times. The medieval folds possess a "mineral quality, like the edges and facets of crystallized masses." In this they manifest "spiritual energy, a fullness of efficient force." They reflect a process of "organizing all of life in accordance with the spirit."[87] During the rise of Muscovy, a time of cultural formation, people made clothes that prolonged the unity in their souls. By contrast, folds on icons from the subsequent Time of Troubles, a period of discord, have a "deliberate straightness, a deliberate stylization." They become "abstract."[88]

Permafrost realism—"Makovets" realism—is self-realization, a bodying forth. Florensky's writings on organ projection build to the essay "Macrocosm and Microcosm." Here he states that the "world is the revelation of the Human, his projection." Nature may be no more macrocosm than it is *microcosm*. Anthropomorphic myths the world over witness the ancient truth that "Human and Nature are mutually like and intrinsically one."[89] He concludes by pointing out that even landscape painting, seemingly so distant from an artist's inner life, exists only insofar as it can assimilate or transform scenery into the artist, into his moods and aspirations. "Look closely," he says. "Any song, any poem, any picture will reveal its *thoroughly* human nature. They are sublimations of human feeling, the enfleshed dreams of our soul—and that alone is why we and others understand them."[90] In "Oro," Florensky repaints the "accidental landscape" of exile, assimilating it to his inner harmony—reintegrating its isolated "crystalline rocks," so to speak.[91] At Solovetsky, nothing coheres. But in his work, and in what remained of his life, Florensky tried to project the image of crystalline perfection he carried within. "Although I'm in seaweed," he writes, "I live by permafrost."[92]

NOTES TO CHAPTER 9

1. P. A. Florenskii, *Sochineniia,* 4 vols., ed. Igumen Andronik (A. S. Trubachev), P. V. Florenskii, and M. S. Trubacheva (Moscow: Mysl', 1994–99), 2:99, 102, 107. The essay originated in lectures written and delivered in 1909. The epigraph to this chapter is quoted in ibid., 4:492.

2. Ibid., 3[1]:378–79.

3. Quoted in Carl Mitcham, *Thinking Through Technology: The Path Between Engineering and Philosophy* (Chicago: University of Chicago Press, 1994), 23–24.

4. Quoted in Florenskii, *Sochineniia,* 3[1]:419.

5. Ibid., 3[1]:420–21.

6. Ibid., 427.

7. Ibid., 2:115–18.

8. Ibid., 121.

9. Ibid., 3[1]:365.

10. Ibid., 3[2]:484–85. In an earlier essay, "Reverse Perspective," Florensky cites Dürer's 1525 study *Underweysung der Messung* as evidence of the prevalence of Euclid's geometric principles by the early sixteenth century. Ibid., 3[1]:66, 75–76.

11. Judith Deutsch Kornblatt and Richard F. Gustafson, eds., *Russian Religious Thought* (Madison: University of Wisconsin Press, 1996), 14. See also John Anthony McGuckin's chapter in this volume.

12. P. A. Florenskii, *Stat'i i issledovaniia po istorii i filosofii iskusstva i arkheologii,* ed. Igumen Andronik (Trubachev) (Moscow: Mysl', 2000), 252.

13. Jonathan Crary, *Techniques of the Observer: On Vision and Modernity in the Nineteenth Century* (Cambridge, Mass.: MIT Press, 1990).

14. Florenskii, *Sochineniia,* 3[1]:90, 60.

15. Ibid., 3:90; 4:379.

16. Ibid., 3[1]:60.

17. Ibid., 1:39.

18. Ibid., 3[1]:88.

19. Florensky himself noted that research on binocular vision led to the invention of the stereoscope. Ibid., 3[1]:411.

20. Ibid., 3[2]:484–85.

21. Ibid., 2:442.

22. Ibid., 4:317–19.

23. Aristotle considered touch the primary sense: "Without the faculty of touch none of the other senses exists. . . . For without touch [an animal] cannot have any other sense-perception. . . . Indeed even the other sense-organs perceive by touch." Aristotle, *De Anima, Books 2 and 3,* trans. D. W. Hamlyn (Oxford: Clarendon Press, 1977), 16.

24. Florensky emphasized that the icon does not mediate between this reality and higher reality; rather, it points out higher reality for the spiritually impaired. He famously said of beholding an icon, "There is a board with paints and there is the Mother of God Herself." The sight of infinity is not subjective; beholders see the same objective reality of God that the icon painter saw. Florenskii, *Sochineniia,* 2:447.

25. Ibid., 2:442.

26. Ibid.

27. James H. Billington, *The Icon and the Axe: An Interpretive History of Russian Culture* (New York: Alfred A. Knopf, 1966).

28. Florensky referred to Pushkin frequently, and quoted from *The Bronze Horseman.* Florenskii, *Sochineniia,* 3[1]:372; 4:493.

29. Ibid., 3[1]:88.

30. Ibid., 3[2]:484.

31. Ibid., 2:628–29.

32. Ibid., 503.

33. Ibid.

34. Ibid., 3[1]:60.

35. Ibid., 3[2]:117.

36. Ibid., 2:107.

37. Ibid., 118.

38. Ibid., 1:40.

39. Florenskii, *Stat'i,*155–56.

40. Florenskii, *Sochineniia,* 3[1]:407–8.

41. P. A. Florenskii, *Detiam moim. Vospominaniia proshlykh dnei. Genealogicheskie issledovaniia. Iz solovetskikh pisem. Zaveshchanie,* ed. Igumen Andronik (Trubachev) (Moscow: Moskovskii rabochii, 1992), 59–60.

42. Florenskii, *Sochineniia,* 2:629.

43. Ibid., 534–36.

44. Ibid., 3[1]:76.

45. Ibid., 2:536.

46. Ibid., 4:703.

47. Ibid., 380–81.

48. Ibid., 3[1]:62.

49. Richard F. Gustafson, *Leo Tolstoy: Resident and Stranger: A Study in Fiction and Theology* (Princeton: Princeton University Press, 1986), 460.

50. Florensky's "childlike constitution" is comparable, for example, to Alexei Khomiakov's "integral reason" or "free willing reason" and to Vladimir Soloviev's "mystical knowledge" or "direct perception."

51. Florenskii, *Sochineniia,* 1:40.

52. Kornblatt and Gustafson, *Russian Religious Thought,* 14.

53. Florenskii, *Sochineniia,* 3[2]:151.

54. Ibid., 4:159, 453, 493, 531, 627, 688.

55. Florenskii, *Stat'i,* 155.

56. Florenskii, *Sochineniia,* 4:492–93.

57. Ibid., 307.

58. Ibid., 3[1]:72.

59. See Henri Bergson, *Creative Evolution,* trans. Arthur Mitchell (New York: Random House, 1944), 361.

60. Florenskii, *Sochineniia,* 3[2]:91; idem, *Stat'i,* 234–37.

61. Florenskii, *Sochineniia,* 2:353.

62. Ibid., 354–55.

63. Ibid., 356.

64. Ibid., 359.

65. Ibid., 369.

66. Ibid., 371.

67. Ibid., 3[1]:415–16.

68. Ibid., 2:382.

69. Ibid., 4:179, 201, 303, 411, 513.

70. Ibid., 155–56.

71. Oro's parents both consult shamans and venerate icons.

72. Ibid., 733–34.

73. Florensky actually had little contact with the Orochons. In an April 1934 letter, Florensky relates an encounter with two on a trip to the Tukuringr Pass to study ice crust. He notes his great interest in the people and that he has begun a poem called "The Orochons" for his youngest son, Mikhail. Florenskii, *Sochineniia,* 4:115. A hoped-for trip to an Orochon village does not materialize, but in a May letter Florensky tells of running after two Orochons who rode past the Experimental Permafrost Station on their reindeer. He invited them in, photographed them, and took down words of the Tungus-Manchu language they speak. He planned to write an Orochon dictionary, grammar, and textbook. Ibid., 122, 130.

74. Ibid., 714.

75. Florenskii, *Detiam moim,* 192; idem, *Sochineniia,* 4:158, 437. Florensky urged Mik to study Faraday. Ibid., 175, 195.

76. Ibid., 159.

77. James Clerk Maxwell, *A Treatise on Electricity and Magnetism* (New York: Dover, 1954), ix.

78. Ibid., 490.

79. Ibid., 651.

80. Ibid., 2:359.

81. Ibid., 4:733–34.

82. Ibid., 503.

83. Ibid., 734.

84. Ibid., 339–40.

85. Ibid., 503.

86. Ibid., 1:161.

87. Ibid., 2:489.

88. Ibid., 489.

89. Ibid., 3[1]:441–42.

90. Ibid., 3[1]:448.

91. Ibid., 4:503.

92. Ibid., 4:394.

JOHN ANTHONY MCGUCKIN

10
FLORENSKY AND ICONIC DREAMING

A LIFE LIVED IN THE INTERSTICES

On 8 December, in the bitter winter of 1937, the priest Pavel Florensky was taken by the NKVD from his labor camp on the Solovetsky Islands in the White Sea,[1] brought by lorry to the suburbs of Leningrad, and executed by close-range pistol shot at the Rzhevsky artillery range near Toksovo. The day of his death, according to reports by the human rights group Memorial,[2] saw the execution of a total of 509 dissidents in the Leningrad area. It had earlier been presumed that his body lay somewhere in the killing fields of Levashevo,[3] but in August 2002 the remains of thirty thousand victims were unearthed at Toksovo, another suburban area of St. Petersburg, finally settling an old question as to what had happened to the many thousands of unaccounted-for victims of Stalin's Leningrad-based terror.[4] That cold December morning, in the Orthodox calendar, was the feast of Saint Patapius the Recluse, whose entry in the liturgical Synaxarion notes that he was a "source of healing and comfort to many people" and had "spent many years in the wilderness." The coincidence would have struck Florensky as not inappropriate. Like Patapius in his own time, Florensky continues to move out from his "seclusion" and "wilderness experience" under Soviet oppression to an expanding international audience. From the 1960s onward, Russian dissident religious intelligentsia began to take note of his work, and today, with a growing amount of his writing available in English,[5] his name is becoming more familiar among diaspora Orthodox theologians and other interested scholars.

Florensky's life had begun on 9 January 1882, in Yevlakh, Azerbaijan, in a railroad worker's family that was not particularly religious, but certainly literate, cultured, and very closely bonded, as his autobiographical writings reveal.[6] The young Florensky showed an early aptitude for academics; he was well versed in mathematics and scientific studies (especially physics) from his gymnasium years in Tbilisi. In his autobiographical notes, he speaks of a crisis he had over a passionately held view of his childhood—that empirical science could be a macro theory for the meaning of existence. He was shaken by his teenage reading of Tolstoy, which shocked him into a deeply felt realization of "the limits of knowledge." This early "loss of faith" in physics deepened his interest in mathematics as a purer metaphysical guide, and in August 1900 he was accepted into the mathematics department of Moscow University, where he graduated in 1904 with the reputation of being the most brilliant student in recent generations.[7] His thesis won the highest honors,[8] and on the strength of it the university offered him an academic post, which he turned down (for what was widely regarded as an utterly mad reason) in order to enroll in the Moscow Theological Academy; however, he never ceased working in science, which became a dominant intellectual obsession. He also developed a strongly Symbolist philosophy, and (progressively) a distinctive religious vision that attempted to synthesize apparently opposed realms of experience. His well-known adherence to the Sophiological movement is part of this, for example. Florensky was the only leading member of that school to remain in Russia, and it cost him greatly. His thought, from the time of his growing rapprochement with the Orthodox Church, was marked by a deep interest in antinomies as descriptive of the inner character of being. His notoriously difficult writing style, his delight in ambiguity, his love of marginality in thought and practical existence, and his strong use of paradox and oppositional figuration as methods of pursuing insight—these are all part and parcel of this overarching philosophical journey to an experience of Truth through and in antinomy. The second part of this chapter will consider Florensky's theory of iconic dreaming in that context.

After Florensky left the mathematics department, two of his professors remained important influences on him personally: Nikolai Luzin, the doyen of the Moscow school of mathematics, and his calculus teacher Nikolai Bugaev. Florensky came into Bugaev's circle, which included his son, Andrei Bely (Boris Bugaev). Viacheslav Ivanov and especially Bely, both Symbolist poets, exerted a strong effect on Florensky, the latter encouraging his growing desire to enter into an explicit communion with the Orthodox Church, into which he had been baptized as an infant. Bishop Anthony Florensov became his confessor and guide at this period of his life,[9] arranging for his entrance into the seminary course of the Moscow Theological Academy in 1904 and steering the young convert away from his expressed desire to enter monastic life, which would have meant, Florensov saw, a suppression of his many academic gifts and cultural potentialities. Since the episcopal blessing was essential for Florensky's ambition to enter the ascetic state (the bishop had spoken to him glowingly of the famed Solovetsky Monastery), the plan was apparently terminated. It would, however, like so many of the strange antinomies that Florensky saw printed onto the pattern of existence, actually come to fulfillment much later in his life. The monastic life is described in Orthodox tradition as the election of a "premature death" to the world, and in some sense the man's solitary vocation to the "death to self" was indeed completed when he was led, years later, through the doors of that same Solovetsky Monastery in Siberia (after it had been transformed into the most feared prison camp in all Soviet Russia).[10]

Florensky's growing desire to find a synthetic worldview that would embrace all material phenomena led him to develop a strong interest in Orthodoxy in his early twenties—something he would habitually refer to later as the discovery of the "ecclesial" mind, or *tserkovnost'*, a term that is sometimes badly rendered as "churchliness" but that is far more substantial a concept than mere ecclesiasticism.[11] It is comparable to what other Slavophiles, such as Berdiaev, Khomiakov, and Bulgakov,[12] meant by *sobornost'*—that essential unity that lay behind the diffracted variety of material phenomena. It was a religious impetus and aspiration as old as the church itself, and had been taken up by foundational Christian theorists of antiquity in a conscious reaction to Neoplatonic and Gnostic attempts to resolve the issue of the relation of the One and the Many.

The issue of cosmic unity-in-diversity was a dominant theme of the most significant intellectual tradition of early Christian thought, a line that stretched from Origen of Alexandria[13] through Athanasius,[14] Gregory of Nazianzus,[15] Maximus the Confessor,[16] and Dionysius the Areopagite. This, the so-called Alexandrian tradition of mystical theology,[17] was also the chief intellectual lineage transported to Rus when the Byzantine Empire first planted the Orthodox Church in Slavic lands. It gave a profound shape and form to the entirety of later Russian theology and philosophy. It was, accordingly, no surprise that Florensky's desire to discover the deeper "ground and unity" of being should correspond with his growing interest in, and discovery of, the Russian Orthodox Church, in its practical (iconic and liturgical) as well as its noetic (patristic, ethical, and mystical) manifestations. Here he found embodied, in sophisticated theory and praxis, a tradition of religious thought and action where the concept of deification (*theosis*) was seen as a primary energy and end goal (*telos*) of the inner springs of all material and personal existence.[18]

In 1908, Florensky graduated from the Theological Academy with a thesis titled "On Religious Truth" and was immediately appointed to its faculty as professor of philosophy.[19] Following the advice of Bishop Anthony, he was married soon after,[20] in 1910, and his close family was a source of great joy for him. He demonstrated his belief that the power of love was the main synthesizing energy of a reunified cosmos in two primary activities: his priestly Eucharistic ministry[21] and his enthusiastic role as loving father of a family of five children.[22] In 1911, he was ordained as one of the "white clergy" (married priests), and 1914 saw the publication of one his most important religious studies, *The Pillar and Ground of Truth*. His intellectual life from that time on was characterized by a dizzying array of interests, from art history to Indic languages; but scientific research remained his grounding theme, and he maintained a serious commitment to empirical research.

One of the reasons Florensky's reputation has taken some time to spread is that he was never afraid to think creatively, resulting in several decidedly odd (and sometimes unpalatable)[23] ideas. He irritated an array of scholars (not least, conservative theologians in Russia, who opposed the Sophiological movement) by his constant desire to display the essential unities among different areas of knowledge. His linking of fields was based on the belief that underpinned all his philosophy and mathematical studies: all truth is antinomic in character; a thing is always such, and it is not such, simultaneously. He saw the primary truth, God's own being, as the fountainhead of all antinomy in the ontological structure of creation, since God is ever One and Not-One (being a Trinity), transcendent yet immanent, enfleshed (incarnationally) yet pure spirit.

After the revolution, Florensky was removed from his theological post (the Bolsheviks simply commandeered the Academy buildings), but throughout the 1920s he was allowed to operate in public academic life as a scientific lecturer and an art historian. He continued, where rooms could be found, to give some theological lectures and to advise seminarians. He also publicly demonstrated his priesthood wherever he went, regularly and provocatively wearing the cassock, even when he gave lectures or attended committees. In 1919, Florensky was appointed head of a plastics-producing factory by the Bolsheviks, and in 1921 was named professor of physics and engineering at the new Moscow Technical Institute, where he inaugurated a series of new initiatives in research and practical science. In 1922, he completed his aesthetic-theological reflections on metaphysics, which he titled *Iconostasis*.[24] He had continued to write theology since 1917, even though he saw no immediate prospect of it ever being published, and the 1922 deportation of dissident intelligentsia gave him little grounds for optimism. In 1927, he announced his invention of a noncoagulating machine oil (of immense advantage in a cold climate), which was given the suitably revolutionary name "Dekanite" (in honor of the tenth anniversary of the October Revolution). From 1927 to 1933, Florensky was the editor of the important *Technical Encyclopedia*, but his "oddity" (a very obvious liminality in all he did and said) and his persistent public witness to his ecclesiality were starting to draw unwelcome attention. In 1928, he was dismissed from his academic offices and given a low-level laboratory job in Nizhny Novgorod as a humiliation. The following year the demotion was reversed and he was reinstated at the institute and given other senior responsibilities in Moscow's academic life.

If the reinstatement had been a warning to mend his profile, Florensky was not willing to take it; to scientific committee meetings he still wore his dramatic priestly robes. In February 1933, he was arrested, made to sign a manufactured confession,[25] and given, in June of that year, a ten-year sentence in a Siberian labor camp. After his first year of incarceration, he was transferred to the Solovetsky Gulag, which was allocated for "unreformables." Even here in this outpost of hell his work was vital and innovative. He produced significant research on permafrost and invented a new method for the production of iodine from seaweed. His most important work perhaps was the constant manner in which he tried to affirm hope and love among the camp's starving inmates.

After his execution on 8 December 1937, by special order of the secret police, Florensky's family was merely informed that communication with an unreformable was no longer permitted. It was not until 1944 that his wife was notified by the state simply and blankly that her husband had died on 15 December 1943. The anti-Stalin revisionist movement of the next generation saw Florensky's exoneration of all charges in a municipal courthouse of the city of Moscow on 5 May 1958. His works began to be circulated in *samizdat* soon after, under the close direction of his immediate family.

Albeit a brief sketch, this biographical synopsis is meant to show that Florensky's life is not incidental to his thought; on the contrary, Florensky deliberately attempted to live out his totalist vision. A life in art has wholly merged in his case with the art of life. That carefully elaborated life, his work, and his ideas are linked in a metaphysical nexus he found to be energized by a state of liminality. That liminal state was, ultimately, fatal for one who lived as Stalin's scientific adviser and attended party meetings in his cassock. I shall now turn to Florensky's aesthetic theory of dream perception in order to show how it illuminated his understanding of the icon (a most highly charged sacramental synopsis of life in the Orthodox intellectual context). The relation of art and biography, however, is not accidental. The life of the man, considered as a substantive icon, is part and parcel of his concept of the icon as a substantive (*hypostatic*) revelation of his life.[26] He is, at one and the same moment, both the icon and its commentary.

THE INTERSTICES AS DREAM REVELATION

More than merely a preface, Florensky's discussion of dreams and their spiritual structure occupies the place of "gateway" to his work *Iconostasis*.[27] His opening remarks create a cosmically large canvas for stating the metaphysical issue under consideration: the problem and mystery of creation lies in its ambivalent nature; reality is material and physical, yet simultaneously something more. Its two aspects, two worlds, overlap and interpenetrate each other. Using markers drawn from Genesis and the Creed, which affirm God's creation of "both heaven and earth" and of "things visible and invisible," Florensky presents the boundary between the two states as something that at one and the same moment "separates them; yet, simultaneously . . . joins them" (33). The dream life of the soul offers insight into the nature of the overlap of the worlds, where we can expect either a revelatory experience or an artistic-philosophical insight to occur.

His initial image is of a veil—palpitating, diaphanous, and porous to light. The image is highly suggestive of the biblical paradigms behind Florensky's imagination here, for the etymological root of the concept he ostensibly discusses (removing the veil) is "apocalypse." The word doubles in Greek—*Apo-* (away) and *kalyptein* (to cover, conceal)—as a term for "revelation," especially as the experience of epiphany is given in a critical moment of seeing (the

Latin *revelatio* means the removal of the *velamen* [veil] itself). The term Florensky actually uses in his text, it should be noted, is "tearing" (*razryvat'sia*). This is evocative of the literarily paired moments in the Gospel of Mark: when the "temple veil was rent in two" at the death of Jesus (Mark 15:37–38); and when the "veil of the heavens was rent in two" at the manifestation of Sophia—the Divine Wisdom—on earth (Mark 1:9–11, the Baptism in the waters, which for Orthodox theology is a highly charged symbol of Transfiguration).[28] The Gospel of Mark is structured around these two epiphanic moments: spirit and flesh are symbolically joined, then sundered. For the Evangelist, the idea of the "rent veil" turns on the ancient Christian notion that the body of the incarnate Wisdom was itself the New Temple of God on earth, decisively replacing the Jerusalem temple.[29]

In its turn, the idea of the body of the Lord as the New Temple is closely related in the Johannine narrative to the Genesis account of Jacob falling asleep and dreaming at Bethel (the ancient site of the northern Temple),[30] where he rests his head on the sacred stone (understood in ancient Jewish mysticism as the Stone of Anointment,[31] which prefigures the altar of the Holy Temple). Jacob sees the divine world in his dreams and wrestles with the Great Angel very much in his flesh. The interplay between the two narratives (the Dream of Jacob and the Temple of Incarnate Sophia) is seen clearly in John 1:51, where the "ascending and descending" angels of God evoke the "ascent and descent" of the angels at Bethel, the awesome holy place depicted in Genesis 28:10–19 as a porous aperture for the interpenetrative engagement of the worlds of "spiritual seeing" and "material grappling."

All this symbolism of dream and revelation is complex and elevated theology behind Florensky's interweaving of the symbols of ascentive and descentive dream in *Iconostasis.* As a learned Russian priest, versed in his scriptures, he presupposes this context of ascent and descent (echoed in the biblical motif of the humiliation/exaltation of the Son of Man). It is, however, a large presupposition, which often eludes those less versed in his biblically and patristically coded symbolism. This is typical of Florensky's difficult, highly allusive Symbolist style of writing. Like the biblical writers, and the Greek Fathers after them, Florensky expects his readers to know the root of the symbols he will now begin to reuse in a "modernist" context. He does not believe in stating them except as mysterious symbols framing his analysis. It is almost as if he deliberately sets a preliminary test of initiation for his readers. So much for necessary prelude. Passing on to the argument itself, this is what he says in elaboration of his theory of dreaming:

> How do we understand this boundary [of the visible and invisible worlds]? Here, as in any difficult metaphysical question, the best starting point always is what we already know in ourselves. The life of our own psyche, yes, *our own soul's life,* is the truest basis upon which we may learn about this boundary between the two worlds. For within ourselves, life in the visible world alternates with life in the invisible, and

> thus we experience moments—sometimes brief, sometimes even the tiniest atom of time—when the two worlds grow so very near in us that we can see their intimate touching. At such fleeting moments in us, the veil of visibility is torn apart, and through that tear—that break we are still conscious of at that moment—we can sense that the invisible world (still unearthly, still invisible) *is breathing*: and that both this and another world are dissolving into each other. Our life in such moments becomes an unceasing stream in the same way that air when warmed streams upward from the heat. (33)

Dreaming, to which we are so used, is the correct place to start with an initiation, "the simplest entry into the invisible world" (34). But while all dreams serve as gateways into the invisible world (a dimension that can be "made visible" only to psychic perception), many of them are of the lowest order of perception, being chaotic in form, and fueled by material needs, desires, and sense-colorations. Even so, the dream itself functions without fail as a gateway; as Florensky says, "Yet we know this too: that when we stand on the threshold between sleep and waking, when we stand at the boundary between the two worlds, our soul is engulfed by dreams" (34). He takes the datum that dream activity is seen to be most active at the boundaries of entering deep sleep, and again on reentering waking consciousness, as sufficient proof of dream's liminal revelatory power. Time itself follows new rules—determined no longer by chronological sequence and measure but instead by psychic perception. *Chronos,* as it were, has been transformed into *kairos,* that is, a moment of grace:[32] "A dreamer passes into another system, another dimension, another measure wherein time is understood and experienced in ways completely unlike the ways of time in the visible world. In this new experience of time, the dreamer's time, compared to time in the visible world, runs at infinite speed" (34–35).

This, as Florensky points out, is a common experience, by which ordinary people can gain a sense of relativity theory, which would be beyond them if they had to rely only on the rhetoric of the mathematicians. He attributes the first important modern theorizing of new time, or "instantaneous time," to the obscure Baron Carl Duprel (1839–1899), omitting to name Einstein. Duprel fell short, however, of the more substantial discovery that instantaneous time flows *backward* as well.[33]

Florensky complains (in his day with some justification) that the role of dreams in psychic development is not yet appreciated. Seen as random events, dreams have been deemed "unworthy of consideration and thought" by serious philosophers (35–36). But what is most significant for him is the "internal structure" of the dream, which is always overlooked in favor of the more amusing or memorable dream narrative. It is the sequence of dream images, however, that demonstrates his chief epistemological point. Here at first sight is the most random and nonsensical aspect of the dream. One who recalls the sequence of dream images can attest how remarkable twists of dream events are set off by preceding images in an apparently superficial way. For Florensky, however, a deeper perception of this seemingly random set of associative ideas is given in the structure of the dream itself; the external cause of the dream (noise, light, or other environmental stimuli that effect the sequence of images), which he designates Ω, is related to the internal sequence of dream images A–X, where A is the initial image of the sequence and X represents the "conclusive dream event" or the "denouement," in which the dream's inner logic is brought to full and final resolution in a satisfactory way. He is particularly interested in pursuing the notion that the Omega event and the denouement coincide:

> What makes the dreamer awaken? When we look at this question from the viewpoint of waking consciousness, we might want to say that it is Ω (the noise or the light) that awakens us. From within the dream, however, it is plainly the conclusive dream event X—the *denouement*—that, precisely because it ends the dream, awakens us. Taken together, we can see that Ω and X almost perfectly coincide in such a way that the *dreamed-content* and the *wakened-cause* are one and the same. This coincidence is usually so exact that we never even wonder about the relation of X and Ω: the *denouement* is unquestionably a "dream paraphrase" of some external stimulus invading our dream from without. (36–37)

Florensky gives the example of a series of dream narratives taken from Friedrich Wilhelm Hildebrandt's *The Dream and Its Utilization* (1875) to illustrate this (39–40). (Hildebrandt's book had been useful to Freud as well.) Florensky's central point is that the episode of the external stimulus Ω that wakens the dreamer (say a pillow falling on the chest) synchronizes with the inner world of the dream when it is timelessly (almost without a faltering of sequential rhythm) absorbed into the dream itself to overprint the final X event of denouement (the dreamer wakes at that moment from a frightening encounter with someone who has fallen on him in an attempt to asphyxiate him). The waking perception of the accidental quality of the external event (whether it was a falling pillow or a noise in an adjacent room) is given the lie by the dream structure when such an event is entered into the entire fabric of the timeless sequence in an organic (nonaccidental) way. This insight enables Florensky to correlate the two distinct spheres of consciousness and to connect them with aesthetics:

> But note what we are saying: the same event is being differently seen by two consciousnesses: by waking consciousness, it is Ω, while by dream consciousness, it is X. This would scarcely be worth our notice at all except for the extraordinary fact that X has a contradictory double status: in waking consciousness, it is a dream effect of external cause Ω, while, in the dream, it is the final effect of the dream's strongly welded causal chain begun by trivial event A. Thus, X concludes two entirely distinct lines of causation, lines whose respective starting points (the external noise and dream event A) have no connection whatever: plainly, Ω cannot in any sense *cause* A to occur. But we can say that if A and all its chain of

> circumstances did not exist, then the whole dream would not occur, and consequently there would be no X—which means that Ω did not reach our consciousness. (37–38)

The narrative structure of dreaming thus implies for Florensky that the denouement is "predetermined from the very start": "A dream, in other words, is wholly coherent; it cannot be sundered anywhere without destroying it entirely. Just as is always the case with the well-written play, where a plot without its conclusive consequences lacks all significance, so we may say that the composition of the dream is teleological: its events occur because of its *denouement*" (38).

As Florensky notes, this issue of the dream sequence absorbing the denouement that is "pressed on it" as it were from outside (where X and Ω overlap) would not be particularly illuminating if it were not for the manner in which this absorption takes place seamlessly and timelessly within dream consciousness. He gives a long and final example of a renowned dream narrative, where a whole sequence of French Revolutionary events are concluded by the touch of the guillotine on the neck of the dreamer, an act that coincides with his waking to find that a piece of the cold metal bed frame had fallen on him. For Florensky, this demonstrates the principle of time flowing in reverse:

> The spiritual cause of the whole dream is this event X. . . . In other words, in the time of the daylight world, event X should be the start of the dream's drama and event A its *denouement*. But here, in the time of the invisible world, it happens inside out, and cause X appears not prior to all the consequences of A and (in general) not prior to the entire series of consequences (b, c, d . . . r, s, t) but following them, concluding the whole row and determining it not as its efficient cause but its final cause: τελος. (41)

The spiritual importance of this is the revelatory force that dreaming can bring to bear because of its teleological character. The connectedness of the dreaming psyche to the spiritual cosmos, which lies behind the veil of waking awareness, suggests Gregory of Nyssa's idea of *epektasis*—the soul's innate desire to ascend to higher levels of perception; dream is a Jacob's ladder to another world order. The aesthetic importance of this is the potentiality it gives to the initiated dreamer to enter the domain of imaginary space, which normally lies hidden from conscious awareness and reflective analysis, something that Florensky says "usually . . . only very dimly reaches our waking consciousness":

> Dream time is turned *inside out,* which means that all its concrete images are also turned inside out with it: and that means we have entered the domain of *imaginary space.* The very same event that is perceived from the area of actual space as actual is seen from the area of imaginary space as imaginary, i.e., as occurring before everything else in teleological time, as the goal or object of our purposiveness. Contrarily, the

> goal seen from here appears (in our failure to appreciate goals rightly) as something cherished but lacking the energy of the ideal; but seen from *there,* through the other consciousness, the goal is comprehended as living energy that shapes actuality as its creative form. (41)

On this point, the dreamer-poet Florensky is the most wide awake philosophically. The dream structure, he is suggesting, points to a form and method of articulating the spiritual teleology of the universe that is far wider and (potentially) much deeper than waking consciousness. I would express the aesthetic implications like this: the artist, who by definition is the "poet of vision," must learn to be the skilled practitioner of this method of analyzing form; otherwise, he is bound (and doomed) to reproduce his own merely surface impression of reality. His art will have merely a decorative effect—the spiritual significance of a pretended bowl of fruit hung over an artificial fireplace, and the philosophical equivalent of existential *trompe l'oeil,* wanting for true connectedness. Here Symbolist aesthetic theory coincides with the classical Christian vision that the invisible world informs and directs the visible.

For Florensky, the unity God has established in the "making of all things visible and invisible" guarantees the possibility of transit between worlds in the dream state.[34] Far from being a peripheral investigation, or merely a psychotherapeutic tool, the dream analysis is indicative of ontological "progress" (*epektasis*) to a higher condition of perceptivity. Far from being meaningless, it is, in essence, deeply revelatory of metaphysical meaning: "Although it is something perceived, the dream is wholly teleological, saturated with the meanings of the invisible world, meanings that are invisible, immaterial, eternal yet nevertheless visibly manifest and (as it were) vividly material. A dream is therefore pure meaning wrapped in the thinnest membrane of reality; it is almost wholly a phenomenon of the other world . . . the boundary where the final determinations of earth meet the increasing densifications of heaven" (43).

Liminality is the key to the comprehensibility of the experience. Florensky notes that since the boundary possesses the characters of both sides of ontology (visible and invisible) and follows the logical rules of existence characteristic of both sides, there can often be occasions when the different logics become muddled. To describe this, he applies the old Philokalic principle of "beguilement" (*prelest'*)—the state of mental and spiritual self-delusion where a person prefers his or her (wrong) estimation of reality to reality itself. Based upon a wrong initial premise (that one can sing, or paint, or write beautifully, for example), prideful clinging to wrong notions can lead a person ever deeper into blindness of the true order of existence (people who have little talent often dream their lives away in pursuit of inappropriate life goals). To puncture this dangerous delusion the Russian Philokalic tradition insisted on the need for a guiding *starets,* a spiritual adviser, whose higher spiritual consciousness and perception could serve as a guide and a corrective. For Florensky, the dangers in the aesthetic domain are comparable to those of the mystical life. He is aware that many people might find it much to their taste to inhabit the borderland domains of the interstices all their lives, as if dreaming their lives away. He regards the level of spiritual vision that is given on the borderland as not ultimately fulfilling—being neither purely actual nor entirely spiritual, but having, as it were, a narcotic element derived from the refinement of matter (or subtle materialization of spirit). He even suggests that the border domain is haunted by lower-level elemental spirits who, sirenlike, have the desire to entrap and hinder human spiritual consciousness from its true teleological vocation—which is the progressive ascent into spiritual freedom, through "spiritual sobriety" (45–46). Without ascetic "sobriety," Florensky argues, the iconic face of reality cannot be perceived, and all one will see is seductive masks.

The contrast between the "vacant mask" and the "iconic face," which reveals spiritual grandeur and beauty, is one of the last elements of his dream theory, and one that relates to the art of the icon proper (50–54). Of course, Florensky is well aware of the complex and rich Orthodox theology of the icon as sacramental representation of the divine. In this art form, above all others perhaps, we see an explicit attempt to depict in earthly colors and using artistic devices the shape of things that makes sense in the spiritual world. The icon is (and is often described as such in Orthodox writing) a "gateway" between heaven and earth. This is why correlating dreaming and the art of the iconographer is a natural step for Florensky to make, though it seemed in the Russian Silver Age a highly unusual (typically Florenskian) set of ideas.

Florensky is much taken with the idea of the ascent and descent in the dreaming state. This is that "crossing of the threshold" that dreaming connotes, since without a transition between the two worlds, no dream is remembered or memorable: "We might say, then, that a dream happens whenever we cross from one shore to another: but it may be more accurate to say that the dream happens whenever our consciousness *hugs the boundary of the crossing* and therefore sustains the double perceptiveness that occurs when we either lightly dream or drowsily keep awake. For there is where all significant dreaming occurs" (43–44). But the crossover between the worlds means that the characteristics of the dream can be primarily marked by either ascent or descent. It is the dreams of descent that are charged with spiritual meaning and from which the icon painter needs to learn, as a method for the articulation of spiritual types and forms in his painting. The dreams of ascent still bear in themselves the material elements of sensuous consciousness and have a primarily earthly, chthonic, character. Florensky calls them "psychic effluvia," like the "outworn clothes" of earthly consciousness the psyche is trying to shed from itself as it rises, what he also describes as "the images of our everyday emptiness." The dreams of descent, those that occur before awakening, when the soul has been freed from the constraints of material rational consciousness for a longer time, preserve the characteristics of the spiritual realm, and are more clearly remembered by waking reason. The spiritual movement becomes synchronous with the exercise of the highest level of artistic creativity:

> What we say about the dream holds true (with minor changes) about any movement from one sphere to another. In creating a work of art, the psyche or soul of the artist ascends from the earthly realm into the heavenly; there, free of all images, the soul is fed in contemplation by the essences of the highest realm, knowing the permanent *noumena* of things; then, satiated with this knowledge, it descends again to the earthly realm. And precisely at the boundary between the two worlds, the soul's spiritual knowledge assumes the shapes of symbolic imagery: and it is these images that make permanent the work of art. Art is thus materialized dream, separated from the ordinary consciousness of waking life. (44)

The artist, especially the icon painter, is thus the waking dreamer, the liminal seer. The dream images that come to the painter and enter into the flow of the artistic work must, of necessity (if they are to carry the charge of the spiritual world), be descentive images: "An artist misunderstands (and so causes us to misunderstand) when he puts into his art those images that come to him during the uprushing of his inspiration—if, that is, it is only the imagery of the soul's ascent. We need, instead, his early morning dreams, those dreams that carry the coolness of the eternal azure. The other imagery is merely psychic raw material" (45).[35] In the coincidence of the dream and the artistic grappling with the archetypes of the spiritual world (which icon painters then have to translate into prototypes recognizable to Orthodox believers),[36] the icon painter thus emerges as the true theologian, fulfilling a priestly task, symbolically and authoritatively communicating the Word by transmission of the archetype through artistic and sacramental prototypes. What Florensky evokes here is fundamentally the Orthodox economy of salvation; as the Word descends (archetypally in the Incarnation) for the revelation of the divine to the material world, so the iconographer, celebrating that mystery of revelation in the symbolic representation of the economy, reveals to the church the images glimpsed in descentive consciousness. For Florensky, the aesthetic-spiritual entrance into such a perception shows the artist-dreamer to be one and the same as the mystic-theologian:

> What is true of art and dream is also true of mystical experience: a common pattern holds everywhere. In mystical experience, the soul is raised up from the visible realm to where visibility itself vanishes and the field of the invisible opens: such is the Dionysian sundering of the bonds of the visible. And after soaring up into the invisible, the soul descends again into the visible—and then and there, before its very eyes, are those real *appearances* of things: ideas. This is the Apollonian perspective on the spiritual world. (45)[37]

For Florensky, the actual icon, crafted from wood and the careful synthesis of colors, using reverse perspective to signify its dissonance from the materialist trend of simple representational art, is the culmination of all this symbolic discourse on the structure of vision and revelatory experience. The artistic work is a complex synthesis in and of itself, not least because it is the work of the seer attempting to elaborate the inner vision at one remove. It thus cannot be the vision itself, which is not directly communicable in the waking reality of material existence:

> Although the most sensitive of us can sense the powerful motions of the angelic wings, we can experience these great motions only as the very faintest breathing. An icon is the same as this kind of heavenly vision; yet it is not the same, for the icon is the outline of a vision. A spiritual vision is not in itself an icon, for it possesses by itself full reality; an icon, however, because its outline coincides with a spiritual vision, is that vision within our consciousness; finally, therefore, the icon—apart from its spiritual vision—is not an icon at all but a board. (64–65)[38]

Florensky's concept of the icon within the context of dream-vision is clearly part of the modern Russian Symbolist agenda in aesthetics. It likewise overlaps powerfully and positively with a profound restatement of traditional Orthodox theology on iconography, economic soteriology, and sacramental witness. In addition to all these complex layers of his argument, he certainly displays a considerable amount of innovative psychological and metaphysical speculation.

Florensky was undoubtedly a seer, poet, and dreamer himself. His greatest iconic statement, without doubt, was his own life, the witness of a perennially liminal figure, exercising what he called the necessary "spiritual sobriety" to safeguard the soul's purity of perception from all manner of seduction, both material and psychic. His own sobriety brought him, in the end, to a bitter personal ascesis where, like the icon of the Trinity by Rublev (which he so admired as a canon of descentive, azure-cool painting), he was stripped down to the essentials and became transparent, symbolical, and clean, in the purposefulness (or teleology) of his life's trajectory and his mind's vitality. In short, by no small degree of conscious elaboration, his own life became iconically organized. In Florensky the modernist, the ancient hope that icon, iconographer, and archetype be bound in communion was graphically and startlingly made manifest, like a radiant color epiphanically shining out in one of the gloomiest periods of the history of Russia.

NOTES TO CHAPTER 10

1. The precursor of the KGB.

2. Irina Titova, "'Russian da Vinci' May Be Among Remains," *St. Petersburg Times,* 1 October 2002.

3. There was also a tradition that Florensky had been killed by a falling tree at Solovetsky while on a work duty. This tale is related to the (seemingly apocryphal) story that inmate-survivors remembered instinctively kneeling as his body was carried out of the camp to its burial. After the opening of the KGB files in 1990, Florensky's file from Solovetsky was found to contain the order on 25 November 1937 for his execution by shooting, issued unanimously by the "Special Triad" of the Leningrad branch of the NKVD. Lt. Polikarpov, the Leningrad secret police commandant, signed an additional note that the order had been accomplished on 8 December.

4. Interviews in the 1960s with truck drivers who had brought bodies of purge victims to the Levashevo fields near Leningrad had determined that an estimated 8,500 people had been taken there after execution in the cellars of the NKVD headquarters on Liteiny Prospect. The discovery of the thirty thousand bodies accounts in the main for the total estimate of forty thousand people who were known to have disappeared from the Leningrad area during the Great Terror. The number of people executed on that day (8 December) suggests, according to the Memorial spokesperson Irina Fligye, that Florensky was not taken from the cellars of the NKVD to the normal site of Levashevo, but was transported directly to the artillery range, where executions and burials took place when larger numbers were involved. The method of death for all concerned was a bullet (9 or 11 mm) at the base of the skull, the preferred means and method of the NKVD. Titova, "'Russian da Vinci' May Be Among Remains."

5. Pavel Florensky, *The Pillar and Ground of The Truth: An Essay in Orthodox Theodicy in Twelve Letters,* trans. Richard F. Gustafson and Boris Jakim (Princeton: Princeton University Press, 2004); *The Trinity–St. Sergius Lavra and Russia,* trans. Robert Bird (New Haven: Variable Press, 1995); *Iconostasis,* trans. Donald Sheehan and Olga Andrejev (Crestwood, N.Y.: St. Vladimir's Seminary Press, 1996); *Beyond Vision: Essays on the Perception of Art by Pavel Florensky,* ed. Nicoletta Misler, trans. Wendy Salmond (London: Reaktion Books, 2002) (this collection contains Florensky's article on "reverse perspective" in the icon); *The Salt of the Earth,* trans. Richard Betts (Platina, Calif.: St. Herman Press, 1987).

6. Florensky's own account, "Memoirs of Childhood, Religion, Nature," was published in *Vestnik* (Paris), nos. 99–102, 1970–71. For Florensky's biography in English, see Robert Slesinski, *Pavel Florensky: A Metaphysics of Love* (Crestwood, N.Y.: St. Vladimir's Seminary Press, 1984); and Judith Deutsch Kornblatt and Richard F. Gustafson, eds., *Russian Religious Thought* (Madison: University of Wisconsin Press, 1996), 14–16, 91–131. The biographical material in Donald Sheehan's preface to *Iconostasis* is an English digest (in the main) of N. A. Struve, *Sobranie sochinenii / Pavel Florenskii,* vol. 1 (Paris: YMCA Press, 1985). (The account of the death in Sheehan's preface is drawn from an article by Vitaly Shentalinsky in the magazine *Ogonek,* Moscow, November 1990, and is inaccurate.)

7. In his second year, Florensky edited and published *Integral Calculus,* the advanced mathematical lectures of his professor N. V. Bugaev.

8. "On the Peculiarities of Flat Curves as Places of Interrupted Discontinuity."

9. Florensky was also put under the guidance of the monastic recluse Elder Isidore (Gruzinsky) of the Gethsemane Hermitage. Within twelve days of each other, in early 1908, both Florensky's father and his spiritual father, Isidore, died. Florensky composed the short book *Salt of the Earth* as a tribute to Isidore. Close spiritual guidance, in the Optina monastic tradition, would always mark Florensky's church career after that point. He became a spiritual guide and elder for a close circle of his own disciples and correspondents.

10. Solzhenitsyn's description of Florensky can be found in *The Gulag Archipelago,* vols. 3–4, trans. Thomas P. Whitney (New York: Harper & Row, 1975).

11. In a famous essay by Berdiaev, Florensky was given a drubbing for his attack on Khomiakov and dismissed as having a "servile sense of ecclesiality . . . as if he wants mystically to justify and intensify the condition of groveling." Berdiaev was angered because of his perception of Florensky's "betrayal" of Khomiakov; he clearly regarded Florensky as being a "parvenu in Orthodoxy," newly converted and "more Orthodox than the Orthodox," as he put it. See N. Berdiaev, "Khomiakov i sviashch. Florenskii," *Russkaia mysl'* (February 1917): 72–81.

12. Florensky was responsible for initiating Bulgakov into the church and also influenced his desire to enter the priesthood.

13. For an introduction to the thought of this most fecund of all early Christian thinkers, see John A. McGuckin, ed., *The Westminster Handbook to Origen* (Louisville: Westminster John Knox Press, 2004).

14. See J. Rebecca Lyman, *Christology and Cosmology: Models of Divine Activity in Origen, Eusebius, and Athanasius* (Oxford: Clarendon Press, 1993); J. Roldanus, *Le Christ et l'homme dans la théologie d'Athanase d'Alexandrie: Étude de sa conception de l'homme avec sa Christologie* (Leiden: Brill, 1977).

15. See John A. McGuckin, *St. Gregory of Nazianzus: An Intellectual Biography* (Crestwood, N.Y.: St. Vladmir's Seminary Press, 2001).

16. Texts of Maximus in English translation include George Berthold, *Maximus Confessor: Selected Writings* (New York: Paulist Press, 1985); and G. E. H. Palmer, Philip Sherrard, and Kallistos Ware, eds., *The Philokalia: The Complete Text,* vol. 2 (London: Faber & Faber, 1979). Studies of his expansive cosmology and deification theology can be found in Lars Thunberg, *Microcosm and Mediator* (Lund: C. W. K. Gleerup, 1965); Andrew Louth, *Maximus the Confessor* (London: Routledge, 1996).

17. Only the first two in the line were actually Alexandrians themselves. For more on this tradition, see Vladimir Lossky, *The Mystical Theology of the Eastern Church* (Crestwood, N.Y.: St. Vladimir's Seminary Press, 1976); for a broad consideration of the Alexandrian mystics in the context of Byzantine ecclesial thought, see John A. McGuckin, *Standing in God's Holy Fire: The Byzantine Tradition* (London: Darton Longman, 2001).

18. See John A. McGuckin, "Deification," in *The Oxford Companion to Christian Thought,* ed. Adrian Hastings (Oxford: Oxford University Press, 2000), 156. The Hesychast tradition of Byzantium, which arrived with great force in the monastic tradition of the Russian Church from its origins, saw in the *telos* of deification the whole momentum of the material order. The transfiguration of Jesus' earthly body on Mount Tabor (Mark 9) was taken by the medieval Hesychasts as the chief symbol of the whole cosmic destiny to be "transfigured in light," as it achieved a glory beyond its present material limitations. That tradition was sustained in Russian Orthodoxy by the monastic Hesychast culture of the church. See also Jules Gross, *The Divinization of the Christian According to the Greek Fathers,* trans. Paul A. Onica (1938; repr., Anaheim, Calif.: A & C Press, 2002).

19. The thesis would be the foundation of his main literary work finally issued (after two earlier recensions) in 1914 as *The Pillar and Foundation of Truth* (*Stolp i utverzhdenie istiny*).

20. To Anna Giatsintova, the sister of a university friend. The marriage between the brilliant Florensky and the quiet peasant teacher raised more eyebrows, but proved to be a strong and deep bonding.

21. The transformation of the Eucharistic elements is a paradigm of the Transfiguration—the divine refashioning of material existence.

22. His grandson, the priest Andronik Trubachev, is a professor at the Theological Academy of Sergiev Posad, near Moscow.

23. Florensky was imbued with some degree of a then-pervasive Russian anti-Semitic prejudice, and had an unfortunate tendency to categorize ideas racially (for example, through his application of Iranian and Kushite "types"—preferring the latter to the former as a type of "church").

24. The book would not appear in an English edition (*Iconostasis*) until 1996.

25. It is possible that Florensky signed to save the life of his "accuser," Moscow law professor Gudulianov, who had named him as a leader of a (fictitious) fascist cell under his own direction intent on undermining the state. See Sheehan, "Introduction," in *Iconostasis,* 19–21.

26. The word *hypostasis* is central to Orthodox theology of the emergence of "person." Etymologically, it denotes "substantive" (*hypo-stasis;* literally, that which stands under a thing), but the word takes on a powerful new meaning in the context of the patristic-conciliar Christology debate, where it becomes the primary word denoting the divine personhood that subsumes flesh and deifies it. See John A. McGuckin, *St. Cyril of Alexandria and the Christological Controversy* (Crestwood, N.Y.: St. Vladimir's Seminary Press, 2004). Florensky's understanding of the sacrality of the icon turns around the belief in Orthodoxy that the sacred image is charged with the "grace of presence" of that which it represents to the believer—that the *hypostasis* of Christ, or the Virgin, or the saint, is timelessly rendered present to the believer through the sacred medium of the icon, which therefore (though merely material in form) becomes an open gateway to heavenly reality. The icon is thus Florensky's ideal image of liminal transparency or the "porousness" of the two worlds, visible and invisible.

27. Florensky, "The Spiritual Structure of Dreams," in *Iconostasis,* trans. Donald Sheehan and Olga Andrejev, 33–44. All parenthetical references are to *Iconostasis.* All italics are Florensky's.

28. As indicated, for example, in the ritual service for the Feast of Epiphany, 6 January, when the Great Blessing of Waters takes place. The Blessing centers on the notion of the metamorphosis of all material elements by divine grace, in the symbol of Jesus' purification of the Jordan.

29. See Hebrews 6:19–20; Mark 14:58, 15.29; John 2 18:22.

30. Genesis 28:10–19.

31. This ancient Christian theology, evident in John's Gospel, equating Jesus' consciousness of God with the claim to be the holy ground of the New Temple (in the sense that the new consciousness of the divine presence will mediate that presence to others) is far older than the text of the Gospels. It turns on a punning metathesis that works only in Hebrew, one that predates and informs the Greek text: the claim that Ben Adam (The Apocalyptic Son of Man) is Eb^{e}n Dam (the Stone of the Anointment, that is, the stone of divine encounter that Jacob witnessed at Bethel). The confession "Ben Adam—Eb^{e}n Dam" was thus one of the most succinct creedal elements of the earliest Jewish Christians, to the effect that Jesus was himself the "ascending and descending," the place of divine encounter. The Evangelist John renders this highly compacted concept into the more Hellenistically comprehensible one of anabasis and katabasis (ascending/descending; humiliation/exaltation) in his account of the Passion of Jesus. Florensky, of course, is aware of both the Jacob typology and the Johannine scheme adapting it.

32. The biblical and patristic theological writers use the word *chronos* (time as sequence) to denote the world order as it lies in bondage and hostility to the spiritual powers; this world (*kosmos*) is distinct from the Kingdom of God (*Basileia*), which is ushered in apocalyptically as a New Time—a *kairos* (moment of grace), which is both the ending of time (the end time of the *eschaton*) and its fulfillment, perfect communion with the spiritual world. Florensky's theory, as we can see again, is highly personal, yet constantly rooted in the ancient patterns of Orthodox patristic eschatological theology, which it presupposes.

33. "[Duprel] approached this discovery; but he grew always more and more uncertain: he finally did not comprehend the invisible that lay before him" (35). The instantaneity of the moment of *kairos* was what the biblical and patristic writers spoke of as the "eternity" of the Next Age, where temporal boundaries did not apply. Gregory of Nyssa, in the fourth century, denoted the extension of the eternal *kairos* by the term *epektasis,* describing it as the paradox of a bounded infinity, whereby the creature could stretch out (endlessly growing) in the limitless experience of the divine, and thus approach the ontologically impossible *stasis* of creaturely infinity. "To allow participation in God," Gregory says, "there must, of necessity, be something in the nature of the participant which is akin to that in which it participates. This is why Scripture says that man was born in the image of God. It was surely that he could see as like does to like. For the vision of God is unquestionably the life of the soul." Gregory of Nyssa, "Discourse on Children," in *Gregorii Nysseni Opera,* ed. Ekkehard Mühlenberg, vol. 3.2 (Leiden: Brill, 1996), 79. Gregory's conception of *metousia theou,* the participation of the material in the immaterial divinity, is a basis of Florensky's logic at this juncture. See Jean Daniélou, *L'Être et le Temps chez Gregoire de Nysse* (Leiden: Brill, 1970), 223; and J. A. McGuckin, "The Strategic Adaptation of Deification in the Cappadocians," in *Partakers of the Divine Nature: The History and Development of Deification in the Christian Traditions,* ed. Michael J. Christensen and Jeffery A. Wittung (Madison, N.J.: Fairleigh Dickinson University Press, 2007), 95–114.

34. This creedal affirmation, which dates to the second century, was an explicit rejection of the Gnostic principle that the two worlds were antipathetic or contrary.

35. Azure is the color of the soul, as described by the Christian mystic Evagrius (*On Discrimination,* 18). English text in Palmer, Sherrard, and Ware, eds., *Philokalia,* 1:49. In the iconic tradition, the symbolic color of azure blue always depicts the heavenly dimension.

36. In icon theory, the archetype of an icon is the hypostatic reality of the spiritual presence it depicts (Christ, the Virgin, Sophia, or saints, for example), while the prototype of an icon is the recognizable quality that makes this icon communicate that hypostatic presence to others. This is the qualitative spiritual character of the icon. In icon theory by formalists and woodenly historical icon painters, this has very often been taken to be a matter of the repetition of old prototypes (copying old icons to ensure that the image remains classically recognizable). Yet the inner spiritual vitality of iconic painting, suggests Florensky, is more a matter of communicating the substantive hypostasis of the iconic archetype correctly by the authenticity of the icon painter's vision of the archetype. In this sense, the old adage that the icon painter is a theologian in the Orthodox tradition is truly fulfilled. It is as a mystical theologian, a *vates* or "seer," that the iconographer must fulfill that task, not as a copyist.

37. The Greek philosophical concept behind Florensky's reference to the "real *appearance* of things" here is *phainoumena,* that is, reality as it appears as an epiphanic mystery.

38. The Greek Christian technical term for the icon's being an "outline" of a vision, as used in icon literature, is *skiagraphia,* or "drawing with shadows."

ROBERT BIRD

11

TARKOVSKY AND THE CELLULOID ICON

The "Russian Golgotha" is a central scene in Andrei Tarkovsky's film *Andrei Rublev* (1966/1969). Set off from the main narrative, which comprises episodes from the life and times of medieval Russia's foremost icon painter, Andrei Rublev, the scene begins suddenly, in the midst of a theological dispute between Andrei and his elder colleague, Theophanes the Greek, on a languid summer day. They are observed by the apprentice Foma, who crouches at the riverbank rinsing his paintbrushes. After an extremely long take, during which the camera executes a graceful dance around Andrei's and Theophanes' static figures, the film cuts to a shot of a cloth being rinsed in a river. The camera zooms out to reveal a Russian Christ in peasant clothes carrying his cross over a barren winter landscape. He is accompanied by sobbing women, somber attendants, and winged angels, nearly invisible against the snow. While a drum beats in the background and a chorus begins to intone a quasi-liturgical chant, the viewer continues to hear Andrei expounding his idiosyncratic understanding of Christ's sacrifice. The cross is raised at the summit of the hill, and the action cuts back to Foma, who is still rinsing paint off his brushes in the river as he listens to Andrei's radical theology (fig. 21).

This scene raises most urgently a question that pervades all of Tarkovsky's *Andrei Rublev:* How do the film's images stand vis-à-vis the icon? Shot in widescreen black-and-white, *Andrei Rublev* is less a biography than a sustained study in the landscape and milieu of its subject, as imagined by the young screenwriters Andrei Tarkovsky and Andron Mikhalkov-Konchalovsky. Rublev is often a mere observer of events occurring around him; indeed, for a large part of the film he is under a vow of silence, as if refusing

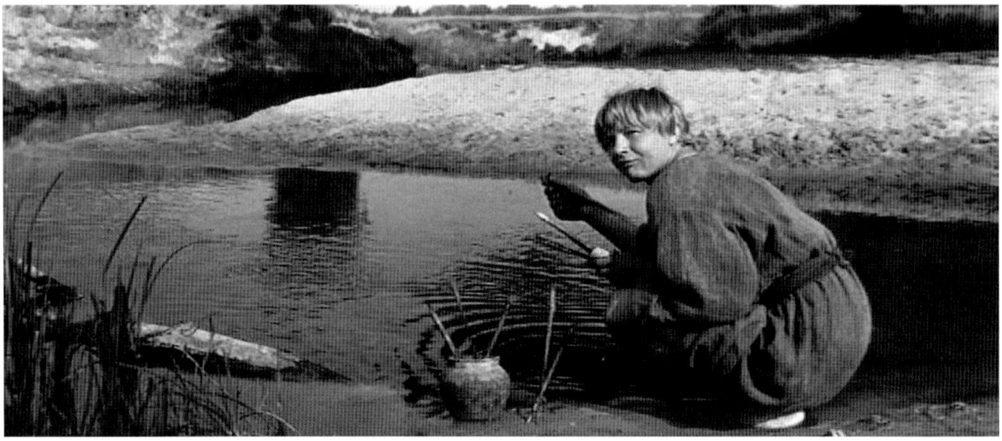

FIG. 21 Foma cleaning his paintbrushes in *Andrei Rublev,* dir. Andrei Tarkovsky (1966/1969).

truculently to participate in the spectacle that has been arranged in his honor. This sullen, pensive narrative, which in both of its major versions runs for more than three hours, culminates in a glorious display in color of some of the icons attributed to Rublev, again set to a choral score. However, the film does not end on this triumphal note; the cinematic exhibition fades into a final scene of four horses grazing on a spit of land. They are bathed in sun, viewed through a film of rain, which renders the cinematic image elusive and enigmatic. The arrival of the icon has infused the dour world with color, but has also removed it from direct gaze. It is as if the icon has overpowered the film, turning the cinematic image into a mere shadow.

In the "Russian Golgotha" and the epilogue, the film might appear to be presenting itself as an icon. It depicts holy people in static poses; their ascetic faces gaze mutely at one another and at the viewer with both appeal and admonition. The supernatural seems ready to intervene at any moment, signaled unambiguously by the angels. Mark Le Fanu writes: "Tarkovsky's facial portraits (Ivan, Daniel, Theophanes), like Rublev's portraits of Christ and the saints, are concerned with the expression of noble, inner rapture. The piercing gaze of the cinema is not, primarily, in Tarkovsky's work, the search for psychological truth, so much as a search for what he terms 'spirituality.'"[1] Le Fanu admits, however, that this is dangerous ground. The characters in the "Russian Golgotha" are statuesque, as on an icon, but their overwrought tears reek of a cheaper sort of melodrama. Those angels have closer ties to a school pantomime than to the Russian icon, which eschews anthropomorphism. How can a celluloid fiction aspire to the kind of veneration reserved for the icon? This would either sacralize the cinema or secularize the icon.

Any single scene in Tarkovsky's film can yield evidence to support either interpretation—the film as icon or anti-icon. In the "Russian Golgotha," the sign that the guards nail to the cross reads, "Jesus Christ, the Crucifixion of Our Lord," just as it would on an icon (and in contrast to the title "King of the Jews" in Matt. 27:37

and John 19:19). However, the landscape is reminiscent of Pieter Bruegel's *Procession to Calvary,* where everyday life bustles, indifferent and unaffected, around the crucified Christ. Drawn into a sacred realm (that of the icon), the viewer is encouraged, at the same time, to question the profane, impoverished medium (that of the cinema). In this manner, *Andrei Rublev* dramatizes the ineluctable tension between art image and icon, which has been a central concern in the aesthetics of modern Russian religious thought. I will argue that, if the narrative suspense of *Andrei Rublev* focuses the viewer on projected images of intense potentiality, the constant suspension of its narrative elevates the viewer's gaze to what remains beyond even the visual resources of film: the icon as imprint of the divine.

SACRED IMAGES AND PROFANE NARRATIVES

Wedged uneasily between devotion and secular drama, Tarkovsky's *Andrei Rublev* addresses the fundamental question concerning the icon in our day, namely, how the icon stands vis-à-vis modern image culture. When, after centuries of decline and neglect, the icon was rediscovered and unveiled in early twentieth-century Russia, Maximilian Voloshin's enthusiasm was tinged with a dawning awareness of the icon's new fragility:

> The glaze [*olifa*], having hardened, formed a thick glasslike surface [on the icons] from underneath which the outlines of the images were only just visible. . . . Who knows whether this freeing of the cleaned icons from the glaze might not cause their final ruin? But now, for an instant, just like the ancient world for the people of the Renaissance, ancient Russian art has arisen in its full stature and radiance before our eyes. It now seems so radiant, so contemporary, and it provides so many clear and direct answers for the contemporary tasks of painting, that it not only allows, but it even requires that we approach it not archeologically, but aesthetically, without mediation.[2]

Voloshin frankly acknowledges the possibility that, revealing its beauty, the icon *as such* might perish when set to work for modern aesthetics. In 1846, A. N. Muraviev viewed Andrei Rublev's *Old Testament Trinity* and noticed only its rich decoration, as a token of the devotion with which it was regarded.[3] In 1866, Fyodor Buslaev, one of the first modern scholars to take note of the icon, still saw the virtue of the icon in its unsightliness, which preserved it from the aesthetic fetishization and profanation that had long since spoiled religious painting in the West.[4] Buslaev argued that the icon lacked any "conscious striving for elegance" and therefore "will never satisfy an aesthetically refined taste."[5] By 1919, Pavel Florensky had reversed the entire system of values by centering the devotional system of modern Orthodoxy on the aesthetic impact of Rublev's icon and, at the same time, holding up the medieval Russian icon as the absolute paradigm of all art.[6] The aesthetic appreciation of the icon secured its physical preservation under the new Soviet government, which was quick to establish Rublev as a great Russian artist. In 1960, the celebration of the six hundredth anniversary of Rublev's purported birth crowned his reputation and sanctioned such tributes as Tarkovsky's film.[7] Unusually for his time, Tarkovsky did not simply accept the incorporation of the icon into a modern aesthetic framework; rather, he used his film to question anew where the icon stood vis-à-vis the modern image and how it can be approached in its very distinction from art.

The unveiling of the icons issued a challenge to the Orthodox tradition of icon veneration that has yet to be answered by theological aesthetics. In modern times, the option of outright iconoclasm is rarely exercised, yet discussion of the icon's aesthetics continues to be framed by the polemics of the eighth and ninth centuries. Meanwhile the icon has become exposed to another hazard, no less serious than the image breakers of old. As it has proliferated as an object of appreciation and research, the icon has lost its specificity; it has become an image in the sense of modern art. As with the art image, aesthetic appreciation has led to mass reproduction and even digitization, allowing for endless dissemination and manipulation, to the point that parodies of the icon have even appeared in mainstream Western media (pl. 15). For art lovers and historians, for collectors and governments, the distinction between icon and painting may not appear crucial; both kinds of work submit equally to analysis, interpretation, and appreciation. For Orthodox Christians and for Orthodox cultures, by contrast, it has proven vital to preserve a distinction between secular art and the icon in order to resist both sacralizing the aesthetic realm and dissolving religious tradition into the history of artistic style. The controversy surrounding the icon is no longer whether the icon is possible, but rather how it can be distinguished from the images that assault the modern viewer from all sides. In 1997, the Tretiakov Gallery opened a special church, Saint Nicholas in Tolmachi (which had been closed as a church in 1929), to display the Vladimir Mother of God in its natural habitat, as is done with exotic animals at modern zoos. The exclusive focus of all visitors on this one icon inadvertently renders invisible the rest of the church, including the many other icons displayed within, and therefore conceals the icon's functionality within its sacred habitat. In such cases it seems that the icon *qua* icon makes no claim on our aesthetic judgment, while an icon that has become an object of artistic regard loses its ritual function. The icon can be ritual object or artwork, but never both at the same time.

For Tarkovsky, there were two distinct issues at play in this dilemma: the status of the icon vis-à-vis the art image, and the ability of the cinematic medium in particular to approach the icon. Buslaev's naive dismissal of the icon makes the very valuable point that, while it is undoubtedly a form of painting, the icon remains indifferent to many central aesthetic categories, including originality, authenticity, authorial design, and interpretive license. The icon is not an "original"; it is always a copy, the faithfulness of which ensures its devotional valence. The often-cited comparison of the icon to the minted coin bearing Caesar's image (based on Matt. 22:17–21) and the tradition of icons "not made by human hands" both suggest mechanical reproduction as a precondition for images of the divine. In 1551, the

Stoglav Council of the Russian Church, called in part to address growing Western influence, mandated that icons be painted "from the ancient standards, as Greek icon painters painted and as Andrei Rublev painted along with other famous icon painters."[8] In modern times, the Orthodox Church has gone a step further by tacitly endorsing the use of mechanical reproductions both in personal and liturgical devotion. Although connoisseurs like Florensky abhorred this development, it makes theological sense as a method of producing faithful images of the divine.[9] Paradoxically, mass reproduction may strengthen the perception of authorship insofar as it is now possible for everyone to own Rublev's *Old Testament Trinity* (pl. 2), if only in a cheap paper reproduction or as a digital screensaver. Icons today are rarely anonymous painted copies. However, in its religious function, the icon remains indifferent to authorship and manufacturing technique, as long as the image remains true in its shape to the hallowed models and is accorded proper reverence in its display and regard.

This openness to mechanical reproduction suggests a surprising kinship between the icon and the photographic image. Both photograph and icon are produced by processes of imprinting, rather than imaginative renderings projected by the artist and interpreted by the viewer.[10] It is the imprintedness of the cinematic image that Tarkovsky saw as a productive link and tension between icon and cinematic image.

The cinema, this spectacle projected onto a blank screen, has not often been considered an appropriate medium for the religious image. As Tarkovsky once noted, "cinema was born . . . at the fairground with the goal of pure profit."[11] Its profane origin has traditionally allied it with progressive, nonreligious (and often overtly antireligious) culture. Many traditionally minded thinkers and artists viewed the cinema as the soulless mechanization of art, especially since early film was dominated by melodrama and sensationalist spectacles. In a text written for the Council of the Russian Orthodox Church in 1917, the artist Viktor Vasnetsov opposed the use of electricity in churches not because of its natural qualities ("there is no sin in it"), but because of its profane associations with "the theater, the railway station, the cinema, the restaurant, and such places of entertainment."[12] The separation of church and cinema was enforced by the religious sensitivity of Russian governments prior to February 1917 and by the Bolsheviks' hostility to religion after October 1917.[13] Between 1918 and 1971 (when *Andrei Rublev* was finally released in the USSR), Orthodoxy was typically represented in Soviet cinema in a negative light. For example, in 1919, Dziga Vertov filmed the desecration of the relics of Saint Sergius, while Eisenstein included antireligious demonstrations in his *The Old and the New* (1929) and fanciful caricatures of icons in *Ivan the Terrible* (1943–46). The Soviet cinema was explicitly presented as a substitute for religious ritual, with many shuttered churches being converted into cinemas (as well as into skating rinks, gymnasiums, and the like).[14] The period of the Thaw saw a sharp increase in the number of antireligious films, such as Vladimir Skuibin's *The Miracle Worker* (*Chudotvornaia,* 1960), based on a novel by Vladimir Tendriakov, in which a young pioneer discovers a wonder-working icon, is forced by the elder female villagers to adopt a religious life, and ends up attempting suicide. In Georgy Daneliya's *I Stroll Around Moscow* (*Ia shagaiu po Moskve,* 1963), shot by Tarkovsky's director of photography, Vadim Yusov, the protagonist (played by Nikita Mikhalkov) enters a church to find the owner of a barking dog, and it is as if he has entered the world of the dead. Against this background, Tarkovsky's *Andrei Rublev* represented the first substantial encounter between film and the icon.

ENVISIONING ICONS

Andrei Rublev is full of icons. They are visible not only in Daniil's monastic cell and in the cathedrals in Vladimir. They are stacked against the walls of Theophanes' and Kirill's workshops. They are discussed by Andrei and Daniil in the field outside Vladimir, and by Andrei and Theophanes after the cathedral is torched by a raiding party of Mongols and treacherous Russians. Specific iconic subjects are echoed in the mise-en-scène and blocking of numerous scenes; for instance, when Andrei and Daniil repeat the poses of the angels in Rublev's *Trinity* and when Andrei's face emerges from between two trees in an apparent allusion to the *Savior in the Wood,* commonly attributed to Rublev (fig. 22). In all of these contexts, the icon is a passive, auxiliary element in the audiovisual narrative. Only in the film's epilogue is the icon unveiled as the central subject, but even then the camera's variable motion and distance prevent the icon from coming into clear focus. The viewer is challenged not so much to make sense of the icon as to establish an appropriate attitude calibrating its disparate manifestations against an absent ground.

One approach is to sort through the characters in search of an authoritative point of view on the icon. The first character to impose himself on the viewer is Kirill, a frustrated monk, whose acute vision is constrained by moral blindness. Kirill demonstrates both learning and acumen as he remarks on the spiritual power of Theophanes' "simplicity without ostentation."[15] When he returns to the monastery after years of abject wandering, his eyes almost fused shut, he notices the shadows of people and beasts upside down on the wall opposite a boarded-up window. This camera obscura reveals to Kirill the secret of projection, but he is helpless to appropriate this discovery for the production of icons or for his own moral healing.

Andrei's young apprentice, Foma, suffers from an overly vivid imagination. Just before the scene of the "Russian Golgotha," Foma is shown idly lifting the wing of a dead swan. He then imagines himself soaring like a bird over the waterlogged Russian landscape. When this inset sequence ends, the camera shows Foma crouching by a river; as he rises, the camera ascends with him, suggesting that—for the moment at least—we are seeing with Foma's eyes. The focus shifts to Andrei and Theophanes, who conduct their choreographed disputation until the camera comes to rest on the back of Andrei's head and cuts to the shot of the white cloth in flowing water, which begins the "Russian Golgotha." After the Russian Christ is nailed to the cross, we cut back to Foma, who is still rinsing the white paint off his paintbrushes. The white paint flows in the stream as a visual echo of

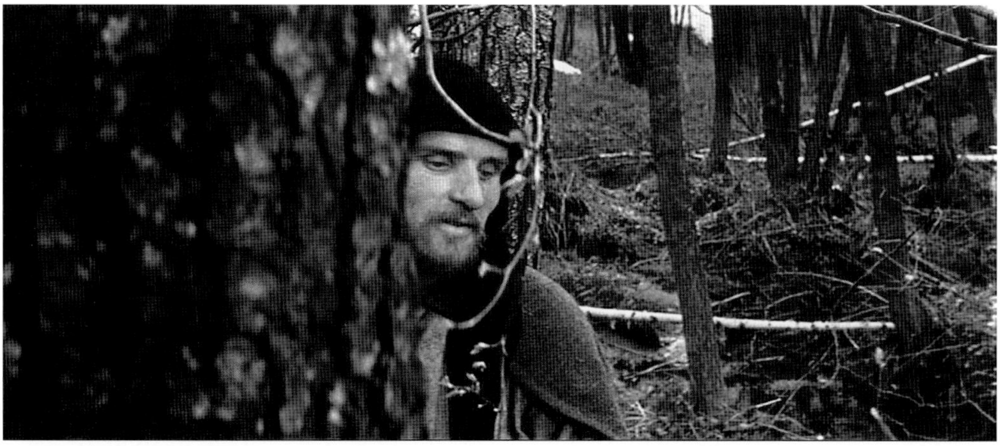

FIG. 22 The titular character in *Andrei Rublev,* dir. Andrei Tarkovsky (1966/1969).

the cloth in the first shot of the crucifixion sequence. The visual echo between this shot and the first shot of the crucifixion scene allows one to read both as representations of the same event seen by Foma, first in his fantasy and then in reality. The dual representation of the event recalls Florensky's discussion of the temporality of the icon. The "real" event Ω elicits a dream event X, which in retrospect the dreamer interprets as the *telos* of a narrative progression A–X; as a result, the actual origin of the dream appears as the conclusion to its narrative.[16] Florensky's nomenclature hints at a Christological model for this narrativization of the singular instant: the crucifixion of Christ (X) is not the culmination but the very beginning, the cause even, of God's history in the world. Returning to the film, the crucifixion that Foma imagines in a momentary flash of inspiration can only be projected as a sequential narrative.[17] The actual moment of seeing is thus divided in two, enfolding the transcendent within an envelope of time. Despite his inspired imagination, Foma's projection is clichéd and melodramatic, lacking the imprint of hard-won experience. Foma's superficial comprehension is confirmed when he quits Rublev's crew in Vladimir. He slams shut the book of icon patterns and walks off to assume a minor commission: "No great honor, but it's something," he says. The cinema can only depict transcendent insight projected as a flat, degraded image in a temporal sequence.

Throughout these unsuccessful approaches to the icon, Andrei remains an observer, increasingly despondent of ever rendering transcendent vision in paint, that is, projecting a spiritual imprint. It seems to him that rendering the divine would cruelly rend the fragile fabric of the human world. Andrei's frustration comes to a head in his conversation with his friend Daniil, whose somewhat naive faith in the iconic canon renders him impervious to Andrei's doubts about the ethics of painting the Last Judgment: "On the left we can paint sinners boiling in tar that will give you goose bumps," Daniil explains as Andrei frets. Their argument is followed by a scene set somewhat earlier, at the charred palace of the Prince of Vladimir. As Andrei cleans an icon of Saint George vanquishing the dragon (pl. 16), the stonemasons leave for a job at the palace of the prince's brother. The prince's henchmen set off in pursuit and blind them, violently and rather gruesomely. This inset scene ends when we see Andrei, back in Vladimir, smearing a dark substance (identified in the screenplay as soot)[18] on the white wall. Vida Johnson and Graham Petrie see the smear as an expression of Rublev's frustrated inactivity, which itself has been caused by the trauma that is revealed in the flashback; his crisis is resolved only by the appearance of the holy fool, who gives him "the confidence to paint a 'happy' Last Judgment."[19] However, Andrei does not actually witness the blinding, as far as we know, and in any case the entire flashback (or fantasy) is shot in a way that makes it surreal. Moreover, assuming the blinding occurred at some point in the past, the smearing of the paint would be quite a delayed reaction. Besides, the frescoes have been finished by the next episode, which takes place that very autumn (Rublev's work with Daniil at Vladimir in 1408 is one of the few reliably documented facts about his life). It is therefore more logical to see Andrei's imagined recollection of the murder of the stonemasons not as the *cause* of his painter's block, but rather as its *cure*. The indescribably horrible event gives Andrei a preview of the Last Judgment (never a "happy" affair) and instructs him how to reshape it as a fresco. The paint smear is admittedly not yet an image, but it is Andrei's first attempt to render his raw horror as visible form. Curiously, when the holy fool looks at it in anguish, the smear has a different shape, suggesting that it appears differently to each pair of eyes. This unlocks for Andrei one of the secrets of his craft: that the transcendent vision, unimaginable to the mind but imprinted indelibly on the soul, can be projected as image that renders it available to individual perception. These projected imprints both link the viewer to transcendent vision and provide a measure of distance from it.

The idea of the icon as an imprint of the transcendent is confirmed by Theophanes the Greek. In life, Theophanes does not seem a model icon painter. He admits to Kirill that he gets bored if he spends too long on an icon. In his riverbank conversation with Andrei, Theophanes is cruel and condescending to his public. Nonetheless, his workmanlike attitude toward icon painting attains unexpected authority when he returns from the dead after the destruction of the cathedral in Vladimir. Theophanes nonchalantly dismisses Andrei's grief over his burnt iconostasis: "Do you know how many iconostases I have had burnt?" he asks. Answering Andrei's question about heaven, he says, "It doesn't look at all as you imagine it." This, it must be stressed, is said to Russia's greatest icon painter, who *saw* the Holy Trinity and other spiritual entities like no one before him. After calling into question the accuracy of Rublev's icon, Theophanes adds, "Still, it's all so beautiful!" Theophanes demotes the icon to an approximation of the truth that imprints transcendent reality as aesthetic beauty. At first, Andrei takes this entire experience as a denial of the word and the image, and he responds by disavowing speech and icon painting. But at this point, *Andrei Rublev* becomes a film about the resurrection of the word and image through Andrei's purgative silence. He must rediscover the burnt word and image as imprints of a spiritual shape without mistaking them for transcendent reality itself.

INCINERATING THE IMAGE

For the character Andrei, the icon's transcendent power would rend the fabric of life unless filtered through the crucible of personal experience. The filmmaker Andrei Tarkovsky faced the opposite dilemma: how to raise the profane art of the cinema to the level of the icon. Tarkovsky achieved this end by discovering the dual nature of the cinematic image, as both projection and imprint. An important role in this was played by *Rublev*'s original narrative form, in which the lack of an authoritative point of view forces the viewer constantly to recalibrate his or her perspective on—and distance from—events on screen.

From the very beginning of the film's development, though he had to present it as a biopic, Tarkovsky described the narrative as a loosely interconnected series of episodes: "The film will consist of several novellas that are not interconnected directly by plot lines. They will be linked by the movement of the idea, which is internally unified. We don't know yet in what order the novellas will be arranged; perhaps chronologically, perhaps not. We would like to offer the episodes in order of their growing dramatic tension according to the degree of their internal significance for our characterization of Andrei Rublev and according to the degree of their importance for the maturation of his plan for the great *Trinity*."[20] Tarkovsky's search for a new narrative form was influenced both by literary models ("novellas," "dramatic tension") and by the portrait icon (specifically Rublev's *Trinity*). The narrative was not supposed merely to bring these genres together in a mechanical fusion, as a story about a picture or a static picture of a story:

> Often films about people of art are constructed according to the following scheme: an event occurs, the hero observes it. Then the viewer sees him think it over, and then he expresses his ideas about the event in his works.
>
> In our film there will not be a single shot of Rublev painting his icons. He will simply live, and he won't even be present onscreen in all episodes. . . .
>
> This plot structure in our film is dictated by its task: to reveal the dialectic of the personality, to study the life of the human spirit. I think that the literary and theatrical principle of organizing the plot material has nothing in common with the specific nature of the cinema. . . . In cinema it is necessary not to explain, but to act upon the viewer's feelings, and the emotion that is awoken is what provokes thought.[21]

The projected image is not the end but the beginning of vision: "For us the story of Rublev is really the story of a 'taught' or imposed concept which burns up in the atmosphere of living reality to arise again from the ashes as a fresh and newly discovered truth."[22] The projected image cancels itself out in its narrative gesture beyond its own limits, to the icon. It brings the viewer to the very edge of meaninglessness and extorts from him or her a decisive act of faith or of dereliction. "The divine painting that appears as the film's finale is presented as the result of Andrei's entire life, which was wholly devoted to gazing at the world, to a contemplative insight into its essence, and a silent grasping of the meaning of each phenomenon from the perspective of the ideal fullness of being. And in relation to this main 'deed' of his life, all his personal affairs, including the technical process of 'completing' artistic images in their material form, appear as relatively insignificant details."[23] The narrative, projected on screen, is revealed as the imprint of an absent original (here the icon), which remains suspended beyond the film and can only be approached through cinematic mediation.

Calling the painter's brush a "seismograph of the unseen," Jean-Luc Marion writes that it "records . . . the cracks of the unseen, such that they disrupt the already visible." In this manner, the painting (like the film *Andrei Rublev*) directs the gaze toward the unseen and establishes the distance that separates the two realities: "Thus it transmits to our gaze its own movement as the imprescriptable condition to be able, precisely, to follow with one's eyes the ascent of the unseen in it to the visible." The icon, by contrast, actually returns the viewer's gaze from beyond the visible painting; the icon looks back. The icon as a visible object is cancelled out by the "visible transit where two gazes cross each other and are exposed to each other." When the viewer's gaze is answered by the icon's gaze, "the visible surface must, paradoxically, efface itself, or at least efface within it every opacity that would obfuscate the crossing of gazes." Marion likens the suspension of the image in the icon to Christ's passion: "The dwelling of the image, which is accomplished in the disfiguration of Christ, delivers the first icon: the veil of Veronica wipes away not a visible image but the kenosis of every figure—the kenosis of the image, 'the condition of a slave' (Phil. 2:7)—and allows the trace of the invisible to appear, which envisages us. . . . It is precisely at the moment that he loses his human appearance [*figure*] that Christ becomes the figure of the divine will."[24] Just as Christ must be disfigured in order for God to appear, so must the image be effaced in order for the icon to appear through it.

Tarkovsky stresses that the narratable and visible history is not merely an incidental feature of the icon as we know it, but the preeminent condition for the icon's appearance in our world at all. The film projects this imprint as narrative spectacle, translating the material trace into temporal categories, which results in a cinema that Tarkovsky calls "imprinted time."

TARKOVSKY AND THE THEOLOGY OF THE ICON

Tarkovsky's resolution of the dichotomy of icon and the art image must be recognized as a major innovation vis-à-vis the tradition of Russian religious philosophy, which here will be represented by Vasily Rozanov and Pavel Florensky. While these two thinkers held substantially different views of aesthetics, I shall argue that both theorized the icon as the suspension of the religious narrative that supports it. Tarkovsky appropriates this resolution but shifts the emphasis squarely onto the interchange between art and icon.

Vasily Rozanov firmly rejected the "dark visage" of the ancient icon in favor of a modern art that opens itself up to worldly life, in particular via technologies of mass reproduction and dissemination. His emphasis was squarely on the side of narrative, which projects the transcendent as narrative spectacle. In his 1908 essay "Religion and Spectacle," Rozanov claims that "the very idea of the church service is to *imprint* before the people and repeat before it visually, in character, that main event which occurred 1900 years ago and which still nourishes the people religiously." Therefore, according to Rozanov, "Theater and the essence of theater do not at all contradict the essence of sacred history because the theater even arose precisely for the presentation in character and images of nothing other than sacred stories, 'mysteria.'"[25] To illustrate his point, Rozanov recalls a "panorama" of painted panels illustrating Christ's crucifixion, which was on display in St. Petersburg: "A panorama is a commercial matter, a secular matter; the topics of panoramas are all secular; but here we find an ecclesiastical topic, and everyone ran to see it in a great crowd, and priests visiting from the provinces first of all rush to see 'Golgotha' as 'something of their own,' as their 'native' picture, and as an object in the field of their discourse [*slovo*] and activity. Everyone views it as an illustration, auxiliary to a book, a spectacle that might have a more powerful effect than an abstract book."[26] Rozanov's emphasis lies squarely on the pedagogical value of religious representations. For him the problem is not the importation of religion into the popular culture, but religion's exile from the culture of the populace. Accordingly, he advocates the maximal spread of religious spectacles: "Isn't this why the *Savior* descended to earth, in order to *mix* with the earth and with the earthly, and *through this mixing* to heal and save everything of the earth, and the earth itself?"[27]

From this standpoint, Rozanov makes a hard distinction between art and the icon. In a short essay on the Cathedral of Saint Vladimir in Kiev, Rozanov criticizes Viktor Vasnetsov's romanticized icons: "*I can go to a museum to admire painting;* but I go *to church* for divine instruction, for an ideal, *for a path of life, for a model.*"[28] Similarly, Rozanov insists that "[Mikhail] Nesterov is not iconic. It is not his task to paint 'God,' only 'how man comes to God.'" Despite the stridency of his argument, Rozanov famously remained "by the church walls," and his interest remained wholly with the question of "how man comes to God." Thus he defines the icon only negatively, by its invisibility as art:

> I shall finish speaking about "iconicity." . . . In its very tasks and essence, it is something "canonic" and "immobile," that to which anyone's prayer—of everyone, of the nation, in whatever condition, *can* and *should* be addressed "without obstacle." . . . I say "without obstacle" and this is the whole thing. There should not be any individual traits here, no incompatibility between venerator and venerated: and *everyone* venerates, the nation. . . . The icon is an "epic" being, it "stands in the corner" and is "looked up" at. The need for generality and opacity in the icon is so evident that the best "icons" are the darkened old images where you can't see the features of the "visage," they are outlined and only slightly visible: and

even that is concealed, hardly visible, in the hole for the "face" in the gold or silver "robe" [*riza*]. . . . God should be *invisible,* and He is of course *invisible:* but if history and custom and regulation have made him "visible," then "a bit less so, please," and best of all if "you can't make anything out."[29]

Rozanov accepts only invisible icons, but he insists that they should be recognizable to those who already know what they represent. Icons require faith, but they do not evoke it. Rozanov finds this limitation typical of Orthodoxy, which rewards hope but has expelled anything that inspires it, including "music" and "color." Although critical of the icons they painted for display within churches, Rozanov admires Nesterov and Vasnetsov for bringing people back to the church by issuing a loud call: "To heaven! To heaven! Everyone has turned to heaven."[30]

At the opposite extreme to Rozanov is Pavel Florensky, who considered the icon a mimetic depiction of the transcendent realm, a medium of divine grace, and a paradigm for all creative activity. Accordingly, Florensky stressed the antithesis between icon and narrative. Florensky calls the "plot" (*siuzhet*) "a superficial . . . element of construction." He identifies the icon's "plot" (*siuzhet*) with its "name" (*naimenovanie*), a single word that tells the entire story immediately, through the spatial composition of the work. He is predictably hostile toward narrative paintings such as Nesterov's *The Soul of the Nation* (1914–16), which shows a procession of Orthodox saints and Russian cultural notables following a young boy. In his hierarchy of genres, the portrait icon reigns supreme precisely because it expresses the entirety of its subject's temporal existence in what Florensky calls "deep" or "dense" time. Next is the artistic portrait, which captures a multitude of impressions of a face, filtered through an artist's creative vision and crystallized in what Florensky calls a "form in time."[31]

However, Florensky is obliged to incorporate narrative into a more nuanced account of the icon and its effect on the viewer. While he largely ignores festal and other narrative icons, Florensky does consider the type of portrait icon where the saint is framed by "scenes" from his life. This, for Florensky, unites the singularity of the noumenal image with its "unfolding" or "elucidation" in time.[32] The effect of the icon "with scenes" is analogous to the way a well-made book imparts unity to its disparate contents: "The pages that pass sequentially before the reader should with their very look [*vid*], with the look of their arrangement [*postroenie*], facilitate the sequentially unfolding but inwardly interconnected unity of the work [*sviaznoe edinstvo proizvedeniia*]." Florensky cites as an example the famed illuminated manuscript of Epiphanius's *Life of Saint Sergius* (the source of unique iconographic material about Andrei Rublev). This manuscript "has an illustrative miniature on every page" of its "musical composition," which in its totality communicates "a *single* depiction of the life of Saint Sergius, integral and united, expressing the heartbeat of time." The book requires and facilitates an active kind of attention that allows the viewer to "overcome" narrative time from within, by uniting its disparate sequence into a single composite image.[33]

Still, one might not expect Florensky to engage positively with film given his hostility to modern technologies of image creation and reproduction. Florensky critiques engraved images for reducing reality to a mere outline and for their indifference to the material on which they are imprinted. As a "mechanically reproducible work," the engraving "is a schema of the image, constructed on the sole basis of the laws of logic . . . deprived of both spiritual and sensuous givenness."[34] It is, in sum, less imprint than projection. The lowest form of representation is the photograph, which might imprint reality but "only in a random and dislocated fashion."[35] The photograph is pure naturalism and, therefore, in Florensky's parlance, "pure abstraction," since "the moment is torn from its process and taken by itself, without past or future."[36] In contrast to technologies of engraving and photography, the icon imprints a total image, free of the arbitrary effects of projection and abstraction.

Nonetheless, Florensky's incorporation of narrative temporality into his reading of the iconic image leads him directly to a consideration of film. Notwithstanding his argument concerning the superficial naturalism and illusionism of the photographic plate, he writes, "The cinematic method *as such* does not necessarily lead to the naturalistic obtrusiveness of an illusionary imitation of reality and may, in certain conditions, require the greatest spiritual effort, and the unity it communicates may be contemplated by an intelligent gaze [*vzor umnyi*], and not a sensual one."[37] For Florensky, the result of this composite image, synthesized by the "intelligent gaze" of the spectator, is still predetermined by the "original," that is, the spiritual reality that is depicted mimetically in the symbolic image. However, it is possible to extract from Florensky's argument the point that the narrative artwork performs the crucial task of projecting an imprint of spiritual reality and thus structuring the "spiritual gaze" toward its transcendent original, suspended beyond the image.

THE SUSPENDED IMAGE

In the course of this chapter, I have repeatedly been led to the idea of suspension, which is inspired by images of suspension that dominate the opening and closing scenes of Tarkovsky's *Andrei Rublev.* These scenes are commonly interpreted as allegories for Andrei's creative ordeal, but I would like to suggest that they also provide a key to understanding the peculiar suspension of the icon above Tarkovsky's narrative and beyond his images.

The film opens with a shot of a crude hot-air balloon being inflated above a fire. Soon there arrives on the scene the peasant Efim, with an angry mob in hot pursuit. After clambering up the bell tower, Efim launches the balloon and succeeds in traveling some distance before coming to a crash landing, dramatized in a freeze frame. This scene is literally packed with cultural allusions that ground it in the narrative of Russian history,[38] but Tarkovsky brings the historical legend back to earth, dwelling less on the iconic achievement than on its concrete experience in lived time. The physical immediacy of the representation forces the viewer not only to share the experience but also to recalibrate it vis-à-vis its reflections in other temporalities, such as those of national history and legend.

Tarkovsky instills the legend with suspense, but then suspends the culminating event as a frozen image, as if to remind the viewer that his or her own position as spectator is just as precarious as Efim's.

A similar pattern is observable in the final episode in Tarkovsky's narrative, "The Bell." Here Rublev is once again a mere bystander as the young Boriska bluffs his way into directing the construction of a huge bell, which is demonstrated triumphantly before an audience that includes chattering Italian dignitaries. The bell itself is fabricated from a mold that Boriska hardly touches, except to smash it. Its tolling is an aural icon, repeated identically each time the bell is rung. Here again, the crude machinery that is used to suspend the bell in the air can be taken as a clear analogy for Tarkovsky's camera, but in this case suspension is achieved, and it is as if the entire cosmos rings out in celebration. This new suspension is only a triumph because of the long, frustrated anticipation of a resolution to the creative ambitions that fill the movie; the icon of Saint George, which was desecrated by the grand prince's murder of the stonemasons, is redeemed by being embossed on the raised bell (fig. 23). This restoration of the image is rendered even more significant in that it takes place on the same hill as the "Russian Golgotha," at the symbolic center of the world. However, just at the moment of triumph, the narrative effaces itself to reveal Rublev's icons, which outshine even Boriska's bell. Tarkovsky's film cancels itself out in the face of the icons whose story it tells. So, Tarkovsky suggests, does the icon efface itself to render the invisible.

Suspension has been conceptualized in the most detail by Roland Barthes and Giorgio Agamben. In his brutal analysis of Balzac's story "Sarrasine," Barthes speaks of the way the overt narrative of the text, propelled forward in a linear fashion by its enigmas, gradually brings itself to a thoughtful halt before unspeakable truths. This halting makes audible the inverted voice of the text: "What sings, what flows smoothly, what moves by accidentals, arabesques, and controlled ritardandos

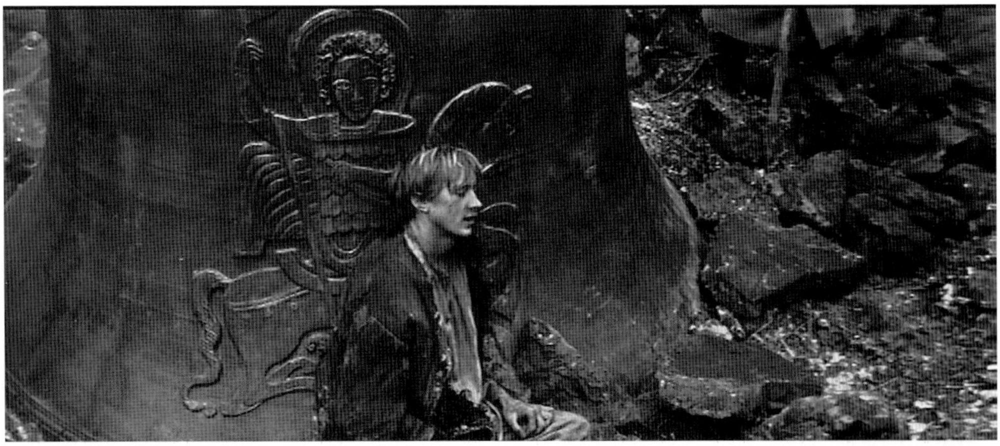

FIG. 23 Boriska's bell in *Andrei Rublev*, dir. Andrei Tarkovsky (1966/1969).

through an intelligible progression (like the melody often given the woodwinds) is the series of enigmas, their suspended disclosure, their delayed resolution."[39] When this voice becomes dominant, the narrative gradually forms itself into a suspended, "pensive" text:

> Just as the pensiveness of a face signals that this head is heavy with unspoken language, so the (classic) text inscribes within its system of signs the signature of its plenitude: like the face, the text becomes *expressive* (let us say that it signifies its expressivity), endowed with an interiority whose supposed depth compensates for the parsimony of its plural. At its discreet urging, we want to ask the classic text: *What are you thinking about?* but the text, wilier than all those who try to escape by answering: *about nothing,* does not reply, giving meaning its last closure: suspension.[40]

Barthes sees the suspension of the narrative as a closure of meaning, but Tarkovsky creates a very similar effect in order to investigate the profound openness of meaning within reality, specifically within lived time.

The existential openness of aesthetic suspension has recently been extended by Giorgio Agamben. Agamben begins with Martin Heidegger's analysis of "profound boredom," which breaks down into two structural moments: being-left-empty (*Leergelassenheit*) and being-held-in-suspense (*Hingehaltenheit*). Being-left-empty results in a superficial captivation (*Benommenheit*) with inert reality; this is a state of distraction. By contrast, being-held-in-suspense is a "deactivation of the concrete possibilities" that "makes manifest for the first time what generally *makes* pure possibility *possible* (*das Ermöglichende*)—or, as Heidegger says, 'the originary *possibilization* [*die ursprüngliche* Ermöglichung].'"[41] Simply put, this state of suspended animation renders visible what it means to be animated, or to have a soul. In addition, it engenders a state of attention that is no longer distracted captivation, but rather is the absorption of total concentration (*Eingenommenheit*). Elsewhere, Agamben has applied this idea of suspension to the way that art establishes a tradition that places man before eternity: "By transforming the principle of man's delay before truth into a poetic process and renouncing the guarantees of truth for love of transmissibility, art succeeds once again in transforming man's inability to exit his historical status, perennially suspended in the inter-world between old and new, past and future, into the very space in which he can take the original measure of his dwelling in the present and recover each time the meaning of his action."[42] The drama in Tarkovsky is not Andrei's creation of an icon, but the viewer's own learning to see the imprint of the transcendent in projected images, and to feel the eternal moment within time. Thus Tarkovsky's interest is not to impose an interpretation on the icon, but to restore the very possibility of the icon as an eternal image open onto time.

CONCLUSION

In Arthur Conan Doyle's story "The Adventure of the Six Napoleons," Sherlock Holmes is confronted by an unusual crime:

someone is amok in London smashing busts of the late Napoleon Bonaparte. It sounds like mania, but, as Inspector Lestrade comments, "When the man commits burglary in order to break images which are not his own, that brings it away from the doctor and on to the policeman." Lestrade begins with the question of identity, both that of the busts' prototype and that of the culprit of their destruction, whom he tries to trace by various signs left at the crime scenes. When a man is found murdered alongside another decimated bust of Napoleon, Lestrade identifies him by following up on the "Catholic emblem round his neck." The dead man was also bearing a snapshot, probably of the murderer: "Probably the photograph we found in his pocket *is* the man himself," Lestrade concludes, thereby anticipating Florensky's theology of the icon with an assertion of identity between person and image. In accordance with this logic, Lestrade interprets Holmes's interest in the busts themselves as objects as a misguided fascination with Napoleon, the prototype of the images. However, Holmes rejects out of hand the idea of a "promiscuous iconoclast" guided by "a general hatred of Napoleon"; instead, he seeks the solution to the mystery in the images' mode of production. Holmes confides in Watson, "I am . . . endeavouring to trace these busts to their source, in order to find out if there is not something peculiar which may account for their remarkable fate."[43] Holmes eventually arrives at the truth: the culprit has secreted the "black pearl of the Borgias" in one of the identical busts and is now obliged to break them all open to discover the real treasure, which lies not in the prototype or in the beholder's attitude toward it, but within the image itself.

Tarkovsky follows Holmes's methods. Cast adrift amid a sea of images, the viewer espies the distinctive copy (the icon or, more specifically, Rublev's icons), but in order to understand what makes it distinctive, we must burn it up in the crucible of experience, letting it tell us its story. The key difference between Holmes's and Tarkovsky's iconoclasm arises at the end of their respective quests. When the last remaining bust is brought to 221B Baker Street, Holmes acts decisively: "He picked up his hunting crop and struck Napoleon a sharp blow on the top of the head. The figure broke into fragments, and Holmes bent eagerly over the shattered remains," from which the black pearl is plucked (fig. 24). Watson and Lestrade promptly applaud "as at the well-wrought crisis of a play"; Holmes takes a bow, "like the master dramatist who receives the homage of his audience."[44] Like Holmes, Tarkovsky weaves narrative drama out of the exceptional image, leading up to a cathartic revelation of the secret. Like the bust of Napoleon, Boriska's cast is smashed to extract the treasure within. But in this case, the secret treasure *is* the icon, which emerges from within the historical conflagration of images. Tarkovsky's achievement was to uncover the tension that allows the icon to remain a distinctive, holy image even while it is proliferated in copies and reproductions, including even icons imprinted on celluloid.

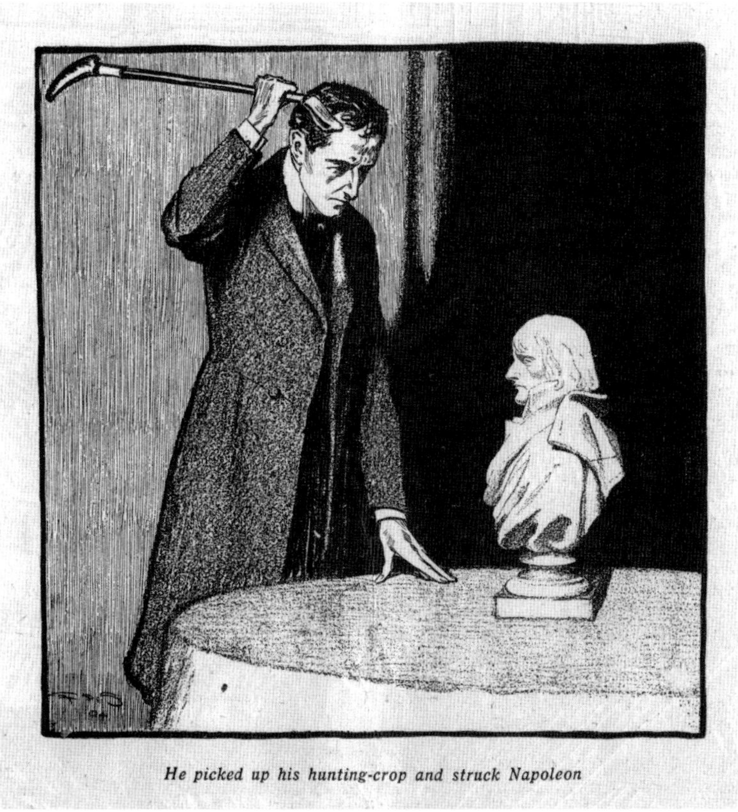

FIG. 24 Frederick Dorr Steele, illustration in Arthur Conan Doyle, "The Adventure of the Six Napoleons," *Colliers Illustrated Magazine,* 30 April 1904, 15.

NOTES TO CHAPTER 11

1. Mark Le Fanu, *The Cinema of Andrei Tarkovsky* (London: British Film Institute, 1987), 52. See also Angela Dalle Vacche, "Andrei Tarkovsky's *Andrei Rublev:* Cinema as the Restoration of Icon Painting," in *Cinema and Painting: How Art Is Used in Film* (London: Athlone, 1996), 135–60.

2. M. V. Voloshin, "Chemu uchat ikony?" in *Liki tvorchestva,* ed. V. M. Manuilov, V. P. Kupchenko, and A. V. Lavrov (Leningrad: Nauka, 1988), 291–95:292. See also Oleg Tarasov, *Icon and Devotion: Sacred Spaces in Imperial Russia,* ed. and trans. Robin Milner-Gulland (London: Reaktion Books, 2002), 369–77; Verena Krieger, *Von der Ikone zur Utopie: Kunstkonzepte der russischen Avantgarde* (Cologne: Böhlau Verlag, 1998), 67–86.

3. O. Iu. Tarasov, *Ikona i blagochestie: ocherki ikonnogo dela v imperatorskoi Rossii* (Moscow: Progress-Kul'tura, 1995), 77. See also G. I. Vzdornov, *Istoriia otkrytiia i izucheniia russkoi srednevekovoi zhivopisi. XIX vek* (Moscow: Iskusstvo, 1986), 49–50, 76, 286.

4. F. I. Buslaev, "Obshchie poniatiia o russkoi ikonopisi," *Drevnerusskaia literatura i pravoslavnoe iskusstvo* (St. Petersburg: Izdatel'stvo Russkogo Khristianskogo gumanitarnogo instituta, "Liga-Plius," 2001), 36–186: 42, 55–57, passim.

5. Buslaev, "Obshchie poniatiia o russkoi ikonopisi," 56.

6. See especially Pavel Florensky, *The Trinity–St. Sergius Lavra and Russia,* trans. Robert Bird (New Haven: Variable Press, 1995); Pavel Florensky, *Iconostasis,* trans. Donald Sheehan and Olga Andrejev (Crestwood, N.Y.: St. Vladimir's Seminary Press, 1996), 66–84.

7. Tarkovsky freely borrowed elements from Vladimir Pribytkov's rabidly anticlerical "biography" of Rublev, including much of the episode "The Last Judgment" and the character of Patrikei. See V. Pribytkov, *Andrei Rublev* (Moscow: Molodaia gvardiia, 1960), 103, 141–55.

8. V. N. Lazarev, *Andrei Rublev i ego shkola* (Moscow: Iskusstvo, 1966), 77.

9. See Tarasov, *Icon and Devotion,* 345–51.

10. Nicholas Wolterstorff, "Would You Stomp on a Picture of Your Mother? Would You Kiss an Icon?" Unpublished manuscript. It is notable that the most strident opposition to the mechanical reproduction of icons has been motivated by aesthetic, not religious, considerations. See especially N. P. Kondakov, *Sovremennoe polozhenie russkoi narodnoi ikonopisi* ([St. Petersburg]: Tipografiia I. N. Skorokhodova, 1901); Viktor Vasnetsov, "Bozhestvennyi smysl ikon," in *Pravoslavnaia ikona: kanon i stil'. K bogoslovskomu rassmotreniiu obraza,* ed. Aleksandr Strizhev (Moscow: Palomnik, 1998), 121–43. For more on this topic, see Robert Bird, "The Imprinted Image," in *Tarkovsky,* ed. Nathan Dunne (London: Black Dog, 2008), 206–29.

11. Andrei Tarkovskii, "Slovo ob Apokalipsise," *Iskusstvo kino* 2 (1989): 95–100: 97.

12. Vasnetsov, "Bozhestvennyi smysl ikon," 141.

13. See Yuri Tsivian, *Early Cinema in Russia and Its Cultural Reception,* trans. Alan Bodger, foreword by Tom Gunning, ed. Richard Taylor (London: Routledge, 1994); Tsivian, "Censure Bans on Religious Subjects in Russian Films," in *Une invention du Diable? Cinéma des premiers temps et religion,* ed. Roland Cosandey, André Gaudreault, and Tom Gunning (Sainte-Foy: Presses de l'Université Laval, Éditions Payot Lausanne, 1992), 71–80.

14. A classic statement of this policy was Lev Trotsky's essay "Vodka, the Church, and the Cinema," *Pravda,* 12 July 1923.

15. The quotation attributed to Epiphanius (but actually occurring only in later versions of Epiphanius's *Life of Saint Sergius*) can be found in "Zhitie Sergiia Radonezhskogo," in *Pamiatniki literatury drevnei Rusi: XIV-seredina XV veka* (Moscow: Khudozhestvennaia literatura, 1981), 290.

16. See Florensky, *Iconostasis,* 33–44. For more on Florensky's theory of dreams, see John Anthony McGuckin's chapter in this volume.

17. On another scene in *Andrei Rublev* with similar temporality, see Igor' Evlampiev, *Khudozhestvennaia filosofiia Andreia Tarkovskogo* (St. Petersburg: Aleteiia, 1991), 95–96.

18. Andrei Tarkovsky, *Andrei Rublev,* trans. Kitty Hunter-Blair, intro. Philip Strick (London: Faber & Faber, 1991), 108.

19. Vida T. Johnson and Graham Petrie, *The Films of Andrei Tarkovsky: A Visual Fugue* (Bloomington: Indiana University Press, 1994), 270.

20. Andrei Tarkovskii, "Iskat' i dobivat'sia," *Sovetskii ekran* 17 (1962): 9, 20.

21. Ibid., 9.

22. Andrei Tarkovsky, *Sculpting in Time,* trans. Kitty Hunter-Blair (Austin: University of Texas Press, 1984), 89.

23. Evlampiev, *Khudozhestvennaia filosofiia Andreia Tarkovskogo,* 67.

24. Jean-Luc Marion, *The Crossing of the Visible,* trans. James K. A. Smith (Stanford: Stanford University Press, 2004), 36, 43, 60, 61–62.

25. V. V. Rozanov, *Sredi khudozhnikov* (Moscow: Respublika, 1994), 271, 274. The passages quoted from "Religiia i zrelishcha" were unchanged from the original publication of the essay in 1908; for a reprinting of the original version and discussion, see Pavel Rudnev, *Teatral'nye vzgliady Vasiliia Rozanova* (Moscow: Agraf, 2003), 129–34, 291–302.

26. Ibid., 275; see 408.

27. Ibid., 273.

28. Ibid., 186. Rozanov's italics.

29. Ibid., 254, 256. Rozanov's italics.

30. Ibid., 258.

31. P. A. Florenskii, *Stat'i i issledovaniia po istorii i filosofii iskusstva i arkheologii,* ed. Igumen Andronik (Trubachev) (Moscow: Mysl', 2000), 150, 214, 231–32, 233, 235, 239, 244.

32. On the origin and development of such icons, see Tarasov, *Icon and Devotion,* 75–77.

33. Florenskii, *Stat'i i issledovaniia,* 213, 224, 226. Florensky's italics.

34. Florenskii, *Ikonostas,* 104–5, 101.

35. Florensky, *The Trinity–St. Sergius Lavra and Russia,* 4.

36. Florenskii, *Stat'i i issledovaniia,* 234.

37. Ibid., 223; Florensky's italics.

38. On the cultural context of Efim's flight, see Robert Bird, *Andrei Rublev* (London: British Film Institute, 2004), 18–22.

39. Roland Barthes, *S/Z: An Essay,* trans. Richard Miller (New York: Hill & Wang, 1974), 29.

40. Ibid., 217; see also Jacques Derrida, *Acts of Literature,* ed. Derek Attridge (London: Routledge, 1992), 47–50.

41. Giorgio Agamben, *The Open: Man and Animal,* trans. Kevin Attell (Stanford: Stanford University Press, 2004), 66. Agamben is referring to the book by Martin Heidegger, *The Fundamental Concepts of Metaphysics: World, Finitude, Solitude,* trans. William McNeill and Nicholas Walker (Bloomington: Indiana University Press, 1995).

42. Giorgio Agamben, *The Man Without Content,* trans. Georgia Albert (Stanford: Stanford University Press, 1999), 114.

43. Arthur Conan Doyle, "The Adventure of the Six Napoleons," in *The Return of Sherlock Holmes,* ed. Richard Lancelyn Green (Oxford: Oxford University Press, 1993), 176–98, 17–77, 185, 189.

44. Ibid., 195.

VERA SHEVZOV

AFTERWORD

As the chapters in this volume have so vividly shown, far from being relegated to the annals of antiquity or marginalized as a symbolically repressive ecclesiastical trapping, the icon in Russia found new life in modern times. Although remaining a dynamic phenomenon within its "natural habitat"—the environs of church and prayer—the icon emerged as a valued commodity in the global world of art historians, artists, and commercial entrepreneurs. Debased, destroyed, or driven underground in the Soviet period, the icon nevertheless remained a prominent fixture in the native worlds of ethnographers, museum curators, and Russian statesmen as well as a charged symbol that hovered just beneath the surface of official art and Communist propaganda. The millennial celebration of the Baptism of Rus in 1988 and subsequent fall of Communism helped to pull the icon "from under the rubble" back into the public sphere of Russian life. No longer shackled by Communist political correctness, Russia's citizens, believers and nonbelievers alike, have once again rediscovered and reclaimed the icon and have done so (and continue to do so) in often daring and dramatic ways. Yet, when viewed against the backdrop of this volume, many of the most salient contemporary challenges posed by and to the icon in contemporary Russia pick up familiar thematic strands from the nineteenth and early twentieth centuries.

As the chapters by Robert Nichols and Elena Boeck have illustrated, icons played a crucial role in sacralizing historical memory and undergirding the notion of the chosenness of the Russian nation. Drawing on a deep tradition shared by church and state of associating icons with major political events in Russia's history, tsar and people alike often embraced the icon as national monuments with a complex mix of piety and patriotism. A famous case in point at the end of the ancien régime involved an icon found by Evdokiya Andrianova, a peasant woman from the Kolomensk region outside Moscow, on 2 March 1917, the day of Tsar Nicholas II's abdication. Within days, believers, first locally, then nationally, interpreted Evdokiya's discovery as a collective sign: in the absence of a tsar, Mary, the Mother of God, had assumed the sovereignty of Russia. Portraying a seated empress with a scepter and orb in her hands and the Christ Child on her lap, the icon She Who Reigns (*Derzhavnaia*) joined a wide array of prerevolutionary Marian images that affirmed Russia's special status among the nations. Icons in this context provided a reassuring continuity with the past and stood as symbols of hope and resistance in the face of wrenching change.

The icon She Who Reigns has re-emerged in a contemporary mythmaking that links post-Soviet Russia with the political glories and cultural lure of its imperial past. In 2007, this icon was featured in an ambitious, highly publicized yearlong procession to celebrate the reconciliation among Russians whose histories had been severed by the 1917 Revolution and subsequent civil war. Organized by the Orthodox Church and endorsed by President Vladimir Putin, the procession had unity as its guiding theme—the unity of Russians at home with those abroad as well as the unity of the peoples of the CIS.[1] It was a sociopolitical march as much as a religious pilgrimage, with thousands joining and departing, and often rejoining again. The procession began in eight different regions in May—Vladivostok, Yakutsk, Barnaul, Rostov-on-Don, Arkhangelsk, St. Petersburg, Jerusalem, and Mount Athos in Greece—and eventually converged in Moscow a year later. Each procession was led by an image of the icon She Who Reigns.

Attempts to capitalize on the icon's unifying power are widespread in contemporary Russia. Commenting on a 2008 exhibit at the Tretiakov Gallery in Moscow titled "The Orthodox Icon: Russia, Ukraine, Belarus," Sergei Kroletvets, director of the National Kyiv-Pechersk Historical Cultural Preserve, noted that "icons are an entire world that unite our peoples. For centuries, the icon was a consolidating principle."[2] Given such sentiments, it is little wonder that Russia's newest state holiday, the Day of National Unity on 4 November, falls on the date of the celebration of one of Russia's most famous icons—the Kazan Mother of God. Signed into law by Vladimir Putin in 2005, the new holiday, a direct response to the tragic events in Beslan in September 2004, commemorates Russia's victorious emergence from the Time of Troubles at the end of the sixteenth and beginning of the seventeenth century. Recalling an event from Russia's deep prerevolutionary past, the holiday is meant to reinvigorate historical memory among the peoples of the CIS, "to fill a gap in [that] memory."[3] Aiming to delineate a latent "national ideal," the rhetoric surrounding the Day of National Unity calls on "civil solidarity," "civic responsibility," and "civil society" in the face of foreign threat.[4] Once again, an icon, by virtue of its centuries-long association with pivotal events in Russia's past, has become involved in the discourse and rituals of post-Soviet Russian state building.[5]

Although the icon in post-Soviet Russia has proved to have tremendous ability to unify and consolidate people, hopes, and identities, it has also revealed its potential to arouse sharp discord. The iconic underpinnings of the Day of National Unity, for instance, prompted almost immediate dissent. Journalists quickly pointed to the "camouflaged" nature of the new holiday and questioned the propriety of having it so closely linked with a prominent Orthodox and imperial symbol.[6] Others, including the head of the Russian Union of Evangelical Christian Baptists and the Communist Party leader, have openly called the Day of National Unity a provocation that would lead only to divisions.[7] Tatar nationalists have referred to the Kazan icon as "a symbol of the colonial yoke."[8]

While the relationship between the icon and Russian national identity continues to be publicly negotiated on various fronts, the incident points to the complex and often sensitive position of the icon in contemporary Russia. The ideological vacuum left by the demise of the Soviet Union has resulted in an environment of heightened cultural competition in which no one group can claim "to own" the icon. Since the time of its decoupling from the church in late imperial Russia, the icon has become a globally recognized art form that can be altered, adapted, and appreciated by many different audiences. As a result of competing claims to its ownership and interpretation, the icon can often be found at the forefront of post-Soviet culture wars.[9]

The infamous exhibit "Caution! Religion" was a recent example of such a battleground. Consisting of approximately forty-five works by contemporary artists from Russia, the United States, Europe, Japan, and Cuba, the 2004 show at Moscow's Sakharov Museum ignited heated public debates comparable to those stirred in America by Andres Serrano's *Piss Christ* in 1989 and by Chris Ofili's *Holy Virgin Mary* in the "Sensation" exhibit at the Brooklyn Museum in 1999.[10] Installations such as an image of Christ on a Coca-Cola billboard with the message "This is my blood," as well as a life-size icon into which the viewer could insert his own face, demonstrated that disputes over the relationship and differences between art and icon continue to be a source of contention.

The icon in post-Soviet Russia—no less than art in the United States—has become a part of the broader contemporary discourse concerning civil liberties. Supporters of the short-lived "Caution! Religion" show included such human rights activists as Elena Bonner, physicist Lev Ponomarev, Orthodox dissident Gleb Yakunin, and Sergei Kovalev, a founding member of the Moscow chapter of Amnesty International. They defended the exhibit's participants as "critical, prophetic voices against abuses of power."[11] One artist compared the exhibit's participants to John Huss, Lev Tolstoy, and the archpriest Avvakum; they, too, were social critics warning of the dangers of religion and religious institutions.[12] The icon, in this context, tested the boundaries of perception. Accordingly, the poster for the exhibit depicted an *oklad* or ornate metal covering under which precious icons were often kept. The show, maintained one of its organizers, addressed whatever was placed under this cover; it challenged believers and nonbelievers alike to distinguish form from content.[13] In pseudoreligious hands, icons, others contended, became a form of "spiritual terrorism" that had little to do with God.[14] The museum's director, Yury Samodurov, who was eventually charged by a Moscow court with inciting religious and ethnic hatred by allowing the exhibit, insisted that the artists rightfully protested a false religious consciousness that they believed was being instilled in citizens in post-Soviet Russia.[15]

The exhibit also had its equally passionate detractors. They felt repulsed by what in their eyes was little more than hackneyed iconoclasm and blasphemy publicly displayed under the canopy of a human rights center. A group of intellectuals that included such well-known figures as filmmaker Nikita Mikhalkov, mathematician Igor Shafareevich, and writer Vasily Belov referred to the exhibit as a new level of "conscious Satanism."[16] The Moscow Patriarchate of the Russian Orthodox Church issued a statement protesting the exhibit and the stereotypes of Orthodoxy that it believed it fostered. In part, church officials were disturbed by the artistic use of icons to advance an essentially political and social agenda. Artistic license that condoned "playing with the holy," in their estimation, posed potential harm to the human soul.[17]

The clamor over the show "Caution! Religion" and a similar exhibit, "Forbidden Art—2006," reflected at least two other issues relevant to the icon in post-Soviet Russia: the conflict between contemporary art and religion and the relationship between the icon and the museum. Before the revolution, artists and iconographers—not to mention futurist poets, as Sarah Pratt's chapter has shown—were engaged in a complex interplay when it came to depicting Christian themes. The icon did not lose its power to influence; the sensibilities that informed even Russia's avant-garde art in the early twentieth century were profoundly spiritual. Many figures in the movement were inspired by the brilliance of ancient Orthodox iconography, including its colors, poetics, and metaphysics.[18] In the years following the revolution, however, the purpose of official art was to overthrow, not to engage, "the old" in the hope of constructing a new reality. The official atheism of the Soviet state left no room for academic artists to experiment openly with the development of a religious art based on Orthodox ideas. Consequently, overt interaction between academic artists and iconographers ceased following the Bolshevik Revolution. Public exhibits of art that explored explicitly religious subjects only began to appear, and then only sporadically, in the 1980s. As a result, religious art in Russia even today remains defined almost exclusively by the icon. Many young artists remain skeptical and cautious when it comes to religious themes that fall outside the frame of Orthodox culture.[19]

The exhibit "Caution! Religion" also spurred debate about museums, the sacred and the profane, and the limits of art. As John-Paul Himka and Shirley Glade have shown, museums played a tremendous role in preserving the icon—as both folk art and masterpieces—in the late imperial and Soviet periods. The icon's modern transformation into "art" prolonged the life of numerous icons that might otherwise have been destroyed, either through decay or iconoclastic zeal, during the Soviet period. Yet the politics of restoration and preservation, even in the early decades of the twentieth century, was fraught with tensions. Today, tensions have flared once again over competing definitions of art and the sacred and the use and misuse of the icon.

From a traditional Orthodox perspective, the icon's proper place—its "home"—is the sacred space of a church, chapel, or devotional icon corner. Yet from a broader cultural perspective, as a "monument of early Russian painting," an icon's appropriate viewing place might also be a museum, on display for the aesthetic appreciation of everyone. Curators and museum employees often approach their work in their own spiritual terms. For both Orthodox faithful and museum curators, the conditions of an icon's display are of utmost importance because the icon's life is at stake. Curators worry about climate and lighting; clergy about liturgy and prayer. Precisely what signals life for an icon from the Orthodox perspective—candles, incense—can eventually spell death for an ancient work of art. Caught between museums and churches, ancient icons in post-Soviet Russia often end up involved in a tug-of-war between competing notions of ownership and belonging.[20]

Recently, clergymen and curators from the Tretiakov Gallery found a mutually satisfactory solution regarding the Vladimir Mother of God icon (pl. 1). Sensitive to its fragility, the gallery's curators became understandably concerned when, in 1993, President Boris Yeltsin issued a directive allowing the Vladimir icon to be used in liturgical services. After one such outing, the icon was returned damaged. In response, the director of the Tretiakov's division of Old Russian art insisted, "The icon has protected us for many centuries; now it is our turn to protect it. It has already put in its time and there is almost nothing left of the painting." The eventual compromise was a "museum-church" located on museum grounds. In addition to an active liturgical space in which the icon can thrive, the building also boasts a controlled climate and a special case for the icon that preserves it from harmful smoke and incense.[21]

Whether located in churches or museums, icons pose a visual challenge to those who gaze upon them no less now than in prerevolutionary Russia. The sheer variety in style and technique prompts a reconsideration of the now-classic narrative of the history of the Russian icon. The standard history situates the icon's developmental high point in the fifteenth century and then traces a gradual decline that accelerates with the influence of Western art from the seventeenth century onward. This narrative raises the question of the relationship between style, perceived quality, and iconic "authenticity." What visually distinguishes an icon from art or a painting that depicts scenes or persons from the history of Orthodox Christianity? In her work on Russian icons in the twentieth century, the art historian Irina Yazykova maintains that the answer to this question today remains murkier than ever. As a case in point, she examines the images in Moscow's recently rebuilt Cathedral of Christ the Savior. The iconographic style of most of its images, she maintains, does not in fact correspond to what most Orthodox traditionalists would deem authentic. In her estimation, its wide array of styles might best be categorized as "ecclesial postmodernism."[22]

One of Russia's most well-known and respected iconographers, Archimandrite Zinon (Theodor), has been less diplomatic in his evaluation of the disparate images that pass for icons in contemporary Russia. Iconographic style and iconicity, in his view, are related. Citing Patriarch Alexis I's (d. 1970) antipathy toward artificial flowers in churches, Zinon argues that poorly executed icons are no less "false"; thus many of those sold in local kiosks "do not have the right to exist."[23] Despite attempts to reestablish the canons of Orthodox iconography through the founding of iconographic divisions in theological schools and the cultivation of the iconographic vocation in monasteries, Orthodox churches in contemporary Russia present the believer with a remarkable assortment of styles and a wide range of quality. And assortment often necessitates assessment. Are all icons equally iconic? In 1922, philosopher and theologian Pavel Florensky suggested that placement in a church does not by itself ensure an image's iconicity: "Some contemporary icons publicly cry out lies in the midst of churches."[24] Zinon echoes this concern, maintaining that "Orthodox churches are often filled with the most unexpected and foreign icons. Many of them . . . are written in ways that hinder prayer" rather than motivate it.[25] Florensky's and Zinon's observations are reminiscent of the often harsh criticism that educated believers in the nineteenth century directed toward the iconographic work of local craftsmen, who were often disparaged as "god-daubers" (*bogomazy*) for the low quality of their work.

At the same time, Zinon's observation also raises the more complex question concerning Western influences on Russian icon painting in the eighteenth and nineteenth centuries. Are images executed in a Western style "foreign" to Orthodoxy, and hence outside the purview of what can be considered iconically authentic? Oksana Gubareva, art historian and member of the Russian Union of Artists, suggests that by allowing such images in churches, the Orthodox Church's hierarchy is engaging in a latent form of iconoclasm.[26] Icon collector Viktor Bondarenko disagrees. In his view, such images bear witness to natural processes of cultural appropriation as well as to a church receptive to the world in which it lives.[27]

In short, the "authenticity" of an icon—what lends an icon its iconicity and thereby sets it apart from other forms of art—is a topic of renewed interest in contemporary Russia. It surfaces in the discourse of church and museum officials who claim the icon; it is discussed in treatises on the theology of the icon and the philosophy of aesthetics.[28] Perhaps most immediate in terms of Russia's viewing public, however, are the challenges that consumer culture, technology, and the marketplace pose. In the nineteenth century, the machine production of icons in Russia elicited unease among some believers. Without the direct involvement of the human hand and spirit, in their estimation, the machine-produced images could not help but be a qualitatively different product.[29] Analogous concerns arise today with regard to icon production and the Internet. While computer technology has contributed substantially to technical advancements in icon restoration, it has also raised concerns about iconographic production. Is an image of an icon downloaded off the virtual space of the Internet, for instance, indeed an icon suitable for prayer?[30]

Consumer culture and technology have also raised questions about the reception of icons and the qualitative shift in the way we see. Douglas Greenfield has described how Pavel Florensky considered the medieval gaze more authentic and unified than the "half-blind" modern gaze. Zinon, whose own work has been compared with that of Andrei Rublev, seems to concur with Florensky when he expresses his amazement that people can gaze at Rublev's *Trinity*—acknowledged by Florensky as the most convincing argument for the existence of God—and not be moved by it.[31] While the factors that inform visual reception are highly complex and difficult to gauge, Zinon's comments remind us of Wendy Salmond's chapter, which traced the transformation of the icon into a commodity in Western consumer culture. A sale of icons at Scruggs-Vandervoort-Barney in St. Louis or at Lord & Taylor in New York posits a different set of visual criteria as the standard of engagement. Almost a century later, Zinon bemoans the impact of such commercialization on the act of seeing. In his view, the sale of icons in the global market, devoid of any confessional context, along with their "branding" on postage stamps, candy boxes, postcards, and souvenirs, has contributed to numbing the human gaze to the imprints of the sacred.[32]

As Robert Bird's chapter on Tarkovsky and the "celluloid icon" has shown, issues involving iconicity become even more problematic where the medium of film is concerned. Church and cinema have a history of tension, and that relationship has entered a new phase in the post-Soviet era. Renewed interest in Orthodoxy among certain cinematographers, coupled with a missionary mind-set, has resulted in the proliferation of Orthodox film festivals and in discussions about Orthodox forms of film. Two relatively recent cinematic events in Russia draw particular attention to the problems associated with the icon and film—Mel Gibson's *The Passion of the Christ* (2004) and Pavel Lungin's *The Island* (*Ostrov*, 2006). The popularity of recent Jesus films harks back to Jefferson Gatrall's chapter and the sensibilities that spurred Russian writers, painters, and archeologists in the late nineteenth century to seek out the origins of the Christ image. Similar to the novels spawned by the various quests for the historical Jesus, films based on the New Testament story challenge Orthodox thinking about the relationship between the icon and history. Despite the fact that Russia's public was rarely exposed to cinematic portrayals of Jesus under Soviet rule, viewers, including Orthodox viewers, displayed the same range of reactions to Gibson's cinematic "icon" of Christ as did their more Hollywood-savvy American counterparts. Some viewers, including Orthodox clergy, judged it a remarkably accurate presentation of the last twelve hours of Jesus' death and saw no reason not to watch it.[33] Others, however, were more reserved in their response. One reviewer, for instance, argued that Orthodox viewers in particular have difficulty watching films about Jesus since their gazes are conditioned from youth by iconography. A cinematic Jesus, in this sense, could never be viewed as an authentic depiction of Christ comparable to an icon.[34] Similarly, though recommending the film on various levels, Andrei Kuraev, an Orthodox deacon and public intellectual, voiced his overall misgivings about the "Jesus film" genre. No cinematic depiction of Christ, in his estimation, could ever be iconic. The face of the actor takes the place of the genuine Face (*Lik*), thereby making it easy to forget that "the Christ of prayer is not the Christ of film." As an art form, film, Kuraev maintains, is too dictatorial, its detailed graphics too forceful in their lasting impression. Icons, by contrast, with their elusive language, do not pose these dilemmas.[35]

What if, however, a film happened to be expressly *Orthodox*? The question is becoming more relevant in contemporary Russia as a specifically Orthodox film industry develops. The recent unexpected success of Lungin's *The Island,* which garnered five Nika awards, has stirred such musings, even in the mainstream press. Hailed as "the first Orthodox film," the film drew wide praise from Orthodox believers, including Patriarch Alexis II; it also spurred tourism and pilgrimages to monasteries.[36] *The Island* depicts the story of Father Anatoly, a holy fool and type of elder with a haunting past who lives in the remote frozen regions of the Russian north. The film drew unexpected numbers of believers and nonbelievers alike because, as one reviewer noted, it not only concerns such themes as the nature of faith, sin, and holiness but also forces one to consider the notion of the potential "ontology of film."[37]

Despite its broad appeal and despite the fact that the film is now sold in churches alongside icons, some reviewers have challenged its perceived iconicity. According to Sophia Ishchenko, a nun and president of the annual film festival Vstrecha held in Kaluga, Orthodox films in general are characterized by three components: theocentricity, Orthodox ethics, and an Orthodox aesthetic informed by iconography.[38] Lungin's film, in the eyes of some, failed on the first front. Instead of lifting the viewer's gaze beyond the boundaries of this world, *The Island,* maintain critics, fixes the gaze on Father Anatoly himself. Applying Florensky's analogy of the dream state described in the chapter by John McGuckin, the film stopped short of "hugging the boundary of the crossing" between two worlds. In this sense, the film fails the test of "cinema-hagiography."[39]

Writing on the eve of revolution in 1917, his impressions still fresh following the rediscovery of the Old Russian icon, the philosopher Evgeny Trubetskoy agreed with Arthur Schopenhauer in maintaining that, as great works of art, icons are best approached as royalty: "It would be impertinent to speak to them; one must stand before them and deferentially wait for them to speak to us first."[40] By shifting the faculty involved in the beholding of icons from sight to hearing, Trubetskoy captured the sense of relationality that the icon presupposed. In so doing, he anticipated the complexities that the study of the icon would come to entail. Embracing both image and beholder, a comprehensive understanding of the icon in modern and postmodern times invariably includes an examination of response and respondent, as much as the perceived language of the object itself. Before 1917, in its celebration of the Triumph of Orthodoxy, the Orthodox Church made an annual attempt by means of anathemas to clear the conceptual air so that the universal language of the icon could most clearly be heard by its listening community. At the outset of twentieth century, however, as the chapters in this volume have shown, it was evident that the icon was also speaking in contexts that lay beyond the boundaries of that community. It had entered the discursive worlds of philosophy, art, cinematography, politics, and economics, in which deference and waiting were not necessarily viewed as virtues. Still situated in these various worlds, the icon continues to beckon the beholder in ways it leaves to us to understand.

NOTES TO AFTERWORD

1. Sergei Aleksandrov, "Vosem' luchei zvezdy Bogoroditsy," *Tverskaia zhizn'* 70, 15 April 2008; Elena Chembaeva, "Krestnyi khod dobralsia do Kazani," *Respublika Tatarstan* 83, 24 April 2008. For information about the She Who Reigns (*Derzhavnaia*) icon of the Mother of God, see A. N. Kazakevich, comp., "'V podvale khrama poiavilas' ikona Bogomateri.' Dokumenty Tsentral'nogo istoricheskogo arkhiva Moskvy o Derzhavnoi ikone Bozhiei Materi, *Otechestvennye arkhivy* 1 (2004): 102–8; Sergei Fomin, comp., *Derzhavnaia pravitel'nitsa zemli russkoi* (Moscow: Palomnik, 1999).

2. Tat'iana Khoroshilova, "Priamaia rech' istorii," *Rossiiskaia gazeta* 120, 5 June 2008.

3. "We Must Be United Today as Never Before: Message from the Interreligious Council in Russia," 22 September 2004, http://www.groupsrv.com/religion/about76612.html; "Slovo Sviateishego Patriarkha Aleksiia na otkrytii pamiatnika v Nizhnem Novgorode," 4 November 2005, http://www.patriarchia.ru/db/text/55730.html; "S Dnem narodnogo edinstva!" *Nasha Penza* 47 (30 October 2008); Denis Babichenko, Evgenii Zherebenkov, and Andrei Kamakin, "Guliaem! Smutnyi den' kalendaria," *Itogi* 4, 31 October 2005, 16.

4. Egor Kholmogorov, "Nesoglasie s primireniem," Radio kompaniia Maiak, 4 November 2004, Aleksandra Glukhova, "Krivye analogii," *Kommuna,* 11 October 2005; Dmitrii Vladimirov, "Prazdnik bez min i pozharov," *Rossiiskaia gazeta* 246, 2 November 2005, 3; Georgii Il'ichev, "Den' raboty narodnogo dukha," *Izvestiia* 205, 3 November 2006, 1; Nail' Gafutulin, "Gde edinenie, tam pobeda!" *Krasnaia zvezda* 204, 3 November 2006; Vladimir Konoplitskii, "Ot Bozhiei Materi—k pobede kommunzima i obratno," *Vladivostok* 165, 7 November 2008.

5. For the role of the Kazan icon in prerevolutionary Orthodox discourse involving the Russian nation and peoples, see Vera Shevzov, "Scripting the Gaze: Liturgy, Homilies, and the Kazan Icon in Late Imperial Russia," in *Sacred Stories: Religion and Spirituality in Modern Russia,* ed. Mark D. Steinberg and Heather J. Coleman (Bloomington: Indiana University Press, 2007), 61–92.

6. Sergei Maksudov, "Minin i Pozharskii vmesto Marksa i Engel'sa: Den' natsional'nogo edinstva mozhet razdelit' Rossiian," *Nezavisimaia gazeta* 18, 6 October 2004, 1; "Metamorfozy: Prazdniki kak instrument politicheskoi bor'by . . . neizvestno s kem," *Moskovskaia pravda* 243, 7 November 2005, 3; Mikhail Romanov, "Sego Dnia: Ty po-russkii ponimaesh'?" *Moskovskii komsomolets* 252, 7 November 2005, 2.

7. G. Ziuganov, "Smena prazdnikov mozhet stolknyt' pravoslavnykh s veruiushchimi drugikh religii," *Mir religii,* 23 November 2004; "Bol'shinstvo Rossiian protiv perenosa prazdnika 7 noiabria," *Religiia i SMI,* 4 November 2004, http://www.religare.ru/article11611.htm; Andrei Fetisov, "Smutnoe edinenie," *Russkii kur'er* 78, 31 October 2005, 3.

8. Iuliia Glezarova, "Chudotvornaia ikona kak simvol russkogo iga," *Nezavisimaia gazeta* 14, 4 August 2004, 1.

9. Vladimir Legoida, "Politkorrektnost'—udobnaia forma molchaniia," *Nevskoe vremia,* 26 October 2007.

10. For controversies concerning religion and art in America, especially those involving the work of Andres Serrano, see Richard Bolton, ed., *Culture Wars: Documents from the Recent Controversies in the Arts* (New York: New Press, 1992). For controversy surrounding the work of Chris Ofili, see Donald J. Cosentino, "Hip-Hop Assemblage: The Chris Ofili Affair," *African Arts* (Spring 2000): 40–50; David Halle, "The Controversy over the Show *Sensation* at the Brooklyn Museum, 1999–2000," in *Crossroads: Art and Religion in American Life,* ed. Alberta Arthurs and Glen Wallach (New York: New Press, 2001), 139–87.

11. "Tvorcheskaia intelligentsiia o sude po delu vystavki *Ostorozhno, Religiia!*" www.demos-center.ru/publications/416.html; "Otkrytoe obrashchenie k General'nomu prokuroru Ustinovu, V. V." 4 March 2003, http://www.sakharov museum.ru/museum/statements/civilcenter_statement_ustinovu.htm.

12. Alina Gurevich, "O vystavke *Ostorozhno, religiia!*" http://www.sakharov-museum.ru/museum/exhibitionhall/religion_notabene/hall_exhibitions_religion_replies_gurevich.htm; Aleksei Lampsi, "Pravoslavie stanovitsia agressivnym," *NG Religii* 14, 20 August 2003, 2.

13. Natal'ia Magidova, "Plakat k vystavke, *Ostorozhno, religiia!*" http://www.sakharov-museum.ru/museum/exhibitionhall/religion_notabene/hall_exhibitions_religion_plakat.htm.

14. "*Ostorozhno! Provokatsiia!* Obrashchenie deiatelei kul'tury," *Slovo* 3, 24 January 2003, 3. For another letter of protest by a group of intellectuals against the exhibit, see "Otkrytoe pis'mo k prezidentu v sviazi s provokatsionnoi vystavkoi v Sakharovskom tsentre," *Sovetskaia Rossiia* 14, 6 February 2003, 2.

15. "Tvorcheskaia intelligentsiia o sude po delu vystavki *Ostorozhno, Religiia!*" www.demos-center.ru/publications/416html; Lampsi, "Pravoslavie stanovitsia agressivnym"; Aleksandr Ures, "Prinadlezhit li iskusstvo narodu?" *Nevskoe vremia* 63, 13 April 2005; Sviashchenno-sluzhiteli N-skoi eparkhii, "Marksizm-Leninizm zhivet i pobezhdaet v tserkvi," *Novaia gazeta* 65, 4 September 2008. In 2008, Mr. Samodurov resigned as director of the Sakharov Center. For a discussion of the controversial exhibit in relation to current trends in religion and society in Russia, see Alexander Agadjanian, "The Search for Privacy and the Return of a Grand Narrative: Religion in a Post-Communist Society," *Social Compass* 53 (June 2006): 169–84.

16. "Organizatorov vystavki *Ostorozhno, Religiia!* trebuiut privlech' k ugolovnoi otvetstvennosti," 21 January 2003, http://www.pravoslavie.ru/news/030120/07.htm.

17. "Vera i sviatynia—samoe dorogoe, chto est' u istinnogo khristianina," 11 March 2004, http://www.moral.ru/Sakh_OVCS.htm.

18. Andrew Spira, *The Avant-Garde Icon: Russian Avant-Garde Art and the Icon Painting Tradition* (Burlington, Vt.: Lund Humphries, 2008).

19. N. K. Gavriushin, "Vekhi russkoi religioznoi estetiki (predislovie)," in *Filosofiia russkogo religioznogo iskusstva XVI–XX vv.: Antologiia,* ed. N. K. Gavriushin (Moscow: Izdatel'skaia gruppa "Progress-Kul'tura," 1993), 30–33; R. V. Bagdasarov, "Khristianskaia zhivopis' v Rossii vtoroi poloviny XX veka," *Chelovek* 5, 1 September 2000, 54–67.

20. For examples of these issues, see Olesia Nikolaeva, "Restitutsiia tserkovnoi sobstvennosti," *NG Religii* 3, 18 March 1998; Oleg Nedumov, "Chernye doski: spasi i sokhrani," *NG Religii* 6, 4 February 2004; Irina Mak, "Trogat' li 'Troitsu?'" *Izvestiia,* 228, 5 December 2008, 30; Stanislav Minin, "Muzeiu ukazali na dver'," *NG Religii* 1, 16 January 2008; Irina Kusova, "Riazan': Boi federal'nogo znacheniia," *NG Religii* 1, 16 January 2008, 8.

21. Kseniia Luchenko and Grigorii Zaslavskii, "Bogomater' Vladimirskaia: Otkryta dlia moliashchikhsia, *Nezavisimaia gazeta* 167, 9 September 1999.

22. Irina Iazykova, *Se tvoriu vse novoe: Ikona v XX veke* (Milan: La Casa di Matriona, 2002), 214–15.

23. Viktoriia Serdiukova, Mikhail Serdiukov, and Vasilii Tolstunov, "Po retseptam drevnikh," *Rossiiskaia gazeta* 86, 14 May 2009, 26.

24. Pavel Florensky, *Iconostasis,* trans. Donald Sheehan and Olga Andrejev (Crestwood, N.Y.: St. Vladimir's Seminary Press, 1996), 83.

25. Serdiukova, "Po retseptam drevnikh," 26.

26. Iuliia Zaitseva, "Na konferentsii 'Ikonologiia i ikonichnost'," 26 January 2007, http://www.blagovest-info.ru/index.php?ss=2&s=4&id=11423.

27. Irina Mak, "Predprinimatel', kollektsioner Viktor Bondarenko: Vot v etom i est' nasha russkost'," *Izvestiia* 228, 5 December 2008, 29.

28. Valerii Lepakhin, *Ikona i ikonichnost'* (St. Petersburg: Uspenskoe podvor'e, 2002); Tat'iana Kasatkina, "Prostranstvo kartiny i ikona v prostranstve," *Novyi mir* 5 (May 2007): 151–60.

29. Robert L. Nichols, "The Icon and Machine in Russia's Religious Renaissance, 1900–1909," in *Christianity and the Arts in Russia,* ed. William C. Brumfield and Milos M. Velimirovic (Cambridge: Cambridge University Press, 1991), 131–44.

30. "Glava Ekaterinburgskoi eparkhii razreshil prikhozhanam molit'sia na ikony iz Interneta posle ikh osviashcheniia," *Interfax-Religiia,* 10 November 2005, http://www.interfax-religion.ru/index.php?act=news&div=7450.

31. Serdiukova, "Po retseptam drevnikh," 26.

32. Ibid.

33. Anton Pomeshchikov, "'Strasti' startovali v Strastnuiu nedeliu. Fil'm Mela Gibsona vykhodit v Rossii," *Izvestiia* 63, 8 April 2004, 9; Oleg Nedumov, "'Strasti Khristovy' splotili radikalov," *NG Religii* 7, 21 April 2004, 2; Anastasiia Petrakova, "Strasti po 'Strastiam Khistovym,'" *Rabochii put'* 138, 23 June 2004.

34. M. Drozdov, "'Strasti Khristovy': ili apologenetika ili koshchunstvo," *Pravoslavnaia Moskva* 5, 1 March 2004, 4; Elena Staf'eva, "Strasti po Gibsonu," *Profil'* 12, 29 March 2004, 70–71.

35. Andrei Kuraev, "Evangelie na kinoekrane," *Literaturnaia gazeta* 14, 7 April 2004, 10.

36. Olga Chernova, "Ostrov Lungina reklamirovali v khramakh," NTV, 16 November 2006, http://news.ntv.ru/97895/; Svetlana Solodskikh, "Angely v dushe zapeli," *Stavropol'skaia Pravda* 14, 26 January 2007; "Ne pora li v monastyr'?" *Vecherniaia Moskva* 44, 15 March 2007; "Sviato mesto bol'she ne pusto," *Komsomol'skaia Pravda* 15, 2 February 2007, 8.

37. Dmitrii Bykov, "Chudo ostrova," *Iskusstvo kino* 10, October 2006, 26–29; Andrei Kuraev, "Fil'm 'Ostrov'—eto kino o chestnom, a ne o 'eleinom' pravoslavii," *Interfax-Religiia,* November 2006, http://www.interfax-religion.ru/?act=news&div=15211.

38. Andrei Sigutin, "Otkrovennyi razgovor o pravoslavnykh kinofestivaliakh," 4 February 2009, http://www.pravoslavie.ru/guest/29164.htm.

39. Alena Solntseva, "'Ostrov' pokaianiia v okeane podsoznaniia," *Vremia novostei* 12, 25 January 2007, 10; "Dlia kinoiskusstva pravoslavie—terra incognita," *Vremia novostei* 12, 25 January 2007, 10; Zaitseva, "Na konferentsii 'Ikonologiia i ikonichnost'.'"

40. Eugene N. Trubetskoi, *Icons: Theology in Color,* trans. Gertrude Vakar (Crestwood, N.Y.: St. Vladimirs Seminary Press, 1973), 27.

SELECTED BIBLIOGRAPHY

Akinsha, Konstantin, and Grigorij Kozlov, with Sylvia Hochfield. *The Holy Place: Architecture, Ideology, and History in Russia.* New Haven: Yale University Press, 2007.

Anisimov, Aleksandr I. *O drevnerusskom iskusstve. Sbornik statei.* Edited by G. I. Vzdornov. Moscow: Sovetskii khudozhnik, 1983.

———. *Our Lady of Vladimir.* Translated by N. G. Yaschwill and T. N. Rodzianko. Prague: Seminarium Kondakovianum, 1928.

———. "Russian Icon-Painting: Its Bloom, Over-Refinement and Decay." In *Masterpieces of Russian Painting,* edited by Michael Farbman, 61–91. London: Europa, 1930.

Belting, Hans. *Likeness and Presence: A History of the Image Before the Era of Art.* Translated by Edmund Jephcott. Chicago: University of Chicago Press, 1994.

Benua, Aleksandr. "Russkie ikony i zapad." *Rech'* 97 (1913): 2.

Betz, Margaret. "The Icon and Russian Modernism." *Artforum* 15, no. 10 (1977): 38–45.

Bird, Robert. *Andrei Rublev.* London: British Film Institute, 2004.

Bowlt, John E. "Neo-primitivism and Russian Painting." *Burlington Magazine* 116, no. 852 (1974): 133–40.

———. "Orthodoxy and the Avant-Garde: Sacred Images in the Work of Goncharova, Malevich, and Their Contemporaries." In *Christianity and the Arts in Russia,* edited by William C. Brumfield and Milos M. Velimirovic, 145–50. Cambridge: Cambridge University Press, 1991.

Bulgakov, S. N. *Ikona i ikonopochitanie: dogmaticheskii ocherk.* 1931. Reprint, Moscow: Russkii put', 1996.

Buslaev, F. I. "Obshchie poniatiia o russkoi ikonopisi." 1866. In *Drevnerusskaia literatura i pravoslavnoe iskusstvo,* 36–186. St. Petersburg: Izdatel'stvo Russkogo Khristianskogo gumanitarnogo instituta, "Liga-Plius," 2001.

Cracraft, James. *The Petrine Revolution in Russian Imagery.* Chicago: University of Chicago Press, 1997.

Florenskii [Florensky], Pavel A. *Beyond Vision: Essays on the Perception of Art by Pavel Florensky.* Edited by Nicolette Misler. Translated by Wendy Salmond. London: Reaktion Books, 2002.

———. *Iconostasis.* Translated by Donald Sheehan and Olga Andrejev. Crestwood, N.Y.: St. Vladimir's Seminary Press, 1996.

———. *The Pillar and Ground of The Truth: An Essay in Orthodox Theodicy in Twelve Letters.* Translated by Boris Jakim. Introduction by Richard F. Gustafson. Princeton: Princeton University Press, 2004.

———. *The Salt of the Earth.* Translated by Richard Betts. Platina, Calif.: St. Herman Press, 1987.

———. *Sochineniia.* 4 vols. Edited by Igumen Andronik (A. S. Trubachev), P. V. Florenskii, and M. S. Trubacheva. Moscow: Mysl', 1994–99.

———. *The Trinity–St. Sergius Lavra and Russia.* Translated by Robert Bird. New Haven: Variable Press, 1995.

Freeze, Gregory L. "Institutionalizing Piety: The Church and Popular Religion, 1750–1850." In *Imperial Russia: New Histories for the Empire,* edited by Jane Burbank and Daniel L. Ransel, 210–49. Bloomington: University of Indiana Press, 1998.

Gatrall, Jefferson J. A. "The Icon in the Picture: Reframing the Question of Dostoevsky's Modernist Iconography." *Slavic and East European Journal* 48, no. 1 (2004): 1–25.

Gavriushin, N. K., ed. *Filosofiia russkogo religioznogo iskusstva XVI–XX vv. Antologiia.* Moscow: Izdatel'skaia gruppa "Progress-Kul'tura," 1993.

Glade, Shirley A. "A Heritage Discovered Anew: Russia's Reevaluation of Pre-Petrine Icons in the Late Tsarist and Early Soviet Periods." *Canadian-American Slavic Studies* 26, nos. 1–4 (1992): 145–95.

Grabar' [Grabar], Igor' E., ed. *Istoriia russkogo iskusstva.* 6 vols. Moscow: I. Knebel', 1910–14.

———. "Scientific Restoration of Historic Works of Art." In *Masterpieces of Russian Painting,* edited by Michael Farbman, 95–105. London: Europa, 1930.

Gur'ianov, V. P. *Dve mestnye ikony Sv. Troitsy v Troitskom Sobore Sviato-Troitsko-Sergievoi Lavry i ikh restavratsiia.* Moscow: Pechatnia A. I. Snegirevoi, 1906.

Himka, John-Paul. "Episodes in the Historiography of the Ukrainian Icon." *Journal of Ukrainian Studies* 29 (Summer–Winter 2004): 149–67.

———. *Last Judgment Iconography in the Carpathians.* Toronto: University of Toronto Press, 2009.

———. "On the Left Hand of God: 'Peoples' in Ukrainian Icons of the Last Judgment." In *State, Societies, Cultures East and West: Essays in Honor of Jaroslaw Pelenski,* edited by Janusz Duzinkiewicz et al., 317–49. New York: Ross, 2004.

———. "The Propagation of Orthodoxy in Galicia on the Eve of World War I." *Ukraina: Kul'turna spadshchyna, natsional'na svidomist', derzhavnist'. Zbirnyk naukovykh prats'* 9 (2001): 480–96.

———. "'Social' Elements in Ukrainian Icons of the Last Judgment (Through the Eighteenth Century)." In *Letters from Heaven: Popular Religion in Russia and Ukraine,* edited by John-Paul Himka and Andriy Zayarnyuk, 235–50. Toronto: University of Toronto Press, 2006.

Hughes, Lindsey. "Inventing Andrei: Soviet and Post-Soviet Views of Andrei Rublev and His Trinity Icon." *Slavonica* 9, no. 2 (2003): 83–90.

Icone Russe. Edited by Carlo Pirovano. Milan: Electa, 1999. An exhibition catalog.

Kondakov, Nikodim P. *Ikonografiia Bogomateri.* St. Petersburg: Tipografiia imperatorskoi akademii nauk, 1914–15.

———. *The Russian Icon.* Translated by Ellis H. Minns. Oxford: Clarendon Press, 1927.

———. *Russkaia ikona.* 4 vols. Prague: Seminarium Kondakovianum, 1928–33.

———. *Sovremennoe polozhenie russkoi narodnoi ikonopisi.* St. Petersburg: Tipografiia I. N. Skorokhodova, 1901.

Krieger, Verena. *Von der Ikone zur Utopie: Kunstkonzepte der russischen Avantgarde.* Cologne: Böhlau, 1998.

Kyzlasova, I. L. *Aleksandr Ivanovich Anisimov (1877–1937).* Moscow: Izdatel'stvo Moskovskogo gosudarstvennogo gornogo universiteta, 2000.

———. *Istoriia otechestvennoi nauki ob iskusstve Vyzantii i Drevnei Rusi 1920–1930 gody: Po materialam arkhivov.* Moscow: Izdatel'stvo Akademii gornikh nauk, 2000.

Lazarev, V. N. *Russkaia ikonopis'—ot istokov do nachala XVI veka.* 6 vols. Moscow: Iskusstvo, 1983.

Leskov, N. S. "Zapechatlennyi angel." In *Sobranie sochinenii,* vol. 5, edited by L. Anninskii, 222–79. Moscow: Ekran, 1993.

Likhachev, Nikolai P. *Materialy dlia istorii russkogo ikonopisaniia.* 2 vols. St. Petersburg: Ekspeditsiia zagotovleniia gosudarstvennykh bumag, 1906.

Lossky, Vladimir. *In the Image and Likeness of God.* Edited by John H. Erickson and Thomas E. Bird. Crestwood, N.Y.: St. Vladimir's Seminary Press, 1985.

Mudrak, Myroslava M. "Sheptyts'kyi as Patron of the Arts." In *Morality and Reality: The Life and Times of Andrei Sheptyts'kyi,* edited by Paul R. Magocsi, 289–311. Edmonton: Canadian Institute of Ukrainian Studies, 1989.

Nichols, Robert L. "The Friends of God: Nicholas and Alexandra at the Canonization of Serafim of Sarov, July 1903." In *Religious and Secular Forces in Late Tsarist Russia,* edited by Charles E. Timberlake, 206–29. Seattle: University of Washington Press, 1992.

———. "The Icon and the Machine in Russia's Religious Renaissance, 1900–1909." In *Christianity and the Arts in Russia,* edited by William C. Brumfield and Milos M. Velimirovic, 131–44. Cambridge: Cambridge University Press, 1991.

———. "Orthodox Spirituality in Imperial Russia: Saint Serafim of Sarov and the Awakening of Orthodoxy." *Modern Greek Studies Yearbook* 16–17 (2000–2001): 19–42.

Ouspensky, Leonid. *Theology of the Icon.* Translated by Anthony Gythiel. 2 vols. Crestwood, N.Y.: St. Vladimir's Seminary Press, 1992.

Ouspensky, Leonid, and Vladimir Lossky. *The Meaning of Icons.* Translated by G. E. H. Palmer and E. Kadloubovsky. Crestwood, N.Y.: St. Vladimir's Seminary Press, 1982.

Pozdniaia Russkaia ikona konets XVIII–XIX vek. Edited by I. Iarygina. St. Petersburg: AO "Kinotsentr," 1994. An exhibition catalog.

Punin, Nikolai. "Vystavka drevne-russkogo iskusstva (ustroennaia Moskovskim Arkheologicheskim Institutom imeni Imp. Nikolaia II)." *Apollon* 5 (1913): 38–42.

Rovinskii, D. A. *Obozrenie ikonopisaniia v Rossii do kontsa XVII veka.* 1856. St. Petersburg: Izdatel'stvo A. S. Suvorina, 1903.

Salmond, Wendy R. *Arts and Crafts in Late Imperial Russia: Reviving the Kustar Art Industries. 1870–1917.* Cambridge: Cambridge University Press, 1996.

———. "Russian Icons and American Money." In *Treasures into Tractors: The Selling of Russia's Cultural Heritage, 1918–1938,* edited by Anne Odom and Wendy R. Salmond, 237–63. Washington, D.C.: Hillwood Museum and Gardens, 2009.

Shchekotov, N. M. "Ikonopis' kak iskusstvo. Po povodu sobraniia ikon I. S. Ostroukhova i S. P. Riabushinskogo." *Russkaia ikona* 1 (1914): 115–42.

Shevzov, Vera. "Chapels and the Ecclesial World of Prerevolutionary Russian Peasants." *Slavic Review* 55, no. 3 (1996): 585–613.

———. "Iconic Piety in Russia." In *Modern Christianity to 1900,* edited by Amanda Porterfield, 178–208. Vol. 6. of *A People's History of Christianity.* Minneapolis: Fortress Press, 2007.

———. "Icons, Miracles, and the Ecclesiastical Identity of Laity in Late Imperial Russian Orthodoxy." *Church History* 69, no. 3 (2000): 610–31.

———. "Miracle-Working Icons, Laity, and Authority in the Russian Orthodox Church, 1861–1917." *Russian Review* 58, no. 1 (1999): 26–48.

———. *Russian Orthodoxy on the Eve of Revolution.* Oxford: Oxford University Press, 2004.

———. "Scripting the Gaze: Liturgy, Homilies, and the Kazan Icon in Late Imperial Russia." In *Sacred Stories: Religion and Spirituality in Modern Russia,* edited by Mark D. Steinberg and Heather J. Coleman, 61–92. Bloomington: Indiana University Press, 2007.

Smirnova, Engelina. "Simon Ushakov—'Historicism' and 'Byzantinism.' On the Interpretation of Russian Painting from the Second Half of the Seventeenth Century." In *Religion and Culture in Early Modern Russia and Ukraine,* edited by Samuel H. Baron and Nancy Shields Kollmann, 169–83. DeKalb: Northern Illinois University Press, 1997.

Snegirev, I. M. "Vzgliad na pravoslavnoe ikonopisanie." In *Filosofiia russkogo religioznogo iskusstva XVI–XX vv. Antologiia,* edited by N. K. Gavriushin, 101–12. Moscow: Izdatel'skaia gruppa "Progress-Kul'tura," 1993.

Snessoreva, Sof'ia. *Zemnaia zhizn' Presviatoi Bogoroditsy i opisanie sviatykh chudotvornykh ee ikon,* 1898. Reprint, Yaroslavl: Verkhne-Volzhskoe knizhnoe izdatel'stvo, 1993.

Spira, Andrew. *The Avant-Garde Icon: Russian Avant-Garde Art and the Icon Painting Tradition.* Burlington, Vt.: Lund Humphries, 2008.

Svientsits'kyi, I., ed. *Ikonopys' halyts'koi Ukrainy XV–XVI. vikiv, Zbirky Natsional'noho muzeiu u L'vovi.* Lviv, 1928.

Tarabukin, N. M. *Smysl ikony.* Moscow: Izdatel'stvo Pravoslavnogo bratstva Sviatitelia Filareta Moskovskogo, 1999.

Tarasenko, O. "K probleme natsionalnykh istokov v russkoi zhivopisi kontsa XIX–nachala XX veka," *Sovetskoe iskusstvoznanie* 27 (1991): 157–82.

Tarasov, Oleg. *Icon and Devotion: Sacred Spaces in Imperial Russia.* Edited and translated by Robin Milner-Gulland. London: Reaktion Books, 2002.

———. "The Russian Icon and the Culture of the Modern: The Renaissance of Popular Icon Painting in the Reign of Nicholas II." *Experiment: A Journal of Russian Culture* 7 (2001): 73–101.

Tarkovsky, Andrei. *Andrei Rublev.* Translated by Kitty Hunter-Blair. Introduction by Philip Strick. London: Faber & Faber, 1991.

Trubetskoi, Eugene N. *Icons: Theology in Color.* Translated by Gertrude Vakar. Crestwood, N.Y.: St. Vladimir's Seminary Press, 1973.

Uspensky, Boris. *The Semiotics of the Russian Icon.* PdR Press Publications in Semiotics of Art 3. Edited by Stephen Ruby. Lisse: Peter de Ridder Press, 1976.

Vasnetsov, Viktor. "Bozhestvennyi smysl ikon." In *Pravoslavnaia ikona: kanon i stil'. K bogoslovskomu rassmotreniiu obraza,* edited by Aleksandr Strizhev, 121–43. Moscow: Palomnik, 1998.

Voloshin, M. V. "Chemu uchat ikony?" In *Liki tvorchestva,* edited by V. M. Manuilov, V. P. Kupchenko, and A. V. Lavrov, 291–95. Leningrad: Nauka, 1988.

Vzdornov, G. I. *Istoriia otkrytiia i izucheniia russkoi srednevekovoi zhivopisi. XIX vek.* Moscow: Iskusstvo, 1986.

CONTRIBUTORS

ROBERT BIRD is Associate Professor of Russian Literature at the University of Chicago. He is the author of *Russian Prospero* (2006), a comprehensive study of the poetry and thought of Viacheslav Ivanov, and *Andrei Tarkovsky: Elements of Cinema* (2008). His translations of Russian religious thought include *On Spiritual Unity: A Slavophile Reader* (1998), Pavel Florensky's *The Trinity–St. Sergius Lavra and Russia* (1995), and Viacheslav Ivanov's *Selected Essays* (2001). His works in progress include *The Soviet Imaginary* and a book on Dostoevsky.

ELENA BOECK is Assistant Professor of Art History at DePaul University. Her research interests range from artistic exchange in the medieval Mediterranean to innovative icons in early modern Russia. She is completing a monograph on illustrated histories that re-vision the Byzantine past for patrons in Bulgaria and Sicily. Her next project will be devoted to icon types that merge medieval piety and modern concerns.

JEFFERSON J. A. GATRALL is Assistant Professor of Russian at Montclair State University. His publications include articles on Chekhov, Tolstoy, Proust, and Nikolai Ge as well as on the visual arts in Dostoevsky. He is completing a book on representations of the historical Jesus in nineteenth-century European and American prose fiction.

SHIRLEY A. GLADE is an independent researcher who specializes in Russian icons and folk art. She has written and lectured widely on Russian art, especially the history of icon restoration in late imperial, Soviet, and post-Soviet Russia.

DOUGLAS GREENFIELD is Assistant Professor in the Intellectual Heritage Program at Temple University. He is the editor of *Depictions: Slavic Studies in the Narrative and Visual Arts in Honor of William E. Harkins* (2000) and is completing a book on Russian philosophers and the visual imagination.

JOHN-PAUL HIMKA is Professor of Ukrainian and East European History in the Department of History and Classics as well as director of the Research Program on Religion and Culture of the Canadian Institute of Ukrainian Studies at the University of Alberta. He is the editor, with Andriy Zayarnyuk, of *Letters from Heaven: Popular Religion in Russia and Ukraine* (2006) and the author, most recently, of *Last Judgment Iconography in the Carpathians* (2009).

JOHN ANTHONY MCGUCKIN is Professor in Late Antique and Byzantine Christian History at Union Theological Seminary and Professor of Byzantine Christian Studies at Columbia University. His many books on historical theology include *The Transfiguration of Christ in Scripture and Tradition* (1986), *St. Cyril of Alexandria: The Christological Controversy* (1994), *St. Gregory of Nazianzus: An Intellectual Biography* (2001), *The Westminster Handbook to Patristic Theology* (2004), and *The Orthodox Church: An Introduction to Its History, Doctrine, and Spiritual Culture* (2008). He is executive editor of the forthcoming three-volume *Blackwell Encyclopedia of Eastern Orthodoxy.*

ROBERT L. NICHOLS is Professor of History Emeritus at St. Olaf College. He has written widely on Russian Orthodoxy and is the translator of Father Georges Florovsky's *Ways of Russian Theology* (1978). He is also the editor, with Georg Michels, of the forthcoming *The Old Belief and Russian Religious Dissent, 1650–1950.*

SARAH PRATT is Professor of Slavic Languages and Literatures at the University of Southern California. She is the author of *The Semantics of Chaos in Tjutcev* (1983), *Russian Metaphysical Romanticism: The Poetry of Tiutchev and Boratynskii* (1984), and *Nikolai Zabolotsky: Enigma and Cultural Paradigm* (2000). She has also published several articles on the Russian critic Lydia Ginzburg and on Russian women's autobiography.

WENDY R. SALMOND is Professor of Art History at Chapman University. Her publications include *Arts and Crafts in Late Imperial Russia: Reviving the Russian Kustar Industries, 1870–1917* (1996), *Russian Icons at Hillwood* (1998), *Pavel Florensky. Beyond Vision: Essays on the Perception of Art* (2002), and *Treasure into Tractors: The Selling of Russia's Cultural Heritage, 1918–1938* (2009). She has curated exhibitions on Russian icons (Hillwood Museum, Estate and Gardens, 2004) and on Fyodor Solntsev (New York Public Library, 2007).

VERA SHEVZOV is Associate Professor of Religion at Smith College. Her book *Russian Orthodoxy on the Eve of Revolution* (2004) won the Frank S. and Elizabeth D. Brewer Prize of the American Society of Church History. Her recent publications include an essay titled "Iconic Piety in Modern Russia," in volume 6 of *A People's History of Christianity* (2007). She is completing a book on Marian devotion in late imperial and contemporary Russia.

INDEX

Page numbers in *italics* refer to illustrations.